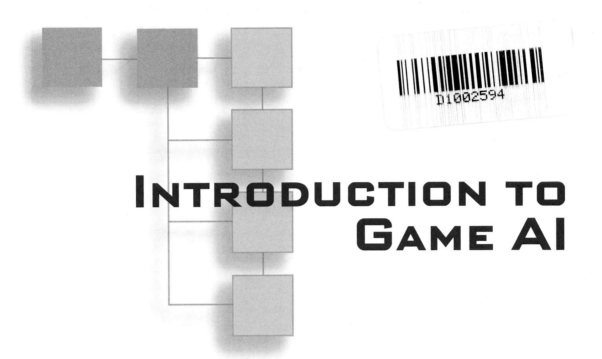

INTRODUCTION TO GAME AI

NEIL KIRBY

Course Technology PTR

A part of Cengage Learning

COURSE TECHNOLOGY
CENGAGE Learning

Australia • Brazil • Japan • Korea • Mexico • Singapore • Spain • United Kingdom • United States

COURSE TECHNOLOGY
CENGAGE Learning™

Introduction to Game AI
Neil Kirby

Publisher and General Manager,
Course Technology PTR: Stacy L. Hiquet

Associate Director of Marketing:
Sarah Panella

Manager of Editorial Services:
Heather Talbot

Marketing Manager: Jordan Castellani

Acquisitions Editor: Heather Hurley

Project Editor: Kate Shoup

Technical Reviewer: Kevin Dill

Copy Editor: Kate Shoup

Interior Layout Tech: MPS Limited, A Macmillan
Company

Cover Designer: Mike Tanamachi

Cover Photograph: Henry Kempker

CD-ROM Producer: Brandon Penticuff

Indexer: Larry Sweazy

Proofreader: Gene Redding

For product information and technology assistance, contact us at
Cengage Learning Customer & Sales Support, 1-800-354-9706

For permission to use material from this text or product, submit all requests online at **www.cengage.com/permissions**
Further permissions questions can be emailed to
permissionrequest@cengage.com

All trademarks are the property of their respective owners.

All images © Cengage Learning unless otherwise noted.

Library of Congress Control Number: 2009942392

ISBN-13: 978-1-59863-998-8

ISBN-10: 1-59863-998-6

Course Technology, a part of Cengage Learning
20 Channel Center Street
Boston, MA 02210
USA

Cengage Learning is a leading provider of customized learning solutions with office locations around the globe, including Singapore, the United Kingdom, Australia, Mexico, Brazil, and Japan. Locate your local office at: **international.cengage.com/region**

Cengage Learning products are represented in Canada by Nelson Education, Ltd.

For your lifelong learning solutions, visit **courseptr.com**

Visit our corporate website at **cengage.com**

Printed in the United States of America
1 2 3 4 5 6 7 12 11 10

This book is dedicated to my spouse Theresa Kempker and our son Henry.
Thanks to you both for giving me the time to do this.

ACKNOWLEDGMENTS

This book would not exist without the support of the game AI crowd that gathers every year at the Game Developers Conference. The late Eric Dybsand inspired many of us by example. I would also like to thank every person who has ever dined with me at one of the AI Programmers Dinners. Thanks go to Steve Woodcock and Steve Rabin for helping me moderate the AI Roundtables at GDC. Dave Mark and Laurie Reynolds proved that you can write a book and stay happily married, something I needed to know before setting off on this adventure. Thanks also go to the AI Game Programmers Guild, a group of experts who were only an e-mail away if I got into trouble. Kevin Dill deserves special attention in that regard. Jenifer Niles and Heather Hurley have supported me and the rest of the game AI community over the years. Many of us would not be in print without them.

About the Author

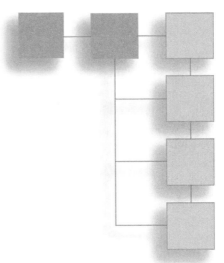

Neil Kirby is a Member of Technical Staff at Bell Laboratories, the R&D arm of Alcatel-Lucent. He currently develops solutions used to support CMMI certification. He also provides software architecture consulting services and teaches the course "Avoiding the Software Performance Crisis." His previous assignments have included building speech-recognition software and teaching at the university level. He has been a judge of the Ohio State University Fundamentals of Engineering Honors robot competition for many years on behalf of Alcatel-Lucent. Neil holds a master's degree in computer science from Ohio State University.

Neil started writing multiplayer tactical combat computer games in 1987. These included a computer version of ADB's *Star Fleet Battles* board game and games of his own design, most notably the futuristic armored ground combat game *Bots*. These were publicly played at the Ohio State University CACON conventions from 1987 until 1992 but never published. The methodology used to develop the AI in *Bots* led to his 1991 Computer Game Developers Conference talk, "Artificial Intelligence Without AI: A Darwinistic Approach." He was under NDA as a consultant to Quicksilver, Software, Inc., during the early phases of development of *Star Fleet Command*. Neil moderates the AI Roundtables and hosts the AI Programmers Dinners at GDC. He has contributed articles to *AI Game Programming Wisdom* volumes 1, 2, and 4 and is a member of the AI Game Programming Guild. Neil also serves on the board of the IGDA Foundation and was a driving force behind its creation.

Contents

INTRODUCTION

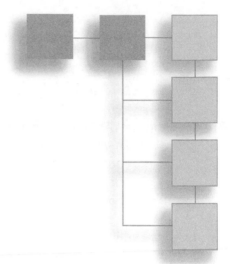

The goal of this book is to get readers who are new to game AI to the point where they can usefully consume "regular" books on game AI. It is aimed at those who do not have a hard-core programming background, particularly those coming from other areas of game development. The book achieves this through a series of projects based on small and understandable games. Because AI is about decision making, the projects and topics selected for the book are measured against the question, "Can a beginner understand the decision-making process?" The projects may present some challenges, but with the help of this book, beginners should always be able to say, "I might have trouble getting the AI to *act*, but I have no trouble getting the AI to *decide*."

The very basics of game AI are covered in the first three chapters of the book. Chapter 1, "What Is Game AI?" introduces game AI and Visual Studio. Chapter 2, "Simple Hard-Coded AI," covers the simplest AI method of all. Chapter 3, "Finite State Machines (FSMs)," is about one of the simplest formal structures for AI, finite state machines. These chapters provide grounding in the most basic of AI techniques, but they should not be overlooked as these techniques are very widely used in game AI.

More-sophisticated techniques begin with Chapter 4, "Rule-Based Systems." Chapter 5, "Random and Probabilistic Systems," covers computing odds on the fly and random-selection decision making. Planning is introduced in Chapter 6, "Look-Ahead: The First Step of Planning." The next step in planning, pre-planning, is covered in Chapter 7, "Book of Moves." A relatively new topic for game AI is covered in Chapter 8, "Emergent Behavior." Chapter 9, "Evoking Emotions on the Cheap," opens the topic of emotions, keeping the material at an introductory but still useful level. Finally, Chapter 10, "Topics to Pursue from Here," wraps things up with a look ahead at more sophisticated AI techniques that are beyond the scope of this book.

The projects use the Microsoft Visual Basic programming language. The Express Edition of VB is a free download from Microsoft. While most professional AI code is written in C++, VB is less threatening to people who do not have a hard-core programming background. Students, artists, animators, managers, and even producers who need to take their first steps in game AI should find the language easy to work with. All the code is included on the CD, which can save you a great deal of typing. If your typed-in code is not working, just consult the code on the CD. All the code for the projects is also included in the text of this book; if you lose the CD, you can still do all the projects.

CD-ROM Downloads

If you purchased an ebook version of this book, and the book had a companion CD-ROM, we will mail you a copy of the disc. Please send ptrsupplements@cengage.com the title of the book, the ISBN, your name, address, and phone number. Thank you.

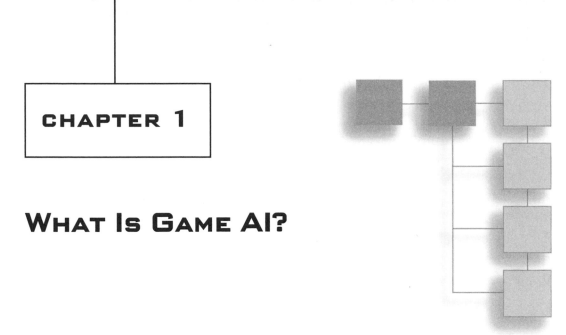

CHAPTER 1

WHAT IS GAME AI?

Our working definition for AI is the ability to act intelligently in the face of changing conditions. Embedding such capability in a game makes it game AI. We will return to this definition throughout the book to make sure that we can identify how any given AI meets the definition. We will also take care to examine what is *not* game AI. While this definition seems simple enough, all three parts of it—the ability to act, the requirement that the action be intelligent, and the requirement that the action be in response to changing conditions—are worth separate inspection.

First, as mentioned, the AI should have the ability to act in some fashion. AI that has no output is wasted computation. In a game context, this means that the actions of the AI must have the possibility of being noticed by the player. Games that are noted for good AI often have an AI that is no better than other games, aside from the fact that the game gives the player the ability to see the AI acting intelligently. For example, if, in a game, the player sees a room with an AI-controlled character working at a computer, the player may conclude there is nothing special about the AI. Even if the AI character happens to be playing a world-class game of chess in real time, it is all wasted unless the player gets a chance to notice this amazing ability of the AI. The player does not necessarily have to see the intelligent behavior at the time a decision is being made, but evidence of the intelligence should be made available to the player in time for the player to enjoy it.

The second part of our definition requires that the AI decisions be intelligent ones. Making the AI decisions appear intelligent is a recurring challenge. The hardest part is not always making the AI look smart; often, it is preventing the AI from looking dumb. At an AI roundtable many years ago, I dubbed this "avoiding artificial stupidity." Even purely random decision making may fit this criterion. Pundits describe insanity as "doing the exact same thing and expecting different results." In this light, random decision making gives the appearance of an AI that is learning from past mistakes or one that is changing how it plays to keep the player from countering the AI's past successes. If players cannot detect the purely random nature, they often interpret it as highly intelligent. The final judge of "intelligence" is the player.

Note

It may seem unfair that AI will be judged by how stupid it is in its low points instead of how smart it is in its high points, but other aspects of games are judged in a similar way. For example, Id Software spent well over a year perfecting the graphics engine for one of the very first full 3D games, *Quake*. The hard part was not hitting 30 frames per second at the top end, but keeping the frame rate above 10 frames per second at all times [Abrash96].

The third part of our definition requires the game AI to react to changing conditions. It is generally accepted that a core part of what makes computer games fun is a high degree of interactivity. Quality interactivity requires that the players' decisions matter—that they change the state of the game. Players are free to make whatever choices they find agreeable and to change the game state in such ways as they can. This is the changing world in which game AI must exist. This changing world places great pressure on the ability of the AI to appear intelligent. If the AI cannot act differently in different situations, it will be only slightly more interesting than watching a stick fall to the ground when you let go of it.

Those three parts give us a working view of AI, but this book is about *game* AI. As an entertainment product, everything must further the player's enjoyment. Our AI must make the game more fun. A harder challenge appeals to only one of the four basic ways people have fun [Lazzaro04]. Even worse, a harder challenge lacks fixed definition—one player's "harder" is another player's "frustrating." A game AI programmer must never lose sight of fun as the primary goal. Making the AI smarter and more sophisticated often makes the game more fun, but not always. An online game that programmed the monster AI to target healers and mages preferentially proved to be far more effective at defeating the players but far less fun for the players.

Having a reasonable definition of what game AI is, it is worth considering what game AI is not. AI is not physics. The code that decides whether a virtual rock on the edge of a cliff should stay on the cliff or fall off the cliff is not AI. The rock has no free choice in the matter and no options to pick from, no matter how smart it is. Forces of a certain magnitude always push the rock off the cliff, and forces below that level cannot. The rock is not free to make a sub-optimal choice in the short term that better suits its long-term goals. The code may resemble AI—the rock evaluated changing conditions and the decision was made to fall off the cliff—but it had no choice in the matter.

AI need not always be complex. While there is a need for complex AI methods, a large amount can be accomplished with simple methods. These simple methods are still AI, despite a feeling in academia and industry that, "stuff we know how to do isn't really AI and stuff we can't do yet is real AI." This book has many basic techniques for game AI. All of them, even the simplest, are in widespread use by professional game developers.

An Introduction to Visual Basic

The rest of this chapter deals with where to find Visual Basic and using Visual Basic to create your first project. If you have experience programming with Visual Basic .NET, you may be able to skip ahead to Chapter 2, "Simple Hard-Coded AI." If you are an experienced programmer who is new to Visual Basic, you should be able to fly through the rest of this chapter. The projects and material in the rest of the book will be far less elementary than this introductory project.

Getting Visual Basic

The projects in this book were written in Visual Basic .NET using Microsoft Visual Basic 2008. VB.NET, like VB before it, is easy to learn and write, and yet quite powerful. With the advent of VB.NET in 2001, VB no longer carries an inherent performance penalty compared to other languages. You will need to install VB to use the software on the CD that is included with this book. Once you have installed it, you'll bring up the development environment and proceed through the walk-through example in this chapter.

Note

There is extensive support for VB on the Internet. Many questions can be answered with a few careful Internet searches; you will usually need to include VB and .NET as keywords. The Microsoft Developer Network (MSDN) library is another valuable resource for Windows developers. It can be viewed online at http://msdn.microsoft.com/en-us/library/default.aspx; you can download it or the Express Library from http://www.microsoft.com/express/download/msdn/Default.aspx.

Visual Basic 2008 requires a Microsoft Windows XP or later operating system. Older versions can run on Windows 2000. The Visual Basic 2008 Express edition is free for non-commercial use. Further details and the software itself are available at http://www.microsoft.com/Express/default.aspx. In addition to the software, the Express Web site offers tutorials and other information that may be valuable to first-time Visual Basic users.

VB is included in the retail versions of the Visual Studio development environment. The screens will be similar, but will carry more options. If you have Visual Studio, you can safely substitute "Visual Studio" wherever you read "Visual Basic" in this book with few problems. Note that the dialog boxes will not match exactly; Visual Studio is more sophisticated than the Express versions of the languages it supports.

If you are an experienced C programmer, you may prefer to use C# or C++. Download Visual C# 2008 Express Edition or Visual C++ 2008 Express Edition instead of Visual Basic. The C# and VB languages both utilize the .Net Framework Common Language Runtime, making them utterly interchangeable. C++ requires modest translations that should not prove taxing for an experienced programmer who happens to be new to AI.

For those new to Windows programming, a few brief words of description are in order. A Windows application starts with forms (the windows in Windows are forms). On the forms are controls such as buttons and text boxes. When the user interacts with a control, an event is fired and the application software handles that event. When the application software is done handling the event, it gives control back to the operating system. There is no "main," familiar to C programmers, only a startup form that is shown to the user when the application launches. Giving control back to the operating system after handling an event does not mean that the application finishes execution and exits, only that it is done handling the last event and is ready to handle another. This is called event-driven programming.

The game projects in this book will be Windows forms applications written in VB. The forms will display the game and take user input. We will separate the AI for the game from the user interface. Not only is this an industry-accepted good practice, but it will also help provide focus and clarity on the AI portion of the code. Separating the AI from the rest of the code will make interfaces between the two explicit. One of the more important jobs of a game AI programmer is to make sure that the rest of the game will provide the AI with the information it needs to work effectively. In addition, the game AI programmer must insist that the rest of the game provide ways for the AI to manipulate the world and the interactive experience.

The Hit Point Calculator Project

Our first project will be a hit point calculator. The user will input a character class and level, and the software will compute the maximum number of hit points for the character. The values match those used in numerous familiar fantasy role-playing games.

This project will familiarize you with creating a project, adding forms to it, adding controls to the forms, and writing code to handle events. Start by launching Visual Studio. From the File menu, select New Project. Visual Basic will show a dialog box similar to the one in Figure 1.1.

On the left side of Figure 1.1, Windows Forms Application is selected. Instead of using the default name, WindowsApplication1, change the name of this application to HitPoints and click OK. Your screen should resemble the one shown in Figure 1.2.

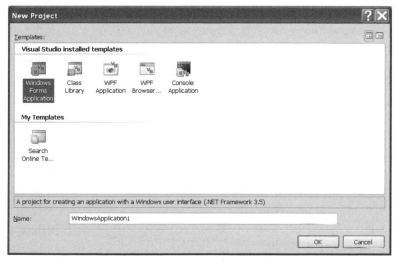

Figure 1.1
This New Project dialog box is for creating a new project.

Figure 1.2
Visual Studio, showing a new project.

Note

If you happen to have version control software such as Visual Source Safe, Subversion, or Git, it is always a good idea to use it. Version control enables you to go back to any of the ideas you have tried out without losing any work. In general, programmer time is more expensive than disk space, so professionals keep everything they produce under version control. Another good argument for version control is the fact that predicting the best idea out of many cannot be done without trying all of them out.

The large area contains a window marked Form1. This is the editing pane. To the right is the Solution Explorer, showing all the files in the project. (A solution in Visual Basic can have more than one project, but we will not use this capability.) Below the Solution Explorer is the Properties window.

The Properties window lists the properties of whatever object was most recently in focus. Buttons near the top of the Properties window control what you see and how it is organized. Starting from the left, the first two buttons control how the window is organized. Click the first button (marked with two plus signs) to organize the properties by category; click the second button (marked with an A and Z and an arrow) to arrange the properties alphabetically.

If the focus is on a form, you will see five buttons. The third and fourth buttons control what is displayed. The Properties window usually shows properties, which you select with the third button. Clicking the fourth button, marked with a tiny lightning bolt, shows events and event handlers. These two buttons are not visible in Figure 1.2 because the focus is on the file Form1.vb in the Solution Explorer. The form has one set of properties, and the file the form is stored in has a different set. These buttons will show up shortly when we change the properties of the form itself.

Note

The last button in the row is always the Property Pages button. We will not need to use it.

Figure 1.2 shows all the files with room for more but only part of the Properties window. You can adjust the height of the Properties window by clicking and dragging the area between the Solution Explorer and the Properties window. This is just one way in which Visual Basic is extremely adjustable; another is the way you can choose to hide or display various window elements. For example, note the pushpin icons. The Solution Explorer and Properties window are pinned in Figure 1.2, so you can see their contents. To the left of the editing pane is the Toolbox; click it, and it slides open. Clicking the Toolbox's pushpin will pin it open. Clicking outside the Toolbox when it is unpinned slides it back out of the way.

Visual Basic created a default form and named it Form1. This is typical of Visual Basic, so one of the first tasks when creating a new form or adding a control to a form is to give the new object a more useful name than the default. Visual Basic also gives default values to other properties, some of which we will also change.

1. Click anywhere on Form1 in the editing pane.

2. Look for the Properties window on the right side. Here you will find the names of all the properties of the current object and their values. Note that the row of buttons went from three buttons to five.

3. Change the Text property from Form1 to Hit Points Calculator; this text will be displayed in the title bar of the form. The value Form1 is bold and easy to find; values that have been changed from the default are marked in bold, as are Text and Name properties. Simply click where it says Form1 and type over it. If you are having trouble finding the property, it

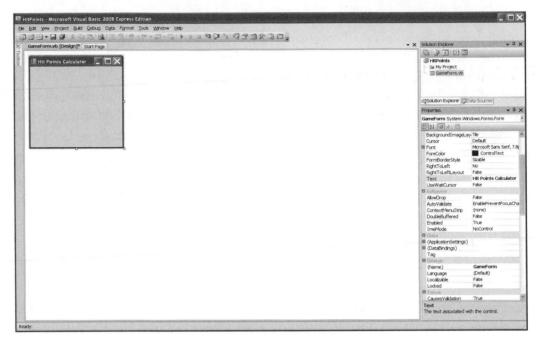

Figure 1.3
The project, after renaming and property changes.

is in the Appearance category near the top. If you alphabetize the properties instead of grouping them by category, it will be near the bottom.

4. Scroll down to the Design category and change the Name property to
   GameForm. This name is used in code and should be selected for enhanced
   clarity.

5. Change the name of the form in the Solution Explorer from Form1.vb to
   GameForm.vb. Do this by clicking the letters of the name and then typing
   the new name or by right-clicking and selecting Rename from the context
   menu that appears and then typing the new name. If you click the form in
   the editing pane, your project should resemble Figure 1.3.

Our next task is to place controls on the form and operate them.

1. Click the Toolbox to slide it open. If your monitor has enough room, pin it
   open. The Toolbox has many categories of controls. The controls we will use
   are in the Common Controls category. Click the minus signs by the names
   of all of the other categories to close them, simplifying what you see. In

general, all controls appear twice; once in a particular category and again in the All Windows Forms category at the top.

2. Scroll down the Common Controls to find the Label control. Then drag a Label control onto the form and place it near the upper left corner of the form. Little helper lines appear and disappear while the control is moving to aid in the placement of the control.

3. Visual Basic names the Label control Label1 and makes its Text property Label1 as well. Change the Text property of the label to Character Level.

4. Find the NumericUpDown control in the Toolbox and drag one to the form. The helper lines make it easy to line up beneath the label we just added.

5. Change the Name property from NumericUpDown1 to Level.

6. Find the Data group in the Properties window and change the Maximum property from 100 to 12.

7. Change the Minimum property from 0 to 1.

8. Drag another Label control from the Toolbox and place it below the Level control.

9. Change the Text property of this Label control to Class.

10. Drag four RadioButton controls from the Toolbox one at a time and put them below the Class label. Your project should look something like Figure 1.4.

11. At this point, we have invested some effort into the project, so it's a good idea to save it. Click the File menu, select Save All, navigate to an appropriate location, and save the files. There will be two HitPoints folders in the file system. The parent folder is for the solution and contains the HitPoints.sln file. The child folder is for the project and contains HitPoints.vbproj. Recall that a solution can have more than one project; each project in a solution has its own folder.

12. Click the RadioButton1 control and change its Text property to Mage.

13. Change the Text property of RadioButton2 to Thief.

Figure 1.4
The project, after adding character class radio buttons.

14. Change the Text property of RadioButton3 to Cleric.

15. Change the Text property of RadioButton4 to Fighter.

16. In a similar manner, change the Name property of the controls to MageRadio, ThiefRadio, ClericRadio, and FighterRadio, respectively.

17. Drag another Label control from the Toolbox and place it to the right of the Character Level label.

18. Change the Text property of this new label to Maximum Hit Points.

19. The end of the label may go past the edge of the form. To fix this, click the form's title bar. Small white boxes appear on the edges and corner of the form; drag the little white box on the right edge of the form to the right to make the form bigger.

20. Drag another Label control from the Toolbox and place it below the Maximum Hit Points label.

21. Change the Text property of this Label control to 888.

22. Change the Name property of this new label to HitPointsLabel. (You cannot have any spaces in a control name, so mixed case is used. We want this label to stand out.)

23. Type over the BackColor property to change it to White.

24. Use the drop-down list to change the BorderStyle property to FixedSingle.

This finishes the user interface part of the project. Your application should resemble Figure 1.5.

Note that we did not change the name of Label1 or any of the other labels, but we did change the name of this last label. We did so because code that we will write later will need to refer to the label, so it needs a clear name. Label1 will never be referenced by code we will write, so since life is short, we did not bother to rename it. We added the word Label at the end of the name so that the name will tell us what kind of control this particular one is. Complex projects employ many controls. Often, they will have similar names; by adding the control type on the end of the name, we can distinguish them easily.

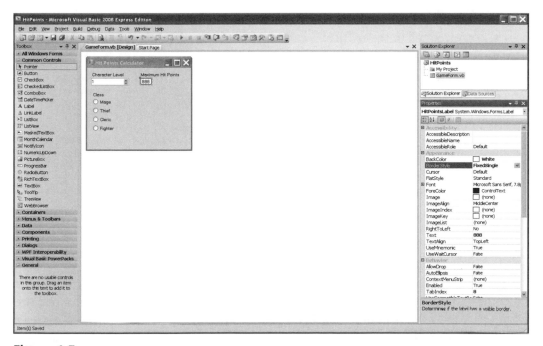

Figure 1.5
The project, with a completed user interface.

You may have noticed that there are many properties that can be set. One of the advantages to VB is that you can generally get away with setting the ones you need and safely ignoring the rest. The Toolbox offers more controls than we need, and we can safely ignore the extras as well. Curious students will want to learn more about them by using the help system and the MSDN library. By now, it should be getting obvious how this project will work.

It is time to write code. Our application needs code to handle three things: events associated with the NumericUpDown control, events associated with the RadioButton controls, and gracefully starting up. The easiest way of getting from a form or a control on a form to the code that handles the events for the form or the control is to double-click the form or the control. We start with handling the events related to startup.

Double-click the GameForm form background, taking care not to double-click one of the controls. Visual Basic brings up a tab labeled GameForm.vb. The code for the form and all its controls live here. Visual Basic added the skeleton of the event handler for the form's `Load` event. The `Load` event is the most typical place to put startup code for a form. When the application launches, the form will be created, and the form's `Load` event will fire. Let us look carefully at the code for the form.

All of the code lives between the `Class` and `End Class` lines. If you are unfamiliar with classes, we will expand on them in Chapter 3, "Finite State Machines (FSMs)." For now, all the code for the form goes inside the class. We are more interested in the event handler.

```
Private Sub GameForm_Load(ByVal sender As System.Object, _
       ByVal e As System.EventArgs) Handles MyBase.Load
```

Going from left to right:

- The first keyword is `Private`. `Private` conceals this routine, making it visible only inside the class. You can safely ignore it for now; we will not change it.

- `Sub` implies that the code does not return a value. If we need to return a value, we would use the `Function` keyword instead.

- VB needed a name for this routine, so it used the name of the form and the name of the event being handled to come up with `GameForm_Load`. We could change this name if we wanted to, but the name the system picked is clear enough.

- Next, you will find a comma-separated list of parameters inside a pair of parentheses. Each parameter is declared the same way as all variables in VB are declared. There is a modifier (`ByVal`), the name of the parameter (`sender`), the keyword `As`, and finally the parameter's type (`System.Object`). Our code will ignore both parameters. (Note that these are preceded by an underscore character; this is the line-continuation character in VB, used when a single line of code spans multiple lines in text.)

- The `Handles` keyword tells the system that this routine is an event handler, and the event it handles is what comes after the `Handles` keyword. The name suggests to the programmer that this is the `Load` event handler, but the `Handles` keyword is authoritative.

We will add our initialization code between the `Sub` and `End Sub` lines shortly. We can ignore the complexities safely as long as we remember that the code we add here will run when the form is loaded, which for us means once, at startup.

Our application will want to compute the correct value of maximum hit points and show it as the text in the HitPointsLabel field instead of 888. To do this, the code needs to compute the product of the level of the character times the size of the character's hit dice. It would be nice if the radio buttons would directly tell us the size of the character's hit dice, but they do not. The Level control will give us a numeric value for level, but we need an integer variable to hold the die size. Just like on a car radio, we have to program the number we want to associate with each button. To make life easier, we will store that number away whenever a button gets clicked.

Below the Public Class GameForm and above the handler for `Load`, type the following and press Enter:

```
Dim dieSize as integer
```

Visual Basic will reformat and color the text as you go.

Note

> As you type, Intellisense will offer various options that you can select. Pressing Ctrl+spacebar brings up Intellisense if it is not already there, and pressing Esc makes Intellisense go away. When Intellisense offers an option list, you can scroll to the one you want and press Tab to select it. The help system and Wikipedia can tell you more.

We want our software to "wake up sane." That means the value shown for maximum hit points should be based on the level and class selected on the user interface. We could have set the Maximum Hit Points label Text property to 4 instead of 888 and selected Mage as the character class, knowing that we set the Level control to start with a value of 1. Doing so would force us into keeping all three controls synchronized whenever we reprogram any of them. It also means that the formula to compute maximum hit points would exist in two places: invisibly implied by the value we use in the Maximum Hit Points label Text property and explicitly stated somewhere in our code. If we change the formula, we would also have to remember to change the label.

There is a better way to ensure that our software wakes up sane. We are going to write code that changes the Maximum Hit Points label Text property whenever the user changes the level or class. Our Load event handler will act like a user and set the user interface to sane values. Then, all the code we have to write anyway will work on our behalf to wake up sane. We will be able to see at a glance that our code works.

We want the formula to exist in only one place. Add the following code between the end of the form Load event handler and the end of the class:

```
Sub ComputeHitPoints()
    HitPointsLabel.Text = CStr(dieSize * Level.Value)
End Sub
```

Adding this code sets the label text to the product of the character level (from the Level control) and their die size (the variable) all converted to a string, since the Text property is of type string and not of type integer. We need to call this code any time the user interface changes the level or class settings. How will our code know the user interface changed?

Whenever the controls are changed by the user, VB will fire events for the controls. We have an event handler for the form's Load event; now we need handlers for the Level and Class controls.

1. Click the GameForm.vb [Design] tab.

2. Double-click the NumericUpDown control.

3. Visual Basic creates a handler for the ValueChanged event. This is the exact event we need to handle. Add a line to the handler to compute the new maximum hit points:

```
Call ComputeHitPoints()
```

4. The Call keyword is not required, but it does help beginning programmers understand that the code is invoking a subroutine. Click the Design tab again.

5. Double-click the Mage radio button. Visual Basic again takes us to the code, and this time it creates a handler for the radio button's `CheckedChanged` event. This event fires when the checked status changes, which includes when the button goes from checked to unchecked. We only want to act if the button was checked. Add the following code for the event handler:

```
If MageRadio.Checked Then

    dieSize = 4
    Call ComputeHitPoints()
End If
```

6. Add similar code for each of the other radio buttons. When finished, your new code should look like the following:

```
Private Sub Level_ValueChanged(ByVal sender As System.Object, _
        ByVal e As System.EventArgs) Handles Level.ValueChanged
    Call ComputeHitPoints()
End Sub

Private Sub MageRadio_CheckedChanged(ByVal sender As System.Object, _
        ByVal e As System.EventArgs) Handles MageRadio.CheckedChanged
    If MageRadio.Checked Then
        dieSize = 4
        Call ComputeHitPoints()
    End If
End Sub

Private Sub ThiefRadio_CheckedChanged(ByVal sender As System.Object, _
        ByVal e As System.EventArgs) Handles ThiefRadio.CheckedChanged
    If ThiefRadio.Checked Then
        dieSize = 6
        Call ComputeHitPoints()
    End If
End Sub

Private Sub ClericRadio_CheckedChanged(ByVal sender As System.Object, _
        ByVal e As System.EventArgs) Handles ClericRadio.CheckedChanged
    If ClericRadio.Checked Then
        dieSize = 8
        Call ComputeHitPoints()
    End If
End Sub
```

```
Private Sub FighterRadio_CheckedChanged(ByVal sender As System.Object, _
        ByVal e As System.EventArgs) Handles FighterRadio.CheckedChanged
    If FighterRadio.Checked Then
        dieSize = 10
        Call ComputeHitPoints()
    End If
End Sub
```

That code takes care of all of the user interface events our code will need to handle. Let us see how well it works.

From the Visual Basic main menu, select Debug→Start Debugging or press F5. You should see something like Figure 1.6. Note that the application changed the value of 888 to 4 as expected. You can stop debugging by clicking the Close button (the red button with an × inside) in the upper-right corner of the application window or by selecting Stop Debugging from the Visual Basic Debug menu.

We can tell at a glance that our code does not wake up sane. It shows no class selection, and 888 is probably not the right number of hits points for a first level character of any class. At least the Level control is sane. Click one of the radio

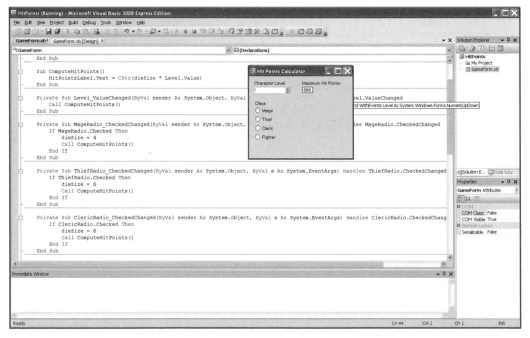

Figure 1.6
The project, running for the first time.

buttons to select a class and see the number of hit points change to the correct value. Change the Level and Class settings and verify that the code properly handles user input. Stop debugging so that you can edit the code.

We need our code to wake up with a class selected. The Level control wakes up sane, but the Class settings do not. We could set the Checked property to true for one of the radio buttons using the Properties window, but there is a better way. Add the following line to the empty GameForm_Load routine:

```
MageRadio.Checked = True
```

Now when our code wakes up, it will check the MageRadio radio button. This means that the radio buttons will appear to the user to wake up sane. One button will be selected. Run the application again. Notice that the maximum number of hit points is shown as 4 and not as 888. We did not directly change the label text, so why did it change? When our code selected the radio button, the system did as we asked and selected the button. The system also did as it always does and fired the CheckedChanged event for the control. The event handler we added for that event of that control ran, setting the die size to 4 and calling ComputeHitPoints. ComputeHitPoints set the label for us, using the formula. Not only will user interaction cause events to be fired, but actions by our code cause them as well.

We exploited the capability of our code to raise events in order to let it use the regular code for operation to also work for initialization. This cut down on the coding and the complexity. We eliminated a hidden dependency between the formula and the initialization code. Getting rid of special initialization code gets rid of potential bugs; there are no bugs in code that is not there.

Chapter Summary

In this chapter, we established a working definition for game AI. Game AI must act intelligently in the face of changing conditions. Unlike physics, game AI has choices when making its decisions. This chapter also gave us our first project, providing a grounding in Visual Basic that we will build upon in future chapters.

Chapter Review

Answers are in the appendix.

1. What are the three parts to our definition of game AI?

2. Why is game physics not game AI?

References

[Abrash96] Abrash, Michael, "The Quake Graphics Engine." In lecture, Computer Game Developers Conference, Santa Clara, California, April 2, 1996.

[Lazzaro04] Lazzaro, Nicole, "Why We Play Games: Four Keys to More Emotion Without Story." XEODesign, Inc., 2004. Available online at http://www.xeodesign.com/xeodesign_whyweplaygames.pdf. See also http://www.xeodesign.com/whyweplaygames.html.

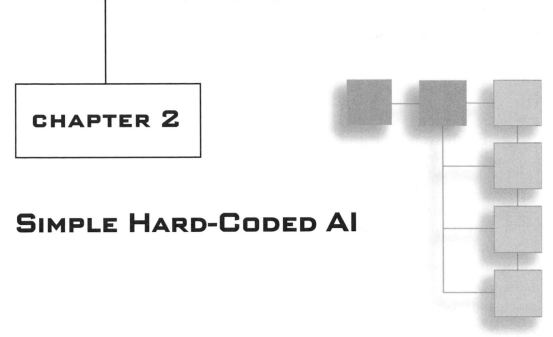

CHAPTER 2

SIMPLE HARD-CODED AI

If the answer to the question, "How will I do the AI?" is "Just write the code," chances are you will write hard-coded AI. Also known as scripted AI, this method has good and bad points. The most serious challenge with hard-coded AI is knowing when to use it and when not to use it. Because hard-coded AI is the most straightforward of all AI techniques, most of this chapter is devoted to facing that challenge, covering the advantages and disadvantages of using hard-coded AI rather than the methods for hard coding.

The Good, the Bad, and the Ugly

When the code fits the situation well, hard-coded AI is often the fastest and most intelligent AI code possible. When the code is not appropriate, the decisions that result from hard-coded AI are often so bad that they disrupt the player's suspension of disbelief. Hard-coded AI gets complex very quickly, can be difficult to debug, and scales extremely poorly. Its brittle nature can quickly lead programmers to think there has to be a better way. These are software-engineering issues in addition to being AI issues, but the demands placed on game AI bring the issues out quickly.

The Good

It is very hard to improve on simple, straightforward code for implementing an algorithm. Properly designed and implemented, this kind of code benefits from minimal overhead and fast execution. Simplicity brings many other benefits. Programmers writing this kind of code find it easy to write and debug. Indeed, this is exactly the kind of coding method that is taught to beginners and perfected by the time they become professionals. As long as the code keeps a reasonable level of simplicity and straightforwardness, this kind of code represents the first and best way of getting the job done.

Sophistication is not always a virtue. Imagine a nail-driving tool that is more sophisticated than a hammer but less sophisticated than a power nail gun. Such a tool would fail in the marketplace because it would fail to displace either hammers or power nail guns. AI code is similar. Any methodology more sophisticated than simple hard-coded AI must be sophisticated enough to bring benefits that outweigh its costs. There is no place for methods that fall in between "simple" and "sophisticated enough."

To extend the nail-gun analogy, consider the fact that hardware stores still sell a wide variety of hammers. Nail guns have not destroyed hammer sales. Carpenters and even roofers still carry and employ hammers. In games, sophisticated AI methods have not wiped out simple AI methods. Professional AI programmers employ both. Beginning AI programmers start with simple methods and move on as they learn more sophisticated ones. That being said, after learning to use sophisticated methods to implement AI, beginning AI programmers should not ignore the simple methods they first learned. It is a beginner's mistake to forget to check if the simplest way to implement AI is also the best way. Many times it will not be, but surprisingly often, the simple methods are the best.

The Bad

Perhaps the most critical issue for hard-coded AI is that it must determine when its behaviors are appropriate. For tiny behaviors, the determination is so obvious and easy to compute conclusively that the programmer can forget to deal explicitly with the issue when the AI grows more complex. The code, no matter how good, must fit the situation.

Consider the AI for a simulated opera singer—a tenor. We will name him Horatio and refer to him in future chapters. The AI for Horatio evaluates his current situation. He is dressed in a dark formal suit. He is standing before a seated, mostly quiet group of formally dressed people. The lights over the audience are low. Quiet, formally dressed ushers direct people to their seats. Music begins to play. So of course his AI directs Horatio to break into the opening song of the latest opera. Unfortunately, the scene described is a funeral home, not a small theater. No matter how good the AI is at making Horatio sing and portray emotion and move on stage, it is behaving inappropriately. As mentioned in Chapter 1, "Introduction," one of the overriding goals of any AI programmer is to avoid artificial stupidity.

No matter how good the AI is at the things it does well, players will recoil when the AI is stupid. Inappropriate behavior destroys suspension of disbelief. Simple, hard-coded AI carries with it the risk of selecting an inappropriate behavior. If the AI for Horatio could reason, it might be thinking, "You mean I am not supposed to be singing right now?" Hard-coded AI also tends to exhibit poor default behaviors: "This is what I do when I don't know what to do." A simple AI can be hamstrung by having a set of behaviors that is too limited: "These few things are all that I know how to do." While hard-coded AI lacks formal structures that lead the programmer to deal with any of these issues, action selection is the most noticeable.

Thus, the first challenge when writing hard-coded AI is to make sure that the AI reasons correctly that the action it is about to take is the right one. It should not decide to sing opera at funerals. The second challenge for hard-coded AI is to fake it gracefully when it does not know what it should be doing. The third challenge for the AI programmer when creating hard-coded AI is to give it a sufficiently broad set of behaviors. Answering this third challenge helps mitigate the second one if the additional behaviors have different situations where they are appropriate.

The Ugly

The major enemies of hard-coded AI are size and complexity. Code organization is ad hoc unless the programmer actively takes steps to regularize it. Changes to the code often entail a full rewrite or major refactoring of the code—and failing to refactor the code carries the risk that the new code will never work properly. This kind of code is said to be "brittle." It has certain strengths, but beyond a certain point, the method fails catastrophically. Ad-hoc organization provides no clear guidance for the programmer with respect to where more code should be added as new capabilities are required. This method fails to scale up.

Reconsider hard-coded AI when size and size-related complexity threaten to become overwhelming. Hard-coded AI is a good place for small, complex algorithms, but it is not well suited when the complexity is mostly due to large size. "Overwhelming" will mean different things to different programmers, and it will change for the same programmer in different parts of his or her career. An evaluation of what is too complex should be made in real time by the people who have to deal with the code. Hard and fast rules in this area are suspect, but in general you should take pains to organize your code and be wiling to refactor it readily.

Note

Refactoring means that you improve the internal structure of the code without changing its external function. It's saying "knowing what I know now, and knowing what I have to change in this code today, I should have written it differently," and then taking the time to rewrite it accordingly.

Refactoring might not get rid of complexity, but it should make it more manageable. The ability to visualize complex software is a very saleable skill. Companies seek and attempt to retain programmers who can keep a clear picture of a large and complex program in their heads and reason about it, but all people have limits.

Projects

The projects for this chapter are based on the AI for a series of household thermostats. While the simplest of thermostats hardly requires a computer, the most sophisticated thermostats certainly depend on the tiny computers inside them.

Note

If you are new to using Visual Studio, you may want to review the projects in Chapter 1 before proceeding.

At first blush, a thermostat may seem to be far removed from game AI. But although it may not seem like it does, a thermostat does meet our definition of an AI insofar as it reacts intelligently to changing conditions. Yes, game AI tends to bring to mind images of the clever, hard-to-overcome bosses found on the last level of a 40-hour game. It is worth noting, however, that such games do not start with the boss level—and for good reason. So it is with learning to program AI. AI game programmers are responsible for turning what would otherwise be a museum walkthrough into an entertainment experience. Their tasks include programming many small, less obvious decision-making capabilities, such as camera AI.

Consider camera AI. Some aspects of camera AI are readily handled by simple, short, hard-coded scripts. A small chunk of AI allows game designers to create a compelling dramatic experience by taking temporary control of the camera. Imagine a first-person-perspective game. The camera shows what the player's character in the game sees. The character deals with the last enemy in a stairwell, opens the door to the roof, and steps out, hoping that the promised helicopter will come and pick him up. At this point, the game freezes and the camera pulls back, showing the character standing there, up high and alone. It then pans a full circle, allowing the player to see the burning city below. Then the camera moves forward and jumps back to the character's perspective. The player walks that character around the roof and gets a bad feeling about the helicopter before giving up and heading back down the stairwell. Halfway down, however, he decides that one last look for the helicopter is in order. The player's character opens the door to the roof and steps out—but this time the AI does *not* take control of the camera.

The hard-coded script for that bit of camera AI is an if-then statement with two conditions. *If* the character is walking out the door and is doing so for the first time, *then* the camera AI should take control and run the pan script. The core decision-making logic is well within the capabilities of a beginning programmer. It is not a great teaching example, however, because it demands that a complex game program—complete with compelling art assets and good interfaces for the AI programmer—already exist.

Thermostat AI places low demands on the programmer in terms of the amount of effort needed to handle the software that is *not* the decision-making part of the thermostat. While few games use thermostat code, many games use code of similar complexity, as seen in the camera example. For example, level designs often involve traps and triggers, and they use AI comparable to our thermostat examples.

A Simple Thermostat

Consider the AI of a very simple thermostat. A mechanical switch in the thermostat decides whether the heating system should run or not run. We will create this type of a thermostat AI as part of a new project.

1. Using Visual Studio, create a new Windows Forms Application and call it Thermostat.

2. Double-click My Project in the Solution Explorer.

3. VB will bring up a window with a column of tabs such as Application and Compile on the left side of the window. Click the Compile tab if it is not already selected.

4. One of the Compile options is Option Strict. Click the drop-down and set it to On.

5. Right-click Form1.vb in the Solution Explorer and rename it House.vb.

6. Click the form in the designer and change the Text property from Form1 to House Simulator, as shown in Figure 2.1.

Next, we will place the controls that make up the house simulation. This will correspond to the "game" in which our AI will operate. As the projects get more complex, we will rely more on the code on the CD, but doing them step-by-step here ensures familiarity with Windows applications written in VB.

We need a reasonably rich world for our AI to operate. The split between what is part of the AI and what is part of the rest of the game is a game-design issue. We will consider all decision making as part of the AI, but will minimize the amount

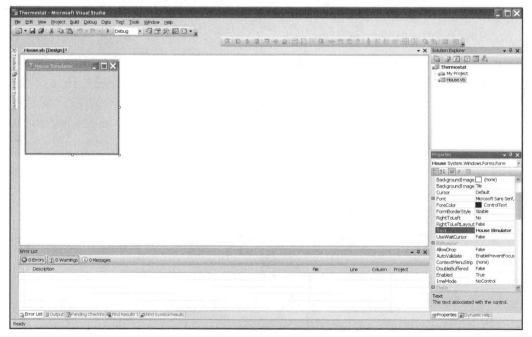

Figure 2.1
The Thermostat project, before the placement of controls.

of AI code devoted to carrying out the decisions of the AI. Once the decisions are made, implementation of the actions is deemed to be something the game world provides. For now, we will also minimize the amount of AI code devoted to sensing the world. Reasoning about the world is the purview of the AI, but the raw state data about the world is something the world should provide to the AI. Professional AI programmers have to be vigilant to ensure that the world will indeed provide the AI with critical data it needs. "Vigilant" in this usage often means that professional game AI programmers wind up writing a large portion of the sensing and action code needed by their reasoning code.

The rich world for the thermostat AI begins with the room temperature. The room temperature will provide the changing conditions that prompt the AI to react intelligently. The AI also needs a furnace to control in order for it to react. The AI itself will do the intelligent part, but that code will be separated out and not part of the simulation.

Note that our AI keeps no memory of the past. Our AI deals only in the current temperature. If the AI needed knowledge about prior temperatures to help it reason, it would have to remember them itself. The world simulation should not keep this data because it exists solely to help the AI. More sophisticated AI will retain memories of the past or suppositions about the future.

Small amounts of data are well served by ad hoc organization, but larger amounts need formal organization. This is known as knowledge representation (KR). Our thermostat AI cannot directly change the world temperature; it can only turn on the furnace. If our AI needed to reason about a world that was warmer, it would need to simulate or partly simulate that world and reason using the simulation. As the programmer, we would need to design the simulation, and that design would be the KR for it. (We will cover KR more explicitly in future chapters.)

1. Drag a Label control to the top-left part of the form and change the Text property to Ambient.

2. Drag another Label control to the right of the first label and change its Text property to Set Point.

3. Drag a third Label control to the right of the others and change its Text property to Status.

4. Drag a NumericUpDown control below the Ambient label.

5. Drag the tiny box on the right side to the left to make the control small enough to fit under the label.

6. Change the Name property of NumericUpDown to AmbientUpDown.

7. The default value of 0 for the Minimum property and 100 for the Maximum property do not need to be changed for a thermostat using the Fahrenheit scale. If you use Centigrade, change the Minimum property to −15 and the Maximum property to 45.

8. Similarly drag a NumericUpDown control below the Set Point label and rename it SetPointUpDown.

9. Resize SetPointUpDown and optionally change the Minimum and Maximum properties.

10. Drag a Label control below the Status label.

11. Change the Label control's Name property to StatusLabel and its Text property to Undefined.

12. Change its BackColor property to White and the BorderStyle property to FixedSingle. Note that when you go to change the color, there will be three tabs showing: System, Web, and Custom. The default tab is System, and White is not listed as an option in the drop-down for that tab. Instead, White is listed in the Web tab, along with many common color names. You can pick it from the drop-down for the Web tab or you can simply type over the existing color with the name of the color that you want. Your project should resemble Figure 2.2.

13. We are ready to add the code. We will put the AI code in a separate file to help differentiate between the world simulation and the AI. Right-click the Thermostat project in the Solution Explorer, choose Add, and choose Module.

Tip

You could also add the module by opening the Project menu and choosing Add Module.

14. The Add New Item dialog box opens with the filename highlighted at the bottom. Change the name to AI.vb and click Add.

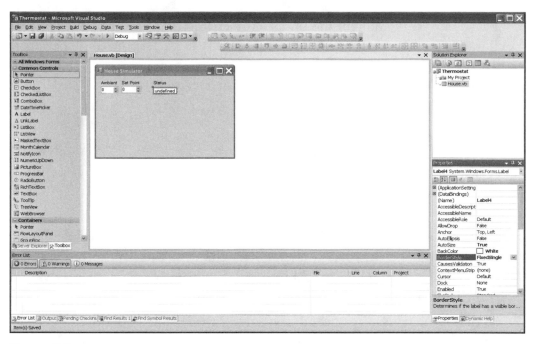

Figure 2.2
Thermostat project, ready for code.

15. We will start with the core AI routine. Designing it first will show us what inputs the AI needs from the world and what outputs it will want to implement. Add the following code to the AI.vb file between the `Module AI` and `End Module` lines:

```
'This function evaluates world conditions and gives back a
' response for the furnace as a string
Private Function CoreAI(ByVal currentTemp As Integer, _
        ByVal desiredTemp As Integer) As String
    If currentTemp < desiredTemp Then
        Return ("Heat")
    Else
        Return ("Off")
    End If
End Function
```

This is only the core code. We need additional code to extract the inputs from the world and to implement the output. The function is marked `private` because we expect it to be called by other AI code that will provide the translations. Note that comment lines in VB start with a single quote character. As mentioned, the underscore character is the line continuation character in VB. Since the language does not use a termination character, like the semi-colon in C, it has a continuation character for when a single line of code should span multiple lines for readability.

16. Now add the following wrapper function to AI.vb:

```
'This is the public wrapper. It knows about the world.
Public Sub RunAI(ByVal World As House)
    World.StatusLabel.Text = CoreAI(CInt(World.AmbientUpDown.Value), _
        CInt(World.SetPointUpDown.Value))
End Sub
```

The wrapper isolates the AI implementation from the world implementation. If how the world is implemented changes, then only the wrapper needs to change, not the core AI routine. CInt converts the UpDown values from decimal to integer.

17. All that remains is to connect the world to the AI. When does the AI need to run? It needs to run upon startup and whenever either of the two temperatures changes.

18. Right-click House.vb in the Solution Explorer and select View Code.

19. We need to get to the form load event. Above the code-editing pane (the big center area) are two drop-down lists. Change the selected entry in the drop-down list on the left from House to (House Events).

20. Change the selected entry in the drop-down list on the right from Declarations to Load. Visual Studio takes you to the event handler or creates the skeleton for it if it does not exist. (This procedure is useful for creating event handlers other than the default event handler and to navigate to a particular event handler.)

21. Change the selected entry in the left drop-down list to AmbientUpDown.

22. Change the selected entry in the right drop-down list to ValueChanged. Visual Studio will create the skeleton for the event handler.

23. Change the selected entry in the left drop-down list to SetPointUpDown.

24. Again change the selected entry in the right drop-down list to Value-Changed. Visual Studio will create the skeleton for this event handler.

25. Add the following line of code to all three event handlers:

```
Call AI.RunAI(Me)
```

26. The `Me` in this case refers to the running instance of the form. Observant readers will have noticed that the `Sub` that handles the form load event is marked as `Handles Me.Load` in the code. Add a comment, and your code should look like the following:

```
'We check the furnace at startup and whenever conditions change.

Private Sub House_Load(ByVal sender As Object, ByVal e As System.EventArgs) _
        Handles Me.Load
    Call AI.RunAI(Me)
End Sub

Private Sub Ambient_ValueChanged(ByVal sender As Object, ByVal e As _
        System.EventArgs) Handles AmbientUpDown.ValueChanged
    Call AI.RunAI(Me)
End Sub

Private Sub SetPointUpDown_ValueChanged(ByVal sender As System.Object, _
        ByVal e As System.EventArgs) Handles SetPointUpDown.ValueChanged
    Call AI.RunAI(Me)
End Sub
```

27. Run the application in the debugger. Note that the status label has the value Off even though the label starts with the value Undefined. This means that the form load event triggered. Manipulate both temperature controls and watch the status change back and forth between Off and Heat. If we had forgotten either event handler, our furnace would ignore changing conditions of interest to it.

Analysis

The AI code, especially the core AI code, is fast, simple, and reasonably bullet-proof. But suppose the thermostat were also asked to control the windows, closing them whenever the furnace is running. The window AI knows exactly the right thing to do and can execute that action so well that it is a given. (We are not considering how easy or hard opening or closing the windows might be.) At first blush, this makes good sense. The windows should be closed when the furnace is running. But the thermostat will also leave the windows open all summer, even when it rains, and it may open the windows when it is cold outside if the room is comfortably warm. Piggybacking the window AI onto the furnace AI results in a poor window AI. The AI response does not fit the conditions.

Making sure that the AI response fits the conditions makes or breaks hard-coded AI. It is rather easy to forget to guard against all the situations where the AI acts inappropriately; indeed, it can be impossible to be completely effective in all cases. Beginning AI programmers must learn to always do the analysis. Hard-coded AI is simply too fast and effective to be discarded out of hand, but knowing when *not* to use it takes practice.

Complexity is the enemy of hard-coded AI. As the number of decisions that govern a particular behavior rises, complexity explodes. Complexity also increases as the number of actions needed to implement a behavior increases and with the number of inputs and the amount of state data that must be examined to make the decisions. At a certain point, the complexity overwhelms the ability of the programmer to write, debug, or modify the code. Usually, the ability to modify the code is the first to succumb, followed by the ability to debug the code.

The thermostat we just coded has one decision to make: whether to call for heat. It can implement that decision with a single action. It has one item of state data: the desired temperature. It has one input from the outside world: the current temperature in the room. So the answer to each of the "how many" questions is 1, the lowest possible number that can still expect an intelligent decision to be made. Is it too low for it to meet our definition of AI?

To react intelligently to changing conditions, the AI must be able to act. This thermostat has one output action. For it to detect changing conditions, it must be influenced by at least one outside piece of data: the current temperature. For it to act intelligently, it needs guidance on the decisions—and that guidance is the set point of the thermostat. This AI is almost the simplest possible AI; it is no surprise that hard-coded design is more than adequate to the task. A more complex design would be overkill. It would be harder to write and debug. The overhead of a more complex method would certainly make it slower to run. It is hard to beat simple methods!

Consider, though, a very simple set-back thermostat with a day setting and a night setting. It still has only one decision to make: whether to call for heat. The internal state data has gone up, however, because there are two set points to track. And the set points themselves have become more complex: Instead of a simple number for the temperature, each set point also has a start time. One number has become four numbers. Also, this thermostat has two inputs from the outside world: the current temperature and the current time.

Real thermostats usually rely on their own clock instead of asking the outside world what time it is. That said, real thermostats, depending on their implementation details, often fail to stay synchronized with the correct time. Power failures, daylight saving time, and even changes in which weekend daylight savings time changes conspire to make real thermostats make bad decisions. To avoid this form of artificial stupidity, our thermostat will lack a time-of-day clock and will ask the outside world what time it is whenever it wants to know.

At first glance, our original thermostat had three things to deal with: one action, one piece of state data, and one piece of world data. This new thermostat has more. It has one action, four pieces of state data, and two pieces of world data. If the different categories do not interact, overall complexity relates to the sum of the different elements. In that case, our complexity has gone up seven-fold. Life for an AI programmer is rarely so kind, however. If the different categories *do* interact, we multiply to get a gauge of complexity. In that case, our complexity has gone up eight-fold. Not surprisingly, this new thermostat is hard to find on the market. While it saves money compared to the first one, it is not intelligent enough to compete with more complex offerings.

Implementing this thermostat is left as an exercise for the reader. Note that the core AI function call does not need to be changed, only the wrapper. Readers taking the slow and steady approach will want to take the time and help cement their skills with Visual Studio and VB. More advanced readers will hold off until we get to a more realistic example.

Our first two thermostats deal with only heat. Adding air conditioning means adding another output and another piece of state data. Our complexity count is then two actions, five pieces of state data, and two pieces of world data. These interact at least partially, giving us a potential comparative complexity product of 20. The code can no longer be written without thought or debugged at a glance. And like the heat-only version of this thermostat, this thermostat is not intelligent enough to compete in the marketplace. Implementation is again left to the reader.

Our fourth thermostat has four set points instead of two. This level of complexity is suitable for many households, and such thermostats are widely available. The set points are matched to getting up in the morning, being away all day, being home in the evening, and being asleep at night. The amount of state data has gone from five items to nine. There are four set points, each with a time and temperature. There is also the mode switch, which decides between heating and cooling. This sums to nine pieces of state data. So two actions, nine pieces of state data, and two pieces of world data multiply to 36. Care must be taken in the coding and design to minimize the number of interactions between all of the data.

A More Sophisticated Implementation

We could implement a fully generalized user interface for this thermostat, but that would go beyond what is needed to illustrate the point. Our implementation will have the expected four set points, but we will not create a user interface for setting them. At this point, it is worth asking, "Where does the state data live? Is it part of the world or is it part of the AI?" The ambient temperature and the time are clearly world data. Our set points could be in either place. If the thermostat needed to remember what it was doing the last time it ran, that data would be part of the AI. It would be part of the AI's knowledge representation of how the world used to be—a piece of data it is remembering to help it think about how it wants to act now.

1. Go to the code for House.vb and delete the three lines that make up the `SetPointUpDown ValueChanged` event handler. We will keep the four set points in the world data.

2. Add the following three lines to House.vb:

```
'Here are the thermostat programmed values.
Public ReadOnly SetTemps() As Integer = {70, 64, 68, 60}
Public ReadOnly SetTimes() As Integer = {6, 9, 17, 21}
```

The () by the names denote that the variables are arrays. The arrays are public so that they can be accessed by the AI code in a different file. They are read-only because we do not expect to change them, and any attempt to do so is a bug we want to catch. The arrays are initialized with the values shown in { }. The temperature values are in Fahrenheit degrees. The times are in hours, using a 24-hour clock familiar to people who have experience with the military or a European train schedule. Our thermostat will not bother with minutes, only the hour. The sequence of values corresponds to morning, day, evening, and night.

3. Click the House.vb[Design] tab.

4. Click the SetPointUpDown control.

5. Right-click it and delete it.

Note

At some point, the error list will show an error because the AI wrapper function as currently written references the deleted control. For now, we will ignore the errors, work on the user interface elements, and update the AI last.

6. Drag a Label control to where the deleted control used to be.

7. Change the label's Name property to SetPointLabel and the Text property to Not Set.

8. Change the BackColor property to White and the BorderStyle property to FixedSingle.

9. Drag a Label control just below the Temperature controls.

10. Change the Text property to Time.

11. Drag a NumericUpDown control just below the new label and make it smaller.

12. Change the Name property to TimeUpDown and the Maximum property to 23.

13. Drag another new Label control just below the Time controls.

14. Change the Text property to Mode.

15. Drag two RadioButton controls onto the form and stack them below the Mode label.

16. Change the Text property of the first RadioButton control to Air and the Name property to AirRadio.

17. Change the Text property of the second RadioButton control to Heat and the Name property to HeatRadio.

18. Change the Checked property of the Heat radio button to True. The form should resemble Figure 2.3.

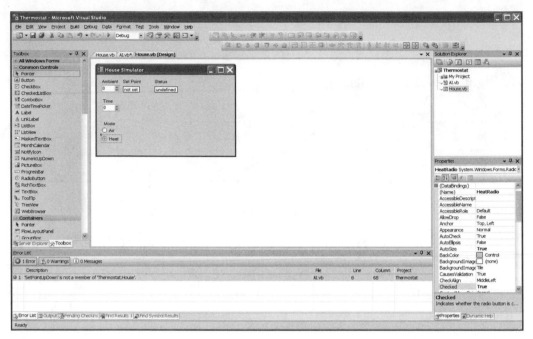

Figure 2.3
The complete user interface for the set-back thermostat.

19. With the new controls, our application needs to handle new events. Double-click the TimeUpDown, AirRadio, and HeatRadio controls. Before each double-click, you will have to switch to the Design view of House.vb. Visual Studio will create the skeletons of the three event handlers we are interested in. Double-clicking the control in the Design view is an alternative to using the drop-down lists at the top of the Code view. Double-clicking takes you to the most commonly used event; to get to other events, you will have to use the drop-down menus.

20. Add the following familiar line of code to all three event handlers:

```
Call AI.RunAI(Me)
```

The code for House.vb should now look like the following:

```
'Here are the thermostat programmed values.
Public ReadOnly SetTemps() As Integer = {70, 64, 68, 60}
Public ReadOnly SetTimes() As Integer = {6, 9, 17, 21}

'We check the furnace at startup and whenever conditions change.
Private Sub House_Load(ByVal sender As Object, _
```

```
            ByVal e As System.EventArgs) Handles Me.Load
        Call AI.RunAI(Me)
    End Sub

    Private Sub Ambient_ValueChanged(ByVal sender As Object, ByVal e As _
            System.EventArgs) Handles AmbientUpDown.ValueChanged
        Call AI.RunAI(Me)
    End Sub

    Private Sub TimeUpDown_ValueChanged(ByVal sender As System.Object, _
            ByVal e As System.EventArgs) Handles TimeUpDown.ValueChanged
        Call AI.RunAI(Me)
    End Sub

    Private Sub AirRadio_CheckedChanged(ByVal sender As System.Object, _
            ByVal e As System.EventArgs) Handles AirRadio.CheckedChanged
        Call AI.RunAI(Me)
    End Sub

    Private Sub HeatRadio_CheckedChanged(ByVal sender As System.Object, _
            ByVal e As System.EventArgs) Handles HeatRadio.CheckedChanged
        Call AI.RunAI(Me)
    End Sub
```

21. Now we move to AI.vb to create our more sophisticated AI. We will work from the wrapper toward the core AI. The core AI will need to know what operating mode to use, so the wrapper will need to get that from the world. Likewise, the core AI will need to know the right set-point temperature. The wrapper will need to know what time it is to get the right temperature value, but once that value is available, the core AI does not care what time it is. Change the wrapper to match the following code (every line changed):

```
'This is the public wrapper. It knows about the world.
Public Sub RunAI(ByVal World As House)
    Dim mode As CurrentMode
    Dim desired As Integer

    'interrogate the world about our settings
    desired = DesiredTemp(World)
    mode = FurnaceMode(World)
```

```
    'and let the core AI figure out what to do.
    World.StatusLabel.Text = CoreAI(CInt(World.AmbientUpDown.Value), _
        desired, mode)
End Sub
```

22. We have not yet written the code that gets the mode and desired temperature, so Visual Studio will quietly complain about the names not being declared. We have not yet defined what CurrentMode means either. It will also complain about the fact that we added an argument to the wrapper function's call to the core but we have not yet changed the core AI. These complaints appear in the Error List tab at the bottom. They are also marked in the code the same way Microsoft Word marks spelling errors. First we will interrogate the world. Add the following code to get the mode of operation:

```
'These modes should match up with radio buttons
Private Enum CurrentMode
    Heat
    Cool
    'Off would go here
    Unknown
End Enum
Private Function FurnaceMode(ByVal World As House) As CurrentMode
    'we put all of the modes into parallel arrays
    'They MUST have the same number of entries

    Dim ModeRadios() As RadioButton = {World.AirRadio, World.HeatRadio}
    Dim ModeValues() As CurrentMode = {CurrentMode.Cool, CurrentMode.Heat}

    'we need a variable to iterate the arrays
    Dim i As Integer

    'Go through the array. Find the one that is checked
    'This code automatically adjusts to adding
    For i = 0 To ModeRadios.GetUpperBound(0)
        If ModeRadios(i).Checked Then
            Return ModeValues(i)
        End If
    Next

    'In case we forgot to check one of them
    Return CurrentMode.Unknown
End Function
```

The GetUpperBound function returns the highest valid subscript for the array. Writing the code this way means fewer things to keep synchronized. The loop always goes from the beginning of the array to the end. As long as the two arrays have the same number of items, the same subscript can be used for both.

Note

The function knows about the radio buttons we added to the form and puts them in an array. If we wanted to add a third mode, such as an explicit off mode, we would add another radio button to the form and add the name of that radio button to the array. We would also add a corresponding entry into the Enum and put that entry in the ModeValues array. On the form, VB groups all radio buttons that have the same container, such as a form, so that checking one unchecks all of the others.

Note

It is worth noting that explicit knowledge of the world implementation is creeping into the AI code. We will be successful at keeping it out of the core AI, but the wrapper and the world are two different files that have to be kept in sync.

23. We still need to interrogate the world about the desired temperature. Add the following code to AI.vb:

```
Private Function DesiredTemp(ByVal World As House) As Integer
    'We need some subscript variables
    Dim ss As Integer

    'the hours after midnight but before morning count as night
    '02:00 is after 21:00 but before 06:00, use the 21:00 value
    Dim foundss As Integer = 3

    'exploit the fact that we know that there are exactly 4 points
    'and that they are in time-sorted order
    For ss = 0 To 3
        'if it is at or past this set time, use this set time.
        If World.TimeUpDown.Value >= World.SetTimes(ss) Then
            foundss = ss
        End If
    Next

    'The times and temps are parallel arrays. A subscript for one
    'can be used on the other
```

```
        'Side effect: show what temp we are using
        World.SetPointLabel.Text = CStr(World.SetTemps(foundss))

        'pass that same value back to the AI.
        Return World.SetTemps(foundss)
End Function
```

This code also knows more than is healthy about how the world implemented the set points, but since that data is directly related to the AI code, it is not as likely to cause problems. The side effect of setting the text of the label is intentional. In this project, it helps debugging by showing that the right set point was selected. In a much broader sense, this is an important part of game AI. As pointed out in Chapter 1, the intelligence must be made noticeable to the player. In addition to finding ways to make the AI smarter or less stupid, the AI programmer must always be looking for ways to make the AI visible to the player.

24. Having gathered data from the world, it is time to upgrade the core AI to make use of it. We will change the signature to include the mode and then make the rest of the code mode aware. Here is the new core code:

```
'This function evaluates input temperatures and mode and gives back a
'response for the furnace as a string
Private Function CoreAI(ByVal currentTemp As Integer, _
        ByVal desiredTemp As Integer, _
        ByVal mode As CurrentMode) As String
    Select Case mode
        Case CurrentMode.Heat
            'the same exact code as before
            If currentTemp < desiredTemp Then
                Return ("Heat")
            Else
                Return ("Ready")
            End If
        Case CurrentMode.Cool
            'note that we flipped the comparison
            If currentTemp > desiredTemp Then
                Return ("Cool")
            Else
                Return ("Ready")
            End If
```

```
        Case Else
            'this helps debug in case we forget to add
            ' a new mode here as well as everywhere else.
            Return "Bad Mode"
    End Select

        'this helps debug because we should never get here
        Return "Broken"
    End Function
```

25. Run the application in the debugger and change the settings. Does the operation seem reasonable?

The heat side is perfectly reasonable, especially for a drafty old house that loses heat quickly and is expensive to heat. The air-conditioning settings seem positively frigid, especially the night setting. A more realistic implementation would have different temperatures for each mode, even if they kept the same times. Doing so adds four more numbers—easily done as another parallel array, but now the numbers interact with the mode. The DesiredTemp function now has to be mode aware. This means that the wrapper has to be changed to get the mode first before it gets the temperature, when before it did not matter. The existing code, which currently works, would have to be changed and the order of the calls fixed. When the two pieces of data were independent, there was less complexity. If we make them interact, the complexity increases. The increased complexity does not show up as increased length of code the way it did in the core AI, but in a nearly hidden way pertaining to statement order. The statements are currently close together, and the interaction would be obvious, but as the code grows, this might now always be the case.

State of the Art

Our last thermostat is modeled after those found in the author's home. It has up to four set points per day, with each day having independent set points, giving 28 set points for heating and 28 more for cooling. It controls a geothermal heat pump that has two stages of cooling and three stages of heating. It also has a fan-only setting. The set points in this thermostat are treated differently. This thermostat anticipates the set points and attempts to have the temperature of the house at the set-point temperature by the set-point time. If the set point is for 68 degrees F at 06:00, this thermostat tries to have the room hit 68 degrees F at 06:00.

The other thermostats we have analyzed so far used their set points as start times, not end times. These latest thermostats determine the stage of heating or cooling required based on the number of degrees between the set point and the current temperature, the amount of time the current staging level has been running, and the current stage of operation.

Recall the discussion from Chapter 1 that AI is not physics. With our latest thermostat, we now have two different methods of operation. Old-style thermostats *start* heating at the set point time, and newer thermostats attempt to *finish* heating at the set point time. The fact that both methods of operation are valid can be seen as evidence that our thermostat example is more like AI than like physics. Rocks on cliffs do not get to choose the method of their falling.

The addition of more set points does not raise the level of complexity in the operation of the thermostat very much. The prior thermostat isolated the set points reasonably well, so the number of them will influence the speed of the code but not the complexity. This decoupling allows the code to scale up without increasing in complexity.

The increase in the level of complexity in this example comes from the implementation of anticipation and the staged output. The thermostat knows that large swings require a second stage. The first stage can almost always hold the house at a given temperature, but changes larger than five degrees are best satisfied with a second stage. The thermostat also calls for the next stage if the temperature does not climb rapidly enough. To make this calculation, the thermostat must track run time at the current stage and well as temperature gain at that stage. The stage called for also depends on the current output, because the unit will not revert to a lower stage if the set point has not yet been met. This algorithm calls for new data and many interactions. The thermostat is thinking about the process, so once again, knowledge representation creeps into the picture.

Implementation is left to the student.

Chapter Summary

The projects in this chapter lead the programmer from simple and effective if-then statements to a more data-driven approach. Hard-coded methods start out simple, fast, and effective, but can wind up brittle and hard to manage. Hard-coded AI can be both the smartest possible AI and the stupidest.

Chapter Review

Answers are in the appendix.

1. What are the common drawbacks to hard-coded AI?

2. What are the advantages to hard-coded AI?

3. Complexity can be as low as the sum of the parts and as high as the product of the parts. What is the relationship between the parts when complexity is the sum? What is it when complexity is the product?

4. What is the design of the data called when the data is information the AI uses to help it think about (or even imagine about) the world?

5. Critique the expediencies in the code that interrogates the world in the four-set-point thermostat. Comment on the dangers versus the additional complexity needed to mitigate the risks.

6. Why is the side effect in the code that gets the set-point temperature in the four-set-point thermostat important?

Exercises

1. Add an explicit Off mode to the thermostat. You will need a additional radio button on the form, an Off entry in the Enum, and an entry in each of the two arrays that are used to turn a checked radio button into a mode value, and you will need to deal with the new mode in the core AI.

2. Implement as many of the features of the last thermostat described as you can. If the specifications seem incomplete, search the Internet or document your reasonable assumptions.

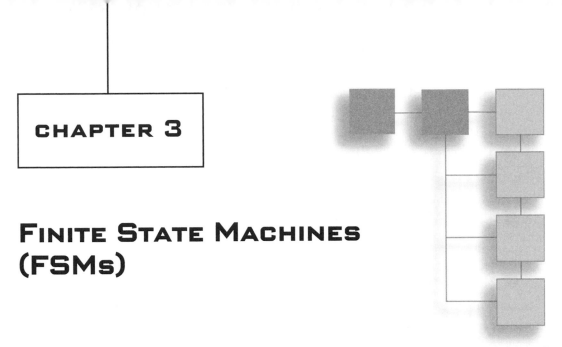

CHAPTER 3

Finite State Machines (FSMs)

Finite state machines are our first formal structure for game AI. The regularity of the structure helps us to manage program complexity, a major problem of hard-coded scripts. Using FSMs, we break down the AI into a fixed—hopefully small—number of states and the transitions between those states. If you have studied formal FSMs in classes, our usage may differ. "It's important to understand that when game developers speak of *state machines* or *finite state machines*, they are only loosely referring to the traditional Computer Science definition." [Rabin02]

This chapter looks at what FSMs are and considers their design and analysis. The analysis includes single-transition review and multiple-transition review. (Multiple-transition review unearths the problems of ambiguous transitions and race conditions.) We will touch briefly on complexity and examine three failure modes. At the end of the chapter are projects to implement an FSM for a game-related AI.

What Are FSMs?

Finite state machines have a finite number of states and a set of transitions between those states. So what do we mean by states? The easiest way to think of states is to think of different ways to finish the statement that begins, "I am. . . ." We could create a list of verbs: flying, walking, running, or sitting. Another way to model uses adjectives: tired, happy, or angry. The set of states might represent nouns: egg, worm, dragon. All of these lists are different ways of doing or being or existing in some way. We build the states in an FSM to model these ways. For game AI, the key idea is that different states imply different behaviors. We expect dragons to behave differently from dragon eggs.

That leaves the transitions. The transitions answer the question, "What would make the AI change from one state to a different state?" Since we are using the states in the FSM to map to behaviors, the question translates to, "What would make the AI change from this set of behaviors to that set of behaviors?"

So can we make our FSMs meet our basic definition of game AI from Chapter 1, "What Is Game AI?" Can they act intelligently in the face of changing conditions? The actions are handled in the states. The transitions provide the mechanism to handle changing conditions. The intelligent part depends on the quality of the fit between the simulated world and the selected states and transitions. Horatio, the simulated opera singer from Chapter 2, "Simple Hard-Coded AI," would still inappropriately break into song if his AI did not correctly differentiate between an opera house and a funeral home. In short, the intelligence is in states and transitions.

Design and Analysis

Besides being a programming method to implement AI, FSMs are an effective AI analysis tool. Before using an FSM, the programmer must ask, "Can I break the AI into concise, independent states?" In order to answer that question, the AI programmer must first solidify his or her idea of what the AI must do. It is imperative to know what the AI must do before an implementation can be selected. The act of determining whether an FSM is appropriate forces the AI programmer to first define the AI.

Look back at the three lists we used to finish the "I am ..." statement. The answers were concise; it is hard to beat single-word answers for brevity. The answers were also independent; that is to say, each one was not like any of the others. More importantly, it would not make sense for the AI to be any two at the same time. Traffic lights and thermostats have concise, independent states and clear transitions. Simulated monsters or very simple simulated people might easily break into a few states, but more complex simulated people do not. A simple monster might be content only to hide, attack, or flee, but a simulated person in the game *The Sims* has to be able to be hungry, lonely, and bored all at

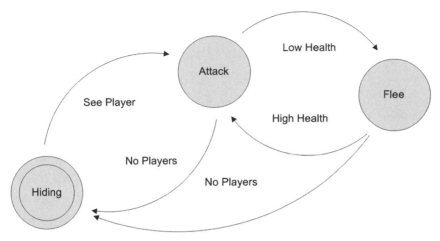

Figure 3.1
First try at a simple monster AI using a finite state machine.

the same time. [Forbus02] If the problem does not easily resolve into independent states, an FSM is not the best solution.

Another question to ask is, "What do the states represent?" For a traffic light, the states might be the color that is currently illuminated. In this case, each state corresponds to an output. This is the most intuitive way of implementing a finite state machine.

FSM machines lend themselves to pictures. One of the better ways to design an FSM is to lay out the states and transitions as a drawing. Figure 3.1 corresponds to our monster AI. It appears quite simple, but it is probably more interesting to analyze than yet another thermostat.

The states are the circles, and the transitions are the arrows. The double circle for the Hiding state means that it is the starting state for our monster. Each transition is an arrow with text showing what causes the transition. There are many drawing programs that make it easy to draw FSM diagrams. This diagram was drawn using Microsoft Visio. In this diagram, the transitions depend on whether the monster can see players or the value of the monster's health. How intelligent is this model? We start reviewing by looking at each single transition by itself.

Single-Transition Review

This model is intelligent, but not intelligent enough. The monster starts out hiding and then attacks when it sees the player. A powerful monster pitted

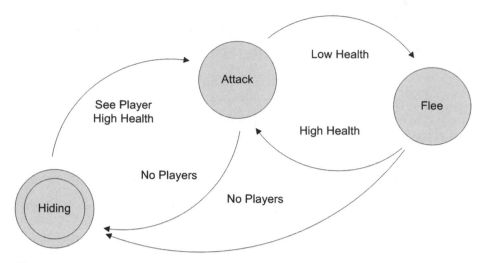

Figure 3.2
AI for a more self-aware monster.

against a weak or inept player will result in quick victory for the monster, which will go back to hiding. If the combat goes against the monster and the monster's health gets too low, it will flee. If the monster is not healed by some means and it successfully evades the players, it will hide. So far, so good. What if the player now wanders into the monster's sight? The monster still has low health. It will attack the player on sight and then immediately flee when it realizes that it has low health. The monster would have been better off if it had remained hidden. So we change the transition from the Hiding state to the Attack state as shown in Figure 3.2.

The change we made between Figures 3.1 and 3.2 improved a single transition to make it better. This change avoids artificial stupidity, and we only had to look at each transition by itself. There is only one transition out of the Hiding state in our FSM. Looking at each transition by itself is the easiest way to review an FSM for potential problems. At first, the original transition looked perfect. The change came after the system left the starting state and ran for a while. The original transition assumed that a monster that was hiding had high health. This is true at the beginning, causing the original transition to seem reasonable, but it was not required to be true. It makes sense for a monster with low health to hide, so we do not want to prevent a low-health monster from hiding. We have already programmed monsters with low health to break away from combat, so it makes sense for us to program monsters with low health to avoid combat.

You should review each single transition of your FSM designs to see that it is always reasonable. It will probably be reasonable during the initial phases of operation, but it may present problems after the data upon which it depends works through the range of possible values. The questions to ask are "Is this transition reasonable from this state in the first place?" and "Is this transition still reasonable when the machine returns to this state from other states?"

Multiple-Transition Review

The second thing to review is multiple transitions. When there is more than one transition out of a state, we face two related issues: disambiguation and race conditions. If two transitions from a single state can be valid at the same time, they are ambiguous. One way that transitions can become ambiguous is if more than one thing in the game world can change before the AI runs again. This gives rise to race conditions. If only one thing can change at a time, Figure 3.2 is perfectly fine. A monster that is in the Attack state can run low on health or it can run out of players, but as long as they do not happen at the same time, the monster AI always does the right thing. If both of those events can happen at the same time, however, the monster AI FSM has two valid transitions to pick from. Transitioning to the Hiding state makes sense, but going to the Flee state does not. The Flee state would transition to the Hiding state as soon as it got a chance.

The problem is that our monster is fleeing from enemies who are not there. A similar condition exists when a monster in the Flee state is healed (perhaps by a more powerful allied monster) at the same time that the players stop pursuit and make themselves scarce (perhaps in order to avoid having to deal with two monsters at the same time). In this case, the FSM in Figure 3.2 will have our monster attack players who are not there. Race conditions like these tend to be subtle and hard to detect at first glance.

In real game development, the AI programmer cannot require that the system change only one thing at a time in order to prevent race conditions in the AI; the AI programmer is forced to deal with race conditions as a fact of life. There are three ways to handle race conditions and ambiguities. You can ignore them, you can fully specify all transitions, and you can prioritize the transitions.

The easiest way to handle ambiguities is to simply not care. In the FSM shown in Figure 3.2, it could be argued that no player will ever see the monster being stupid. The ambiguities all happen when there are no players and some other condition also changes at the same time. We have already noted that if the player never sees great AI, that AI is wasted. Conversely, and to our benefit, if the player never sees artificial stupidity, then for all practical purposes that stupidity did not happen.

This powerful tool fails if the game ever offers the player a chance to see things the player could never see while playing the game. For example, the any-angle instant-replay capability popular in sports games kills this method of handling ambiguities. In our example, we might claim that no player will see our monster being stupid because it only happens when there are no players present. The idea of "no players present" needs closer examination, however. Is the player supposed to be able to hide from the monster? If so, then the player will expect the monster to not detect the hidden player when the player is actually present. If the monster acts like it knows that the player is present when the player is hidden, then the AI is cheating and—more importantly—it is visibly cheating. Players hate visible cheats worse than they hate artificial stupidity. If players can hide and the monster properly ignores them when they do, then the race conditions in the FSM of Figure 3.2 must be dealt with. A player who was hidden from both the monster and the other players will indeed be able to see the monster attack or flee from the other players who are no longer there.

The next simplest way to handle ambiguities is to fully specify every transition in terms of every one of the conditions on which any transition depends. This can be characterized as "Look at all the data every time." "Simple" in this usage does not mean easy or effective, however; it merely means that it is not hard to understand the concept. Full specification adds complexity to the transitions and quickly becomes a nightmare to maintain.

The third and most common way to handle ambiguities is by prioritizing the transitions. If the No Players transitions from the Attack and Flee states are checked before the health-related transitions out of those states, the monster AI will never attempt to attack or flee from players who are not there. The implication here is that the first valid transition found will be the transition taken. This capability is very easy for the programmer to provide by making the code that checks the transitions for validity go through them in a fixed order set by the programmer. The programmer will probably write the code to check the transitions in a fixed order anyway. All that is required is that the programmer thinks about the order and forces it to be optimal. This simple approach often meets a "good enough" criterion.

When there are numerous transitions and states, a fixed order may not always yield the best AI, however. If need be, the programmer can employ a more sophisticated approach and implement dynamic prioritization. With dynamic prioritization, the valid transitions indicate how well they fit the state of the world.

Consider a more sophisticated monster AI. The transition that handles "Flee combat if health is low" might be modified. The modified transition might factor in how fast the player can move compared to the monster when computing priority. A fast player would be able to run down the fleeing monster, so turning to run would be suicidal. It might factor in if the player has missile weapons and there is no cover. So in adverse conditions, the transition from Attack to Flee might still be valid, but with a low priority. Why do this? Our more sophisticated monster AI might have a Berserk state suitable for when all-out attacks are the only hope. Such a behavior has a high entertainment potential for the player. Chances are that the monster will become very scary and dangerous, but only for a very short time. The transitions to the Berserk state have modest priority. The observed behavior is, "When all the normally good ideas look like bad ideas, this normally bad idea is actually the best idea." For a more in-depth coverage of useful techniques for dynamic priorities, see *Behavioral Mathematics for Game AI* [Mark09].

This level of sophistication is not required in all cases, and might not be observable. If it is not observable and the player cannot recognize it, it is wasted effort. Games are an entertainment product first and foremost; everything in them should be there for the player's benefit.

Complexity

Note that not all of the transitions in Figure 3.2 needed to evaluate all of the conditional data. In a good FSM implementation, the transitions do not take into account every possible event or condition in the world, only those needed to cause a particular transition and those needed to disambiguate similar transitions. This simplifies life for the programmer. Note that there is no transition from the Hiding state to the Flee state. It commonly happens that there will be many fewer transitions than are possible, especially when there are many states. This also simplifies life for the programmer. The maximum number of transitions possible is $N^*(N-1)$ where N is the number of states. The only hard rule about transitions is that there should only be one transition out of a state for any unique set of conditions.

In actual implementation, programmers encounter complexity that is hidden by the state diagram. For each state, there can be an entry function, an exit function, and an update function that runs when there is no transition to be made. The entry function runs when the state is entered from another state. It provides any setup capability the state needs in order to run properly. The entry function for the Hiding state might be tasked with picking the hiding spot. The exit function runs when the FSM is leaving the current state and provides clean-up functionality. Upon leaving the Attack state, the monster might want to put away any weapon it is carrying in order to run away faster or to more easily climb into a hiding spot. The update function runs each time the AI gets to think while in the state. In the Flee state, our monster needs to go quickly in a direction that is away from the players, and the update function for the Flee state handles all of that.

Failure Modes

FSMs have some common failure modes. We will touch on three of them: concurrent states, state explosion, and transition explosion. The latter two may be dealt with through careful design practice, but the concurrent states are usually a clear indicator that you should not use an FSM implementation.

Concurrent States

When reduced to an FSM, the AI might need to be in more than one state at once. For example, simulated people may need to be hungry, lonely, and bored all at the same time. The original states are clear and concise, but they are not exclusive from each other. Do not attempt to use FSM machines for this kind of AI problem, because it is better solved by other methods, such as the various agent technologies.

State Explosion

The term "state explosion" describes when the finite number of states becomes too large, especially when the number of states starts multiplying. State explosion is often the result when the original states selected blur into each other and more states are added to better differentiate them. Note that our original states were concise, one-word responses to "I am...." The programmer should be concerned when those answers become full sentences. Plain FSMs are not appropriate when those responses become paragraphs.

One method of controlling state explosion is to use hierarchical state machines. Typically, this involves two levels. Each high-level state runs a low-level state as part of the high-level state's update function. Subtleties within the high-level state are handled by the low-level state machine. If our monster is a fire-breathing dragon, the Attack high-level state might have a few low-level states, such as a Close state in which the dragon charges and breathes fire on far-away targets. When the dragon gets near, it would switch to a Combat state, where it wants to avoid breathing on itself and instead employs claws and teeth. Likewise, the high-level Flee state might involve two low-level states: Running and then Flying. With hierarchical FSMs, the low-level machines from one state have no outside interaction with any of the other low-level FSMs.

Transition Explosion

Transitions can grow in number and complexity. If an FSM design suffers from state explosion, a far worse transition explosion almost always follows. One characteristic of a good FSM is that the states have mostly local, rather than global, transitions. Hierarchical FSM machines enforce this good trait, but regular FSMs benefit from it as well. Any given state has transitions to a small subset of all of the states. In pictorial form, the FSM resembles a flat mesh with few lines crossing. Without this locality, state growth may be manageable, but the transition growth may not. Ask yourself, "If I add this state, how many existing states will have to connect to it?" If the answer is all (or nearly all) of them, it indicates potential problems. If the answer is a few of them, it is a good sign. Recall from the complexity discussion that the number of possible transitions grows much more quickly than the number of states.

Another characteristic of a good FSM is that the transitions are simple. "Simple" here means that of all the data that gets evaluated by all the transitions, a given transition only depends on a few of those items. Disambiguation methods deal with the problem of multiple valid transitions. If the disambiguation methods are inadequate, the complexity of the transitions grows with the number of data items touched by all transitions. When adding a new transition or changing an existing one, ask, "How many transitions need to be updated to consider this new data item?" If the answer is only a few, your disambiguation is solid. If the answer is all (or nearly all) of them, your machine is not effectively exploiting what are called "don't care" conditions. (The "don't care" conditions are all the things that can safely be ignored when evaluating a particular transition. Clever disambiguation simplifies important factors of an evaluation into don't care conditions. For example, in our monster AI, the High Health transition from the Flee state to the Attack state cares about health, but the No Players transition from the Flee state to the Hiding state does not, because the No Players transition is evaluated prior to the High Health transition. If High Health evaluates at all, then players are known to be present; the transition does not need to check for them again.)

Projects

Games are written in many languages, and few of them include out-of-the-box support for FSMs. We will write the structure ourselves. We could write all AI code ad hoc, but the amount of work to build a structure is less than the amount of work needed to debug ad hoc methods. We will write the structure in such a way as to minimize the number of errors we can make in the code.

The project itself will be to implement the simple monster AI in code. Our AI will do more than think; it will think "out loud" for our benefit. That is, our monster will emit text messages for us to read, enabling us to see clearly what it is thinking. Note that as an added benefit, doing so improves our ability to debug the code. More importantly, doing so reinforces the good habit of making the AI programmer look for ways to show the player what the AI is thinking. Games that show the player what the game is thinking are perceived to be smarter than games that do not.

A Brief Foray into Object-Oriented Programming

If you are familiar with object-oriented programming, you can safely skip this section. If not, the "Fundamental Concepts" section of the Wikipedia entry on the subject is quite good as a place to start [Wikipedia09].

In object-oriented programming, behavior and internal data are combined as an object. An object is one of something. The kind, or type, of an object is its class. An object named Bob might be of type Human. The Human class does not by itself do anything; objects of that class certainly do, however. The actions a programmer can ask an object to do are called the methods of that object. From this description, you may have realized that we have been dealing with objects all along. For example, in Chapter 2, we passed a World object of type House to the RunAI subroutine.

For our purposes, we will exploit the fact that objects have control over their internal data. Instead of manipulating the data directly, code outside the object uses the methods the object provides. Using a real-world metaphor, an instance of a Painter object might have a method called `PaintTheTrim(somecolor)`. The Painter object internally decides whether it needs to use masking tape or to paint freehand. The Painter object picks which paintbrush to use. A well-implemented object does not allow direct manipulation of the details, and the programmer using the object does not want to micromanage those details. In short, if the programmer gets the class right, he or she can quit worrying about the internals and use the objects at a much higher level of abstraction.

In our code, the `Public` and `Private` keywords are how a class marks methods that can be called outside of an object. You can make some of the internal data of an object visible outside of the object by marking it `public`, but this should be done sparingly. Consider the complexity discussions of Chapter 2. Object-oriented programming helps keep the internal complexity of our AI additive as it grows instead of multiplicative.

Another common feature of object-oriented programming is inheritance. A class, say of type Dragon, can inherit from another class, say of type Monster. In that case, all object of the class Dragon have all the methods of the Monster class plus the methods specific to the Dragon class. So all objects of the Monster class might have a method to indicate their health, but the ability to breathe fire would be implemented only by objects of the Dragon class. We will use inheritance very sparingly. We will use it to get different kinds of objects that inherit from a common class to act the same way. You should never be able to create an object of certain classes. For example, we might not want there to ever be an instance of a generic monster. In VB, we would mark the Monster class `MustInherit` to enforce this. We can create objects of classes that inherit from Monster, such as Dragon or Orc, but we cannot create an object of type Monster directly.

FSM Objects

So what objects do we need for our FSM AI? We need states, the states need transitions, and the states need some machine that runs them. In addition, that machine needs some changing environment to live in; that environment will be our monster. If the FSM needs data, it asks the monster. The monster will either have that data or get it from the rest of the world. We will not consider the outside world; all the world data needed by the FSM will reside in the monster.

State Objects

Our state objects need four methods for normal operation:

- **An entry method.** The entry method will be called once by the machine when it transitions into a new state.

- **An update method.** The update method will be called when the machine elects to stay in the current state.

- **An exit method.** The exit method will be called to clean up when the machine leaves the current state.

- **A transition-check method.** This method determines if the machine should transition out of the current state. Our states will check their transitions in the order they were loaded and use the first valid transition. This will provide a mechanism for dealing with ambiguous transitions.

Our state objects will also need to initialize themselves. When the state is created, it will load a list of transitions out of the state. In our implementation, transitions are stored in the state that the transition comes from.

Transition Objects

Our transitions will be very simple. They have a method that indicates if they are valid when checked against the current world conditions. That method indicates the state to which the machine should transition.

The Machine Object

The Machine object will present a RunAI method to the world. This is how the world asks the AI to do some thinking. In addition, it needs a way to load the states and transitions. We will do this by loading the Machine object with states. The first state loaded into the Machine object will be the Start state.

The Monster Object

The Monster object will actually be a Windows form, which is also a type of object. It will provide the user interface. The user will be able to adjust whether the monster sees players or not as well as adjust the monster's health between low and high. The Monster object will make both of those adjustments available to the AI. The Monster object will also have an output window to show what it is thinking. Of course, the Monster object will have a button the user can click to make it think.

Creating the MonsterAI Project

The Monster object will be our only Windows form. We will add numerous classes to implement the states and transitions. If we were going to make more than one kind of monster, we would create a class for general monsters first. Each different kind of monster would inherit from the general class. We would reuse the bulk of the software that way. Using inheritance this way is straightforward and easy to understand. Commercial games tend to use a more complex, highly data-driven approach. Since we are only going to do one kind of monster, however, we will not bother generalizing it for reuse. Writing for reuse rarely works unless there are two or better yet three different uses implemented when the software is first written.

1. Launch Visual Basic.

2. Create a new Windows Forms Application project and name it MonsterAI.

3. In the Solution Explorer window, rename Form1.vb to Monster.vb.

4. Click the form in the editing pane and change the Text property to Monster.

5. Resize the form to make it much wider.

6. Open the File menu and click Save All. At this point your project should resemble Figure 3.3. We are going to put the user inputs on the left side of the Monster form and the output of what the monster is thinking on the right side of the form.

7. We can make short work of the user interface from here. By studying the transitions, we see that the monster needs to be able to know if it can detect players and if it has high or low health. We also need to give the monster a place to show us what it is thinking. After we add the controls that make up the visual elements, we will add the code that makes them work. First, drag a CheckBox control from the Toolbox to the top-left corner of the Monster form.

8. Change the Text property of the CheckBox control to Sees Players.

9. Change the Name to SeesPlayersCheckBox.

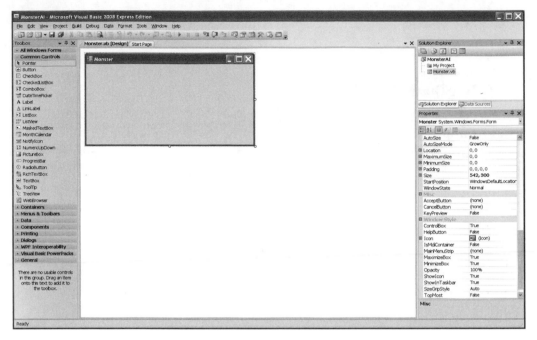

Figure 3.3
Initial FSM project.

10. Drag a Label control from the Toolbox and place it below the Sees-PlayersCheckBox control.

11. Change the Text property of the Label control to Health.

12. Drag a NumericUpDown control from the Toolbox and place it below the Health label.

13. Change the Name property of the control to CurrentHealth.

14. Change the Maximum property to 10 and the Value property to 10.

15. Drag another Label control from the Toolbox to the top middle of the form and change its Text property to Thoughts.

16. Drag a TextBox control to the form just below the Thoughts label. Change its Name property to ThoughtsTextBox.

17. Change the Multiline property to True. This will allow us to resize the control.

18. Drag the lower-right corner of the control to the lower-right corner of the form, using nearly all of the available space.

19. Set the ReadOnly property to True. This keeps the user from editing the text in the control.

20. Set the ScrollBars property to Vertical. Our monster will do a lot of thinking, and we want to see it all.

21. Finally, drag a Button control to the bottom-left corner of the form.

22. Change the Text property to Think and the Name property to ThinkButton. This completes the visible portion of the user interface. Your project should look like Figure 3.4.

Our next task is to provide some code that interprets the meaning of the user interface. Our FSM could look at the controls on the form directly, but we will create a simpler, better-defined interface between the AI and the monster.

Why add this apparent complexity? It will turn out that adding this tiny bit of complexity will make the AI code simpler and easier to maintain. One of the

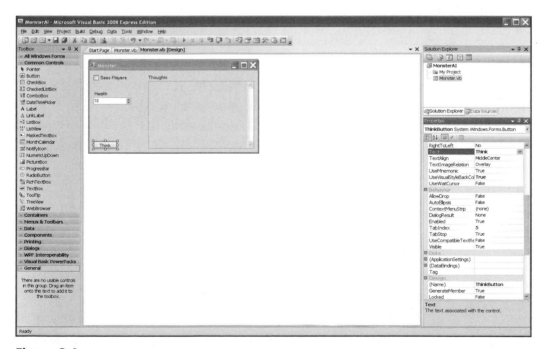

Figure 3.4
Monster user interface.

questions the AI will ask is, "Is the monster's health low?" The evaluation should be made by the monster, not the AI. If the AI looks directly at the controls, it can only ask the question, "What is the value of the CurrentHealth control?" These questions are not the same. If we use the same AI for two different monsters—one that has a maximum health of 10 and another with a maximum health of 100—a value of 10 returned for one monster will probably have the opposite interpretation if it is returned for the other monster. If we change the implementation of our simple monster and use a checkbox for high health/low health, we should not have to change the AI.

Even something as simple as the checkbox for seeing players will go through an interface. A blind monster might hear players and at times be close enough to touch them. The real question the AI wants answered is, "Do I detect players well enough to attack them or flee from them?" Our monster is visually oriented, but our AI interface will be in terms of detection.

We will add a three-part public interface to the monster. The AI will use this interface to ask questions and to supply thoughts. If we do a good job with the interface, we could use it for all kinds of monsters and many kinds of AI to drive them. To begin, right-click Monster.vb in the Solution Explorer window and select View Code. Just below the Public Class Monster line, type the following and press Enter:

```
#Region "Public Interfaces For the AI"
```

Visual Basic will create an End Region line for you. Regions have no effect on the program, but they do help you group like pieces of code together. Note the minus sign to the left; you can collapse a region to hide the code inside while you work on other parts of your code. You can also do this to the individual Sub and Function blocks.

Inside the region, we will add the three parts of the interface. We will start with the easiest one first. Add the following lines of code to the region:

```
Public Function DetectsPlayers() As Boolean
    'If we had more than one way of detecting a player,
    'we would OR them all together.
    Return (SeesPlayersCheckBox.Checked)
End Function
```

We marked the function with the Public keyword because we want outside code to be able to ask the monster if it detects players. Because we return a value, this code is a function instead of a sub. Since it returns a value, we have to specify the type of value returned—in this case a Boolean. Dealing with the monster's health requires similar code:

```
'We will assume that health is either good or bad
Public Function GoodHealth() As Boolean
    'We will use thirty percent as our threshold
    If CurrentHealth.Value >= 0.3 * CurrentHealth.Maximum Then
        Return True
    Else
        Return False
    End If
End Function
```

The core of this function could be compressed to a single line at a modest cost in readability. What remains is to give our monster a place to speak its mind. We will do this by creating a routine to write to the ThoughtsTextBox control:

```
'The output side of the interface:
Public Sub Say(ByVal someThought As String)
    'Everything we thought before, a new thought, and a newline
    ThoughtsTextBox.AppendText(someThought & vbCrLf)
End Sub
```

The & character is used for character string concatenation. Our code takes everything that was already in the text box and adds another line to it.

This completes everything in the user interface except the Think button. Before we can make the Think button do anything, we will have to implement our FSM. We start with the states.

Our states need common parts shared by all states and unique parts for each specific state. We will use classes and inheritance to accomplish this. We will create a class called BasicState to hold all the commonalities. The three classes we will actually use in our FSM will inherit from BasicState. We will never attempt to put a BasicState object into our FSM; our monster only understands Hiding, Attack, and Flee. It does not understand BasicState.

Right-click MonsterAI in the Solution Explorer window and select Add→Class. The Add New Item dialog box appears; name the new class BasicState.vb and click Add. VB will create the file and display it in the Editing pane. The first thing we will do to our new class is make sure that we cannot accidentally try to create an object of this type. Add the `MustInherit` keyword to the very first line:

```
Public MustInherit Class BasicState
```

The three classes we create will inherit from `BasicState`, and we will be able to create objects of those types. The analogy here is that it is correct to create dogs and cats and impossible to create generic mammals. So what are the things that each child class will need to do in its own unique way? Add the following lines below the class statement.

```
'Some state functionality must come from the various child states
Public MustOverride Sub Entry(ByVal World As Monster)
Public MustOverride Sub Update(ByVal World As Monster)
Public MustOverride Sub ExitFunction(ByVal World As Monster)
```

Note that there is no `End Sub` after each `Sub`. The `MustOverride` keyword tells VB that child classes are required to have a member that has this signature. It also means that the parent will not supply any common code for those members. We expect the `Update` function of the class for the `Attack` state to be very different from the `Update` function of the class for the `Flee` state. But we require all of the classes that inherit from `BasicState` to implement an `Update` function.

Not shown in `BasicState` is the unique initialization that each child class requires. That initialization will be where we load the transitions out of each state into the particular states. All states will keep their list of transitions the same way. Add the following code to the class:

```
'All kinds of states keep an ordered list of transitions.
Protected MyTransitions As New Collection
```

The Collection object is very handy in VB. We will exploit many of its capabilities. Since it is an object, we need to ensure that the variable `MyTransitions` points to an actual object. The `New` keyword initializes the variable for us so that it always starts pointing to an object. We will store all of the transitions for a state in this collection. What remains is the code that walks through the collection checking the transitions. Before we can do that, we have to implement transitions.

Our approach for transitions will be similar to the one we use for states. We will create a parent class that describes all Transition objects. We will then create child classes that inherit from the parent class and implement the unique needs of the individual transitions. This will work fine for our simple FSM. Be aware that coding this way can easily lead to an explosion of classes, however.

Note

> There is a different way to implement transitions and states that does not involve a child class for every unique transition or state. Experienced programmers should look up the `Delegate` keyword and the `AddressOf` function. Armed with these two powerful tools, we could store functions the way we store data. Then we could use a single class for all transitions and a single class for all states. This yields less code at the cost of more complicated concepts.

Right-click MonsterAI in the Solution Explorer window and add another class. Name this class BasicTransition.vb and add it. Then add the `MustInherit` keyword to the very first line.

```
Public MustInherit Class BasicTransition
```

There will be only two parts to our transitions. One part is code that will evaluate the current world conditions and decide whether or not to take the transition. That code is unique for every transition, so `BasicTransition` will force child objects to implement it. Add the following code to the class:

```
'If a transition is valid, return the name of the next state as a string
Public MustOverride Function ShouldTransition(ByVal World As Monster) As String
```

The other part of a transition is the state to transition to. We are going to store the name of the next state in a string. It needs be accessible by child classes derived from `BasicTransition`, so we mark it `Protected`. The Transition object will give that string to the state that called it. The state machine will use that string to find the next state in its collection of states. Add the following code to the class:

```
'Store the name of the state to transition to.
Protected NextState As String
```

So how are the states to be named? We could write code that maps each state, which is an object, to a string. Instead, there is a way to do this automatically, which means less code to maintain if we add a new state.

We will exploit the fact that each state in the FSM is an object of a different class than any other state. The FSM will only keep a single copy of the Flee state. The class that implements the Flee state will be a different class than the classes that implements the Hiding and Attack states. So instead of dealing with the hard question, "Who are you?," we will deal with the easier question, "What are you?" in regard to naming the states.

In the .NET languages such as VB, code can ask any object what type of object it is. Every different class of object has a unique type name. Since our FSM will only store one of any given type of state, asking a state what type it is will provide us with a unique string identifier for that state. Our code will be asking the states, but it will be telling the answer to the transitions. So the transitions needed to know what type of data to store.

Since all transitions will need to store something in the NextState string variable, we will take care of it in the parent class. Add the following code to the class:

```
'All child objects should initialize their next state
Public Sub Initialize(ByVal someStateName As String)
    NextState = someStateName
End Sub
```

All code that creates transitions will also need to initialize them. We will do this in the states. While we have not created any specific transitions, we have completed the parent class for all transitions. When we create a Transition object, we care a great deal which transition class we are using. Other than that we rely on the fact that all of them can be treated as a BasicTransition. We have defined transitions sufficiently well that we can finish off the BasicState class.

Now would be a good time to go to the File menu and choose Save All. Double-click BasicState.vb in the Solution Explorer or click the tab for it in the Editing pane. Since all states will use the same method for checking their transitions, we will put it in the parent class. Add the following code to the class:

```
'All states use the same method for checking transitions
Public Function TransitionCheck(ByVal World As Monster) As String
    'We can hold any transition in a BasicTransition
    Dim Txn As BasicTransition
    'We need to store the name of any state returned
    Dim nextState As String
    'Loop through the collection in regular order
    For Each Txn In MyTransitions
        'Store off the state name if any
        nextState = Txn.ShouldTransition(World)
        If nextState <> "" Then
            'The first valid transition is the one
            Return nextState
        End If
    Next
```

```
        'No transition was valid, no state to change to
        Return ""
    End Function
```

`BasicState` is now complete.

Just as finishing the base class used for transitions allowed us to finish the base class for states, finishing the base class for states will allow us to write the state machine object. We only have one kind of state machine, so it does not need inheritance. Open the File menu and choose Save All, and then add a new class to the project. Name it FSM.vb and add the following lines to the class:

```
'We need a place to store the states
Dim States As New Collection
'We need to remember what state is the current one
Dim currentStateName As String
```

You may have noticed that some variables are declared with `New`, and others are not. Visual Basic treats certain types of variables differently than others. Basic data types include integers and strings. In VB, there is always storage created for them, and they are initialized automatically. Strings start with the empty string "", and integers start with 0. Collections are not a basic data type; they are objects. The `New` keyword tells Visual Basic to actually create the object. Variables that deal in objects start with the special value of `Nothing` until they are assigned to an actual object.

Our monster will want to load its FSM with states. We let the monster control the loading so that different monsters can use the same FSM class but load it with monster-specific states. Add the following code to the class:

```
Public Sub LoadState(ByVal state As BasicState)
    Dim stateName As String
    'Get the short name of this state's class
    stateName = state.GetType.Name
    'The first state we get is the start state
    If States.Count = 0 Then
        currentStateName = stateName
    End If
    'Never add the same state twice
    If Not States.Contains(stateName) Then
        'Add the state, keyed by its name
        States.Add(state, stateName)
    End If
End Sub
```

Note

All .NET objects implement the `GetType` method, which returns a Type object. The Type object has a `Name` method that we will use to get the short name of a type. The class name Type is necessarily confusing; it is hard to clearly name an object that holds the type information of other objects. Besides being a method of every object, `GetType` can be called with a class name as a parameter to get a Type object for the class without having to create an object of that class. We will use that capability later to get the name of a state's type without having to create a State object.

This code takes a State object and gets the name of the type of the object. The state was passed in as an object of type `BasicState`. So why won't all objects have the same `stateName`, `BasicState`? The `GetType` method of an object ignores the type of the variable and instead uses the type of the underlying object. In any case, the object passed in can never have been created as type `BasicState` because we marked `BasicState` as `MustInherit`. Put another way, there are no generic mammals, even though dogs and cats are mammals. The object passed in will have been created with a type of `FleeState`, `HidingState`, or `AttackState`, all of which we will create very soon.

Our design called for the first state to be loaded to be the Start state. So we checked the count of items in the `States` collection to see if there were any states already loaded. If the count is zero, we are loading the first state, so we make it the current state.

Our states are different from each other—one of the hallmarks of a good FSM implementation. Before we add a state to the `States` collection, we check to make sure it is not already there. If not, we add the state to the collection, keyed by the `stateName`. If we add an object to a collection and also specify a key string, we can later access the object using that key. Keys must be unique in a collection. What the code actually does is check to see if the key is present in the collection; it does not check the actual objects. Keys are hashed, which means that finding an object in a collection of many objects happens reasonably quickly.

The FSM needs one more member: a way to make the machine run. Add the following code to the class:

```
Public Sub RunAI(ByVal World As Monster)
    If States.Contains(currentStateName) Then
        'Get the object using the name
        Dim stateObj As BasicState
        stateObj = States(currentStateName)
```

```
        'Check for transitions
        Dim nextStateName As String
        nextStateName = stateObj.TransitionCheck(World)
        'Did we get one?
        If nextStateName <> "" Then
            'Make a transition
            If States.Contains(nextStateName) Then
                'Leave this state
                stateObj.ExitFunction(World)
                'Switch states
                stateObj = States(nextStateName)
                currentStateName = nextStateName
                'Enter and run the new state
                stateObj.Entry(World)
                stateObj.Update(World)
            Else
                World.Say("ERROR: State " & stateObj.GetType.Name & _
                    " wants to transition to " & nextStateName & _
                    " but that state is not in the machine!")
            End If
        Else
            'Just run the update of the current state
            stateObj.Update(World)
        End If
    Else
        World.Say("ERROR: Current state " & currentStateName & _
            " is not found in machine!")
    End If
End Sub
```

This code has two error checks. The first makes sure the current state can be found by name in the collection of states in the machine. This error protects against any programming errors involving the name of the current state. This error is unlikely, but by checking first we keep the code from crashing. We use the monster's Say function to complain about the problem. Real game code would have a real error log. The second error check makes sure that any state called for by a transition is present in the machine. This type of error is far more likely; forgetting to load a state into the machine is a data error and not an algorithm or coding error. It will not show up unless a particular transition to the missing state executes. All the FSM code can be correct, but it needs to be correctly initialized.

Note

This type of error checking speeds development. It is faster to read an error message than it is to rerun code in a debugger. We could even ensure that the second kind of error never happens by having the FSM self-check for consistent data. That exercise is left for the student.

We have assembled all the basic parts. We are getting closer to the time, as Dr. Frankenstein puts it, to "give my creature life!" We need to implement a child class for each of the unique states and implement the transitions that will go into our monster. Open the File menu and choose Save All; then add a new class to the project. Name it HidingState.vb and type the following line of code inside the class without pressing the Enter key.

```
Inherits BasicState
```

Now press Enter. VB adds the three routines called for by BasicState. If you look back at BasicState, you see three MustOverride routines. One of the advantages to the Common Language Runtime languages in Visual Studio such as Visual Basic and C# is that the development environment has a deep understanding of classes. IntelliSense exploits this same technology. The whole package is aimed at speeding up development and reducing errors.

Because Visual Basic was kind enough to create the skeletons of our three routines, we should fill them in. In the Entry routine, add the following:

```
World.Say("This looks like a good hiding spot!")
```

In the ExitFunction routine, add the following:

```
World.Say("I can't stay hiding here.")
```

And in the Update function, add the following:

```
World.Say("Shhh! I'm hiding.")
```

At this point, we might want to do the transitions out of the class, but we have not yet defined the classes at the other end of the transitions. We will start on those other states now. Add another class and call it AttackState.vb. Make it inherit from BasicState the same way you did for HidingState. In the Entry routine, add the following:

```
World.Say("Grab weapon and shield!")
```

In the ExitFunction routine, add the following:

```
World.Say("I better put my weapon and shield away.")
```

And in the Update function, add the following:

```
World.Say("Attack!")
```

We have one state left. Add another class and call it FleeState.vb. Make it inherit from BasicState the same way you did for the prior two states. In the Entry routine, add the following:

```
World.Say("Feet, don't fail me now!")
```

In the ExitFunction routine, add the following:

```
World.Say("I better slow down.")
```

And in the Update function, add the following:

```
World.Say("Run away! Run away!")
```

This would be a really good time to go to the File menu and choose Save All.

All three states are defined, but they are not complete. There are no transitions defined, and this makes it impossible for the states to load their transitions. We will store our transitions in the same file that holds the state the transition is from. We start with HidingState. Go to the End Class statement. Hit the End key on your keyboard or click at the end of the line and then press Enter twice. Now type the following line and press Enter:

```
Public Class SeePlayerHighHealthTxn
```

VB nicely adds the End Class statement for you. Exactly as HidingState inherits from BasicState, this transition needs to inherit from BasicTransition. Add the following line inside the class and press Enter:

```
Inherits BasicTransition
```

VB again provides the required skeleton.

Note the squiggly line under the End Function statement. This indicates a problem. Hover your mouse over that line, and Visual Basic will tell you what the problem is. You can easily miss the marking, however; fortunately, Visual Basic provides an easier way to see every issue it has with the code. To display it, open the View menu and select Error List. The Error List window docks at the bottom of the environment, listing errors, warnings, and informative messages. It warns us that we should make sure that this function always

sets a value to return. We will do that now. Add the following code to
`ShouldTransition`:

```
If World.DetectsPlayers And World.GoodHealth Then
    Return NextState
Else
    Return ""
End If
```

The `NextState` variable is declared in the parent class, `BasicTransition`, and is
made available to this child class because we marked it `Protected` in the parent.
Note that this transition class does not know explicitly what state it transitions to.
Not only can any state that wants to use this transition do so, it can point it at any
other state. The state that creates the transition will tell the transition what the
next state should be. Coding this way makes the transition reusable.

Our code for `ShouldTransition` has access to the world, but it makes no calls to
the `Say` function. Right now, our monster speaks only when it is doing something. It does not talk about the thinking process itself. But since each transition
has full access to the world, it could also speak. If your code does not work right
the first time you run it, one of the ways to see what the monster is thinking is to
have all the transitions say that they are running and whether they are valid.

Now that the transition is defined, the states that use it can load it into their
transition collections. This should happen only one time: when the state is
created. The place to do this is in the state's `New()` function. Scroll to the top of
HidingState.vb and click the word HidingState. VB changes the contents of the
drop-down lists at the top of the Editing pane based on where you clicked. The
left drop-down list now says HidingState, and the right one says (Declarations).
Click (Declarations). All the routines in the class are in this list, plus New and
Finalize (whether they have been added or not). Select New from the list. VB adds
the skeleton for you.

`New()` runs once, when an object is created, and it is the perfect place for our State
objects to load their transitions. Add code to the `New()` routine as follows:

```
Public Sub New()
    Dim Txn As BasicTransition
    'Create a specific transition
    Txn = New SeePlayerHighHealthTxn()
    'Set the next state name of that transition
    Txn.Initialize(GetType(AttackState).Name)
```

```
    'Add it to our list of transitions
    MyTransitions.Add(Txn)
End Sub
```

We see in Figure 3.2 that the Hiding state has only one outgoing transition. At this point, we have completed the Hiding state. If we add this state to the FSM, we could test it to see if it works. We have written a great deal of code at this point and tested none of it, so perhaps some testing is in order. We should expect problems because we have not completed everything, but what we have should run. Before we can do any serious testing, however, we need to give the monster an FSM, and we need to load our single completed state into it.

Navigate to the code for Monster.vb. You can do this via a right-click on Monster.vb in the Solution Explorer window or by clicking the tab above the Editing pane if it is present. If a skeleton for the Load event handler is not present, click the top-left drop-down and select (Monster Events). Then click Load in the right drop-down to create the skeleton. Then add the following two lines above the Load event handler:

```
'We need an FSM
Dim Brains As New FSM
```

To the Load event handler itself, add the following lines:

```
'The first state loaded is the start state
Brains.LoadState(New HidingState)
```

Working from in the parentheses out, this asks VB to create a new HidingState object and pass it to the LoadState method of the FSM object we call Brains. All that remains is the ability to ask the FSM to think. Switch to the Design view of Monster.vb and double-click the Think button. VB will switch back to the Code view and create the Click event handler for ThinkButton. Add the following line to that handler:

```
Brains.RunAI(Me)
```

The Me keyword is how the monster form can refer to itself. Brains is an FSM object, and its RunAI member expects to be passed an object of type Monster. We have not loaded every state into the Brains FSM object, but one state is enough for testing. From the Debug menu, select Start Debugging. VB saves all the files and compiles them before running the program. Click the Think button and manipulate the user interface. When finished, close the form or select Stop Debugging from the Debug menu. You should see something like Figure 3.5.

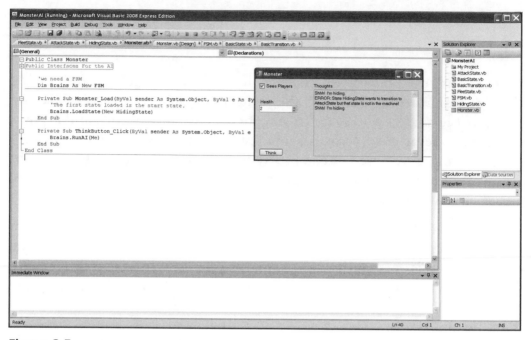

Figure 3.5
An incomplete monster attempts to think.

Our lobotomized monster complains about missing two-thirds of its brain, but other than that, it performs reasonably well. The second error check we added to RunAI in the FSM has proven its worth. If your monster is having trouble thinking even that much, add Debug.Writeline statements anywhere in the code. The output appears in the Immediate window at the bottom of the development environment. (You can see this window in Figure 3.5, although it has nothing written in it.) Now that our monster thinks, we should enhance it with more brain power by finishing the other two states and their transitions.

According to Figure 3.2, the Attack state needs two transitions. Go to Attack State.vb and add the following two classes after the End Class line. VB will help you by supplying End Class lines as well as the skeletons for the ShouldTransition members. There are no new concepts in any of this code; it asks the same questions of the world we saw in SeePlayerHighHealthTxn. With good classes, once the hard part of creating the structure is complete, bolting in the rest is simple and straightforward.

```
Public Class NoPlayersTxn
    Inherits BasicTransition
```

```
        Public Overrides Function ShouldTransition(ByVal World As Monster) As String
            If Not World.DetectsPlayers Then
                'No one to attack or flee from
                Return NextState
            Else
                Return ""
            End If
        End Function
End Class

Public Class LowHealthTxn
    Inherits BasicTransition
    Public Overrides Function ShouldTransition(ByVal World As Monster) As String
        If Not World.GoodHealth Then
            'Stop attacking
            Return NextState
        Else
            Return ""
        End If
    End Function
End Class
```

We need to put these transitions into the `AttackState` class's `New()` routine. Be sure you add the code to the state class and not to either of the transition classes! When complete the `New()` function of the `AttackState` class, it will look as follows:

```
Public Sub New()
    Dim Txn As BasicTransition

    'Order is important - react to players first
    'If no players, hide
    Txn = New NoPlayersTxn()
    'Set the next state name of that transition
    Txn.Initialize(GetType(HidingState).Name)
    'Add it to our list of transitions
    MyTransitions.Add(Txn)

    'Then react to health - if low, flee
    Txn = New LowHealthTxn()
    'Set the next state name of that transition
    Txn.Initialize(GetType(FleeState).Name)
    'Add it to our list of transitions
```

```
        MyTransitions.Add(Txn)
    End Sub
```

Recall that we disambiguate transitions by taking the first valid transition and controlling the order in which they are evaluated. They are evaluated in the order loaded, so reacting to players should be loaded first. We do not want our monster to flee from players who are not there. This completes the Attack state. We will add the Attack state to the FSM after we complete the Flee state.

Switch to FleeState.vb so that we can add the two transitions that leave the Flee state as seen in Figure 3.2. Before we add them, note that the No Players transition in the Flee state has the same decision criteria as the No Players transition in the Attack state. We can reuse the NoPlayersTxn class we created in Attack State.vb as it is. We still have to create the High Health transition and load both transitions into the state. Add the following class to the bottom of the FleeState.vb file below the End Class statement:

```
Public Class HighHealthTxn
    Inherits BasicTransition
    Public Overrides Function ShouldTransition(ByVal World As Monster) As String
        If World.GoodHealth Then
            'Stop flight
            Return NextState
        Else
            Return ""
        End If
    End Function
End Class
```

The only differences between this and LowHealthTxn are the names, the word Not in the comparison, and the comment text. You can save yourself some typing via copy and paste as long as you remember to edit what is pasted.

Now we will add the two transitions to the New() routine for the state. When finished it will look like the following:

```
    Public Sub New()
        Dim Txn As BasicTransition

        'Order is important - react to players first
        'If no players, hide
        Txn = New NoPlayersTxn()
        'Set the next state name of that transition
```

```
        Txn.Initialize (GetType(HidingState).Name)
        'Add it to our list of transitions
        MyTransitions.Add(Txn)

        'Then react to health - if high, attack
        Txn = New HighHealthTxn()
        'Set the next state name of that transition
        Txn.Initialize(GetType(AttackState).Name)
        'Add it to our list of transitions
        MyTransitions.Add(Txn)
    End Sub
```

This is very similar to the New() code for AttackState. The first transition is identical; it has the same criteria and the same next state. The second transition uses a different transition, and it goes to a different state, so of course the comment is changed as well. The final step remaining is to get these states into the machine.

Switch to the Code view of Monsters.vb and go to the Load event handler. Below the existing call that loads the Hiding state, add these lines:

```
        Brains.LoadState(New AttackState)
        Brains.LoadState(New FleeState)
```

Recall that the first state loaded is the Start state, so make sure these lines come after the line that loads the Hiding state. Now select Start Debugging from the Debug menu. Change the settings on the user interface and click Think to watch the monster react. This monster AI is pretty simple, but with a few more states it would be as smart as the monsters in the original version of *Doom*.

Chapter Summary

This chapter shows that a collection of a few simple states and transitions is enough for many simple game AI tasks. Once the framework is created and understood, new behavior states can be added quickly and easily without upsetting existing work. There is an up-front cost, but it pays off quickly with every new capability added. Using this technique, game AI programmers can quickly turn a design diagram into changing behaviors in a game. While experienced programmers often use FSM, they also know when not to use them and how to modify them to control complexity and ensure intelligent behavior.

Chapter Review

Answers are in the appendix.

1. Define a finite state machine and tell what each part does.

2. What are the advantages of a finite state machine compared to hard-coded AI?

3. What are some indicators that a finite state machine is inappropriate to use?

4. What do we mean by ambiguous transitions?

5. What do we call it when ambiguous transitions exist? What are three ways of dealing with them?

Exercises

1. Change the order of the transitions in the Attack state to make the monster flee from players who are not there.

2. Change the monster user interface to have a very low setting for health and implement the Berserk state.

References

[Forbus02] Forbus, Ken; Wright, Will. "Simulation and Modeling: Under the Hood of The Sims," *CS 395 Game Design*, Northwestern University, 2002, online at http://www.cs.northwestern.edu/~forbus/c95-gd/lectures/The_Sims_Under_the_Hood_files/frame.htm.

[Mark09] Mark, Dave. *Behavioral Mathematics for Game AI*, Course Technology PTR, 2009.

[Rabin02] Rabin, Steve. "Implementing a State Machine Language," *AI Game Programming Wisdom*, Charles River Media, 2002.

[Tozour02] Tozour, Paul. "First-Person Shooter AI Architecture," *AI Game Programming Wisdom*, Charles River Media, 2002.

[Wikipedia09] Various. "Object-Oriented Programming," wikipedia.org, Wikimedia Foundation, 2009, online at http://en.wikipedia.org/wiki/Object-oriented_programming.

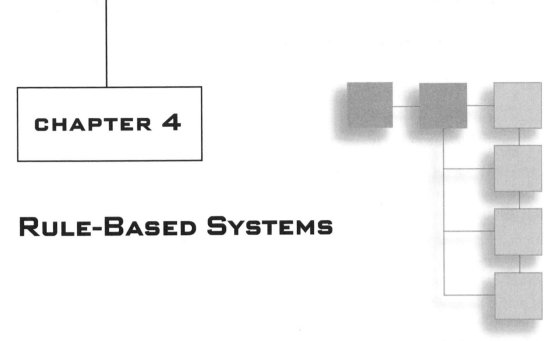

CHAPTER 4

RULE-BASED SYSTEMS

Rule-based systems attempt to use the best qualities of hard-coded AI without their disadvantages—and without constraining the designer to partition the problem into the independent states of an FSM. Rule-based systems provide a formal way to store expert knowledge and use it appropriately. (As in the case of FSM, game AI programmers may use terminology less exactly than researchers.) Regardless of how they are coded, rules can yield a very entertaining game AI; for example, the chase mode AI for the ghosts in *Pac-Man* can be written as four simple rules [Pittman09].

This chapter looks at what rule-based systems are and considers their advantages and disadvantages. To illustrate them, this chapter features a project that implements a rule-based system that plays *Minesweeper*. This project should be the most enjoyable project so far. Not only will it provide you with a playable game including AI assistance, but the presentation is in a "build a little, test a little" style that has more frequent rewards along the way.

What Is a Rule-Based AI?

The basic idea behind a rule-based AI is very similar to a method school teachers use with young children. The teacher presents the students with a question. Some of the children raise their hand. Each student is asked to present his or her idea as to the answer, and the teacher picks the best of them. The teacher can pick one or many of the ideas, or possibly have the children work on all the ideas in parallel—or at least all of them that do not place conflicting demands on classroom resources.

Rule-based systems consist of a collection of rules and the framework to apply them. When the AI is asked to think, the current state of the world is presented to the rules. Each rule determines if it matches the current situation. From among the matching rules, the framework activates one or more of them.

Besides being familiar from classroom experience, you may recognize that the transition checking done by the states in the FSM project of Chapter 3, "Finite State Machines (FSMs)," fits the definition of a rule-based system. The transitions out of a state are checked for a match; the system picks one of the matching transitions and changes the FSM state. Just as in an FSM, where multiple transitions may be valid, there may be multiple rules that match in a rule-based system. Unlike an FSM, however, a rule-based system need not be limited to activating only a single rule. Activating multiple rules forces the programmer to deal with the issues of conflict and efficiency. The activated rules must not conflict with each other; "go left" and "go right" may both be valid responses, but one precludes the other. Evaluating all the rules ensures that the best response can be used, but it has a direct impact on efficiency. Conflict resolution and efficiency concerns suggest that the rules be prioritized in some way, the simplest method being that the first rule to match is the only rule to be activated.

Let us examine what rules are. Done properly, rules are a collection of really good ideas about what to do, combined with the knowledge about when to use them. This means that there are two parts to each rule: the matching part and the execution part. For game AI, intelligence comes from sufficient rules with good execution, and stupidity comes from bad matching or too few rules.

Rules have to determine whether they match the current situation. Recall our simulated opera singer who confused a funeral gathering with a small theater and broke into song. His problem is not in the execution part; we made no comment on his singing skills, and no one at the funeral really cared. His problem is in the matching part. The AI could be missing a rule specifically for funerals; the near match of the funeral situation with a theater situation meant that it was the best-matching rule in the AI, so it was the rule used. Alternatively, if the AI had a rule for funerals, and somehow the rule for theater was selected instead, then the matching part of the funeral rule might be miscoded or poorly prioritized. That is, the framework might not have disambiguated the matched rules properly, or the design of the matching system might not be adequate.

In general, highly specialized rules need to match very strongly or not at all. More general rules need to match often, but not as strongly. Conversationally, this is the difference between asking a person about his or her new baby compared to commenting on the weather. People who actually have a new baby tend to react quite positively when asked about it. People who do not have a new baby tend to react equally poorly when asked about one. Commenting on the weather is a generally safe, if uninspired, conversational gambit.

The execution side of the rules is where the expertise in expert systems really shines. A sports AI that properly recognizes a zone defense needs an effective counter tactic; what's more, it needs to be able to execute that counter tactic. As another example, there are many people who can correctly distinguish between heartburn and heart attack; among those people, a trained cardiologist is more likely to have superior execution in the case of heart attack.

Any existing algorithms make the game AI programmer's job easier when developing the execution part of a rule. The AI is free to exhibit machine-like precision using optimal algorithms if they exist. More abstract games tend to have such algorithms, while more real-world simulations force the AI programmer to do the best that he or she can with other methods. When the AI is very effective, the AI programmer is required to mediate the conflict between an AI that is stupid and boring and one that is too smart and frustrating.

The rules execute in a framework. One of the design decisions that AI programmers need to consider is whether the framework will allow more than one rule to execute at a time. For many systems, executing one rule at a time is sufficient (or perhaps required). However, concurrent rule execution is a neat trick that enhances the richness of the AI. Systems that allow concurrent rule execution need to provide a mechanism to ensure that the demands of all the rules selected for execution can be met. There are many ways to do this. One algorithm repeatedly adds the rule with the best match to the rules selected to run, provided that the rule to be added does not conflict with any of the rules already selected. However it operates, the framework in a rule-based system selects a rule or rules, including breaking ties and conflicts among them.

Design and Analysis

Besides being a programming method to implement AI, rule-based systems require the programmer to think about the AI in a particular way. As with FSMs, this forces programmers to crystallize what they expect the AI to actually do.

Rule-based systems lend themselves to a somewhat Darwinian approach to coding the AI. Game AI programmers add their best rules to the system and test it. Rules that never fire are considered suspect. They address inadequacies in the AI by adding new rules or improving existing ones. Then they balance the rules in the framework with careful tuning.

How many rules are required? This will depend on the game and the desired quality. To play *Sudoku*, two rules will solve any board that has a difficulty level below "evil." To play *Minesweeper*, three rules suffice to play every move of a beginner- or intermediate-level board and nearly every move of an expert-level board [Kirby08]. Yet at one point in time, the SOAR Quakebot had more than 300 rules [Laird].

How complicated will the framework need to be? Simpler games do not allow concurrent rule execution; the AI is expected to pick a single move or do one thing during its turn. Concurrent rule execution is too complex for most beginning game AI programmers doing their first rule-based AI. But without concurrent rule execution, the framework still needs a method to select a rule when more than one rule matches. The rules need a method to report how well they match, and the framework needs a method to select among them. This can be as simple as comparing integers using a fixed algorithm, or it can be very complex. A glance back at the section "Multiple-Transition Review" in Chapter 3 might be in order. Do not make your methods complex until tuning demands it.

Advantages

There are many advantages to rule-based game AI. The rule structure helps contain complexity without the straightjacket of a state-based approach. When the rules are based on human play, the AI plays like a human. When the rules loaded into a rule-based system come from a high degree of expertise, the system usually exhibits that same level of expertise. Simple rule-based systems are within the reach of a beginning AI programmer. The execution part of a rule can be as complex as required to do the job. There are no constraints to get in the way.

Disadvantages

Rule-based systems also have disadvantages. It is very hard to have a good rule for every situation. The method places strong demands on some general rules to cover default behaviors. Writing rules takes human expertise at the task at hand. This is true of most beginning AI techniques. There is no inherent structure to the execution part of a rule. This is the flip side of an advantage; great freedom includes the freedom to create a nightmare. The temptation to drown the system with a rich set of rules must be balanced against the additional cost required to evaluate each new rule.

The *Minesweeper* Project

Our project is based on the ubiquitous *Minesweeper* game. We will implement both the game and the AI to help play it. The game requires more code than the AI, but the game code is generally less complex than the AI code. Not surprisingly, the basic game code will need additions to accommodate the AI. The AI will make moves through the same code pipeline that implements player moves. The added code allows the AI to sense the world. The AI commonly asks the world what squares neighbor a given square. The AI is also interested in the number of mines that need to be placed around a square and the number of unmarked squares surrounding a given square.

In our project, each rule will report the number of moves it can make. This customizes the general idea of each rule, reporting how well it fits the situation. The emphasis here is on how much gain each rule proposes to deliver. The rule with the highest number of proposed moves will be executed. Our project will also order the rules by cost. The costs are fixed and roughly based on the complexity of the rule's matching algorithm. The framework breaks ties by using the lowest-cost rule with the highest proposed gain. Since the lowest-cost rules are checked first, the first rule with the best score can be the rule used.

Implementing the Basic Game

The game itself will have three main components: squares, a playing field to hold them, and a control panel. In addition, we will need an AI to help play it. The AI will assist the human player, helping to spot moves and making them when requested. A fully automatic AI is left as an exercise. We will again use a spiral model of development. We start with the basics of the parts and add sophistication each time we go around rather than writing each part completely before going on to the next part.

The Playing Field

The most basic part of the game is the playing field. The minefield of an expert level game spans 30 columns and 16 rows. Our tiles will be 30-pixel squares, so we will need the minefield to be more than 900 pixels wide and 480 pixels tall. We will put the control panel below the mines, so the form will have to be even taller.

Launch Visual Basic and create a project called Mines.

1. Change the name of Form1 to PlayingField.vb and its Text property to Mines.

2. Resize the form to around 920 by at least 650 pixels. Final sizing will depend on your Windows settings and can be adjusted later. If you have room to make it taller, it is a good idea to do that now.

3. Drag a Panel control to the form from the Toolbox. This will be our control panel. Change its Location property to 0,490 so that it will be below the minefield on the form.

4. Resize the panel so that it takes up all of the bottom of the form.

5. Change the BackColor property to White.

6. Open the File menu and choose Save All and choose an appropriate location on your system.

Your screen should resemble Figure 4.1. The actual proportions will vary according to the resolution of your monitor.

This gives us rudimentary versions of two of our three main components of the game.

Squares

We will base our squares on the Button control. We will create a class called Square, and it can inherit from the Windows Button control. Playing *Minesweeper* involves a lot of clicking and right-clicking, Button controls have all the events we would need to handle the user input and display the results. Our Square class will extend the Button class and add the custom data and code we need.

So far, we have dragged all the controls that we have placed on the forms from the Toolbox, but that's not the only way to get them there. Here we will create Square objects and place them on the form using code. We will write the Square class and add just enough code to test that we can get Square objects onto the form.

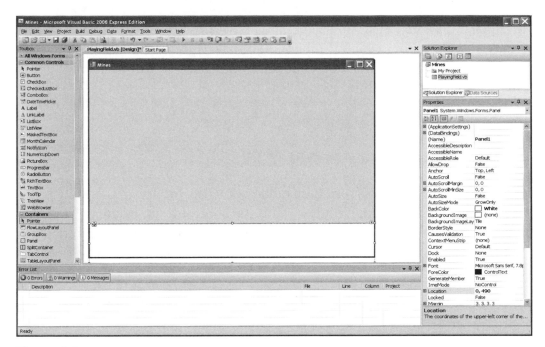

Figure 4.1
Basic layout of the playing field.

Click the File menu and add a class to the project. Name it Square.vb. We need to make the `Square` class inherit from `Button` and we need to control what a Square object looks like when it is created. We also need to have them make sure that they are ready to act like buttons. Our Square objects need to know what row and column they are at so that they can identify themselves. Add the following code to the class:

```
Inherits System.Windows.Forms.Button
Dim Row, Col As Integer
Public Sub New(ByVal R As Integer, ByVal C As Integer)
    MyBase.New()
    'Get a different font and color for the button
    Me.Font = New System.Drawing.Font("Arial", 9, FontStyle.Bold)
    Me.BackColor = Color.White

    Row = R
    Col = C
    Height = 30
    Width = 30
    Text = ""
    FlatStyle = Windows.Forms.FlatStyle.Standard
End Sub
```

Our `Square` class inherits from `Button`. The `MyBase` keyword is how our class refers to the class from which it inherits. To make sure that our class acts like a button, we want the initialization code that buttons use to run when our control initializes—hence the call to `MyBase.New()`.

After doing something new, it is a good idea to test it. We will need a few more controls on the form to do that.

1. Switch to the Design view of `PlayingField`:

2. Drag a Button control from the Toolbox onto the top left of the white panel. The panel is a container, and we want the control to go inside it. That way, we can move it by moving the container if we need to resize the underlying form. If you drop the Button control onto the form, the form will be its container.

3. Change the Button control's Text property to Expert and the Name property to ExpertButton.

4. After you change its properties, double-click the Button control to view the `Click` event handler. Add the following line of code:

```
Call NewGame(16, 30, 99)
```

Adding Squares to the Playing Field

The `NewGame` code does not exist yet, so you will see the name flagged in the code and an error in the error list. If you have played a lot of *Minesweeper*, you know that an expert level board has 16 rows and 30 columns and conceals 99 mines. We want to be able to walk through the tiles and find their neighbors easily, so we will do more than just put the controls on the form; we will hold them in an array as well. Add the following code to PlayingField.vb:

```
Public Field(,) As Square

Dim NumRows As Integer
Dim NumCols As Integer
Dim NumMines As Integer

Private Sub NewGame(ByVal nRows As Integer, ByVal nCols As Integer, _
        ByVal nMines As Integer)
    Dim Sq As Square
    'Put up an hourglass
    Me.Cursor = Cursors.WaitCursor
```

```
    'If we have an existing game, get rid of it
    'Do we have a field?
    If Field IsNot Nothing Then
        For Each Sq In Field
            'If it exists, take it off the form
            If Sq IsNot Nothing Then
                Sq.Parent = Nothing
            End If
        Next
    End If

    'Copy the passed-in parameters to the globals
    NumRows = nRows
    NumCols = nCols
    'Do some error checking
    Dim sqcnt As Integer = NumRows * NumCols
    If nMines > sqcnt Then
        nMines = sqcnt - 1
    End If
    'Then do the last assignment
    NumMines = nMines

    'Create the tiles for the new game
    'VB uses zero-based arrays
    ReDim Field(NumRows - 1, NumCols - 1)
    Dim row, col As Integer
    For col = 0 To NumCols - 1
        For row = 0 To NumRows - 1
            'Create an actual object
            Sq = New Square(row, col)
            'Set the location
            Sq.Top = row * Sq.Height
            Sq.Left = col * Sq.Width
            'Put it on the form
            Sq.Parent = Me
            'Store it in the array as well for easy access later
            Field(row, col) = Sq
        Next
    Next
    'Back to regular cursor
    Me.Cursor = Cursors.Default
End Sub
```

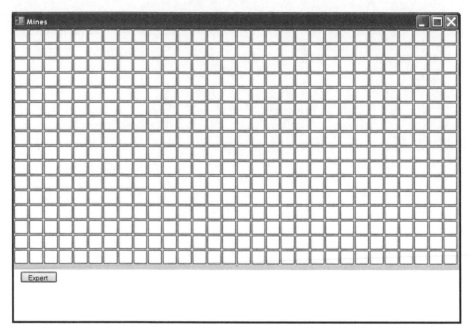

Figure 4.2
A field of blank tiles.

Open the File menu and choose Save All. Then start the project in the debugger and click the Expert button. After a bit of thinking, the form will paint all the Button controls. If you click Expert again, the form will remove them and paint new ones. Remember that you have to stop debugging before you can edit the code. Your application should resemble Figure 4.2.

Note that locations are in terms of top and left, and the values grow as you progress down the form and to the right. Programmers not used to the way Windows does things will need to remember that the Y axis is inverted.

Turning Plain Squares into Mines

At present, these are just clickable buttons, not a minefield. One of the benefits of object-oriented programming is that objects can conceal their inner data. We will design the Square class so that the only way to find out if a tile is truly a mine is to click it. This will ensure that our AI does not cheat. We will, of course, need a way to *tell* the tile if it is a mine or a safe square. We also need a way for safe squares to know how many mines are adjacent to them. Our code will not let the safe squares ask their neighbors if they are mines or not, however, so the mine squares will need to tell their neighbors to increment their count of nearby mines anonymously.

Before we load the Square objects with their ominous data, we have to wait for the user to click the first tile. In *Minesweeper*, the first click is *always* safe. We placed error checking in the NewGame code to make sure that at least one square was open for this very reason. This means that our Square objects have three possible states: They can be mines, they can be safe, or they can be waiting for the first click. They have to exist on the form in order for the user to make the first click, but they cannot have mines loaded until after that first click.

So what we will do next is modify the squares to have three possible states and to start in the uninitialized state. They will have to detect the first click and ask the playing field to tell them all what they contain. The squares will need to tell their neighbors to increment their mine counts. We will use the concept of neighbors a great deal, so the playing field needs some helper functions to create lists of neighbors. Finally, we should test that all of this code works. To test, we will add code that we will later turn into comments.

We start with the Square objects. Under the Inherits line in the Square class, add the following code:

```
Public Enum HiddenValue
    Uninitialized
    Safe
    Mine
End Enum
'Hold the definitions of the button text in one place
Public Const ShowMine As String = "@"
Public Const ShowFlag As String = "F"
Public Const ShowBrokenFlag As String = "X"

'What does this Square object actually hold?
Private contents As HiddenValue
'How many mines are near us?
Private actualNearMines As Integer
```

The contents variable holds the secret value of the square. An Enum is a way of creating an enumerated list of independent values. We do not really care what the values are, we just need for all of them to be different, and we need to be able to tell them apart. A variable of an enumerated type is restricted to hold only values from the enumeration. We want our Square objects to be created with their contents equal to Uninitialized, so we add the following line to the New() routine.

```
contents = HiddenValue.Uninitialized
```

VB initializes integer values to zero, so we do not have to explicitly set actual-NearMines to zero.

While we are working with the Square object, we should create the routine that lets the playing field initialize it. This routine will store the hidden value and tell the neighbors to increment their count of the mines near them. Add the following code to the Square class:

```
'Load the square with its hidden value
Public Sub Init(ByVal HV As HiddenValue, ByVal Neighbors As Collection)
    contents = HV

    'If that was a mine, the surrounding counts need to go up
    If contents = HiddenValue.Mine Then
        'Let the neighbors know
        Dim Sq As Square
        For Each Sq In Neighbors
            Call Sq.IncrementMineCount()
        Next
    End If

    'Debugging code to comment out later
    If contents = HiddenValue.Mine Then
        'Use @ to mark a mine
        Me.Text = ShowMine
    End If
    'End debugging code
End Sub
```

We are calling IncrementMineCount, but we have not written it yet, so it will be marked as an error for now. We have included debugging code so that as soon as possible, we can fire up the application and make sure that what we have so far works. As soon as it does, we will comment out the code because it gives away secret data, but we will leave it in case we need it later. We need to add the IncrementMineCount routine to the class:

```
'Some unknown neighbor is telling us that they have a mine
Public Sub IncrementMineCount()
    'Add one to the existing count
    actualNearMines += 1

    'Debugging code to comment out later
    'If I am not a mine, show my count
```

```
        If contents <> HiddenValue.Mine Then
            Me.Text = actualNearMines.ToString
        End If
        'End debugging code
    End Sub
```

There is an easy way to comment out a block of lines: Highlight the lines you want to make into comments and then hover your mouse over the buttons in the toolbar below the Data and Tools main menu. You are looking for the ones with horizontal black lines and blue lines. The tooltip will indicate which button comments out the lines and which button uncomments the lines. Try them out and watch what they do to your code. Commenting a comment line adds another leading ' character to any that are already there. That way, when you uncomment a block that includes comment lines, the comment lines stay comments.

Our Square objects are ready to be initialized by the form, but they do not yet ask the form to do so. Click the left drop-down list at the top of the Editing pane. This one probably has a current value of Square in bold text. Select (Square Events), which is marked with a lightning bolt. From the right drop-down list, select the Click event; VB will give you the skeleton of the event handler. Add code to the event handler so that it looks like the following:

```
Private Sub Square_Click(ByVal sender As Object, ByVal e As System.EventArgs)
Handles Me.Click
        'We should be part of a playing field
        Dim theField As PlayingField = Me.Parent

        'If not, we can't ask it anything
        If theField Is Nothing Then Exit Sub

        'If this square is uninitialized, all of them are
        If contents = HiddenValue.Uninitialized Then
            'Have the playing field object init all the squares
            Call theField.InitializeSquares(Row, Col)
        End If

        'Make the button look pressed
        FlatStyle = Windows.Forms.FlatStyle.Flat
        Me.BackColor = Color.LightGray

        'Below here is where the player finds out if it is safe or not

    End Sub
```

This block of code introduces a few notational shortcuts. The first is that you can assign a value to a variable on the same line that you declare the variable. The next shortcut is for when you have a single line as the object of an If statement; you can just put the line after the Then keyword. When you do this, there is no need for an End If. (If you are new to VB, use this construct sparingly. It is not advisable to use it inside a nested If statement. The compiler could care less, but the programmer might get confused.) One of the very nice features of VB is that it takes care of indenting nested constructs for you. If you think that you have messed up the indentation, highlight the entire routine (or even the entire file) and press the Tab key. VB will line everything up based on where the compiler places the levels.

At this point there is one error. We have called upon the form to initialize the squares, but that code does not yet exist. The code for this has to walk the field and randomly place mines. Squares that get a mine need to know who their neighbors are. Do not let the length of the code fool you into thinking that it is complicated. Add this routine to the PlayingField class:

```
'After the first click, place the mines
Public Sub InitializeSquares(ByVal ClickedRow As Integer, ByVal ClickedCol As Integer)
        'There is a lot of code that goes here.
        'We will add it in stages.

        'We have to track how many mines are yet to be placed
        Dim minesLeft As Integer = NumMines
        'We track the number of squares to go (one has been clicked)
        Dim squaresleft As Integer = (NumRows * NumCols) - 1
        'Percent and random numbers are floating point
        Dim perCent, roll As Single

        'Reseed the random number generator
        Call Randomize()

        'Our working variables
        Dim Row, Col As Integer
        Dim Neighbors As Collection

        'Walk the grid
        For Row = 0 To NumRows - 1
            For Col = 0 To NumCols - 1
```

```
            If Row <> ClickedRow Or Col <> ClickedCol Then
                'What percent of the squares need mines?
                'Has to be converted to a single precision float
                perCent = CSng(minesLeft / squaresleft)
                'Roll the dice, get a number from 0 to almost 1
                roll = Rnd()
                'If we roll less than the percent, we place a mine
                'Also, we ensure that we place them all
                If (roll < perCent) Or (minesLeft >= squaresleft) Then
                    'It has a mine!
                    'Call init on the square - we need the neighbors
                    Neighbors = NearNeighbors(Row, Col)
                    Field(Row, Col).Init(Square.HiddenValue.Mine, _
                        Neighbors)
                    'We placed a mine, so dec the count remaining
                    minesLeft -= 1
                Else
                    'It is safe - don't bother the neighbors
                    Neighbors = New Collection
                    Field(Row, Col).Init(Square.HiddenValue.Safe, _
                        Neighbors)
                End If
                'We either place a mine or not, but we have one less
                'Square in the computations
                squaresleft -= 1
            Else
                'It is the initial tile, therefore safe
                Neighbors = New Collection
                Field(Row, Col).Init(Square.HiddenValue.Safe, Neighbors)
            End If
        Next Col
    Next Row

    'Error checking:  All mines should be placed by now
    If minesLeft > 0 Then
        MsgBox(minesLeft.ToString & " Mines leftover!", _
            MsgBoxStyle.OkOnly)
    End If
End Sub
```

The new and interesting parts of the code include our first brush with the random number generator and the underscore (_) continuation character. Random number generators are not really random. The call to Randomize uses the system clock to "seed" the random number generator with a reasonably unpredictable value. This means that each game should look different. The Rnd calls return a floating-point number that is greater than or equal to zero and less than one.

The error check at the end should never trip; the code does its best to force all the mines into the field. This type of coding is a good idea, even when it detects errors that are not fatal to the current routine but might be fatal to later routines. The call to MsgBox presents the user with a small dialog box. The underscore is used to break a long line over many lines. If you use the underscore, it should have a space before it and nothing after it. It is most commonly used following a comma, and it cannot be inside an open set of quotes.

Neighbors

We need to code the NearNeighbors function so that the squares can tell their neighbors about mines. The AI will rely heavily upon it as well. The AI will also want a function for neighbors that are two squares away. We will code the NearNeighbors function with this need in mind.

One of the questions the AI will need to ask is if a square is in a collection of squares. To make this question easier to answer, we will combine the row and column numbers for a square into a unique key string to use as an identifier.

Add the following line to the PlayingField class and press Enter:

```
#Region "Neighbor Code"
```

VB will add the End Region for you. All the code we are about to add will go in this region to help organize it. We will do the easy things first. Start with the code to create a unique string key from the row and column values:

```
'Turn two items into a single unique key name for each square
Public Function KeyFromRC(ByVal row As Integer, ByVal col As Integer) _
        As String
    Return "R" & row.ToString & "C" & col.ToString
End Function
```

The next thing we will do is create a list of offsets to compute the neighbors of a square. We will use one set of offsets to compute near neighbors and a different set to compute neighbors two away. Add the following code to the region:

```
'We use this list to compute the row and col of adjacent squares
'Point objects make it easy to store X,Y pairs
```

```
Private NearNeighborOffsets() As Point = { _
    New Point(-1, -1), New Point(-1, 0), New Point(-1, 1), _
    New Point(0, -1), New Point(0, 1), _
    New Point(1, -1), New Point(1, 0), New Point(1, 1)}
```

If you add the X,Y values stored in the Point objects to the row and column numbers of a square, you will get the row and column numbers of the eight surrounding squares. Squares on the border will have fewer than eight neighbors, so our code will have to catch proposed neighbors that are off the board.

```
'We have the idea of near neighbors and far neighbors
    Public Function NearNeighbors(ByVal Row As Integer, ByVal Col As Integer) _
            As Collection
        Return GeneralNeighbors(Row, Col, NearNeighborOffsets)
    End Function

    'Both neighbors' functions use same method on different offsets
    Private Function GeneralNeighbors(ByVal Row As Integer, ByVal Col As Integer, _
            ByVal Offsets() As Point) As Collection
        'Put the neighboring Square objects into a collection
        Dim Neighbors As New Collection

        'No neighbors if no field
        If Field IsNot Nothing Then
            Dim Pt As Point
            Dim NeighborRow, NeighborCol As Integer
            For Each Pt In Offsets
                'Add the values in the point to get neighbor
                NeighborCol = Col + Pt.X
                NeighborRow = Row + Pt.Y
                'It has to be on the board
                If (NeighborRow >= 0) And _
                    (NeighborRow < NumRows) And _
                    (NeighborCol >= 0) And _
                    (NeighborCol < NumCols) Then
                    'It is on the board, add it in with key
                    Neighbors.Add(Field(NeighborRow, NeighborCol), _
                        KeyFromRC(NeighborRow, NeighborCol))
                End If
            Next
        End If
        'We always return a collection, even if it is empty
        Return Neighbors
    End Function
```

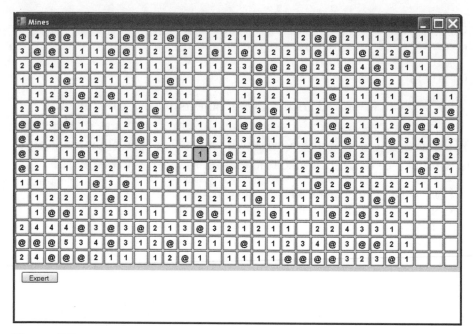

Figure 4.3
A correctly initialized minefield after the first click.

If you have not been doing so regularly, now is a very good time to open the File menu and choose Save All. Note that starting the debugger saves the files as well as providing you a chance to see if this works. Start your application in the debugger. Click the Expert button and, once the field paints all of the tiles, click one of them. The results you see should resemble Figure 4.3. The hard work is paying off—this looks like a *Minesweeper* minefield!

Take the time to carefully evaluate each square of your own running game. Are all 99 of the mines there? Noting that blanks imply zero, does every square that does not have a mine have the right number? If these numbers are not correct, both human and AI players will have a very frustrating time with your game.

Making It Playable

Our next step is to turn what we have into a playable game. First, we must turn off the debug code that sets the text of the Square objects. That was in two places in the Square class. Comment out the debugging sections in Init and Increment. Run the game and click a tile to make sure.

The player needs more than a field to play; the player also needs to know how many mines remain. Switch to the Design view of `PlayingField`. We will drag four labels to the control panel to help the user:

1. Drag a Label control from the Toolbox and drop it to the right of the Expert button.

2. Change the Text property to 888 and the Name property to MovesLeftLabel.

3. Change the BorderStyle property to FixedSingle and the TextAlign property to MiddleCenter.

4. Drag a Label control from the Toolbox and drop it to the right of the MovesLeftLabel.

5. Change the new label's Text property to Moves Left.

6. Drag a Label control from the Toolbox and drop it below the MovesLeftLabel.

7. Change the Text property to 999 and the Name property to MinesLeftLabel.

8. Change the BorderStyle property to FixedSingle and the TextAlign property to MiddleCenter.

9. Drag a Label control from the Toolbox and drop it to the right of the MinesLeftLabel.

10. Change the Text property to Mines Remaining.

After you open the File menu and choose Save All, your screen should resemble Figure 4.4.

Now we need to provide the code to update those numbers. Add the following code to the end of the `NewGame` routine, just above the code that changes the cursor back.

```
'Init the counters
MinesLeftLabel.Text = NumMines.ToString
MovesLeftLabel.Text = sqcnt.ToString
```

As people manipulate the squares, the squares will need to change the numbers as well. When a player clicks a square to reveal it, the number of moves remaining goes down. When the player flags a square, it reduces both the number of moves

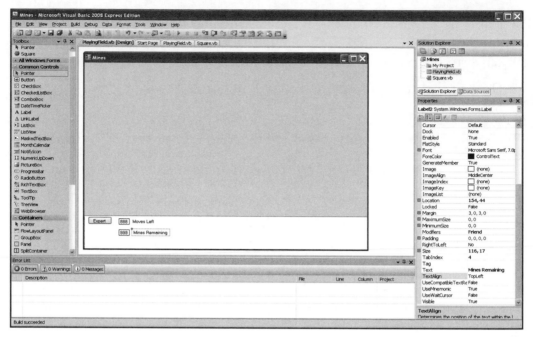

Figure 4.4
Some vital numbers on the user interface.

and the number of mines. Removing a flag increases both. Add the following code to PlayingField.vb to handle those changes:

```
'Code to change the counters - convert the text to int,
'add or subtract one, change back to text. 2 for moves,
'and 2 for mines
Public Sub DecrementMovesLeft()
    MovesLeftLabel.Text = (CInt(MovesLeftLabel.Text) - 1).ToString
End Sub


'If you undo a flag, the resulting blank is a valid move
Public Sub IncrementMovesLeft()
    MovesLeftLabel.Text = (CInt(MovesLeftLabel.Text) + 1).ToString
End Sub


'Usually by placing a flag
Public Sub DecrementMinesLeft()
    MinesLeftLabel.Text = (CInt(MinesLeftLabel.Text) - 1).ToString
End Sub
```

```
'Removing a flag
Public Sub IncrementMinesLeft()
    MinesLeftLabel.Text = (CInt(MinesLeftLabel.Text) + 1).ToString
End Sub
```

Another demand that the squares will place on PlayingField is to end the game if the player clicks on a mine. The field will do this by telling each square that the game is over and letting the squares act appropriately. Add the following code to the PlayingField class:

```
'Something bad happened and a square is calling for the game to end
Public Sub EndGame()
    Dim Sq As Square
    'Tell them all
    For Each Sq In Field
        Sq.Endgame()
    Next
End Sub
```

That dealt with PlayingField. Now onto the squares. A square needs to be able to determine whether its contents have been revealed. It will not want to tell the AI how many mines are near it if it has not been revealed, and it will treat the mouse differently as well. Add the following code to the Square class just below the declarations for contents and actualNearMines:

```
'Have I been clicked or not?
Private Revealed As Boolean
```

Boolean variables initialize to False. The AI will also want to ask the square if it is revealed, so we should support that capability as well while we are at it. Add the following code to the Square class:

```
'The outside world will want to ask us
Public ReadOnly Property IsRevealed() As Boolean
    Get
        Return Revealed
    End Get
End Property
```

We needed to control how the Square object exposes the private variable Revealed to the outside world. Properties allow us to have code between internal data and the outside world. Unlike functions, properties can be either or both directions (read or write) using the same name.

We need to do some work on the `Click` event handler for the `Square` class. Refactor the code that makes the button look pressed as follows. This code uses the existing comment and property changes, but integrates them into a more sophisticated block.

```
If Not Revealed Then
    'Below here is where the player finds out if it is safe or not
    If contents = HiddenValue.Safe Then
        'This square is done
        Revealed = True
        'Make the button look pressed [reused code from before]
        FlatStyle = Windows.Forms.FlatStyle.Flat
        Me.BackColor = Color.LightGray
        'Tell the user how many are near (if any)
        If actualNearMines > 0 Then
            Me.Text = actualNearMines.ToString
        Else
            'Implement free moves here
        End If
        'One fewer move left to make
        theField.DecrementMovesLeft()
    Else
        'Make bad things happen here
        Me.Text = ShowMine
        theField.Endgame()
    End If
End If
```

If the user or the AI does click a mine, the `Square` object asks `PlayingField` to tell all the squares that the game is over. We will now add code to the `Square` class so that it can take end-of-game actions. Add the following code to the class:

```
'It no longer matters
Public Sub Endgame()
    'If it is the end of the game,
    'I cannot be clicked (stops cheats)
    Me.Enabled = False
    If Not Revealed Then
        If contents = HiddenValue.Mine Then
            'If they did not flag me, show the mine
            If Me.Text <> ShowFlag Then
                Me.Text = ShowMine
            End If
```

```
        Else
            'I am a safe square
            If Me.Text <> "" Then
                'If they marked it, they were wrong
                Me.Text = ShowBrokenFlag
            End If
        End If
    End If
End Sub
```

At this point, the code should be playable—aside from the fact that it does not allow the user to mark mines. Run the game in the debugger and see if it plays. Intense concentration and some luck may be required to play for very long. Check that the number of moves decrements and that making mistakes in play not only is fatal, but stops the game. Your game might resemble Figure 4.5 after you make a mistake in play.

There were still deterministic moves available in the game shown in Figure 4.5 when the mistake was made. An AI player would not have missed the moves or

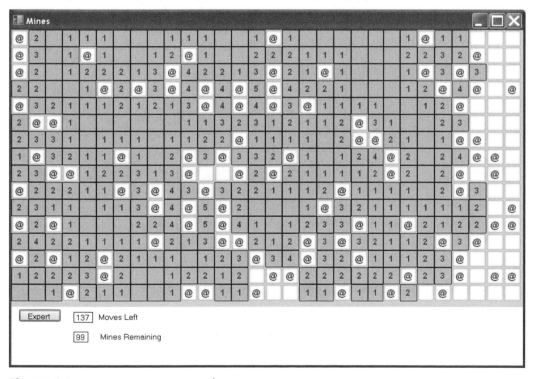

Figure 4.5
After 343 moves and only 38 safe moves to go, one mistake ends the game.

made the mistake. After we add the ability to mark mines with flags, the game will be complete and ready for the AI.

Making It Fun: Adding Flags and a Safety Feature

To flag a blank square, the player right-clicks it. The player right-clicks a second time to remove the flag. It makes no sense to do this to a revealed square.

Examine the events available to the Square class. Note that the Click event is in bold to indicate an event handler is present for it. Scan the list carefully. There is no right-click event. How will we detect a right-click? The list does have the MouseUp event and many other mouse-related events. A control will get a MouseUp event each time the user releases a mouse button, provided the user pressed the button while the mouse was over that control. The MouseUp event always fires for the control that got the MouseDown event. The behavior here is different from a Click event. The Click event will not fire if you move the mouse off the control between button press and button release.

Select the MouseUp event to get a code skeleton. Then add code to complete that skeleton as shown here:

```
    Private Sub Square_MouseUp(ByVal sender As Object, ByVal e As System.Windows.
Forms.MouseEventArgs) Handles Me.MouseUp
        'This is where we catch right-click - but we have to
        'check which button came up
        If e.Button = Windows.Forms.MouseButtons.Right Then
            'We should be part of a playing field
            Dim theField As PlayingField = Me.Parent

            'If not, we can't tell it anything
            If theField Is Nothing Then Exit Sub

        If Not Revealed Then
            'We change the marking on the tile
            'What is on the tile now?
            Select Case Me.Text
                Case ""
                    'Blanks get a flag
                    Me.Text = ShowFlag
                    theField.DecrementMinesLeft()
                    theField.DecrementMovesLeft()
```

```
                    Case ShowFlag
                        'Flags get a blank
                        Me.Text = ""
                        theField.IncrementMinesLeft()
                        theField.IncrementMovesLeft()
                End Select
            Else
                'Placeholder for AI
            End If
        End If
    End Sub
```

Run the game and right-click some revealed and concealed squares. Mark a square that you know is safe with a flag. Watch the counters to see the number of moves and mines remaining decrease. Next, mark a square that you know holds a mine with a flag. Then click the flagged square that holds a mine. Two interesting things happen, one good, one bad. The good thing is the flag on the safe square turns into an X to show that it was incorrectly flagged. We have now tested a bit of code we wrote earlier. The bad thing is that even though we marked the square with a flag, the square let us click it in the first place, ending the game.

We can guard against a click on a flagged square. In the Click event, find the following line of code:

```
If Not Revealed Then
```

Then add the following code:

```
If Not Revealed Then
    'Safety code: if marked, ignore the click!
    If Me.Text = ShowFlag Then Exit Sub
```

Test this code by marking a square with a flag and then clicking it. The square does not reveal itself. If you right-click the square to remove the flag, anything could happen the next time you click it.

Implementing the AI

We now have a complete *Minesweeper* game! When the thrill of playing it wears off, you may wish to review the discussion of a rule-based AI earlier in this chapter. We need to design the classes that we will use for the rules and for the framework and extend the game so that the AI can "see" what the player sees. We also need to extend the game so that we can listen to the AI think. The AI will not do anything if we fail to add code that runs the AI.

The AI Needs to Think Out Loud

We start by giving the AI a place to tell us what it is thinking. The extra space on the right side of the control panel makes a perfect place for messages. Bring up the Design view of PlayingField; then follow these steps:

1. Drag a TextBox control from the Toolbox and drop it to the right of the controls already there.

2. Change its Name property to ThoughtsTextBox.

3. Set the Multiline property to True and resize the control to fill the available space.

4. Set the ReadOnly property to True.

Later on, you may wish to add a vertical scrollbar to the control by setting the ScrollBars property to Vertical. We will create two routines that manipulate this control. Both will add text, but one of them will clear out the old text first. Switch to Code view and create a new region for the AI. Do not put this region inside any other regions. Add code to it to get the following:

```
#Region "AI Related"
    'Let it speak - clear old stuff
    Public Sub FirstThought(ByVal someThought As String)
        ThoughtsTextBox.Clear()
        MoreThoughts(someThought)
    End Sub

    'Say what it is thinking
    Public Sub MoreThoughts(ByVal someThought As String)
        ThoughtsTextBox.AppendText(someThought & vbCrLf)
    End Sub
#End Region
```

Our AI now has a place to say things. We should clear what it is thinking when we start a new game. Add the following line of code to the NewGame routine just above where the cursor is returned to normal:

```
        'Remove thoughts from last game
        ThoughtsTextBox.Clear()
```

Rules

It is time to design the rules and the framework to make use of them. We start with the rules. All the different rules have common elements. For example, every rule proposes a set of moves as part of the matching phase. In addition, every rule needs to execute its proposal when selected for execution by the framework. Add a class to the project and name it BasicRule.vb. Mark it MustInherit and add code to get the following:

```
Public MustInherit Class BasicRule

    'Child classes and outside helpers need this
    Public Enum PossibleActions
        BlanksToFlags
        ClickBlanks
    End Enum

    'We need to remember what move we propose
    Protected SimonSays As PossibleActions
    'And the targets of that action
    Protected SquaresList As New Collection

    'All rules must have tell how well they match
    Public MustOverride Function Matches(ByVal RevealedSquare As Square) As Integer

    'The match routine stores our proposal for possible execution
    Public Sub Execute()
        Dim Sq As Square
        For Each Sq In SquaresList
            'We only ever do unknown blanks
            If (Not Sq.IsRevealed) And (Sq.Text = "") Then
                'What did we propose to do?
                Select Case SimonSays
                    Case PossibleActions.ClickBlanks
                        Call Sq.LeftClick()
                    Case PossibleActions.BlanksToFlags
                        Call Sq.RightClick()
                End Select

            End If
        Next
    End Sub
End Class
```

You can try to see if you can get the `Sq` variable to divulge the hidden contents variable, but VB respects the `private` marking in the Square.vb file. Hidden in this design is the idea that a rule will do only one kind of move. It turns out not to be a limitation; all the rules we will write will boil down to either "Flag a bunch of squares" or "Click a bunch of squares" but never both. This code asks the squares to click and right-click themselves; that code does not exist. We will add that capability to the `Square` class. Switch to the `Square` class and add the following code:

```
'Let code work our UI:
'A regular click of the square
Public Sub LeftClick()
    Call Square_Click(Nothing, Nothing)
End Sub

'Let them mark a square with right-click
Public Sub RightClick()
    'Create the arguments for a right-click
    'All we care about is the button
    Dim e As New System.Windows.Forms.MouseEventArgs(Windows.Forms.
MouseButtons.Right, 0, 0, 0, 0)
    Call Square_MouseUp(Nothing, e)
End Sub
```

The `Click` event handler ignores its arguments, so we can safely pass it `Nothing` for both of them. The `MouseUp` handler looks to see what button was pressed, so we created a new mouse event arguments object with the correct button and zeroes for all the numbers. We do not care about those numbers, and zero is a safe value for them.

There are two types of cheating for game AI: The AI can know things that it should not, or the AI can do things the player cannot. For this reason, there is a very important design decision made here: The AI uses the same user interface as the player, and is restricted to the same actions as the player. The AI has shims between it and the player code, but those shims are very thin and know nothing about the intent of what they transmit. In most commercial games, the shim is usually between the player and the game because the AI can natively speak the command language of the game. Besides preventing cheating, using common code simplifies the evolution of the game by having only one command path instead of two that must be kept synchronized.

A Rule for Single-Square Evaluation

Let us create our first rule. The first rule will ask the question, "Can I tell what goes in the blanks surrounding a revealed square using the revealed count and the number of flags and blanks surrounding the revealed square?" This boils down to two statements: If the number of flags around the revealed number equals the revealed numbers, then any surrounding blanks must be safe. And if the number revealed minus the number of flags is equal to the number of blanks, then any surrounding blanks are all mines. More simply, "These are safe because I know all of the mines already," or "Mines are all that are left."

This rule will require that our AI find out a number of basic statistics. How many flags surround the revealed square? How many blanks? The revealed square itself gives the number of nearby mines. In addition to statistics, the rule will want to know what squares around the revealed square are blanks because the action of the rule, if it executes, will be to click them all or flag them all. It turns out that three of our rules will need this data. It will be a lot easier to get this data if we can get the Square objects to tell us their row and column data so that we can get their neighbors and their key value. Add the following to the `Square` class:

```
'Let the outside world ask but not set our row
Public ReadOnly Property R() As Integer
    Get
        Return Row
    End Get
End Property

'Let the world ask our column, too
Public ReadOnly Property C() As Integer
    Get
        Return Col
    End Get
End Property
```

Since many rules will need the basic data, we should place the code for it in a separate file where all rules can get to it. Add a module to the project (similar to adding a class) and name it AI.vb. Then add the following code:

```
'Note the three ByRef parameters - we write to them
Public Function BasicStatsAndBlanks(ByVal RevealedSquare As Square, _
        ByVal Neighbors As Collection, _
    ByRef sees As Integer, ByRef flags As Integer, _
```

```
            ByRef blanks As Integer) As Collection
        'Look at line above and see the integers are all ByRef!

        Dim BlankSquares As New Collection
        'Text of revealed squares are blank = 0 or a number
        If RevealedSquare.Text <> "" Then
            sees = CInt(RevealedSquare.Text)
        End If


        'Get the counts of what they show
        Dim Sq As Square
        For Each Sq In Neighbors
            'We want hidden squares only
            If Not Sq.IsRevealed Then
                'Count the flags and blanks
                Select Case Sq.Text
                    Case ""
                        blanks += 1
                        BlankSquares.Add(Sq, PlayingField.KeyFromRC(Sq.R, Sq.C))
                    Case Square.ShowFlag
                        flags += 1
                End Select
            End If
        Next
        'The caller often needs the blank squares as a group
        Return BlankSquares
    End Function
```

This routine collects the stats and writes them back onto the passed-in parameters. VB defaults to call by value, so we have to make sure that we use the ByRef keyword. This function returns a collection holding any blank squares. Armed with this helper routine, our first rule is easy to write. Create a class and name it RuleOne. Mark it to inherit from BasicRule. The only code we have to add is the Matches routine.

```
Public Class RuleOne
    Inherits BasicRule

    Public Overrides Function Matches(ByVal RevealedSquare As Square) As Integer
        'Clear out anything from before
        Me.SquaresList.Clear()
        'Do not run on a hidden square!
```

```
If RevealedSquare.IsRevealed Then
    'We should be part of a playing field
    Dim theField As PlayingField = RevealedSquare.Parent

    'Who is around me?
    Dim Neighbors As Collection = theField.NearNeighbors
(RevealedSquare.R, RevealedSquare.C)

    'We keep a bunch of numbers:
    'How many mines do we see?
    Dim sees As Integer = 0
    'And how many flags are around us?
    Dim flags As Integer = 0
    'And how many blanks are around us?
    Dim blanks As Integer = 0
    Dim BlankSquares As Collection
    'Now fill in all of those.   Note that the variables
    'for the three numbers are passed by reference.
    BlankSquares = BasicStatsAndBlanks(RevealedSquare, Neighbors, sees, _
        flags, blanks)

    'No blanks, no work possible
    If blanks > 0 Then
        'Decision time! No worries, it can't be both

        If sees = flags Then
            theField.MoreThoughts(Me.GetType.Name & " sees " & _
                blanks.ToString & " safe squares to click.")
            'Store the result for later execution
            SimonSays = PossibleActions.ClickBlanks
            SquaresList = BlankSquares
        End If

        If blanks + flags = sees Then
            theField.MoreThoughts(Me.GetType.Name & " sees " & _
                blanks.ToString & " mine squares to flag.")
            'Store the results for later execution
            SimonSays = PossibleActions.BlanksToFlags
            SquaresList = BlankSquares
        End If
    End If
End If
```

```
            'This is how many moves we can make
            Return Me.SquaresList.Count
        End Function
End Class
```

The routine declares the numbers it needs and sets them to zero. It gets the neighboring squares from the playing field. Armed with all that, it gets the basic statistics and the collection of nearby blank squares. The decision will be to flag all the blanks as mines, click all of them because they are safe, or do nothing. Since this is the only rule, we can test it without writing the framework.

Switch to Square.vb. Find the MouseUp event handler. Look for the comment about a placeholder for AI. When the user right-clicks a revealed square, that user is asking the AI to run. Replace the placeholder comment with the following code:

```
            'Placeholder for AI
            theField.FirstThought("Thinking about Square at Row=" & _
            Row.ToString & ", Col=" & Col.ToString)
            Dim R1 As New RuleOne
            If R1.Matches(Me) > 0 Then
                R1.Execute()
            End If
            'End placeholder
```

This is sufficient to test the rule. Run the game and right-click every revealed square. If the AI makes a move, you may want to click again on revealed squares previously clicked to see if the AI now has enough information to make another move. Armed with this single simple rule, after you get a game started, the AI can make around 90 percent of the moves needed to solve the game. You will have to help it now and then by using the information of more than one square. This rule proves that *Minesweeper* is less about thinking hard than it is about never making a mistake.

This rule executes perfectly, giving it an advantage over human players. Does it make the game more or less fun? If the fun part of the game is making the hard moves and the thrill of making a non-fatal guess, then the rule takes away the boring, repetitive part of play. If the fun part of the game is the challenge of holding to discipline and demonstrating the perfection of your play, then this rule trashes the fun right out of the game. Recall in the earlier discussion that the programmer must mediate between an AI that is stupid and thus boring versus one that is too smart and thus frustrating. With only one rule in place, we can clearly see this need.

The Framework

The first rule was a great start. It is time to add the framework so that we can add another rule. Add a new class to the project and name it FrameWork.vb. The framework is very easy to code; it depends on the rules being loaded in order of increasing complexity and needs a place to store the rules. It also needs a routine to match and then execute the best rule, as well as a routine for loading rules. Add the following code to the class:

```
Private Rules As New Collection

Public Sub AddRule(ByVal goodIdea As BasicRule)
    'Add it if it is not there
    If Not Rules.Contains(goodIdea.GetType.Name) Then
        'Use its type name as string
        Rules.Add(goodIdea, goodIdea.GetType.Name)
    End If
End Sub
```

Now we need the match and execute routine. It is far less complex than the rules it invokes. Add the following routine to the FrameWork class:

```
Public Sub RunAI(ByVal RevealedSquare As Square)
    'Keep the best rule and its score
    Dim bestRule As BasicRule = Nothing
    Dim bestScore As Integer = 0

    'We want the playfield so that we can talk
    Dim theField As PlayingField = RevealedSquare.Parent

    Dim someRule As BasicRule
    Dim currentScore As Integer
    'Go through the rules we have loaded in order
    For Each someRule In Rules
        currentScore = someRule.Matches(RevealedSquare)
        If currentScore > bestScore Then
            'Best idea so far, at lowest cost
            bestRule = someRule
            bestScore = currentScore
        End If
    Next

    'Did we get a good idea? If so, use it
```

```
        If bestRule IsNot Nothing Then
            theField.MoreThoughts("     Executing " & bestRule.GetType.Name)
            bestRule.Execute()
        Else
            theField.MoreThoughts("     No good ideas found.")
        End If
    End Sub
```

Adding the Framework to the Game

The right place to create and hold a FrameWork object is in PlayingField. We only need one copy of it, and we only need to initialize it once. We will need to make it available to the squares so they can ask to run the AI when they get user input. Switch to the Code view of PlayingField and add the following code to the class just below the declarations for Field and the three Num variables. (We are keeping this kind of data together to make it easier to find.)

```
    'This is the AI.
    Public Brains As New FrameWork
```

Have VB create the skeleton of the Load event handler for PlayingField. Add code to it so that it resembles the following:

```
Private Sub PlayingField_Load(ByVal sender As Object, ByVal e As
System.EventArgs) Handles Me.Load
        'All we have to do is load the rules IN ORDER
        Brains.AddRule(New RuleOne)
    End Sub
```

The framework is available and loaded; next, we need to call it. Return to the MouseUp event handler in Square.vb, locate the placeholder AI code, and replace the placeholder code, including the begin and end comments, with the following:

```
            'Run the real AI
            theField.FirstThought("Thinking about Square at Row=" & _
                Row.ToString & ", Col=" & Col.ToString)
            theField.Brains.RunAI(Me)
```

Now run the game and right-click on the revealed squares. The game plays as expected; we are ready for another rule.

Rules for Two-Square Evaluation

The next two rules are very similar: They use the information from two revealed squares to look for moves. These rules could be combined into a single rule, but we will leave them separate so that we can control how smart our AI appears. We also leave them separate because one version is easier for humans to see than the other. Both of these points are game-design issues. We want our AI to play like a human and we want to easily control how well it plays.

So how will the rule work? It takes a revealed square and attempts to use a nearby square as a helper. In the simpler version of the rule, the nearby helper is adjacent to the original revealed square. The two squares need to share some blank squares, and the original square also needs to be adjacent to some blank squares that are not shared. The helper square computes the minimum number of mines and the minimum number of clear squares that are in the shared squares. These numbers can be zero but not negative. If either number is greater than zero, the helper has provided the original square with potentially new information. The original square already has information about *all* of its squares, but the helper gives information about a *subset* of them. If the minimum number of mines in the shared squares is equal to the number of mines the original square has not yet placed, the original square can safely click all the squares that are not shared because it knows that all of its mines are somewhere in the shared squares. If the minimum number of clear squares in the shared squares is equal to the number of unknown clear squares around the original square, then all the non-shared blank squares around the original square must be mines. This rule does not act on the shared squares; it acts on the original square's private squares. If your brain is in danger of exploding, perhaps a picture will make the situation clear (see Figure 4.6).

The upper 1, with the dark border, is the helper square. The lower 1 is the original square. The rule will not work the other way around because the upper 1 has no private blanks. The lower 1, the original square, has three private blanks, in addition to four shared blanks. The helper can compute that at least one mine must be in the shared squares; it sees one mine, and the only thing around it is shared squares. The original square needs to place one mine, and the helper just told it that at least one mine is in the shared squares. That was all the mines the original square had left to place, so the private squares must all be clear. If there are any flags nearby, they adjust the various numbers, but the method is the same. Note that the move is in the original square's private blank squares. The two squares do not yield enough information to safely determine anything about the shared squares. Note that the move consumes all the private blank squares.

The same method also places mines. If the original square had been a 4 and the helper square remained a 1, the helper would report that there are at least

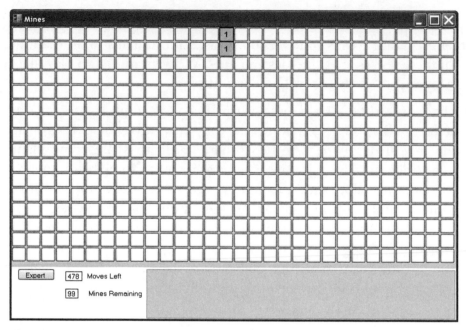

Figure 4.6
Can you spot the three safe moves?

three safe shared blank squares. The original square has seven blanks and four mines to place, leaving three safe blank squares to account for. The original square hears from the helper that all three of the original square's safe squares are among the four shared squares. This means that there are no safe private blank squares around the original square, so those private blank squares are all mines (see Figure 4.7). This is a powerful rule, and together with the single square rule it plays very effectively. Turning the rule into code will be somewhat complex.

A Two-Square Evaluation Rule Using Near Neighbors

Add a class to the project, name it RuleTwoNear.vb, and make it inherit from BasicRule.

```
Inherits BasicRule
```

VB will provide the skeleton for the Matches function. Add code to the Matches function so that it resembles the following:

```
Public Overrides Function Matches(ByVal RevealedSquare As Square) As Integer
    'We use a helper function with near neighbors
```

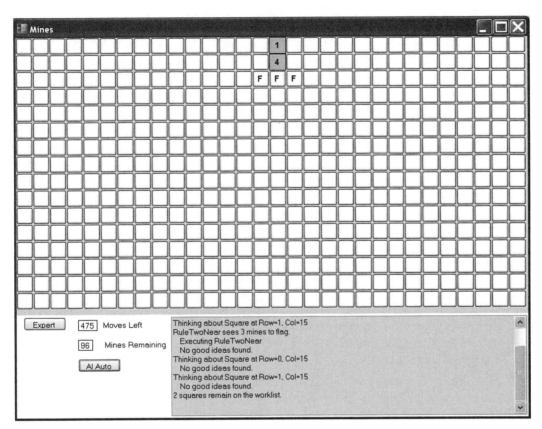

Figure 4.7
The AI places three mines using the second rule.

```
'We should be part of a playing field
Dim theField As PlayingField = RevealedSquare.Parent

'Who is around me that might help?
Dim CloseNeighbors As Collection = theField.NearNeighbors( _
    RevealedSquare.R, RevealedSquare.C)

'Do the work
Call AI.TwoSquareMatcher(RevealedSquare, CloseNeighbors, _
    SimonSays, SquaresList)

'How many moves were found?
If SquaresList.Count > 0 Then
    'Tell the world what we think
    If SimonSays = PossibleActions.BlanksToFlags Then
        theField.MoreThoughts(Me.GetType.Name & " sees " & _
            SquaresList.Count.ToString & " mines to flag.")
```

```
            Else
                theField.MoreThoughts(Me.GetType.Name & " sees " & _
                    SquaresList.Count.ToString & " safe squares to click.")
            End If
        End If

        'Tell the framework how many moves
        Return SquaresList.Count
    End Function
```

This code will depend on a routine in AI.vb that we have not written yet. The important point here is that the rule asks the squares directly adjacent to the revealed square for help. For most squares, that will be eight surrounding squares, and the NearNeighbor function finds them. We store them in the CloseNeighbors collection. Everything else in this routine is generic. Now we turn to AI.vb to implement the matcher. Add the following code to AI.vb:

```
'This function does the work for two rules
'This code tries to use a helper to help find moves
'Two byRef parameters
Public Sub TwoSquareMatcher(ByVal RevealedSquare As Square, _
        ByVal Helpers As Collection, _
        ByRef SimonSays As BasicRule.PossibleActions, _
        ByRef SquaresList As Collection)

    'Clear the list of proposed moves in case we do not find any
    SquaresList.Clear()

    'We should be part of a playing field
    Dim theField As PlayingField = RevealedSquare.Parent

    'Get the basic data of the revealed square
    'Who is around me?
    Dim Neighbors As Collection = theField.NearNeighbors(RevealedSquare.R, _
        RevealedSquare.C)

    'We keep a bunch of numbers:
    'How many mines do we see?
    Dim sees As Integer = 0
    'And how many flags are around us?
    Dim flags As Integer = 0
    'And how many blanks are around us?
```

```
Dim blanks As Integer = 0
Dim BlankSquares As Collection
'Now fill in all of those - note that the
'three numbers are call by reference
BlankSquares = BasicStatsAndBlanks(RevealedSquare, Neighbors, sees, _
    flags, blanks)

'If no blanks, we have nothing to do.
If blanks = 0 Then Return

'Can one of the helpers aid us?
Dim Helper As Square
For Each Helper In Helpers
    'If at any point in the loop we know no help is
    'possible, we continue For to get the next helper

    'To help me, they must be revealed
    If Not Helper.IsRevealed Then Continue For

    'We need the helper's basic data

    Dim TheirNeighbors As Collection = _
        theField.NearNeighbors(Helper.R, Helper.C)
    'How many mines do they see?
    Dim theySee As Integer = 0
    'And how many flags are around them?
    Dim theirFlags As Integer = 0
    'And how many blanks are around them?
    Dim theirBlanks As Integer = 0
    Dim TheirBlankSquares As Collection
    'Now fill in all of those - note that the variables
    'for the three numbers are passed by reference
    TheirBlankSquares = BasicStatsAndBlanks(Helper, TheirNeighbors, _
        theySee, theirFlags, theirBlanks)

    'If they lack blanks, they can't help us
    If theirBlanks = 0 Then Continue For

    'My blanks that they can't see are where my moves will go
    Dim PrivateBlanks As New Collection
    'Shared blanks are how they will help us
    Dim commonBlankCount As Integer = 0
```

```
'Compute and collect those blanks
Dim Sq As Square
'Go through my blanks looking in theirs
For Each Sq In BlankSquares
    'Need the key to search
    Dim sqKey As String = theField.KeyFromRC(Sq.R, Sq.C)
    If TheirBlankSquares.Contains(sqKey) Then
        'It's mine and it's theirs
        commonBlankCount += 1
    Else
        'It's mine alone and a possible move
        PrivateBlanks.Add(Sq, sqKey)
    End If
Next
'Do we have anything to say?
If commonBlankCount = 0 Then Continue For
'Do I have possible moves?
If PrivateBlanks.Count = 0 Then Continue For

'So what do those common blanks tell us?

'We can compute how many private blanks they have
Dim theirPrivateBlankCount As Integer = theirBlanks - _
    commonBlankCount
'From that we can take a crack at their view of the smallest possible
'number of mines in the common blanks
Dim minCommonMines As Integer = theySee - theirPrivateBlankCount - _
    theirFlags
'But it can't be negative
If minCommonMines < 0 Then minCommonMines = 0

'We can run similar numbers for clear squares
Dim minCommonClear As Integer = theirBlanks - _
    (theySee - theirFlags) - theirPrivateBlankCount
'That can't be negative either
If minCommonClear < 0 Then minCommonClear = 0

'If those are both zero, they are no help to us
If minCommonClear = 0 And minCommonMines = 0 Then Continue For

'This is a good point for error checks

'We have useful information - is it useful enough?
'Do the mines help us?
```

```
            If minCommonMines > 0 Then
                If minCommonMines = sees - flags Then
                    'The common mines are all of my mines!
                    'Since both variables were ByRef, we can change them
                    SimonSays = BasicRule.PossibleActions.ClickBlanks
                    SquaresList = PrivateBlanks
                    'Finding one set of moves is good enough
                    Return
                End If
            End If

            'Do the clear squares help us?
            If minCommonClear > 0 Then
                If blanks - minCommonClear = sees - flags Then
                    'The common squares include all of my clear
                    'Therefore, my private blanks must all be mines
                    'Since both variables were ByRef, we can change them
                    SimonSays = BasicRule.PossibleActions.BlanksToFlags
                    SquaresList = PrivateBlanks
                    'Finding one set of moves is good enough
                    Return
                End If
            End If
        Next Helper
    End Sub
```

The first part of the routine reads just like single-square matching. We get the basic statistics for the original square and check for blanks. There is nothing to do if there are no blank squares to act on. At that point, the original square looks for help from the helpers that were passed in.

If the helper is not revealed, the helper square lacks the required numerical information. The Continue For directive tells VB that we are done with this iteration of the loop and to go on with the next iteration. We will make numerous qualifying tests on the helpers as we go. This could be coded with nested If statements, but the nesting level would be extreme.

At this point, we know that the helper has basic data, so we get it the same way we get it for any other square. If the helper has no blanks, it cannot help. If it has blanks, we need to know if any of them are common blanks. We need the count of the common squares but not the squares themselves. We do need the original square's private blanks, however, because those squares are where we will make our moves if we find any.

We loop through the original square's blanks, checking them against the helper's blanks. We count the common blanks and store the private blanks. When we are done, we look at the numbers. Without common blanks, the helper cannot feed the original square any new information. Without private blanks, the original square has no moves to make. If there are common blanks but no private blanks, the original square might be a good candidate to help the helper square, but we do not pursue that. The user told the AI to look for moves for the original square.

We are finally ready to compute the numbers. We compute the minimum common mines and clear (safe) squares among the common blank squares as seen by the helper. We start with the number of mines they see and decrement that count by any flags they see since they may know where some of their mines are. We then decrement by the number of private blanks that could hide mines to determine their view of the minimum number of mines in the shared blank squares. Then we make similar computations for the minimum number of clear squares, starting with the blanks they see and decrementing that by the number of mines they do not know about, which is the number they see less any flags they have placed. Then we decrement again by their private blanks that could be safe, and we are left with their view of the minimum number of safe squares among the common blank squares. It takes a ton of code to get to this point. Adding some `Debug.Writeline` statements might be a good idea here. The output will show in the Immediate window when you run the game in the debugger. Some error checks might be good here as well. The minimum common mines should not be greater than the number of mines the original square needs to place. The minimum common clear squares should not be greater than the number of safe squares that have to be around the original square. If you don't think your code is working correctly, add those error checks. If you are unsure about your code, use `Debug.Writeline` to display all the computed numbers so that you can compare them to the board.

All that remains is to evaluate the quality of the numbers. The numbers could indicate that the private squares are mines or that the private squares are safe. The code sets the two variables passed in by reference to the correct move and to a collection holding the proper squares.

Note

VB does automatic garbage collection, so we do not worry about what happens to an object when no variables point to it.

There is a design decision in the code that the comments point out. We take the first helper who can help and go with it. It is possible that a different helper could come up with more moves for the original square. Rather than evaluate them all, we go with the first one that qualifies. The match portion of a rule needs to be computationally efficient because the framework will run it often.

That completes the rule. The rule will never run if we fail to put it into the framework. Find the `PlayingField Load` event handler and add the following line after the first one:

```
Brains.AddRule(New RuleTwoNear)
```

Run the code. After you get a game started, you can chase the perimeter by madly right-clicking revealed squares. Slow down and watch carefully, and you will see the two-square rule fire and leave a single-square move that another right-click will pick up. If the game ever steps on a mine, you have a bug or the player has manually flagged a safe square. Look at the thoughts output to make sure that the first rule with the most squares is the one that executes. That way, we know that the framework is working properly.

Play a number of games using the AI as much as possible. How much fun is *Minesweeper* now? Is the AI too smart or not smart enough?

Two-Square Evaluation Using Non-Adjacent Squares

The AI can still use more help. If you think about it, you may realize that the helper square does not have to come from the directly adjacent squares (usually eight of them). The helper could be from one of the squares surrounding the directly adjacent squares. There are usually 16 such surrounding squares. The original square and the helper will have common squares directly between them. If one or more of these are blank, and the original square has other private blanks, the same method works from farther away.

All we need is access to the next outer ring of neighbors. Switch to the Code view of PlayingField.vb and find the `NearNeighbors` code. We need a different set of offsets for the new neighbors. Add the following to the class file:

```
Private FarNeighborOffsets() As Point = { _
    New Point(-2, -2), New Point(-2, -1), New Point(-2, 0), _
    New Point(-2, 1), New Point(-2, 2), _
    New Point(-1, -2), New Point(-1, 2), _
    New Point(0, -2), New Point(0, 2), _
```

```
          New Point(1, -2), New Point(1, 2), _
          New Point(2, -2), New Point(2, -1), New Point(2, 0), _
          New Point(2, 1), New Point(2, 2)}
```

We also need a public routine to return a collection of Square objects. GeneralNeighbors will do it for us if we pass in the new offsets. Add the following code to the class:

```
    Public Function FarNeighbors(ByVal Row As Integer, ByVal Col As Integer) As
Collection
        Return GeneralNeighbors(Row, Col, FarNeighborOffsets)
    End Function
```

This capability makes writing the rule refreshingly easy. Add another class to the project and name it RuleTwoFar.vb. Copy *everything* inside the RuleTwoNear class and paste it inside the RuleTwoFar class. Start with Inherits and be sure to get the End Function line. We need to change the code that deals in getting the list of potential helpers.

Change this line:

```
    Dim CloseNeighbors As Collection = theField.NearNeighbors
(RevealedSquare.R, RevealedSquare.C)
```

Into this:

```
    Dim OuterNeighbors As Collection = theField.FarNeighbors
(RevealedSquare.R, RevealedSquare.C)
```

Since we changed the variable name for clarity, we have to change it everywhere. Just below the declaration is the following line:

```
    Call AI.TwoSquareMatcher(RevealedSquare, CloseNeighbors, SimonSays,
SquaresList)
```

That line should be changed to read as follows:

```
    Call AI.TwoSquareMatcher(RevealedSquare, OuterNeighbors, SimonSays,
SquaresList)
```

That completes the rule. Remember to put a copy of the rule into the framework. Find the PlayingField Load event handler and add the following line after the first two:

```
    Brains.AddRule(New RuleTwoFar)
```

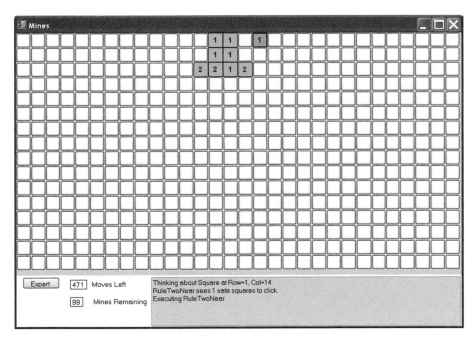

Figure 4.8
Our new rule has three safe moves.

Now run the game. It may be hard to find places where the new rule has moves. Figure 4.8 shows a game example where it can fire.

The lone revealed 1 square can get help from the revealed 1 square two columns to the left. The common blank squares hold all the mines the lone square needs to place, making the three private squares safe moves. The thinking output is from a prior move and can be ignored. After right-clicking the lone square in Figure 4.8, we get Figure 4.9.

In Figure 4.9, the thinking output is current, and we see that our new rule fired. The first two rules we implemented demolish most of a *Minesweeper* game. This third rule keeps the AI from getting stuck. I risked clicking the tile with the lone 1 in Figure 4.8 precisely to take advantage of the power of the new rule. This rule gives the ability to make guesses *productive*. The rule did not change the risk of clicking a random blank tile, but it clearly improves the reward of clicking tiles just past the perimeter.

Do We Need More Rules?

As shown in Figure 4.10, the AI still gets stuck sometimes when there are deterministic moves. Find the pair of 1 squares at the bottom of the group of four

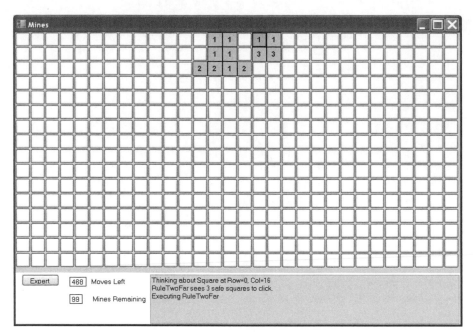

Figure 4.9
Our new rule takes the three safe moves.

revealed squares at the left edge of all the cleared squares. One of them has a darker outline. There is a 2 and a 3 above those 1 squares. Above that are two unknown squares. By looking at the four revealed squares above those unknown squares, we can determine that there is one mine in the two unknown squares. The 2 and the 3 squares then tell us that there is one unknown mine in the pair of squares to the left of the 2 and one unknown mine to the right of the 3, in addition to the flag already there. The 1 under the 2 sees the same mine that the 2 sees, making all squares below it safe. The outlined 1 under the 3 sees the same additional mine the 3 sees, making all squares below the 1 safe. This gives us four safe moves that the AI does not see.

Experienced players sometime use three or more tiles to find a move. We could implement rules that use three or even more tiles, but it begs a question: What's the point? The AI now can play most games either to completion or to the point where all that remains is a handful of purely random guesses. A lucky few games require the player to use some serious brain power or to make the risky guess that will end the game or unleash the AI anew.

If we added the more sophisticated rules, we would want to create a setting for the AI so that we could control how deep into the rule base it could go. This

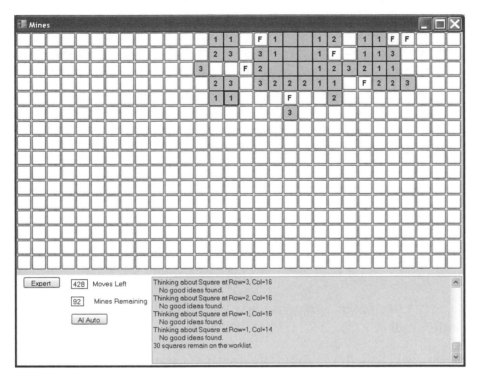

Figure 4.10
There are four safe moves that the AI does not see.

implementation of a rule-based AI is inherently adjustable. One of the advantages to a rule-based system is that it gives an intuitive way for the AI programmer to adjust the degree of difficulty.

There are a few simple rules that could be added to finish the game. If the number of mines left hits zero, then the AI should click all remaining squares. If the number of moves equals the number of mines, the AI should flag every remaining square. The need for these rules did not make an appearance until the AI was well on its way to finishing off most games. We watched it play and noticed an area for improvement.

This illustrates one of the advantages of the method: Working with the rules makes it easier to add new rules. We can evolve the AI by seeing a need and then adding a new rule to cover it. We do not have to implement every good idea we come up with at the very start because we can test as soon as we have one rule. If the AI proves sufficient with a few simple rules, the programmer does not need to risk investing time in more complex ones.

Chapter Summary

This chapter shows that a few rules and a framework to run them go a long way. Once the framework is created and understood, new rules can be added quickly and easily without upsetting existing work. There is an up-front cost to the system, but it pays off quickly with every new capability added. Rule-based systems are inherently tunable and allow for almost Darwinian evolution to cover any deficits. As shown by the project, when the rules fit the game well, they are powerfully effective.

Chapter Review

Answers are in the appendix.

1. What are the two parts of a rule in a rule-based system?

2. What does the framework do in a rule-based system?

3. Why is it that a rule-based system can play like both a human and a machine at the same time?

4. What makes a rule-based AI appear intelligent? What makes it appear stupid?

Exercises

The code for some of these exercises is on the CD.

1. Add buttons below the Expert button for Intermediate (16 row, 16 columns, and 40 mines) and Beginner (9 rows, 9 columns, and 10 mines) games.

2. Add code to track the number of moves made by the player and by each rule. For a more in-depth analysis, keep statistics over many games that include per-move data for all 480 possible moves. When is the game the most dangerous?

3. Modify the framework so that RunAI runs the match-execute cycle repeatedly until it finds no moves around the revealed square. You will need to add a scrollbar to the ThoughtsTextBox control. You might want to make it taller as well. This code is on the CD.

4. Add code to take free moves when a zero is revealed. Recall that the playing field can tell a square who its neighbors are. The following fragment of code may come in handy:

```
Sq.Square_Click(Nothing, Nothing)
```

Our `Click` event handler ignores the parameters that Windows passes in, so we pass in `Nothing` when we call the event handler.

5. Add the two end-of-game rules mentioned earlier. Like our other rules, they need some support from the game. In terms of cost, where do they go in our ordered list of rules?

6. Add code that has the AI search for moves and make all the moves that it can. It may be helpful to keep a work list that holds revealed tiles that have one or more unknown adjacent tiles. It will be far faster to search the work list than to search the entire playing field. This addition will really show how powerful the AI can be, although keeping the work list correct may be a challenge. This code is on the CD.

7. Write a Sudoku game and a rule-based AI for it. Think of the rules you use to find moves when you play Sudoku. Put those rules into a rule-based AI and see how well it plays.

References

[Kirby08] Kirby, Neil. "AI as a Gameplay Analysis Tool," *AI Game Programming Wisdom 4*, Charles River Media, 2008: pp. 39–48.

[Laird99] Laird, John; van Lent, Michael. "Developing an Artificial Intelligence Engine," *Proceedings of the 1999 Game Developers Conference*, San Jose, CA, Miller Freeman.

[Laird] Laird, John. "Part VI: Building Large Soar Programs: Soar Quakebot," date unknown, available online at http://ai.eecs.umich.edu/soar/sitemaker/docs/tutorial/TutorialPart6.pdf.

[Pittman09] Pittman, Jamey. "The *Pac-Man* Dossier," February 23, 2009, available online at http://home.comcast.net/~jpittman2/pacman/pacman-dossier.html.

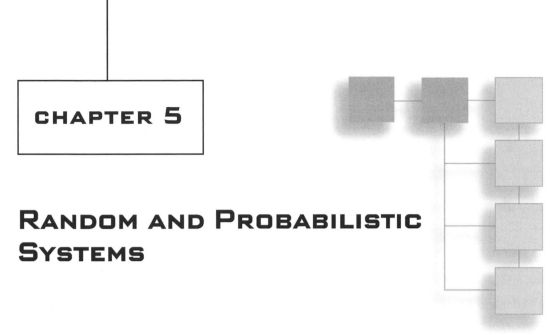

CHAPTER 5

RANDOM AND PROBABILISTIC SYSTEMS

Random systems are easy to understand. Consider the coin toss that starts American football games, the winner of which gets to choose to kick off or to receive the kickoff. The coin toss is not influenced by any consideration that one particular outcome might be "better" or "more entertaining" or "preferred."

Probabilistic systems, on the other hand, consider the odds. In the card game Blackjack, the dealer for a casino hits on 16 or less and stands on 17 or more. This simple rule is based on a known long-term outcome that can be mathematically proven.

Can That Be AI?

Both types of systems appear to conflict with our working definition of AI. What is the intelligent part of random? How does a fixed rule deal with changing conditions? Random decisions can simulate human behavior. Humans get bored and distracted and are subject to the urge to try something different. So an AI that is predictable will seem less intelligent than an AI that is not predictable. At the same time, an AI that randomly picks from equally good choices is just as good in the long term as an AI that picks the first of equally good choices it evaluates. Our *Minesweeper* AI from Chapter 4, "Rule-Based Systems," had a very reliable figure of merit for the available choices, but it could just as easily have picked among the best choices by random selection. A similar argument can be made for FSM: *Random selection is a good way to disambiguate equally good choices.*

Choices are not always equally good, however. When the AI needs to avoid being predictable, it must sometimes select a sub-optimal choice. A real-life Blackjack dealer is required to be predictable; the prediction that must be true is that in the long run, the house always wins. But game AI must balance the flaw of predictability against the flaw of making sub-optimal choices. The game AI needs to consider the odds in order to strike that balance.

Computing the Odds

Odds are situational. The odds for many games of pure chance can easily be precomputed. The methods for doing so are presented in most probability and statistics books. More advanced treatments are available in books on combinatorics, which, while fascinating in its own right, might not be for the faint of heart. We will look at three ways of computing the odds: Monte Carlo methods, precomputing, and faking it. Each method has unique strengths and costs.

Monte Carlo Methods

How can one know the odds in cases where the situation cannot be known in advance? One way is to simulate some or all of the potential game outcomes and compute the odds from the simulated results. This is known as a Monte Carlo method, and it can be directly applied to game AI. If one view of intelligence is that current actions increase future gains, then game AI could surely benefit from the ability to look into the future before making a decision.

The quality of a Monte Carlo simulation depends on how accurately the AI's Monte Carlo simulation models the actual game situation. An AI programmer wishing to use Monte Carlo methods needs to ensure that the simulation is close enough to the situation and make sure the simulation is computationally cheap enough to be worthwhile. Also, the simulation may involve simplifications and assumptions; the programmer must ensure that they are "good enough" and that the results are better than other alternatives. Even if Monte Carlo methods are not employed, probabilistic AI needs to get the odds, also thought of as weights, to apply to the alternatives.

The accuracy of a Monte Carlo prediction depends not only on the quality of the simulation but also on how many times the simulation is run. The simulation may involve multiple points where random events, decisions, or assumptions are employed. In the case of Blackjack, a simulation may pick the next cards to be dealt using random selection from the set of cards not yet dealt. The simulation may involve deterministic decisions with random outcomes. Artillery simulations deal in the real-world concept of "circular error probable," which means "Half the shells land inside this circle." The more often these random points are simulated, the more likely the simulation will converge to an accurate estimation of the actual probability.

Monte Carlo methods are conceptually simple and elegant, but the development time to implement them and the computational cost to run them make them unsuitable for most game AI applications. Their narrow niche is occasional use in NPCs. An NPC that runs a simulation a few times, or only once, is impulsive or short sighted. An NPC that runs the simulation many times, however, has a very good idea of what the future holds.

Precomputing

Given sufficient memory, looking up the odds in a table is so much faster than any other method that it should be employed whenever possible. ("Sufficient" memory is relative; the Wii is particularly constrained for memory compared to PCs used for gaming). In many situations, the odds can be exactly precomputed. In many other situations, the odds can be approximately precomputed. There are two tricks to this. First, the approximation has to match closely enough to be useful. (Think: "This is like X, and the odds for X are. . . .")

The second trick is to validate the odds before the game ships. The only place to get actual numbers is from the game itself. Be warned that during development, the numbers will be change—possibly drastically—as the game evolves. Each time the game is played, it could be logging events and crunching numbers on behalf of the AI programmer. The AI programmer uses these numbers to validate the odds in the table. It is up to the AI programmer to decide if the guidance provided by any particular set of numbers should be followed. This works only if the game has the instrumentation built in early enough to generate the required amounts of data, however. There are many other benefits to building in the instrumentation as early as possible that we will not cover. Real armies need to know the circular error probable of their artillery long before they go to war; AI programmers should heed that lesson.

Known-good numbers are a great thing, but because games are an entertainment product, accurate numbers are not actually required. If the AI plays well with a warped view of its world, there is no inherent problem. The effort required to validate the actual numbers is likely to be substantial and in the long run may not be worthwhile. This brings us to our third method of getting the numbers, which is to simply fake it.

Faking It

Somewhere between random selection and a good set of precomputed odds is the age-old method of faking it. The fact that experience helps is no comfort to the beginning AI programmer, but the beginner should also take heart in the fact that even experts sometimes fake it. All numbers are subject to tuning, so the sooner tuning begins, the better. Faking it means having numbers "as soon as the dart hits the dartboard," which can happen well before the first line of instrumentation code is ever written. Usually, the first set of numbers is thought to be reasonable in some sense by the person making them up. Fewer people turn to a life of daily crime than go to a day job. What is "fewer" in actual numbers: 1 in 10? 1 in 1,000? 1 in 100,000? The numbers from current real life in a first-world country may not match the number from *The Sims*, and that number is probably different from *Grand Theft Auto*. Games are an entertainment product, so the numbers only have to be right *for your game*. Faking it starts by being within one or two zeroes of the final number.

For a beginner, the most serious drawback to faking it and tuning as you go is that tuning can take forever. Hard numbers (or anything close to hard numbers) place bounds on the tuning problem and guide the effort. A hybrid approach is to start by faking it as best you can. Instrumentation is designed into the game, and tuning is guided by the hard numbers as soon as they are available.

For the experienced AI programmer, faking it is actually quite liberating. Tables of numbers can be easier to tune than files of code. The AI does not have to be perfectly rational; it can think that the game world works differently than it actually does. In fact, the AI programmer can negotiate with the game designer how the game world *should* actually work, because that reality is just as mutable as the AI. Not only is the AI being tuned for maximum entertainment value, but so is the rest of the game world. The equations and mathematics used by experienced AI programmers to get their numbers is a book in its own right [Mark09] and will not be covered here.

Using the Odds: Factors to Consider

With precomputed odds or a sufficient number of runs of a good simulation, the AI can accurately determine the odds of future events. The most common way such odds are used is to create weights to influence an otherwise purely random selection. The weights can take in more than the probability of success; they can also factor in potential gains, potential losses, and the cost of taking an action regardless of success or failure.

People weigh decisions this way in real life. Going to a day job each day typically has a very high probability of success, good but not great gain, almost zero potential loss, and modest costs. Buying one lottery ticket with the leftover change from a purchase has an extremely low probability of success, incredible potential gain, no potential loss, and low cost. Cutting in and out of traffic has far lower odds of success than normal driving, small potential gains in saved time, substantial potential losses from accidents and tickets, and modest additional costs in gas and wear on the car.

Impulsive behavior is easy to model with these methods. To get this with a Monte Carlo simulation, run the simulation just one time. With precomputed odds, this happens when a random selection falls outside the most probable outcomes. Much of the time, the system will select a typical response, but occasionally it will select a low-probability outcome. The normally reasonable AI is thinking, "Today is my lucky day."

You can model compulsive behaviors by using different weights on the factors. The compulsive gambler ignores the probability of success and bases decisions on potential gains to the near exclusion of other factors. The gambler says, "I use all of my leftover money on lottery tickets." A miser focuses on minimizing costs. "If you order a cup of hot water, you can use the free ketchup on the table to make tomato soup." A timid person is obsessed with avoiding potential loss. "I won't put money in the stock market or bonds, and I can barely tolerate having it in banks. Those companies could all go bankrupt!"

Slow and steady behavior weighs an accurate probability of success against potential gains, avoids unnecessary risks, and indulges lightly in cheap long-shot activities. In the real world, such people seek steady employment at a good wage, maximize their retirement contributions, carry insurance, and avoid risky behaviors, but are not above entering the occasional sweepstakes. These behaviors may lack entertainment value, but the game AI programmer benefits by knowing how to program "boring and normal."

All the behaviors listed here can be simulated using a set of weights on the various categories. Subtle changes in the weights create richness within a category; there are a lot of different ways to be slow and steady. Gross changes in the weights yield the compulsive or near-compulsive behaviors. Games are entertainment products, so the AI programmer will need to use tools like these weights to create an interesting player experience.

Design and Analysis

If the AI problem at hand does not lend itself to numbers, probabilistic methods are of little help. Like all the other tools we have covered so far, the method forces the AI programmer to try to think of the problem in terms of this kind of solution. Some problems will have an elegant fit, and the AI programmer can orchestrate a rich variety of behaviors by changes to some numbers.

The hardest question to answer is, "Can I get the numbers?" We have covered three basic ways of getting the numbers. Sometimes a number may not tune well; it may need to be lower or higher at different times. In such cases, you replace the number with some code that computes a value based on the situation and include more numbers that will need to be tuned. The idea is to use the simplest methods that do the job and apply sophistication only as needed. (Note that this idea applies to all aspects of game AI, not just methods based on numbers.)

Advantages

Probabilistic methods put a floor under artificial stupidity by coming up with reasonable actions. Random selection among best moves provides interest and removes predictability. The methods enable the AI programmer to provide a range of behaviors, including interesting or possibly baffling moves. Even good moves can be nuanced—possibly too subtly for the player to notice, but far more than we saw with FSMs. In addition, adding such nuances has a lower impact on complexity than we would see with FSMs.

Disadvantages

There are disadvantages to these methods. The greatest is that they literally live and die on good numbers. If you cannot get those numbers, the method will fail or underperform. Not all AI programmers are comfortable with these methods, and tuning the numbers is a learned skill.

Monte Carlo methods generally are computationally expensive. If the simulation does not converge rapidly—or at all—the program will use too much CPU while delivering unreliable numbers. The simulation itself may be difficult or impossible to write. The skills and knowledge needed to write an accurate simulation can be very similar to those needed to write a regular AI in the first place. With luck, the simulation safely ignores or simplifies factors that a regular AI would be forced to deal with, but that luck is never a given.

AI systems based on numbers can drown the inexperienced AI programmer in too many numbers. If only one programmer can tune the AI, then the project is in severe difficulty if anything happens to that programmer. Extra effort is required to document what the numbers mean and how the values were derived. Games that allow user-provided content, such as mods, need to expose these numbers to a wide audience of varying skills. If those numbers are not well organized and well documented, they can be hard to deal with. This disadvantage is easily countered by experience. People who play online games are notorious for rapidly reverse-engineering the numbers and equations used in those games.

The *Day in the Life* Project

Our project is a simulation showing how different people evaluate different possible occupations and the results they get at those occupations. There are three main parts to the project: the simulation, the simulated people, and the occupations available to them. We will use four simple variables to get a wide variety of tunable behaviors. Note that while this looks like a simulation, it is only a game. It ignores all manner of social issues present in real life. Note also that the monetary system is intentionally skewed; not only does $1 mean "one day's wages," but some of the rest of the values are off even by that standard.

The think cycle for the AI revolves around answering the basic question, "What will this character do today?" There are many factors that will go into the answer. Because the simulation deals in money, the first important factor is how much cash the character has. The character will evaluate the available occupations based on four numbers that will have different values for each occupation. The characters do that evaluation based on their own personal equation that handles the four numbers and the amount of cash they possess in a way that fits their personalities. This equation is known variously as a fitness function or an eva-luation function, and we will see it again in future chapters. Here the function can be thought of as a measure of how well each occupation fits the likes of each character.

The Simulation

The simulation starts a person with 10 days worth of wages in cash and runs for 1,000 work days. Each day, the simulation asks the person to pick an occupation from the seven available. This decision will be influenced by the amount of available cash and the person's particular way of evaluating choices. The simulation will not allow the person to pick an occupation unless he or she has at least twice the cost of the particular occupation in cash. If the person picks a different job than the day before, the simulation outputs the results from the prior occupation. Then the simulation takes the selected job and randomly determines success or failure according to the odds. It deducts costs and applies gains or losses to the person's cash. At the end of the day, the simulation deducts living expenses based on the person's cash. The simulation brackets people as rich, doing okay, poor, and almost broke with commensurate expense levels. People who have negative cash are declared bankrupt, and their cash is mercifully reset to zero.

Occupations

There are seven occupations available to our simulated people. An occupation carries a name and four items of numerical data:

- The probability that the simulated person will succeed at the job on any given day, denoted as P. The probability value is given as a percent, such as 99.0 percent, but is stored as a decimal, as in 0.99.

- The fixed cost of each attempt at participating in the occupation, denoted as C. This cost is spent every time the simulated person attempts the occupation, whether he or she succeeds or not.

- The financial gain that the simulated player receives when he or she succeeds at an occupation. Gain is denoted as G.

- The financial loss the player incurs when he or she fails an attempted occupation. The potential loss is denoted as L.

Different evaluations of these data allow the different simulated people to select occupations to their liking. These occupations include the following:

- **Day Job.** The Day Job occupation is used as the balance point for all the others. It carries a 99 percent chance of success. The 1 percent failure rate corresponds to about 2.6 unpaid days per year. It can be thought of as, "I tried to go to work, but when I got there, work was closed." This occupation has a gain of 1.0, which is used as the yardstick for one day's wages. It costs 0.01 day's wages to try to go to the day job. This attempts to factor in the cost of transportation, clothing, and other expenses that directly relate to holding down a job. There is no additional loss for failing to succeed at this occupation; the employer does not fine employees for days they do not work, it simply does not pay them.

- **Street.** The Street occupation models begging or busking on the street and freeloading off friends. This occupation has a 75 percent chance of earning a simulated person 0.2 days' wages, which could be thought of as 1.6 hours of pay. It has no financial downsides; the occupation is free to engage in, and there is no fee for failure.

- **Stunt Show.** The Stunt Show occupation is hard. It has only a 70 percent chance of success. It pays handsomely at 2.5 days' wages; the downside is that a failure costs 1.0 day's wages. (Think of the medical bills!) Even good days have 10 times the cost of a regular job at 0.1 day's wages, due to wear and tear on equipment.

- **Lotto.** The Lotto occupation is not terribly promising. It has a very low chance of success, at 0.01 percent. The payoff of 10,000.0 days' wages certainly exhibits a powerful lure, however. Playing the game costs the same amount as going to a regular job—0.01 day's wages—and there is no additional cost for losing.

- **Crime.** The Crime occupation succeeds 30 percent of the time and, when successful, pays an eye-opening 100 days' wages. It is twice as expensive to do as going to a day job—a mere 0.02 day's wages. The downside is that failure costs 200 days' wages.

- **Rock Band.** The Rock Band occupation has an alluring payoff of 1,000 days' wages. It is not the same as hitting the lottery, but the 0.5 percent chance of success puts it in the reach of the dedicated artist. The lifestyle is nearly as expensive as Stunt Show at 0.05 day's wages in direct costs. Alas, as in real life, bands that fail cannot be fined merely for being bad. No matter how much we would like it to be otherwise, there is no additional loss for failure.

- **Financier.** The Financier occupation really pays, averaging 70 days' wages, net, per day over the long run. It is not smooth sailing, however. Any given day has only a 66 percent chance of success, and every day has the fixed cost of 100 days' wages. Successful days pay 220 days' wages, and failing days cost 100 days' wages in additional losses. A bad run of luck can be catastrophic in the short term. This attempts to model an options trader, who can lose far more than the base price of a stock. It also attempts to model the enormous profits and *unlimited* liability befalling a "Name" backing Lloyd's of London throughout most of Lloyd's history, many of whom went bankrupt in the 1990s [Wikipedia09].

The Simulated People

The simulated people differ in exactly one regard: their method for prioritizing the occupations. In the simulation, each person provides a single equation involving the four variables that pertain to each occupation. While each person is defined in terms of a function F() of our four variables, F(P, C, G, L), we will also attempt to describe their expected behaviors in more human terms. Eddy, or "Steady Eddy," strongly prefers a sure thing. He modulates his choices against loss but is willing to take some risks if the adjusted rewards are still high. Note the $P * P$ terms in his equations to strongly prefer reliable gains. He ignores costs, but that does not prove to be a defect in the current implementation. As you might expect, Eddy gravitates toward the Day Job. Eddy uses the following equation to evaluate occupations:

$$F() = P * P * G - (1 - P) * L$$

Gary is a gambler. All he is after is the payoff, no matter how remote. Gary is a Lotto addict. His equation is quite simple:

$$F() = G$$

Mike is a miser. The only thing he cares about is avoiding costs. He thinks the best way to hoard money is to live on the street. His equation is also quite simple:

$$F() = -C$$

Carl is designed for a life of crime. He wants the easy big score. He does not care about potential losses or costs. His equation is as follows:

$$F() = P * G$$

Larry wants the long shot. He shoots for the big time and accepts the hardships along the way, but he has his standards about what he will and will not do. At first blush, it appears that Larry is taking the most balanced approach of all. It is interesting that he spends as much time as he can in the Rock Band occupation. This is Larry's equation:

$$F() = P * G - (1 - P) * L$$

Barry is bolder than Eddy, but he wants surer things than what Larry will attempt. He has the same P * P terms that Eddy has to prefer reliable gains. The hard knocks of the Stunt Show occupation do not deter him from the higher pay. Note the $(1 - P) * (1 - P)$ terms that Barry uses to deemphasize potential losses; Barry thinks losses are less likely to happen to him than other people. As you might expect, his equation is very close to Eddy's:

$$F() = P * P * G - (1 - P) * (1 - P) * L$$

Complexity

The complexity level of this project appears to be stunningly low. An occupation has four numerical data items. Changing the values of one occupation does not affect the values of another. Adding an occupation takes exactly one short line of code. The simulated people use just one equation of those four variables, although the simulation considers cash on hand as well. Each simulated person is completely independent of any of the others. Adding or removing a person does not change the behavior of any of the others. It appears that there are almost no interactions, making the complexity growth with new additions as small as theoretically possible!

The real complexity is in the selection of those numbers and equations *as a system*. This system must be tuned to give pleasing results. Every added occupation could unbalance the system. You may have noticed that the simulation requires that a simulated person have twice the cost of an occupation in cash before it lets him or her select that occupation. Why twice instead of once? In testing, the Financier occupation kept wiping out people who tried it without sufficient reserves. The simulation is more pleasing with the times-two setting. The 2.5 value for Gain in Stunt Show has a very narrow band of values between spoiling Day Job and never being selected by anyone. The caution here is that tuning is required, even in a relatively simple system like this one. The good news is that the system can be tuned without heroic effort.

The people and occupations in this simulation were developed together, with each occupation aimed toward at least one particular person. When the simulation runs, the people sometimes opt for other occupations that were not explicitly tuned for their selections. These behaviors show up, or emerge, from the simulation. Emergent behaviors are a blessing and a curse. They are a blessing because they are free complex outcomes from simpler parts. They are a curse because there are no direct controls on the behaviors, and the system must be extensively tested to ensure that all such behaviors are pleasing.

Implementing the Basic Game

The basic game is straightforward. We need to create jobs and a simulation to use them. That code will be employed by the AI we implement later so that it can act on the decisions it makes. We start with the project itself.

1. Launch Visual Basic.

2. Create a new Windows Forms Application and name it DayInTheLife.

3. Double-click My Project in the Solution Explorer, click the Compile tab, and set Option Strict to On. This option forces the programmer to make all type conversions explicit.

4. Rename Form1.vb to MainForm.vb.

5. Right-click DayInTheLife in the Solution Explorer, select Add → Class, and name the class Job.vb.

6. Add another class, named Person.vb.

7. Click the File menu and choose Save All.

We have all the files we need. We will hold off on the user interface until we have more of the underlying code completed.

The occupations are the easiest part of the code. The job class stores the five data items used to create it without letting outside code change them. Add the following lines of code to the class to provide storage for the data:

```
'Other than the New call, this is mostly a read-only store of data.
Private myName As String
Private myPSuccess As Double
Private myCost As Double
Private myGain As Double
Private myLoss As Double
```

That takes care of storage. We want the class to be created with the five values it will store. To do that, we add a New routine to the class. It will take the five values, validate them, and store them. Add the following code to the class:

```
'New: store away my values
Public Sub New(ByVal Name As String, _
        ByVal PSuccessAsPerCentage As Double, _
        ByVal Cost As Double, ByVal Gain As Double, ByVal Loss As Double)
    myName = Name
    If PSuccessAsPerCentage > 100.0 Or PSuccessAsPerCentage < 0 Then
        MsgBox("Bad PSuccess value fed to Job.New")
    End If
    'convert from percent to decimal
    myPSuccess = PSuccessAsPerCentage / 100.0
    myCost = Cost
    myGain = Gain
    myLoss = Loss
End Sub
```

Having stored the five values, we need to make them available to outside code. Simple functions will do the trick. Add the following five access functions to the class:

```
'Accessors to allow outside code to read our data.
'We could have exposed them
'as public, but we do not want them changed.

Public Function Name() As String
    Return myName
End Function

'As a decimal; 99% means we return 0.99
Public Function PSuccess() As Double
    Return myPSuccess
End Function
```

```
Public Function Cost() As Double
    Return myCost
End Function

Public Function Gain() As Double
    Return myGain
End Function

Public Function Loss() As Double
    Return myLoss
End Function
```

There is only one thing left to do with the Job class. To make things easier, we want to be able to ask it to use a random number to compute a day's wages or losses. To do this, we will provide the following function:

```
'Return either the gain or loss
'based on the probability.
Public Function Wages() As Double
    If Rnd()< myPSuccess Then
        Return myGain
    Else
        Return -myLoss
    End If
End Function
```

That completes the Job class. Click Save All on the File menu, and we can proceed to the user interface. Go to the Design view of MainForm.vb:

1. Change the Text property to Day In The Life.

2. Resize the form to make it larger. A size of 930 by 450 should suffice.

3. Drag a button to the top-left corner of the form. Change the Name property to EddyButton and the Text property to Eddy.

4. Drag a text box to the form. Change the Name property to Thoughts-TextBox.

5. Set the Multiline property to True.

6. Resize and position the text box to take up all of the form to the right of the Eddy button.

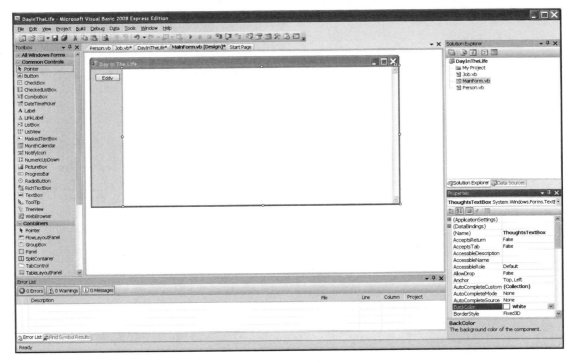

Figure 5.1
Project with a complete basic user interface.

7. Set the ReadOnly property to True and the ScrollBars property to Vertical.

8. Set the BackColor property to White. White is available on the Web Colors tab when you click the drop-down for BackColor.

9. Save all.

This completes the basics of the user interface. Your screen should resemble Figure 5.1.

The name ThoughtsTextBox may be familiar from Chapter 3, "Finite State Machines." We will reuse some of the same code in this chapter. Switch to the code for MainForm and add the following:

```
'The Output side of the interface:
Public Sub Say(ByVal someThought As String)
    'Everything we thought before, a new thought, and a newline.
```

```
        ThoughtsTextBox.AppendText(someThought & vbCrLf)
    End Sub
```

The MainForm will hold our occupations for the simulated people to pick from. Add the following line to the class:

```
Dim Occupations As New Collection
```

Now that we have a place to store them, we need to create our occupations. We will be intentional about which one we load first. We want the Street occupation to be the first one checked because it has a zero cost. Complete MainForm_Load:

```
    Private Sub MainForm_Load(ByVal sender As System.Object, _
                              ByVal e As System.EventArgs) Handles MyBase.Load
        'Load the options - zero cost option must be first!
        'Format is: Occupations.Add(New Job(Name, success as %, Cost, Gain, Loss))

        'Busking/begging is free to do usually gets you almost two hours' pay
        Occupations.Add(New Job("Street", 75.0, 0.0, 0.2, 0.0))
        'Load the rest in any order.
        'Very steady way to get a full day of pay.
        Occupations.Add(New Job("Day Job", 99.0, 0.01, 1.0, 0.0))
        'This pays better but bad days hurt.
        Occupations.Add(New Job("Stuntshow", 70.0, 0.1, 2.5, 1.0))
        'Cheap with high payoff.
        Occupations.Add(New Job("Lotto", 0.01, 0.01, 10000.0, 0.0))
        'Might pay big in the short run, costs in the long run.
        Occupations.Add(New Job("Crime", 30.0, 0.02, 100.0, 200.0))
        'You play and play and one day hit it big.
        Occupations.Add(New Job("Rock band", 0.5, 0.05, 1000.0, 0.0))
        'If you can afford the costs and risks, it pays best over time.
        Occupations.Add(New Job("Financier", 66.0, 100.0, 220.0, 70.0))

        'Reseed the rnd function.
        Randomize()
    End Sub
```

That loads all our occupations. It also makes sure that we get different random numbers each time we run the application. Before we can go on, we need some people.

Implementing the AI

Switch to Person.vb. We will sub-class the parent class for each different person. This will make the code easy to understand. We start by working on the parent class. Add the `MustInherit` keyword to the class definition:

```
Public MustInherit Class Person
```

That forces us to make child classes that inherit from this parent class. The parent class will carry code that is common to all the child classes. Add the following to the class:

```
'Everybody picks the same way; do it here in the parent class
Public Function Pick(ByVal Cash As Double, _
        ByVal Occupations As Collection) As Job
    'Prime the loop
    Dim bestJob As Job = CType(Occupations(1), Job)
    Dim bestValue As Double = Me.Evaluate(bestJob, Cash)
    'Loop values:
    Dim otherJob As Job
    Dim otherValue As Double
    For Each otherJob In Occupations
        'Can I afford 2 days of this job?
        If 2.0 * otherJob.Cost <= Cash Then
            'How much do I like it?
            otherValue = Me.Evaluate(otherJob, Cash)
            'More than what I have?
            If otherValue > bestValue Then
                bestJob = otherJob
                bestValue = otherValue
            End If
        End If

    Next
    Return bestJob
End Function

'Everybody evaluates jobs their own way.
Public MustOverride Function Evaluate(ByVal Task As Job, _
    ByVal Cash As Double) As Double
```

The last line tells any child classes to provide a way to evaluate a given job. This is the member that will use the equations we developed for each person that gives a number describing how much the person likes a given job. Now we need specific people. After the `End Class` line, add the following code:

```
'Real games would not subclass these, but it makes it simpler to understand

Public Class Eddy
    Inherits Person
    'Eddy values a sure thing and balances loss against doubly adjusted gain.
    Public Overrides Function Evaluate(ByVal Task As Job, _
            ByVal Cash As Double) As Double
        Return Task.PSuccess * Task.PSuccess * Task.Gain - _
                (1 - Task.PSuccess) * Task.Loss
    End Function
End Class

Public Class Gary
    Inherits Person
    'Gary is all about the upside potential
    Public Overrides Function Evaluate(ByVal Task As Job, _
            ByVal Cash As Double) As Double
        Return Task.Gain
    End Function
End Class

Public Class Mike
    Inherits Person
    'Mike is a miser
    Public Overrides Function Evaluate(ByVal Task As Job, _
            ByVal Cash As Double) As Double
        Return -Task.Cost
    End Function
End Class

Public Class Carl
    Inherits Person
    'Carl wants easy money and doesn't care about risks
    Public Overrides Function Evaluate(ByVal Task As Job, _
            ByVal Cash As Double) As Double
        Return Task.PSuccess * Task.Gain
    End Function
End Class
```

```
Public Class Larry
    Inherits Person
    'Larry is shooting for the big time but can't afford to lose
    Public Overrides Function Evaluate(ByVal Task As Job, _
            ByVal Cash As Double) As Double
        Return Task.PSuccess * Task.Gain - (1 - Task.PSuccess) * Task.Loss
    End Function
End Class

Public Class Barry
    Inherits Person
    'Barry is bolder than Eddy but needs surer things than Larry
    Public Overrides Function Evaluate(ByVal Task As Job, _
            ByVal Cash As Double) As Double
        Return Task.PSuccess * Task.PSuccess * Task.Gain - (1 - Task.PSuccess) *
(1 - Task.PSuccess) * Task.Loss
    End Function
End Class
```

It may be amazing that we can model people in just one equation of four variables. We are nearly ready to see how they respond. To do that, we must finish the simulation.

Finishing the Code

Return to the code for MainForm. We are going to add the simulation code here. The simulation will start out a person with 10 days' wages. It will then loop through 1,000 days. Each day it will see if the person wants to change jobs. If he or she does, it will give the output from the prior job. Once a job is known, it will be evaluated for success or failure, and living expenses will be deducted. At the very end, it will show us the result of the last job held. Add the following code to the class:

```
Private Sub RunSim(ByVal name As String, ByVal Dude As Person)
    ThoughtsTextBox.Clear()

    'Start with 10 days' wages.
    Dim cash As Double = 10.0
    'Fake out the curJob to get started.
    Dim curJobName As String = "Just starting out"
    Dim curJob As Job = Nothing
    'Working variables:
    Dim wages As Double
    Dim expense As Double
```

```
'A bunch of totals to track:
Dim daysInJob As Integer = 0
Dim wins As Double = 0.0
Dim losses As Double = 0.0
Dim costs As Double = 0.0
Dim living As Double = 0.0

Dim i As Integer
For i = 1 To 1000
    curJob = Dude.Pick(cash, Occupations)
    If curJob.Name < > curJobName Then
        'Print results of last job.
        Say(name & " spent " & daysInJob.ToString & " with job " & _
         curJobName & " ending with $" & Format(cash, "#,##0.00") & _
            " from $" & Format(wins, "#,##0.00") & " gains less (" & _
            Format(losses, "#,##0.00") & " + " & _
            Format(costs, "#,##0.00") & " + " & _
            Format(living, "#,##0.00") & _
            ") in losses+costs+expenses.")
        curJobName = curJob.Name
        daysInJob = 0
        wins = 0.0
        losses = 0.0
        costs = 0.0
        living = 0.0
    End If

    'Go to work.
    daysInJob += 1

    'Account the costs.
    cash -= curJob.Cost
    costs += curJob.Cost

    'And take the wages.
    wages = curJob.Wages
    cash += wages
    If wages > 0 Then wins += wages
    If wages < 0 Then losses -= wages
```

```
        'Do bankruptcy here.
        If cash < 0 Then
            Debug.WriteLine("Bankruptcy")
            cash = 0
        End If

        'Pay living expenses (free if you are broke or almost broke).
        expense = 0.0
        If cash > 500 Then
            'Rich people spend 2.5 days' wages a day on expenses.
            expense = 2.5
        Else
            If cash >= 1 Then
                'Regular people spend 25% of a day's wage to live.
                expense = 0.25
            Else
                If cash >= 0.1 Then
                    'Poor people have expenses too.
                    expense = 0.025
                End If
            End If
        End If
        living += expense
        cash -= expense
    Next

    'Print results of last job.
    Say(name & " spent " & daysInJob.ToString & " with job " & _
        curJobName & " ending with $" & _
        Format(cash, "#,##0.00") & " from $" & _
        Format(wins, "#,##0.00") & " gains less (" & _
        Format(losses, "#,##0.00") & " + " & _
        Format(costs, "#,##0.00") & _
        " + " & Format(living, "#,##0.00") & _
        ") in losses+costs+expenses.")
End Sub
```

All we need now is the code to tie the user interface to the simulation. Get to the EddyButton's Click event handler and add the following line of code:

```
RunSim("Eddy", New Eddy)
```

We are ready to debug! Run the code and click the Eddy button a few times to see how he does. He should work steadily toward becoming a Financier, though it may take him a few tries at it. Once the code is working correctly, adding the rest of the gang is very easy:

1. Add a button to the form below Eddy for Larry. Larry's event handler needs just one line of code:

```
RunSim("Larry", New Larry)
```

2. Add a button to the form for Gary. Gary's event handler needs this line of code:

```
RunSim("Gary", New Gary)
```

3. Add a button to the form for Carl. Carl's event handler needs this line of code:

```
RunSim("Carl", New Carl)
```

4. Add a button to the form for Mike. Mike's event handler needs this line of code:

```
RunSim("Mike", New Mike)
```

5. Add a button to the form for Barry. Barry's event handler needs this line of code:

```
RunSim("Barry", New Barry)
```

Run them all and see how they do. The final running project looks like Figure 5.2.

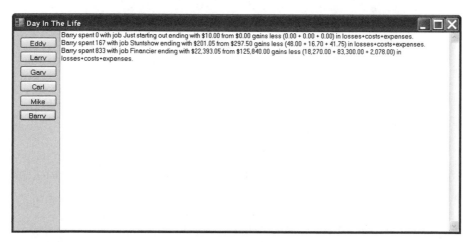

Figure 5.2
Barry has an excellent run.

Results

It is no surprise that Eddy works steadily at Day Job until he has saved up enough money to give Financier a try. The first few days of his new job are critical; Eddy changes jobs with only a minimal cushion against losses. Very often, he winds up back at his Day Job, possibly many times, before he takes off. It would be easy to make an interesting story of Eddy, the steady guy with a fatal flaw of reaching too soon.

Barry, less shy of losses and enamored of higher pay, follows a similar path to Larry, only faster. His Stunt Show days take him to Financier faster, but with an equally small cushion. His setbacks are shorter, and over many runs he appears to do better than Eddy. He tells a similar story.

Gary is pathetic. He gambles his money away until his habit forces him out on the street. There, he scrapes enough money to keep feeding his gambling habit until he is back on the street again. Once in a great while, he wins and retires to Lotto heaven, where the cheap cost of tickets means his winnings last him to the end.

Mike is just as pathetic. Living on the street, he saves money slowly. Alas, when he has saved a small amount, his expenses rise beyond what a street beggar can afford. Let's face it: Even misers are averse to being hungry and cold. Our miser is not immune to spending beyond his means when he has some money saved up.

Larry just might be the most interesting character of the whole lot. He slaves away, pouring his money into his band to no avail. The costs get to him, and he can no longer keep up the lifestyle. Dejected, he spends his last few days of cash in vain on lottery tickets. This is an unexpected emergent behavior. This puts him back to playing on the street, where he saves enough to play again for a while. The cycle repeats until he hits the big-time payoff. Faced with a wad of cash, he changes careers. Unlike Eddy or Barry, Larry has enough cash to survive some initial losses as at Financier. In fact, Larry has the potential to have the highest earnings of all. No one else can get to Financier as fast as he can, and no one else does so with as big a financial cushion. Sometimes, even Larry can get wiped out in the market and go back to playing in the band. A few times, he hits it big a second time.

Carl usually spends his time failing at crime and winding up bankrupt on the street until he can scrape up enough money to try crime again. Oddly enough, sometimes he hits three successful jobs in a row. When this happens, he gives up his life of crime and takes up high-stakes finance. That often succeeds, but if it doesn't, he can always fall back on his evil ways.

We get a great deal of mileage out of single equations of only a few variables. The code and the numbers are simple. We even get sensible unexpected behaviors out of the system.

There are clear ways to extend the simulation. Because each person is implemented as a class, we can replace the single equation with as much code as required as long as the evaluate function eventually returns sensible numbers. There could be more than one equation; there could even be a small finite state machine in there. A simpler extension would be to use the cash value directly, the number of days in job, and the day number of the simulation. The days in job number could feed wanderlust or a feeling of comfortable familiarity. The day number of the simulation could be used as a proxy for age, perhaps to adjust tolerance for risk as the person gets older.

Chapter Summary

With just a few carefully selected numbers and some finely crafted equations, you can use probability to create surprisingly realistic behaviors for game AI. Getting the numbers and equations appears deceptively easy. Tuning them is far harder.

Chapter Review

Answers are in the appendix.

1. What are three ways to get odds for a game?

2. What are the drawbacks to these methods?

Exercises

1. Add more occupations and people. Try to fit the new people to the new jobs without changing how existing people act.

2. Change the equations to include the turn number. Make some of the people tolerate less risk as time goes by.

3. Change the `Jobs` class so that the `Gain` and `Loss` member functions take cash as a parameter. Create a retirement subclass and override those member functions. Treat the `myGain` and `myLoss` values as a percentage to apply to cash to give the values for `Gain` and `Loss`.

References

[Mark09] Mark, Dave. *Behavioral Mathematics for Game AI*. Course Technology PTR, 2009.

[Wikipedia09] Various authors. "Lloyd's of London," available online at http://en.wikipedia.org/wiki/Lloyd's_of_London, last edited September, 2009.

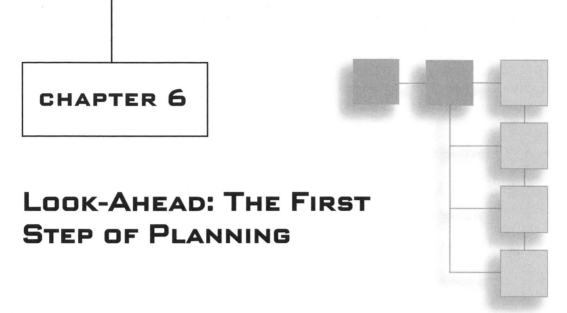

CHAPTER 6

LOOK-AHEAD: THE FIRST STEP OF PLANNING

If you have not memorized all the possible moves in *Tic-Tac-Toe*, you probably play by thinking something like, "If I move here, he could move there, there, or there...." This is the heart of look-ahead. Another way of thinking about it would be to ask the simple question, "If I move here, and then each of us takes our best moves in turn, will I win in the end?" We will revisit the implications of each part of this reasonably simple question throughout the chapter.

The method seems simple on the surface, but even simple games such as *Tic-Tac-Toe* reveal some hidden complexities. Every part of our seemingly simple question is an iceberg hiding many complexities, including evaluation functions, pruning, heuristics, discrete moves, and knowledge representation. By the end of this chapter, it will be clear that look-ahead lives and dies on how well the implementation manages computational complexity. We mentioned combinatorics in passing in Chapter 5, "Random and Probabilistic Systems." We will lightly brush up against it here as well, mostly hidden as determining the product of a bunch of numbers multiplied together. Computational complexity will be a running theme throughout the discussion of other complexities.

After examining look-ahead and its complexities, we will summarize the method's advantages and disadvantages. This will make it easy to discuss the kinds of games for which look-ahead is well suited. This chapter then ends with the *Fox and Hounds* project, which illustrates in depth many of the challenges to using look-ahead.

Evaluation Functions

Evaluation functions are how we turn "...best moves..." in our reasonably simple question given in the first paragraph into code. The simplest evaluation function for *Tic-Tac-Toe* would look at any game and return one of four values:

- **Victory:** Three in a row for our side.

- **Loss:** Three in a row for their side.

- **Tie:** All moves have been taken without a victor.

- **Unknown:** The game is still in play.

While this method always gives a correct answer, we should consider its drawbacks. An AI using this evaluation of the board will always get back unknown until the fifth move. It will not always know with certainty in some games without looking ahead to the ninth move. Looking ahead to the ninth move means looking at all possible games.

How many moves have to be evaluated to get to the end of every possible game? *Tic-Tac-Toe* has nine different beginning moves, eight different second moves, and so on until it has one final move. To get the total number of outcomes, we multiply those numbers together to get 362,880, also know as 9 factorial, which is written as 9!. A 1MHz computer of 25 years ago could do this after a very long pause; modern hardware running a thousand times faster makes it seem nearly effortless. However, any function that has factorial cost must be kept to small numbers. Factorial functions start out slow but grow more rapidly than linear functions, faster than polynomial functions, even faster than exponential functions. Think of a factorial function as a grenade; after a short while, it explodes. When this happens in a game, the player's computer becomes an expensive space heater, appearing to do nothing but blow warm air for very long periods of time.

A more useful evaluation function would attempt to foretell the outcome of an indeterminate game—one not yet played to completion. Our reasonably simple question asked "...will I win in the end?" It would be nice if we could predict the end without playing to the end. We ignore the fact that we can state from the outset that if both sides play to win, *Tic-Tac-Toe* always ends in a tie. But if one side makes a mistake, we would like our evaluation function to be able to indicate victory while using the smallest amount of looking ahead. We want our evaluation function to generate good advice from indeterminate games. *Tic-Tac-Toe* does not provide meaningful insight into this kind of evaluation function.

Fox and Hounds, the game we will use for our project, does provide insights into more complex evaluation functions. We will return in depth to evaluation functions when we take up the project.

Pruning

Our reasonably simple question started out, "If I move here." Think of *Tic-Tac-Toe* as a tree. From the root of the tree, there are nine branches, one for each possible first move. Each of those branches has eight sub-branches, corresponding to the possible second moves that could follow a first move. This is the top of the search space that our AI will look through in search of victory.

If we count the number of possible game boards in the first three levels, there is one empty game board, nine game boards with one move, and 72 boards with two moves on them. As it turns out, while there are nine squares available for a first move, there are only three different *kinds* of first moves: the center, any corner, and the middle of an outer row or column. You can make your favorite corner into any other corner simply by viewing the game from another angle—you do not need to move any marks! From those three first moves, there are 12 kinds of second move. This is shown in Figure 6.1, from Wikimedia Commons [Wikimedia04].

From the figure, we see that there are 12 kinds of boards after two moves, while our naïve method of look-ahead calls for 72 boards. We can get rid of ⅚ of the expected workload if our code is smart enough to realize that most opening moves are the same as some other opening moves, and only the unique ones need to be evaluated. This is called *pruning*, and the numbers show how effective it can be at fighting computational complexity. The idea with pruning is that the numbers that we multiply together to measure complexity are all smaller numbers than before. Our computational "grenade" either takes longer to explode or becomes a less problematic firecracker.

In the *Tic-Tac-Toe* example, there was no loss of information after pruning. There are other kinds of pruning that may cause loss of information, however. One of the most common kinds of pruning is to limit the depth of the look-ahead. *Tic-Tac-Toe* has barely any middle ground where setting a depth limit makes sense. It takes five moves of look-ahead at the opening move to see the first possible victory. After four or more moves have been made, there are five or fewer moves left in the game. In other games, the AI programmer sets the look-ahead "high enough to stay out of trouble, low enough to run quickly." If that limit is too low, the player will observe something like, "Now he sees it coming,

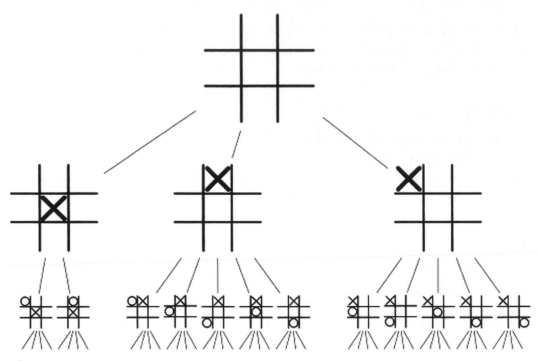

Figure 6.1
First two moves of *Tic-Tac-Toe*.

but it's too late for him to do anything about it." In terms of gameplay, the AI programmer can be tempted to use a variable depth limit to change the skill level of the AI in what seems to be a realistic manner. Be warned that small changes in look-ahead depth can cause major changes in the effectiveness of the AI. In the case of *Fox and Hounds*, we will see that five moves of look-ahead are all the fox ever needs; more depth does not help. With four or fewer moves, the fox may wander too far from the vicinity of effective moves to ever see them. Tuning the AI via look-ahead depth is effective only in games where incrementally more look-ahead produces incrementally better AI.

Heuristics

Heuristics give guidance in ambiguous situations. Think of heuristics as general rules, often based on experience. Heuristics are very helpful in game AI, and evaluation functions need all the help that they can get. At some point, the AI will hit the look-ahead depth limit, and the evaluation function will have to pass judgment on an indeterminate game. Heuristics provide guidance to the evaluation function in otherwise ambiguous circumstances. Pruning methods often need help as well. What moves can safely be ignored? What moves are the most promising? Heuristics provide guidance to pruning as well as to evaluation. Note that risky, high-payoff moves illustrate differences between the needs of evaluation and the needs of pruning. Risky moves evaluate poorly because of the risk. If we prune them, we will not exploit the ones with a high payoff that follows. In short, heuristics are very important to game AI. *Tic-Tac-Toe* is too small for good heuristics, but *Fox and Hounds* is not. A brief description of *Fox and Hounds* is in order.

Fox and Hounds is played on the dark squares of a standard checkerboard. The fox moves like a king in checkers. The hounds move like regular checkers; they cannot move backward. There is no jumping and no capturing. Once a hound reaches the far end of the board, it can no longer move. The goal of the hounds is to pin the fox so that it cannot move. The goal of the fox is to get past the hounds. The fox moves first. The game starts with four hounds at one end of the board and the fox at the other, as shown in Figure 6.2.

Figure 6.2
Opening board for *Fox and Hounds*.

While perfect play always results in a win for the hounds, the game is a pleasant step up in richness compared to *Tic-Tac-Toe*.

There are *many* heuristics. The hounds start as an unbroken line. If they can keep the fox behind their unbroken line, they cannot lose. If the fox does not interfere, there is always a safe move for the hounds that keeps the line unbroken. Early on, when the line is straight or nearly straight, the hound that has only one possible move is the hound with the safe move. That hound is found against an edge when all the hounds are on the same row. When the hounds are in the middle of moving from one row to the next, the hound that has one of its two moves blocked by the hound that moved last is the hound with the safe move. In Figure 6.2, the right-most hound has the safe move. In Figure 6.3, the fox is blocking a safe move from the left-most hound.

One heuristic for the fox is that any time it is behind an unbroken line, any move that forces the hounds to break the line is better than any move that does not. This is shown in Figure 6.3. It is clear that the fox must break the line to win, and experience shows that there is nothing to be gained by waiting to break the line later.

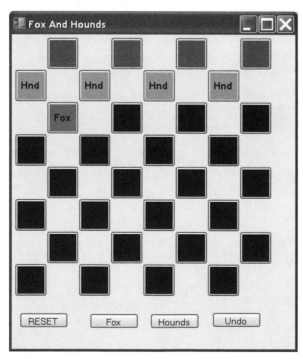

Figure 6.3
The fox forces the hounds to break their line on their next move.

When the hounds are forced to break their line, they use the simple heuristic of picking the move that results in the longest path to freedom for the fox. This gives the hounds the time they need to reform their line and close the hole before the fox escapes. It is clear that having more time to correct a worrisome situation is better than having less time.

Once the line is broken, good hounds' moves are ones that force the fox behind a newly reformed line. They must do this in order to win. As we will see later, the sooner they reform the line the better.

A reasonable heuristic for the fox is to head directly for the nearest hole in the line when the line is broken. We will see later that this heuristic is imperfect. It is clear that the fox must eventually head for freedom in order to win, but in certain circumstances the fox should wait and not head directly for the nearest gap.

Collectively, we can call these the *line heuristics*. A related heuristic is that when the hounds have more than one move that keeps their line unbroken, the move that hems the fox in the most is the best. A less obvious heuristic is that if the fox ever makes it to any square that no hound can make it to, the fox has gotten past the hounds and wins. A final pair of heuristics is that we can safely limit the look-ahead depth to five fox moves or six hounds' moves. The project will use all of these heuristics. We will examine the impact they have on complexity.

Heuristics greatly help the evaluation function. Figure 6.3 shows the fox forcing the hounds to break their line. That move is not sufficient to win, but it is better than any other possible move the fox can make that does not break the line. The heuristics can also help prune the search space. The hounds have at most eight moves to pick from. If any of those moves keeps the fox behind an intact wall, then there is no need for the hounds to do any look-ahead. They still might need to decide between two such moves, but no look-ahead is called for.

Complexity Without Heuristics

In the very first paragraph of this chapter we posed the simple question, "If I move here, and then each of us takes our best moves in turn, will I win in the end?" Now we look at the complexity of " ... takes our best moves in turn." The hounds cannot take more than 28 total moves because each of the four hounds can only move seven times each before it hits the back wall. That yields 28 moves by the hounds. Since the fox moves first, such a game would require a matching 28 more moves from the fox. A fox in the middle of the board with nothing around it has four possible moves. It can have fewer when near hounds or an edge, but it can never have more. Each of the four hounds, when nothing is in front of it and it is not next to an edge of the board, has two possible moves. Setting up the math, we get four possible fox moves times eight possible hounds moves for 32 combinations. We do this 28 times, yielding 32^{28}. This is the same as 2^{140}. Very roughly speaking, this is 10^{42} combinations to evaluate. If somehow our 1GHz computer could do a billion of these per second, it would take 10^{33} seconds, which compares poorly to the age of the Earth, which is around 10^{17} seconds, and to the estimated time until the heat decay death of the universe at 10^{19} seconds. The polite word for this kind of problem is "intractable," although it might not be the first thing AI programmers say when they run the numbers. It should be very clear that heuristics are required to keep the computational complexity of the game manageable. A brute-force look-ahead approach will simply take too long.

It is worth noting that *Fox and Hounds* has only 32 possible combinations for a single move and the following countermove. A move and countermove pair is called a "ply." *Chess* starts out with 32 pieces, and most of them have two or more possible moves to consider each turn. If the pieces were limited to just two possible moves each (a number that is far too small), a single move for one side would involve one of 16 pieces, times two possible moves, for 32 combinations. Not all of the 16 pieces can always move, but half of the pieces have far more than the two moves we limited them to, with eight being a more typical number. If 32 combinations is a reasonable estimate, then there are 32 possibilities for the white times the 32 possibilities for black as a countermove for a product of 1,024 combinations in each ply. This number might seem too large, but *Chess* starts out with exactly 20 possible opening moves followed by 20 opening response for 400 combinations in the first ply. This is called the *branching factor*, and in games such as *Chess* (or worse yet, *Go*), the branching factor is so high that simple look-ahead is quickly overwhelmed. Heuristics and other measures have helped a great deal in the case of *Chess*, but they have achieved far more modest success with *Go*.

There are noteworthy comparisons to be made between the complexity of *Fox and Hounds* and *Tic-Tac-Toe*. *Tic-Tac-Toe* is small enough that its factorial growth never goes on long enough to overwhelm the situation. For small numbers, factorial growth is well behaved. *Fox and Hounds* is more complex, but unlike *Tic-Tac-Toe*, the complexity of the individual turns is fixed. If you increased the number of turns for both games, by playing on a larger board, for example, eventually *Tic-Tac-Toe* would show higher complexity as ever higher numbers are multiplied together. Both show unacceptable growth rates; in *Tic-Tac-Toe*, it is managed by keeping the game small, where in *Fox and Hounds* we will manage it with heuristics.

Complexity with the Line Heuristics

Our project will prove just how much heuristics help. For example, when the hounds have the fox behind an unbroken line and they have moves that keep the line unbroken, the hounds have no need for look-ahead. In the aforementioned calculations, each time this happens, the eight hounds' moves to explore in depth become just one. In terms of a tree, only one of the eight branches will need to be followed. Our heuristic allows us to prune away ⅞ of the work *at each level in the tree that the heuristic can be applied*. After the first move, when the fox is looking to break the wall but is too far away to make contact with the hounds, the complexity computation of three moves of naïve look-ahead without this heuristic gives a sequence resembling the following:

$$\ldots (4*8) \;*\; (4*8) \;*\; (4*8) \ldots$$

The naïve method requires 32,768 combinations to be searched. With the heuristic, the hounds know right away that their best move is the one that keeps the wall intact. The three-move sequence becomes this:

$$\ldots (4*1) \;*\; (4*1) \;*\; (4*1) \ldots$$

With the heuristic applied, there are 64 combinations to be searched.

Careful examination of the board shows that in this part of the game, the hounds have only seven moves available instead of eight. One hound in the line is either against an edge or has another hound in front of it blocking one of its two moves. Using seven instead of eight yields 21,952 combinations to be searched. This is lower than 32,768, but pales when compared to the 64 combinations that the heuristic yields. Good heuristics like this one can be applied at multiple levels in the tree. There are other heuristics that can be applied to the game.

We can do something similar when the line is broken. The heuristic is that the fox takes the shortest path to freedom. This reduces the number of moves evaluated by the fox from four to just one. This allows us to eliminate ¾ of the work at every level of the tree while the hounds are looking ahead to reform their line. We started with our naïve look-ahead sequence:

$$\ldots (4*8) \;*\; (4*8) \;*\; (4*8) \ldots$$

With the heuristic for the fox it becomes:

$$\ldots (1 * 8) \; * \; (1 * 8) \; * \; (1 * 8) \ldots$$

Instead of needing 32,768 combinations to search three turns, we now only need to search 512.

Complexity with Depth-Limit Heuristics

We will allow the fox to look ahead at most five turns and the hounds to look ahead at most six. These numbers come from experience tuning the AI; the fox can always find a way to break the line in five fox moves or fewer if one exists. Six hounds' moves are enough for them to reform their line if it is possible. These make the complexity computations completely different. When the fox is looking ahead, it is trying to break the line. This implies that the line is there, so the hounds know their best move. So we get four fox moves times one hound's move per turn, for five turns.

$$(4 * 1) \; * \; (4 * 1) \; * \; (4 * 1) \; * \; (4 * 1) \; * \; (4 * 1) = 1024$$

This is 1,024 moves, and it can be evaluated in a few seconds even with the debugging output scrolling by. The hounds' computation is similar: eight moves for six turns.

$$(1 * 8) \; * \; (1 * 8) \; * \; (1 * 8) \; * \; (1 * 8) \; * \; (1 * 8) \; * \; (1 * 8) = 262{,}144$$

A quarter million moves might seem troubling, but without the heuristic, the number would be 4,096 times larger—at just over a billion. Heuristics make otherwise impossible look-ahead tasks possible.

Drawbacks to Heuristics

The danger with heuristics is when they fail. "Usually right" is not the same as "always right." One of the heuristics that we will use in *Fox and Hounds* was not always correct for all the given evaluation functions tested. That heuristic is that the best move for the fox when the line is broken is to take the shortest path toward freedom. We use that heuristic to prevent the fox from looking ahead when the hounds are looking ahead; this improves performance considerably. The hounds look ahead when the line is broken, as they look to pin the fox behind a reformed line. The hounds, in their look-ahead, predict the fox's move using the heuristic. The hounds are predicting their opponent's move, but the prediction might not come true. As long as any move the fox might take puts the fox in a worse position, the hounds are fine. As we shall see, this was not always the case; the hounds pruned potential fox moves that the hounds needed to know about.

As it turned out, fixing the problem had an impact on the style of play shown by the hounds. The hounds like it when the fox has fewer moves available to it. So when reforming their line, their look-ahead could see a sequence of moves that reformed the line quickly and a different sequence of moves that reformed the line a few moves later. The first option left the fox more room than the second option. Early versions of the evaluation function preferred the second option because it hemmed in the fox better, which is closer to the winning condition of hemming in the fox completely. As long as the fox took the shortest path, the hounds would "toy" with the fox and slam the door at the last possible moment. It worked fine when the fox behaved as predicted, but could be made to fail if the fox took a different path than expected. The fix meant that the hounds prefer moves that reform their line as soon as possible, with ties broken by how hemmed in the move leaves the fox. The fix makes for more effective but less flashy play by the hounds.

There are two heuristics involved here. One says, "Reforming the line is good"; the other says, "Hemming in the fox is good." A few chapters earlier, we solved the issue of ambiguous transitions in FSM by prioritizing them. Here, we have a similar issue with competing heuristics that also require proper prioritization. Both heuristics apply; neither is broken, but we have to be intentional about which takes precedence.

Discrete Moves

Both *Tic-Tac-Toe* and *Fox and Hounds* benefit from having discrete moves. While this is true of many computer games, it is not true for an even larger number. American football is played in discrete turns, but soccer and hockey feature nearly continuous play. When we have to deal with continuous games, we transform the complex possibilities into as few discrete buckets as we can get away with because we know that the number of buckets is going to get multiplied many times. Terrain is often treated this way. Continuous terrain gets implemented as a set of discrete tiles. All the different possible movements to different points on a given tile can be reduced to a single move, "Move to this tile." The tiles provide our buckets. Sometimes the tiles are even grouped into regions to keep the number of buckets manageable. A small number of buckets is in conflict with the richness of the possibilities; too few, and the AI appears dumb. But too many, and it will run too slowly. Alas for the beginning AI programmer, experience is the best guide. Other AI techniques can be employed, including faking it, to give the look-ahead system a fighting chance.

Knowledge Representation

When the AI looks ahead, it has to think using views of the world that do not exist outside of the AI's thought process. The AI programmer has to make sure that those views are rich enough to allow the AI to answer any questions it is allowed to ask of the current state of the world plus any questions it wishes to pose to its predictions of the future. The AI programmer needs to carefully consider how the AI will deal with knowledge. Besides being rich enough to be useful, the view has to be small enough that it can be passed around, copied, modified, and restored as needed. If the AI is not going to cheat, the view also needs to be properly restricted to keep the AI from having access to information that should be unavailable to it.

One method for dealing with these views of the world is to have just one copy. The AI can edit the world view as needed while it is deciding what to do, but it needs to restore the view to its original state when it is done. If the view takes up a large amount of storage, and no piece of the AI code changes very much of it, this method makes sense. This method dies if the restoration code has any imperfections at all. One part of the AI will consider doing something, and later AI code will treat the earlier consideration as having happened. The computational cost of setting the view back also needs to be considered against the very low cost of discarding a copy.

Another method is to give each part of the AI its own private copy of the view to play with as it sees fit. The act of copying by itself has only modest cost. It is no surprise that computers can copy from memory to memory with good speed. Doing so begs the question, "How many copies exist at one time?" Look-ahead methods are often recursive. How deep is the AI allowed to look? Heuristics that control depth not only save us from computation, they also can save us from excessive memory usage.

Advantages to Look-Ahead

Look-ahead provides a minimum level of competence for the AI even when other methods are used for longer-term planning. With a few moves of look-ahead, the AI will not willingly step into instant disaster. It may not be all that smart, but it's not that dumb either. Controlling the search depth also provides the AI programmer with a good tool for controlling difficulty.

Look-ahead methods are conceptually easy for the AI programmer to understand. Letting the AI search relieves the AI programmer of the burden of crafting an AI that makes good moves for the future by looking only at the current situation. Look-ahead provides a goal-oriented approach; the programmer programs the ability to recognize a goal state or to recognize states that will lead to the goal state, and then the AI searches ahead for them. Dealing with the goals may be easier for the programmer than dealing with alternative methods for getting to them.

Disadvantages

Look-ahead dies when the number of combinations to evaluate grows too high. Complexity can sometime be controlled by pruning, but imperfect pruning methods risk pruning moves that looked poor when pruned but would have led to superior results if followed. Even exact pruning can remove richness of play. Look-ahead gives strange and bizarre results if the player does not play in the manner that the AI is using to model player behavior. The AI "over thinks" the situation and comes up with what would be elegant moves if it were playing against someone else (our implementation can be made to show this trait).

Applicability

Game AI look-ahead can be applied easily to games that have discrete moves and no hidden information. Look-ahead works particularly well for end-game situations for games that would not otherwise use it. A limited look-ahead AI can advise other AI methods, particularly when the other methods are occasionally prone to blunders. Look-ahead by itself is difficult to apply to games with a high branching factor, such as *Go* or *Chess*, without assistance from other methods.

The *Fox and Hounds* Project

The complete code for this project is also on the CD. In addition, there are multiple versions of some of the files reflecting the evolution of the AI code. If you use the code on the CD instead of typing it in, be sure to read the commentary that goes with the code so that you will understand the context in which the AI will operate. Like many of the games we have implemented so far, we will start with a fully playable game and then add AI to it. As we go, we will add code to make the game easier for the AI to play and easier for the programmer to understand. We will start with some design discussions before we get to the game board that contains the squares.

Moves and Neighbors

A checkerboard is more than 64 graphical squares. People have no trouble seeing that the squares of the same color are connected diagonally, but we will need to program that knowledge for the benefit of the AI and the user interface code. Our game only uses squares of one color, so if we do it right, we ignore squares of the other color. As we look at connectivity, we see that the neighbors of any square are also the set of moves that a fox can take from that square if there are no hounds in the way. Continuing that thought leads us to the idea that the half of the neighbors that are "down" as we see the board are potential moves for hounds. The AI will be using this knowledge all of the time, so it is best if we precompute it. While we are at it, moves up are handy to know as well (more on that later). All of this makes us ask, "How do we tell one square apart from another?"

As shown in Figure 6.4, we will tell squares apart by numbering them (ignore the buttons at the bottom for now). For us, the upper-left square is square 0. Our board has four squares in each row, since we are ignoring the off-color squares. The lower-right square will then be square 31. If you have a cheap folding checkerboard, it may have similar numbers that differ by one. Numbering from 0 to 31 makes our code easier, even if we humans have a pesky habit of starting out at 1.

The kind of design we are doing now is the first concrete step toward dealing with knowledge representation. We know that the AI will need to make numerous copies of the boards it considers, so we need to be aware of the performance impact of those copies. There are three standard factors to consider: memory space, computational speed, and programmer time.

The space consideration is worth at least a quick examination. Earlier, we saw complexity numbers such as 1,024 combinations for the fox and 262,144 for the hounds. While we might examine that many boards, we will never store them all at the same time. The number of boards we have in memory at the same time is related to how deep we are looking ahead. The most we look ahead is six moves when the hounds are looking ahead. Since there is a fox move between each

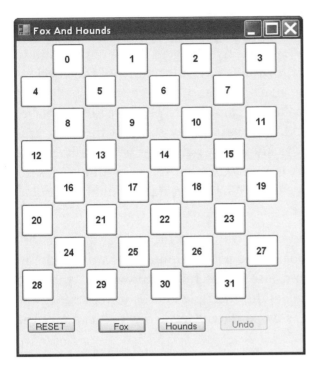

Figure 6.4
Squares showing their numbering.

hound's move, we get six more boards for a total of 12. In our case, 12 is small enough that we can ignore it, but the back-of-the-envelope check is always a good idea.

The speed consideration can be dealt with by a time-honored method: ignoring it unless it proves to be a problem. Unlike the space consideration, where the numbers are trivial, our AI will take the time needed to create over a quarter-million boards. The time required to make determinations about those boards is the concern, not the time spent copying them; modern hardware copies memory extremely rapidly. Ignoring potential speed issues is easy, and the use of the profiling tools needed to find problem areas is beyond the scope of this book.

Programmer time must be mentioned as a third vital resource. Time and care spent along the way that prevent the program from wasting resources are an investment. Time spent trying on early optimizations is wasted. Wasted time has direct costs in terms of money and opportunity costs in terms of features that cannot be added and deadlines that cannot be met. "Premature optimization is the root of all evil." [Knuth74]

What Is Needed for Game State?

The minimum amount of state data we need is five integers. These correspond to four hound subscripts plus one more for the fox. The locations of the checkers are the only way we can tell one game apart from another. We will actually keep far more state data. This data will make the game more pleasant for the player and will make things easier on the AI. We will display some of this data graphically. While the player merely enjoys knowing what the AI is thinking, the AI programmer has a burning need to know exactly what the AI is thinking. Our game will show some of the game state data. What other data would be useful in the game state?

One very important bit of data would be the output of the evaluation function, which we will call the rank, for this board. We will compute it once and store it, trading space to gain speed. It would also be useful to know what the turn number is for the board. As the AI generates multiple boards to represent possible future states of the game, if it sees two different ways to win, it can take the one that comes sooner.

The AI and the display system also benefit from storing some per-square data. We will store what the square holds, which is the fox, a hound, or nothing. We will store what color we are going to paint the square. This color helps more than the display; it will help the AI by providing a fast way to exploit heuristics. We use three colors for our squares: white, black, and green. We color the squares that the hounds cannot get to with green. As the hounds move, they leave behind them a growing area of green, since the hounds do not move backward. If the fox makes it to a green square, the fox wins. We internally mark the squares that the hounds occupy as black, which we show graphically using gray so that we can read the black "Hnd" labels on the buttons. The rest of the squares we color black or white, depending on how the square relates to the hounds and to the green squares. Any square that is not already green or black and has a path that avoids the hounds and leads to a green we color white. Any square that has no unblocked path to a green square is colored black. Figure 6.3 is not in color, but there are green squares behind the hounds and black squares in front of them. If the fox is hemmed in, the squares it can get to are black, which we indicate by using a dark red for the fox as suggested in Figure 6.3. If the fox has a path to freedom, those squares are white, and we use a light red for the fox, as seen in Figure 6.5. Finally, we will store a number that holds the number of steps each white square is away from a green square, also seen in Figure 6.5 As you might expect, coloring and numbering are also used

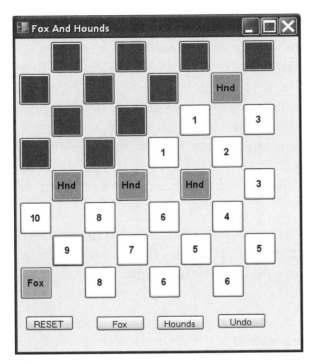

Figure 6.5
Longest possible path to freedom.

by the AI to implement heuristics. The coloring and the numbering will let us see at a glance if the AI is working as we expect.

Evolution of the Evaluation Function

Our evaluation function will be part of the class we use to store the state data instead of being part of the AI. Our evaluation function describes the fox's situation. We use the concept of "big numbers for big decisions" [Dill08] in our evaluation function. Any game board in *Fox and Hounds* can be categorized as either good for the hounds or good for the fox. If the fox is hemmed in, it is good for the hounds; if the fox has a path to freedom, it is good for the fox. There are variations within each category, but there is no confusing middle ground. By making the most important categories numerically far apart, we have sufficient latitude for the variations. Our numbers will reflect this separation of the two categories. A value of 0 means that the fox has won. A value of 127 means that the fox is trapped and has lost. We need in-between numbers as well. Getting those numbers is an evolutionary process.

The first step in the evolution of the evaluation function is quite simple. If the fox can move but not reach freedom, the evaluation function gives a value of 64, which is coded using a constant named UNREACHABLE. If the fox has a path to freedom, the evaluation function returns the length of that path. With only 32 squares on the board, the path can never be long enough to conflict with the value 64 used to mark UNREACHABLE. The highest rank that still allows the fox to reach freedom appears to be 10, as shown in Figure 6.5, where the fox is 10 steps from reaching a square that no hound can get to. The dark solid squares shown with no numbers are green squares, which are winning squares for the fox if it can get to them.

The simple evaluation function is not good enough for the hounds. Some moves that restore or keep the line intact are better than others. These come late in the game, when the hounds are closing in on the fox. One wrong move will let the fox out.

Figure 6.6 shows a sequence of moves illustrating this problem. The sequence starts after the fox takes the 41st move, backing away from the encroaching hounds as it is forced into the lower-left corner. Disaster for the hounds comes on move 42, when they have to pick from two possible moves that keep the fox behind their line. Since the hounds have the fox behind an intact line, they do not use look-ahead to pick between the two moves that keep the fox behind the line. The better move closely presses the fox. But since the simple evaluation function treats all UNREACHABLE moves as equal, the hounds pick the move shown on the

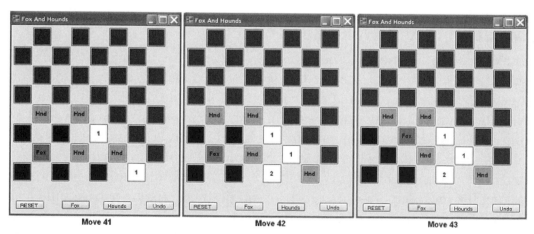

Figure 6.6
All UNREACHABLE moves are not equal.

middle board. Moving the end hound, which is not part of the line, does not improve their position at all. The fox steps forward on move 43, leaving the hounds no choice but to let it out on their next move.

The evaluation function needs a way to judge which UNREACHABLE move is better. One way to describe the better move for the hounds is that the better move keeps pressing the fox. In Figure 6.6, the hounds threw away a chance to close in on the fox in favor of wasting time with a "free" move. We need a way to turn words like "close in" and "pressing" into something our AI can compute. One of the finer arts of AI programming is the ability to turn these concepts into code.

The next step in the evolution is to come up with a number to indicate "better" UNREACHABLE moves, with "better" meaning "fewer black squares." Recall that the black squares have no path to freedom and that the hounds try to keep the fox restricted to black squares. The idea is that the smaller the number of squares left to the fox, the closer the fox is to being pinned by the hounds. There is a subtle difference between "fewer black squares" and "fewer squares available to the fox," however, as we shall soon see.

It is easy to simply count the number of black squares. This gives an evaluation function that generates board rank as follows: If the fox can move but not reach freedom, the value for rank is 127 (the value when the fox is pinned) reduced by the number of black squares. Note that the number of black squares in this situation is at least six; the four squares the hounds sit upon are always black, the fox is on a black square, and since the fox is not pinned, there is one or more black square, to which it can move. The opening board shown in Figure 6.2 has 32 black squares, for a board rank of 95. This is as low as the rank can go and still have the fox behind an unbroken wall. The value of 95 is well above the value of 64 used to mark UNREACHABLE, so all such boards would have a rank that is greater than or equal to UNREACHABLE, making the code changes easy to implement.

This new evaluation makes judgments between different UNREACHABLE boards. Any ties are broken using the idea that good things should happen sooner and bad things should happen later. A rank of 102 is always better than a rank of 104. A rank of 102 on turn 36 is better than a rank of 102 on turn 38.

This step in the evolution fixes the problem illustrated in Figure 6.6. This evaluation function proved to be the most interesting, even though it has flaws. The interesting part is that the hounds appeared to "toy" with the fox after the fox had broken the line. The hounds would see one move that reformed their line early and another move that would reform their line later. The early move would have more black squares, thus a lower board rank, so the hounds would pursue the later move. "Instead of slamming the door in your face now, I'll lead you on and just do it to you later."

Note

The AI.V5.vb file on the CD has the code for this method. The routines of interest are the better move routines in the "Internal Stuff" region. Use it with the naïve method for counting black squares (mentioned later in this chapter) to get the behaviors shown in Figures 6.7 through 6.9.

The hounds can do this if the fox moves the way the hounds expect the fox to move. In games where the fox AI is pitted against the hounds AI, this is always true. Recall that when the hounds are looking ahead, it is to fix their broken line. This is the time that the fox is not looking ahead, but instead taking the shortest path to freedom. The fox is not required to play the way the hounds want it to. A few moves of human intervention helps the fox by ignoring a path to freedom that the hounds will close before the fox escapes. Instead, the fox blocks the hounds from making critical moves on which their plan depends.

This is illustrated in the next few figures. The boards shown are after the hounds make a move, hence the even move numbers. The action starts in Figure 6.7 with

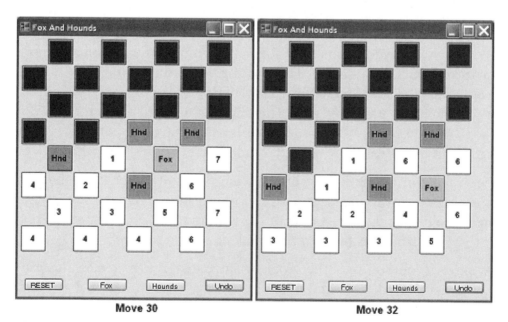

Figure 6.7
The hounds break their line and plan for a glorious future.

move 30. The fox has just forced the hounds to break their line. Move 30 might seem strange, but recall that when the hounds first break their line, they do not look ahead. Instead, they pick the move that puts the fox farthest from the hole. The alternative of moving the left-most hound would have created a shorter path to freedom for the fox.

While move 30 might appear to be strange, move 32 at first glance appears completely insane. Before they made move 32, the hounds looked ahead, expecting the fox to always take the shortest path to freedom. They saw that they could put their line back together at move 34, yielding a board with an evaluation score of 116. They also saw that they could put their line together on move 36 with a score of 117. What they liked best was putting their line together on move 42 with a score of 119. With this evaluation function, the hounds appear to have mastered the concept of delayed gratification.

If the fox moves as the hounds predict on move 33, heading downward for freedom, then the hounds will toy with it. They will open a second hole to tempt the fox, as shown with move 34 in Figure 6.8. If the fox takes this new bait, the hounds close the new hole on move 36, setting up the inevitable enclosure shown a few moves later in move 42. If the fox ignores the new hole opened on move 34 and heads along its original path downward toward freedom, the hounds will be able to block both holes before it escapes (not shown).

The critical move for the fox was move 33, visible in board 34. Is there a better alternative for the fox after the hounds make move 32, as shown in Figure 6.7?

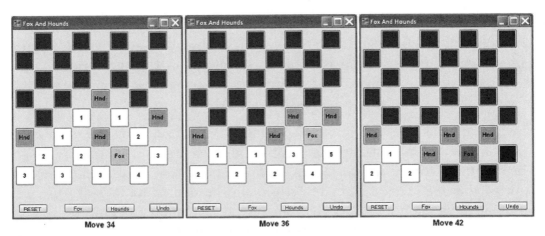

Move 34   **Move 36**   **Move 42**

Figure 6.8
The hounds toy with the fox before crushing it.

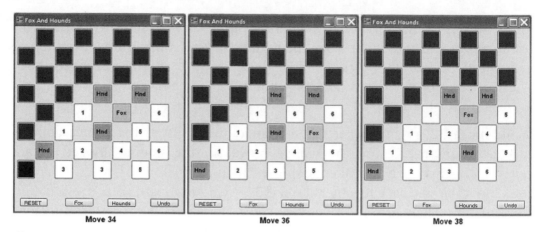

Figure 6.9
Delayed gratification by the fox shatters the hounds' plan.

There is indeed. The fox can pin three hounds if it stays close to them, as shown in move 34 (see Figure 6.9). The hounds will not open a hole with the fox right there to exploit it. The fox AI will not move this way, but the game allows the user to make moves. Instead of moving down toward freedom, the player moves the fox back into the pocket to hold the three hounds fixed. The left-most hound is too far to the left to help, proving that move 32 was an error. The hounds can stall, as shown in move 36, but as long as the fox keeps the pressure on the pocket, that only leads to move 38. With no free moves left, the hounds have to break open the pocket holding the fox. Our fox does not see this because our fox does not look ahead when it has a path to freedom.

The hounds' delayed gratification strategy is flashy but flawed. When writing game AI, avoiding AS—that is, artificial stupidity—is a higher priority than increased brilliance of play. There is also a lesson here about making plans that survive contact with the enemy. The hounds' AI needs to evolve.

The hounds look ahead to reform their line. Rather than change the evaluation function, the hounds' method for comparing different boards needs to change. The best move for the hounds, when the line is broken, is the earliest move that reforms the line. This equates to "slamming the door now to make the win inevitable." The hounds stop "over thinking" the situation and quit toying with the fox. If the line is intact, they take the board with the highest rank, which means the board with the fewest black squares. Things look promising for the hounds, but they still could lose. The subtle difference between the simple-to-compute "fewer black squares" and the more complex "fewer moves for the fox" bites them, so we will fix it.

This last evolutionary step is to change how the black squares were counted. If the fox cannot get to an open black square, that square should not count in the computation. Otherwise, the hounds could be distracted into making a move that reduces the number of black squares but does not reduce the moves available for the fox. Late in the game, most moves for the hounds reduce the total number of black squares by one. All such moves are equally good, and if the line is intact, the hounds do not look ahead. Look back at the sequence of boards shown in Figure 6.6. After the fox has taken move 41, there are two moves for the hounds that do not break their line. The first is to move the hound near the center of the board down and to the left, directly toward the fox. The second is the one shown as move 42 in Figure 6.6: The right-most hound moves down and to the right, placing it on the last row. Using the naïve method of counting black squares, each of these hounds' moves reduces the number of black squares by one, giving them identical evaluation scores. The hounds do not have any moves that reduce the number of black squares more than one; in fact all of their other moves break the line. The two moves we are considering do not give identical results! The first move we considered will bring victory to the hounds on their next move when the fox retreats to one of three squares, each of which allows the hounds to trap it. The second move, shown as move 42 in Figure 6.6, leads the fox to make move 43 as shown, which dooms the hounds.

A more sophisticated way of counting black squares prevents this from happening. We count a black square in the board evaluation score only if it has a hound on it or if the fox can get to it. In Figure 6.6, there is a black square after move 41 in the bottom row that becomes a white square with the number 2 after move 42. In the naïve counting method, this square counted as a black square for the evaluation score. It is the square that lead the hounds to make the ill-fated move shown. Under the better method for counting black squares, this black square does not count in the evaluation score because the fox cannot get to it. The coloring algorithm colors it black after move 41, but it no longer counts in the score. The two moves that do not break the line no longer have identical scores; the hounds will now prefer the winning move of pushing the center hound directly at the fox.

We will implement both ways of counting the number of black squares. The code for this will be described in the next section when we deal with game state. The ColorMe routine will call either NaiveBlackCount or BetterBlackCount to get the number of black squares. You will be able to switch between the two by commenting out the one you do not want to be used.

As we have seen, the AI lives and dies on the quality of the evaluation function. The good news is that simple methods go a long way, and they suggest the areas to improve when they fail. The bad news is that careful testing is required to make sure that the evaluations always behave. The code in the project will have signs of this evolution; presenting the final code in a fully optimized form would reduce the impact of the lesson. We will start with the game board user interface and proceed through to the AI.

Game Board User Interface

We need to start with a new project. That will give us the form that we will use for the board. Use Figure 6.2 or Figure 6.3 as a guide.

1. Launch Visual Basic.

2. Create a new Windows Forms Application and name it Fox And Hounds.

3. Double-click My Project in the Solution Explorer, click the Compile tab, and set Option Strict to On. This forces us to make all potentially risky type conversions explicit. It is not mandatory, but it is a good habit for programmers to be intentional about conversions between numbers with differing precision or objects of differing types.

4. Rename Form1.vb to Board.vb.

5. Change the Text property to Fox And Hounds.

6. Change the size to 450 by 530.

7. Change the BackColor property to Old Lace, which is located in the Web tab of colors.

8. Click the File menu and choose Save All. (Do this regularly as you proceed.)

9. Drag a button from the Toolbox to the lower-left corner of the form. Change its Name property to ResetButton and its Text property to RESET.

10. Drag a button from the Toolbox and place it to the right of the ResetButton. Change the Name property of this new button to FoxButton and its Text property to Fox.

11. Drag a button from the Toolbox and place it to the right of FoxButton. Change the Name property of this new button to HoundsButton and its Text property to Hounds.

12. Drag a final button from the Toolbox and place it to the right of HoundsButton. Change the Name property to UndoButton and its text property to Undo.

This completes the entirety of the graphical elements of the user interface. For squares, we will create a class that inherits from the built-in Button class, but we will not do anything graphical with them. We do need to implement our checkerboard.

Implementing Moves and Neighbors

Right-click Fox And Hounds in the Solution Explorer window (or use the Project menu) and choose Add→Module. Name it Moves.vb. Add the `Public` keyword to the module definition so that the rest of the program can access what we put here:

```
Public Module Moves
```

We will keep the three kinds of possible moves for each square in this module. The number of moves from any given square will differ from square to square, but we know in advance exactly how many squares we have to deal with. Arrays are intuitive when we know how many things there are in advance, and collections are easy to use with a variable number of things, so we will use both. Add the following code to the module:

```
'Three kinds of moves
Public MovesUp(31) As Collection
Public MovesDown(31) As Collection
Public Neighbors(31) As Collection
```

Reading this carefully, we see that `MovesUp` is an array with 32 elements, each of which is a collection. In VB, arrays start with subscript 0 and go as high as the number given. A range from 0 to 31 has 32 elements. So square 0 will have a collection of moves going up, as will every square on the board. Examine Figure 6.4, and you will notice square 0 has no upward moves. We handle this by making sure that the collection has no moves in it. There will still be a collection to look at; it will simply have no moves. Squares that are near any edge of the board will have different numbers of moves than squares in the middle of the board.

When we add moves to the collections, we will add the subscript for every square that connects to a given square. We will mark each added subscript with a key corresponding to its value converted to a string so that we can interrogate the collection using the key to see if it contains the number of a square we are interested in. (VB collections can hold any type of data, but their keys are always strings.) The formula for computing neighbors changes between even- and odd-numbered rows. We will take that into account when we compute the neighbors. Using Figure 6.4, we can see that the square above and to the left of square 22 is square 17, which is a difference of 5. But from square 17, the same move takes us to square 13, a difference of 4. In both cases, the move up and to the right is one more than the move up and left.

An important point to notice is that we can influence the effectiveness of the AI by how we arrange the moves in the collections. We will do two things to help. We will add upward moves first to the neighbors so that the fox tries to go up the board before trying to go down the board. We will also change how we order the upward or downward moves so that even and odd rows do left or right moves in different order. This encourages the fox to zigzag upward instead of going up and left.

The code to initialize all three arrays may appear daunting, but it beats the alternative of 200 lines of mind-numbingly regular initializations that differ from each other only slightly.

```
Public Sub InitMoves()
        Dim row As Integer
        Dim col As Integer
        'The array subscript is computed off row and col.
        Dim ss As Integer
        'The final subscript is what we store in the collections.
        Dim finalss As Integer
        Dim offset As Integer

        'Do moves up first so the fox prefers them.

        For row = 0 To 7
            'Offset will = 0 or 1.
            offset = row Mod 2
```

```
For col = 0 To 3
    ss = row * 4 + col
    'Everybody gets a collection even if it might stay empty.
    MovesUp(ss) = New Collection
    MovesDown(ss) = New Collection
    Neighbors(ss) = New Collection

    'Treat even and odd rows differently.
    'The changing order in which up-left and up-right
    'moves are added is by design to make the fox zigzag
    'upward instead of going up diagonally.
    If offset = 0 Then
        'Do moves up first (helps fox AI).
        'Don't fall off the top of the board.
        If row > 0 Then
            'The last col in even rows lacks the
            'neighbors to the right.
            If col <> 3 Then
                'up and right.
                finalss = ss - 3
                MovesUp(ss).Add(finalss, finalss.ToString)
                Neighbors(ss).Add(finalss, finalss.ToString)
            End If

            'up and left.
            finalss = ss - 4
            MovesUp(ss).Add(finalss, finalss.ToString)
            Neighbors(ss).Add(finalss, finalss.ToString)

        End If
        'Now do moves down.

        'Even rows always have an odd row below
        'down and left.
        finalss = ss + 4
        MovesDown(ss).Add(finalss, finalss.ToString)
        Neighbors(ss).Add(finalss, finalss.ToString)

        'The last col in even rows lacks the
        'two neighbors to the right.
        If col <> 3 Then
            'down and right.
            finalss = ss + 5
```

```
                    MovesDown(ss).Add(finalss, finalss.ToString)
                    Neighbors(ss).Add(finalss, finalss.ToString)
                End If

            Else
                'This is an odd numbered row.
                'Same concepts, different numbers.

                'Always an even row above, do the moves up.
                'The first col lacks the
                'neighbors to the left.
                If col <> 0 Then
                    'up and left.
                    finalss = ss - 5
                    MovesUp(ss).Add(finalss, finalss.ToString)
                    Neighbors(ss).Add(finalss, finalss.ToString)
                End If

                'The move up and right we always get
                finalss = ss - 4
                MovesUp(ss).Add(finalss, finalss.ToString)
                Neighbors(ss).Add(finalss, finalss.ToString)

                'Moves down.
                If row < 7 Then
                    'down and right.
                    finalss = ss + 4
                    MovesDown(ss).Add(finalss, finalss.ToString)
                    Neighbors(ss).Add(finalss, finalss.ToString)
                    If col <> 0 Then
                        'down and left.
                        finalss = ss + 3
                        MovesDown(ss).Add(finalss, finalss.ToString)
                        Neighbors(ss).Add(finalss, finalss.ToString)
                    End If
                End If
            End If
        Next col
    Next row
End Sub
```

Moves and neighbors are only part of the checkerboard. We still have the gra-phical parts, and we still need to decide what we will pass around to the AI. We will do the minimum of both needed to get us to the point where we can begin testing as we go.

Graphical Squares

Our graphical squares will be square buttons that have been adapted to our needs. We need our squares to know their subscript. We do this because we will split the graphical elements apart from the state data that drives them. The state data is going to be copied and passed around and analyzed. We only need one graphical board. People play *Chess* with one board in front of them and many boards in their head; our code follows this pattern as well. Add a class to the project and name it FaHButton.vb. Add the following code to the class:

```
Inherits Button

'Just a button, but we would love to know our subscript in the array
'so that we can tell others when we take events.
Private MySubscript As Integer

'When we drag/drop, we will have a hound number or -1 for fox.
Protected HoundNumber As Integer
```

That last bit is for later, when we will implement player moves using drag and drop. The rest of the code makes our class act just like a regular button except in the ways that we extend it. One way we do that is that our class will keep around a subscript value. We want to make that value available to outside code, but we never want it to change. Add the following code to do that:

```
Public ReadOnly Property Subscript() As Integer
    Get
        Return MySubscript
    End Get
End Property
```

This is the simplest possible property method; it returns our private value and provides no way for outside code to change that value. We need a way to set it in the first place, and we will do that when the class is created. Add the following code to the class:

```
'We need a subscript value when we are created.
Public Sub New(ByVal ss As Integer)
    MySubscript = ss
```

```
    'We use drag and drop for player moves.
    AllowDrop = True
    'Bold looks nicer.
    Me.Font = New System.Drawing.Font("Arial", 9, FontStyle.Bold)
End Sub
```

Again, we are laying groundwork for implementing player moves in the future using drag and drop. Since our class is in all respects a button, we let the code that creates instances of our class manipulate them as though it were a button.

Implementing Game State

We will implement the state data using a class. The code for that class will color the squares and compute the rank of the board. We will also have it mark the buttons on the board when we ask it to. We would normally pull that kind of functionality out of the class, but we will take the expedient route here. Before we can implement the class, we need some helper code.

Constants

Add a module to the project and name it Constants.vb. Add the Public keyword to the module declaration.

```
Public Module Constants
```

We will keep more than just constants in this file, but we will start with the constants. Add the following code:

```
    'UNREACHABLE has to be bigger than any possible count.
    Public Const UNREACHABLE As Integer = 64
    'And TRAPPED needs to be bigger than that.
    Public Const TRAPPED As Integer = 127
```

We use UNREACHABLE as our dividing line between when the fox can and cannot reach freedom. We use TRAPPED to denote the fox has lost. We also will add the per-square data definitions to this module.

```
    'The raw data needed to process a square.
    Public Class SquareData
        Public Holds As Checker
        Public Kind As SquareColor
        Public Steps As Integer
    End Class
```

```
'What, if anything, sits on this?
Public Enum Checker As Integer
    None
    Fox
    Hound
End Enum

'Just the color (used when thinking as well as for display).
Public Enum SquareColor As Integer
    Black
    White
    Green
End Enum
```

GameState *class*

We are finally ready to start on the class for the state data. Add a class to the project and name it GameState.vb. Add the following data to that class:

```
'The fox and hounds are the minimum.
Dim Fox As Integer
Dim Hounds(3) As Integer

'But it is very useful to analyze the board.
Dim Turn As Integer
Dim Rank As Integer
Dim Squares(31) As SquareData
```

Now we want to create a brand-new game state. Later on we will add a method that creates a new game state as a copy of a given state. Since this file will contain a good deal of code, we use regions to be able to group like parts together and to be able to collapse them out of sight. And the following code to the class:

```
#Region "Class New"
    Public Sub New()
        Dim i As Integer

        'New game locations; fox on bottom row.
        Fox = 30
        For i = 0 To 3
            'Hounds go in the top row.
            Hounds(i) = i
        Next i
```

```
          'No one has moved.
          Turn = 0

          'Allocate the squares.
          For i = 0 To 31
               Squares(i) = New SquareData
          Next

          'Make this new board displayable.
          Call ColorMe()

     End Sub
#End Region
```

The system will complain that ColorMe does not exist, so we will do that next. ColorMe is only called within the GameState class, so we will put it in a separate region. Regions cannot overlap, so put the following code between the #End Region and the End Class statements.

```
#Region "Internal Stuff"
     Protected Sub ColorMe()

          'The only given is where the fox and hounds are.
          'Compute everything else.

          'The square in game state.
          Dim StateSquare As SquareData

          'i is for going through squares.
          Dim i As Integer
          'ss is for subscripts of OTHER squares.
          Dim ss As Integer

          'The base state is an all black board.
          'Do all squares (no need for the subscript).
          For Each StateSquare In Squares
               StateSquare.Holds = Checker.None
               StateSquare.Kind = SquareColor.Black
               StateSquare.Steps = UNREACHABLE
          Next

          'Add the fox.
          Squares(Fox).Holds = Checker.Fox
```

```
'Add the hounds.
For i = 0 To 3
    Squares(Hounds(i)).Holds = Checker.Hound
Next

'Start coloring the top row of green.
For i = 0 To 3
    StateSquare = Squares(i)
    If StateSquare.Holds <> Checker.Hound Then
        StateSquare.Kind = SquareColor.Green
        StateSquare.Steps = 0
    End If
Next i

'I am green if all of my parents are green
'and no hound sits on me.
For i = 4 To 31
    StateSquare = Squares(i)

    If StateSquare.Holds <> Checker.Hound Then
        Dim AmGreen As Boolean = True
        For Each ss In Moves.MovesUp(i)
            AmGreen = AmGreen And (Squares(ss).Kind = SquareColor.Green)
        Next
        If AmGreen Then
            StateSquare.Kind = SquareColor.Green
            StateSquare.Steps = 0
        End If
    End If
Next

'Renumber the squares if the hounds left an opening.
'Keep renumbering until the numbers stabilize (at most
'something like 11 times).

Dim NeedsMorePasses As Boolean = True
While NeedsMorePasses
    'We are done unless we do something.
    NeedsMorePasses = False

    'Start at 4, the top row is never white.
    For i = 4 To 31
        StateSquare = Squares(i)
```

```
                    'Don't number hound squares.
                    If StateSquare.Holds <> Checker.Hound Then
                        'Use the neighbors to see if I have a lower number.
                        For Each ss In Moves.Neighbors(i)
                            'Can my neighbor lower my steps count?
                            If Squares(ss).Steps + 1 < StateSquare.Steps Then
                                StateSquare.Steps = Squares(ss).Steps + 1
                                'That makes me a white square.
                                StateSquare.Kind = SquareColor.White
                                'We changed stuff, have to keep looping.
                                NeedsMorePasses = True
                            End If
                        Next ss
                    End If
                Next i
            End While


            'Is the fox trapped?
            StateSquare = Squares(Fox)
            Dim CanMove As Boolean = False
            For Each ss In Moves.Neighbors(Fox)
                If Squares(ss).Holds <> Checker.Hound Then
                    CanMove = True
                End If
            Next


            'Set the game rank (and maybe change fox from UNREACHABLE to TRAPPED).
            If Not CanMove Then
                StateSquare.Steps = TRAPPED
                Rank = TRAPPED
            Else
                'It can move, is it on black or white?
                If StateSquare.Steps < UNREACHABLE Then
                    'Use the steps value if on white.
                    Rank = StateSquare.Steps
                Else
                    'The first version of the code was happy with UNREACHABLE.
                    'See Figure 6.6 to see this fail.
                    'Rank = UNREACHABLE

                    'Rank is higher the fewer black squares remain,
                    'but always lower than TRAPPED (four hounds are black)
                    'and always higher than UNREACHABLE.
```

```
                'The naive black count has issues: see Figure 6.6 and the
                'last part of the discussion of the evaluation function.
                'Rank = TRAPPED - NaiveBlackCount()
                Rank = TRAPPED - BetterBlackCount()
            End If
        End If
    End Sub
#End Region
```

We started by making all the squares black. After adding the checkers, we started coloring in any green squares. The top row is easy to color green; if no hound sits on a top square, it is green. The rest of the board is checked from top to bottom. Note that the code uses MovesUp. The hounds cannot move up, and the fox is never restricted to moving up. But the coloring algorithm needed to know what neighbors are above any given square. After making green squares, we can number any white squares. We keep checking the squares against their neighbors until the numbers settle. We then see if the fox is trapped and if the fox cannot reach freedom. The code and the comments show the three ways of computing board rank that were mentioned in the discussion of the evaluation function. All this work makes the board easy to display, informative for the player, and far easier for the AI to consider. The benefits for the AI programmer cannot be overemphasized.

We need to implement the two ways we discussed to count the number of black squares when computing board rank. The simplest is to just count them, so we will do that one first. Add the following code to the Internal Stuff region:

```
    Private Function NaiveBlackCount() As Integer
        'Just count them.
        Dim NBC As Integer = 0
        For i = 0 To 31
            If Squares(i).Kind = SquareColor.Black Then NBC = (NBC + 1)
        Next
        Return NBC
    End Function
```

This function can distract the AI into making sub-optimal moves as was shown in Figure 6.6. What we really want is to count the number of black squares available to the fox. We saw that in the end game, the hounds can be fatally distracted by reducing black squares that the fox cannot get to. Add the following code to the region for a better way to count black squares:

```
Private Function BetterBlackCount() As Integer
```

```
                'Only the ones that the fox can reach.
                Dim BN As New Collection
                Dim stopAt As Integer = 1
                Dim startAt As Integer = 1
                Dim ss As Integer
                Dim pbs As Integer

                Dim i As Integer
                'Add the fox's square to the collection.
                BN.Add(Fox, Fox.ToString)
                While startAt <= stopAt
                    'Check the members of the collection we've not checked before.
                    For i = startAt To stopAt
                        ss = CInt(BN(i))
                        'My neighbors are potentially black squares.
                        For Each pbs In Moves.Neighbors(ss)
                            If Squares(pbs).Holds = Checker.None Then
                                'Don't add if already there.
                                If Not BN.Contains(pbs.ToString) Then
                                    'Add them to be counted, we'll check
                                    'their neighbors next loop.
                                    BN.Add(pbs, pbs.ToString)
                                End If
                            End If
                        Next pbs
                    Next i
                    'Start at the one after the end of the group we just did,
                    'which is the first new one if we added any.
                    startAt = stopAt + 1
                    stopAt = BN.Count
                    'If we didn't add any, stopAt didn't change, so
                    'startAt is now greater, terminating the loop.
                End While
                'Add in the hounds.
                Return BN.Count + 4
            End Function
```

We need to add the ability to mark the buttons with the values of the game state. There will be a number of methods that the outside world can use to access the game state, so we will create a separate region for them. Add the following code to the class, outside any of the other regions:

```
#Region "Public Methods"
```

```
'Make a graphical board reflect this game state.
Public Sub MarkButtons(ByVal Board() As Button)
    Dim i As Integer
    'The square on the board.
    Dim BoardSquare As Button
    'The same square in game state.
    Dim StateSquare As SquareData

    For i = 0 To 31
        BoardSquare = Board(i)
        StateSquare = Squares(i)

        'Set the back color of that square.
        Select Case StateSquare.Kind
            Case SquareColor.Black
                BoardSquare.BackColor = Color.Black
            Case SquareColor.Green
                BoardSquare.BackColor = Color.Green
            Case SquareColor.White
                BoardSquare.BackColor = Color.White
        End Select

        'Set the text of that square and maybe
        'improve the back color.
        Select Case StateSquare.Holds
            Case Checker.Fox
                BoardSquare.Text = "Fox"
                'Fox needs better colors.
                Select Case StateSquare.Kind
                    Case SquareColor.White
                        BoardSquare.BackColor = Color.LightPink
                    Case SquareColor.Black
                        BoardSquare.BackColor = Color.Red
                    Case SquareColor.Green
                        BoardSquare.BackColor = Color.LightGreen
                End Select

            Case Checker.Hound
                BoardSquare.Text = "Hnd"
                'Can't read text on black.
                BoardSquare.BackColor = Color.DarkGray

            Case Checker.None
```

```
                        Select Case StateSquare.Kind
                            Case SquareColor.Black, SquareColor.Green
                                'Green and black squares are solid.
                                BoardSquare.Text = ""
                            Case SquareColor.White
                                'White have the step number.
                                BoardSquare.Text = Squares(i).Steps.ToString
                        End Select
                End Select
            Next
        End Sub
#End Region
```

With some help from the board, we will be able test what we have. We will return
to add more functionality to the GameState class, but we can leave that for later.

Board Code

The board itself will need to store some data. We need our buttons and the game
state used to paint them. As you may have guessed from the figures, we will
support an undo function, so we will need to stash the prior boards away. View
the code for Board.vb and add the following to the class:

```
'The graphics:
Dim BoardSquares(31) As FaHButton
'Our current game:
Dim ThisGame As GameState
'The boards before this one so we can undo:
Dim PriorBoards As New Collection
```

We will do one-time initializations in the form Load event handler. Once those
are done, we will ask the reset button click handler to start a new game for us.
Add the following code to the class:

```
Private Sub Board_Load(ByVal sender As System.Object, _
        ByVal e As System.EventArgs) Handles MyBase.Load
    Dim i As Integer
    Dim sq As FaHButton
    Const sqsize As Integer = 50

    'Do the once per run stuff.
    Call InitMoves()
    For i = 0 To 31
        sq = New FaHButton(i)
```

```
        sq.Height = sqsize
        sq.Width = sqsize

        sq.Parent = Me
        'Four in every row.
        sq.Top = 5 + sqsize * (i \ 4)
        'Left: 5 for border, i mod 4 term steps through the 4 columns,
        'and the mod 2 term for the offset in alternating rows.
        sq.Left = 5 + (sqsize * 2) * (i Mod 4) + sqsize * (((i \ 4) + 1) Mod 2)
        BoardSquares(i) = sq
    Next

        'Just use the reset function from here to get a new game.
        Call ResetButton_Click(Nothing, Nothing)
    End Sub
```

That provides us with the one-time initializations. We need to add the reset code that we called in order to get a new game. Add the following to the class:

```
Private Sub ResetButton_Click(ByVal sender As System.Object, _
            ByVal e As System.EventArgs) Handles ResetButton.Click
    'Start with a brand new one.
    ThisGame = New GameState
    'Clear the undo collection.
    PriorBoards.Clear()
    'Means we can't undo.
    UndoButton.Enabled = False
    'Have the current game imprint itself on the buttons.
    Call ThisGame.MarkButtons(BoardSquares)
End Sub
```

We are now ready to fire up the game and see if we get the board we expect. Run the code in the debugger, and you should get the board illustrated in Figure 6.2. While the reset button works, we cannot tell because we cannot make any changes to the game. This was a great deal of work for a static picture, so we should let the player have some fun.

Enabling the Player's User Interface

We will use drag and drop to let the player make moves. On the graphical side, there are three parts to a drag-and-drop operation: the mouse button down event, the drag over, and the drop. Since our game board is more than just moveable squares, we also have to change the game state after we make our move.

In addition, we have to prevent moves that break the rules of the game. We will make additions to the code in three areas: the board, the button class, and the GameState class.

The board has to hold the current game state for the game it is showing. Drag and drop is going to happen to the buttons. The buttons will need to ask the board for the current game state to validate potential moves. The buttons will need to tell the board about the new game state after a valid move has been performed. The buttons will need help from the GameState class to generate that new game state. As before, the board will ask the GameState class to paint the new state onto the array of buttons the board is holding.

UI Elements in the *Board* Class

The board code is the easiest to deal with. Add the following code to the Board class:

```
Public Property CurrentGame() As GameState
    'There can be two parts to a property.
    Get
        'Get is very simple for us:
        Return ThisGame
    End Get

    'Set requires some work on our part.
    Set(ByVal value As GameState)
        'Did we have a prior game to save?
        If ThisGame IsNot Nothing Then
            'If one side couldn't move, the undo
            'will need multiple clicks to make a visible change.
            PriorBoards.Add(ThisGame)
            UndoButton.Enabled = True
        End If
        'Store the new current game.
        ThisGame = value
        'Ask game state to paint itself.
        Call ThisGame.MarkButtons(BoardSquares)
    End Set
End Property
```

The outside world calls Get to get the GameState object that represents the current game shown on the board. The outside world calls Set to give the board a new

GameState object to display. Before it displays the new GameState, the board pushes the current game, if any, onto the undo stack. It then paints the UI with the new game state. The AI code will also exploit these new capabilities. For many games, it is a great idea to merge the player input pipeline and the AI input pipeline as early as possible. Doing so prevents you from having to keep two different pieces of code that do the same thing synchronized.

Now that we have enabled the undo button, we should give it something useful to do. Add the following code to the Board class:

```
Private Sub UndoButton_Click(ByVal sender As System.Object, _
        ByVal e As System.EventArgs) Handles UndoButton.Click
    'Do I have a prior board to show?
    If PriorBoards.Count > 0 Then
        'Overwrite the current board with the last board
        'out of the collection.
        ThisGame = CType(PriorBoards(PriorBoards.Count), GameState)
        'Remove it from the collection.
        PriorBoards.Remove(PriorBoards.Count)
        'That might have been the last board.
        UndoButton.Enabled = (PriorBoards.Count > 0)
        'Paint the board.
        Call ThisGame.MarkButtons(BoardSquares)
    End If
End Sub
```

The undo function is very handy when debugging the AI. Human players likewise appreciate the ability to recover from accidentally letting go of the mouse button too soon. That is all of the additions to the board that the buttons need, but they still need help from the GameState class.

Game State Support for the UI

The buttons need to be able to ask the game state where the fox is and where the hounds are. Only those squares can be the source of a valid move. It does not make sense to move an empty square, and we have to allow the fox to move differently than the hounds. Getting the location of the fox is easy. Change to the GameState.vb tab in the editor. Add the following code to the Public Methods region of the GameState class:

```
'Where is the fox?
Public Function FoxAt() As Integer
```

```
        Return (Fox)
    End Function
```

For the hounds, we will return a copy of the game state's array holding the locations of all of the hounds. Add the following code to the Public Methods region:

```
'Where are the hounds?
Public Function HoundsAt() As Integer()
    'Create a new array.
    Dim Locations(3) As Integer
    Dim i As Integer
    'Fill that array from our private copy.
    For i = 0 To 3
        Locations(i) = Hounds(i)
    Next
    'Return that array to protect our private copy.
    Return Locations
End Function
```

To be a valid move, the target square has to be open. If it has a checker on it, it is blocked. We could use the FoxAt() and HoundsAt () functions, but the code is easier to read if we can just ask the game state if a checker is on a given square. Add the following code to the Public Methods region:

```
'Is some square occupied?
Public Function HasChecker(ByVal ss As Integer) As Boolean
    'Is the fox there?
    If ss = Fox Then Return True
    Dim i As Integer
    'Is one of the hounds there?
    For i = 0 To 3
        If ss = Hounds(i) Then Return True
    Next
    Return False
End Function
```

While we are in the Public Methods, we will add some code that the AI will need. Other code might want to know these things, but the AI has to be able to get to them. Add the following code to the Public Methods region:

```
'Fox wants 0, Hounds want TRAPPED (127).
Public Function GameRank() As Integer
    Return Rank
End Function
```

```
'How many turns have been taken?
Public Function MoveCount() As Integer
    Return Turn
End Function
```

Right now, the buttons can ask the game state if there is a fox or a hound on the source square. The buttons can ask the game state if there is a checker on the target square. The buttons can use the arrays in Moves.vb to check for valid moves for the fox or the hounds. What remains is for the buttons to be able to get the new game state from the current game state by asking the current game state to make a move. Then the buttons will be able to set the board's game state with the new one.

We will have the GameState class provide move capability rather than have outside code change the game state. This defensive measure protects the game from AI code bugs as well as user-interface code bugs. We can live with the idea that the AI is not smart enough, but we cannot accept having an untrustworthy game state. The game must work, even if the AI goes off the rails. Our highly defensive way of making a move is to ask the game state to return a clone of itself changed by one move. This lets us do anything we desire with the new game state, including throwing it away, which the AI will do often. This also makes our undo method work as expected.

We will implement the cloning part by providing a different way of creating a new instance of the class. Add the following code to the Class New region. (You may want to collapse other regions to reduce the clutter in the editor):

```
'Clone the passed-in gamestate.
Public Sub New(ByVal GS As GameState)
    Dim i As Integer

    'Copy the positions.
    Fox = GS.Fox
    For i = 0 To 3
        Hounds(i) = GS.Hounds(i)
    Next

    'Allocate the squares.
    For i = 0 To 31
        Squares(i) = New SquareData
    Next

    'Copy the turn number.
    Turn = GS.Turn
```

```
            'We do NOT color. The caller will want to move stuff
            'and after the move, it will call color.
    End Sub
```

We will not call this New method directly from the outside. Instead, we will provide an interface based on the idea of making a move. The fox is slightly simpler since there is only one. Add the following code to the Public Methods region:

```
    'So what do we get if the fox moves to some square?
    Public Function ProposeFoxTo(ByVal targetSqaure As Integer) As GameState
        'Clone me.
        Dim afterMove As GameState = New GameState(Me)
        'Take a turn . . .
        afterMove.Turn = afterMove.Turn + 1
        ' . . . by moving the fox.
        afterMove.Fox = targetSqaure
        'Analyze the new board.
        afterMove.ColorMe()
        Return afterMove
    End Function
```

The only difference when moving a hound is that we have to say which hound moved. Add the following code to the Public Methods region:

```
    'So what do we get if a hound moves to a new square?
    Public Function ProposeHoundTo(ByVal houndNumber As Integer, _
                    ByVal targetSqaure As Integer) As GameState
        'Clone me.
        Dim afterMove As GameState = New GameState(Me)
        'Take a turn . . .
        afterMove.Turn = afterMove.Turn + 1
        ' . . . by moving one of the hounds.
        afterMove.Hounds(houndNumber) = targetSqaure
        'Analyze the new board.
        afterMove.ColorMe()
        Return afterMove
    End Function
```

Drag and Drop in the Button Class

We finally have enough support from the board and the game state to actually make some moves. Now we will do the three parts to the drag and drop: the mouse down, the drag over, and the drop. Change to the FaHButton.vb tab in the editor. We start with the mouse down event. Add the following code to the class:

```
Private Sub FaHButton_MouseDown(ByVal sender As Object, ByVal e _
    As System.Windows.Forms.MouseEventArgs) Handles Me.MouseDown

    'Our parent is the board.
    Dim MainForm As Board = CType(Me.Parent, Board)
    'Get the game state from the board so we can ask it things.
    Dim GS As GameState = MainForm.CurrentGame

    Debug.WriteLine("Mouse Down " & MySubscript.ToString)

    'Is the fox on my square?
    If MySubscript = GS.FoxAt Then
        'Use -1 to signal that it is the fox.
        HoundNumber = -1
        'Tell Windows we want to do drag/drop.
        Call DoDragDrop(Me, DragDropEffects.Move)
        Debug.WriteLine("DragDrop FOx")
    End If

    Dim i As Integer
    'Ask gamestate where the hounds are.
    Dim Hounds() As Integer = GS.HoundsAt()
    'Is a hound on my square?
    For i = 0 To 3
        If MySubscript = Hounds(i) Then
            'Record which hound is moving.
            HoundNumber = i
            'Tell Windows we want to drag/drop.
            Call DoDragDrop(Me, DragDropEffects.Move)
            Debug.WriteLine("DragDrop a Hound")
        End If

    Next

End Sub
```

The debug statements provide text that we can follow in the output window when we run the debugger. You can comment them out or uncomment them to provide the right level of detail. That handles mouse down. We want to provide feedback as the mouse travels over the other buttons. Add the following code to the class:

```
Private Sub FaHButton_DragOver(ByVal sender As Object, ByVal e As System.
    Windows.Forms.DragEventArgs) Handles Me.DragOver
        'Debug.WriteLine("FaH DragOver")
```

```
        'Default to no move allowed
        e.Effect = DragDropEffects.None

        'Only allow F&H buttons to drag over.
        If Not (e.Data.GetDataPresent(GetType(FaHButton))) Then
            Return
        End If

        'We will need the board's game state.
        Dim MainForm As Board = CType(Me.Parent, Board)
        Dim GS As GameState = MainForm.CurrentGame

        'Can't drop on me if I am occupied.
        If GS.HasChecker(MySubscript) Then
            Return
        End If

        'We also need to know where this drop is coming from.
        Dim Source As FaHButton = _
            CType(e.Data.GetData(GetType(FaHButton)), FaHButton)
        If Source.Subscript = GS.FoxAt Then
            'Do the fox's neighbors include me?
            Dim FoxsNeighbors As Collection = Moves.Neighbors(Source.Subscript)
            If FoxsNeighbors.Contains(MySubscript.ToString) Then
                'A valid move!
                e.Effect = DragDropEffects.Move
            End If
        Else
            'So it must therefore be a hound.

            Dim HoundMoves As Collection = Moves.MovesDown(Source.Subscript)
            If HoundMoves.Contains(MySubscript.ToString) Then
                'A valid move!
                e.Effect = DragDropEffects.Move
            End If
        End If
    End Sub
```

Run this code in the debugger. Drag a hound around the board. Drag the fox around the board. You should be able to tell valid moves by the feedback from the system. What remains is to deal with the drop. Add this final routine to the class:

```
Private Sub FaHButton_DragDrop(ByVal sender As Object, _
        ByVal e As System.Windows.Forms.DragEventArgs) Handles Me.DragDrop
    Debug.WriteLine("DragDrop event.")

    'We will need the board's game state.
    Dim MainForm As Board = CType(Me.Parent, Board)
    Dim GS As GameState = MainForm.CurrentGame

    Dim Source As FaHButton = CType(e.Data.GetData(GetType(FaHButton)),
        FaHButton)
    If Source.HoundNumber < 0 Then
        'Fox moved.
        MainForm.CurrentGame = GS.ProposeFoxTo(MySubscript)
    Else
        'Hound moved.
        MainForm.CurrentGame = GS.ProposeHoundTo(Source.HoundNumber,
            MySubscript)
    End If
End Sub
```

Run the code and make moves for the fox and the hounds. Use the Undo button to go backward. Make a number of moves and notice that the board colors correctly and numbers the squares when the line is broken. Our game so far has the same game play as a folding checkerboard and five checkers, but the interactivity is notably better. The coloring and numbering tells the state of the game at a glance. This is more engaging for a human player, and it makes the game far easier on the AI and on the AI programmer.

Adding the AI

The AI in these pages uses look-ahead. It was developed from code that used only the heuristics. On the CD, the AI code will have both versions. The heuristics-only AI has the hounds keeping the wall intact if they can. Without look-ahead, they fail to know how to put it back together when broken. Likewise, the fox AI breaks the wall by getting lucky, but once it is broken, it heads for the hole and freedom. There were many benefits to writing the AI this way. First, it proved that the heuristics worked as expected. Second, it provided experience at writing code that took moves in the game framework. The heuristics-only AI is in the No Lookahead region of the file AI.vb on the CD. If you have trouble with the look-ahead AI, switch to the heuristics-only AI. You can do this by copying the No Lookahead region to your AI.vb code and then changing the calls to Fox2() and

Hounds2() in the `Public Interface` region to `Fox1()` and `Hounds1()`. The look-ahead AI code here has numerous debug statements, not all of which are commented out. All of them are there to aid in debugging the code, so feel free to uncomment them if things go wrong.

This look-ahead implementation uses recursion. Recursion is when a routine directly or indirectly calls itself. "My best move depends on their countermove, which depends on the best move I can take after that," involves recursion. Notice that "best move" is mentioned twice. Our AI will call itself when looking ahead. The limit on search depth or the use of a heuristic will stop the chain from going on infinitely.

Our AI has two parts each for the fox and for the hounds. The first part is asked to pick a move from its available moves. It does this by examining the expected outcomes of each of the moves. In the code, you will see this in terms of the best current move being based on the best future result. The basic request of "give me your best move" has the code looking ahead with each of the possible moves to decide what is best. That is to say that for every candidate move, there is a future result that can be used to rank the candidates. We can use game state for both the candidates and the results.

Since the same code is used to generate both moves and results, we will need to make sure that the program returns the appropriate one. When the outside world calls, it wants the move, not the result. When the fox is looking ahead to consider a candidate move, it will want a countermove from the hounds, not results. When the fox looks ahead for how well things turn out after the hounds take their countermove, the fox wants results.

Connecting the UI to the AI

The first task will be to add code for the Fox and Hounds buttons on the board. Switch to the Board.vb tab in the editor and add the following code to the class. It will generate errors that we will fix shortly.

```
'Move the fox.
Private Sub FoxButton_Click(ByVal sender As System.Object, _
            ByVal e As System.EventArgs) Handles FoxButton.Click
    'Give the user an hourglass.
    Me.Cursor = Cursors.WaitCursor
    'Do some performance measurements.
    Dim startTime As Date = Now
    'Take an actual move.
```

```
        Me.CurrentGame = AI.MoveFox(ThisGame)
        'Show how long it took.
        Debug.WriteLine("Fox move took " & HowLong(startTime) & " ms.")
        'Get rid of the hourglass.
        Me.Cursor = Cursors.Default
    End Sub

    'Move a hound.
    Private Sub HoundsButton_Click(ByVal sender As System.Object, _
              ByVal e As System.EventArgs) Handles HoundsButton.Click
        'Give the user an hourglass.
        Me.Cursor = Cursors.WaitCursor
        'Get the current time for performance.
        Dim startTime As Date = Now
        'Make a move.
        Me.CurrentGame = AI.MoveHounds(ThisGame)
        'Show how long it all took.
        Debug.WriteLine("Hounds move took " & HowLong(startTime) & " ms.")
        'Get rid of the hourglass.
        Me.Cursor = Cursors.Default
    End Sub

    'Do the time math and output the result.
    Private Function HowLong(ByVal startTime As Date) As String
        'Fix the stop time since we compute with it twice.
        Dim stopTime As Date = Now
        'We have to do the seconds and ms seperately...
        Dim secs As Integer = stopTime.Subtract(startTime).Seconds
        '...since the ms roll over to zero each full second.
        Dim ms As Integer = stopTime.Subtract(startTime).Milliseconds
        'Combine them and output the string.
        Return (secs * 1000 + ms).ToString
    End Function
```

We exploit the fact that the AI code will be passing around and returning game state here. If the AI goes off the rails and returns a future result instead of a current move, the board will show that future result. We do this to minimize the amount of code; it's not generally a good idea.

The Public Interface to the AI

We are ready for a deep dive into the AI. Add a module to the project and name it AI.vb. The first thing we will add is the public interface to the AI. It protects the rest of the code from any changes we make to the AI. Add the following code to the module:

```
#Region "Public Interface"
    Public Function MoveFox(ByVal GS As GameState) As GameState
        Debug.WriteLine("")
        Debug.WriteLine("Move #" & (GS.MoveCount + 1).ToString)
        Debug.WriteLine("Move Fox.")

        'The code for this is on the CD.
        'Return Fox1(GS)

        Return Fox2(GS, 1, True)
    End Function

    Public Function MoveHounds(ByVal GS As GameState) As GameState
        Debug.WriteLine("")
        Debug.WriteLine("Move #" & (GS.MoveCount + 1).ToString)
        Debug.WriteLine("Move Hounds.")

        'The code for this is on the CD.
        'Return Hounds1(GS)

        Return Hounds2(GS, 1, True)
    End Function
#End Region
```

Internal Helper Routines for the AI

The actual AI will benefit from some helper routines. The discussion of the evaluation function indicated that the code will not always do a strict comparison between board rankings. So we will need a way to say that one board is better than another, and the fox and the hounds will have different opinions on the matter. That said, often the code will use simple rank, so we should provide a way to keep a sorted list of candidate boards.

We will create a new region called Internal Stuff in the module. Remember that regions cannot overlap. The first thing we will add is code to keep a sorted list. Add the following code:

```
#Region "Internal Stuff"
    Private Sub AddGameStateKeepSorted(ByVal NewGS As GameState, _
            ByVal SortedMoves As Collection)
```

```
                'Compare us to existing moves.
                Dim i As Integer
                Dim GS As GameState
                For i = 1 To SortedMoves.Count
                    GS = CType(SortedMoves(i), GameState)
                    'Smallest first.
                    If NewGS.GameRank < GS.GameRank Then
                        'Add it here and we are done.
                        SortedMoves.Add(NewGS, Nothing, i)
                        Return
                    End If
                Next
                'Add it at the end.
                SortedMoves.Add(NewGS)
        End Sub
#End Region
```

Recall the discussion of the evaluation function and how sometimes we want to use rank and sometimes we want to use how fast something happens. Evaluating the moves by rank alone gives the results we saw in Figures 6.7–6.9. As mentioned in the sidebar, that code is on the CD as AI.V5.vb. The final version of a better move is simpler than the intermediate versions. Let us add code for the fox to the Internal Stuff region:

```
    Private Function BetterFoxMove(ByVal Result As GameState, _
            ByVal BetterThan As GameState) As Boolean
        'Anything is better than nothing.
        If BetterThan Is Nothing Then Return True

        'Smaller rank is better for fox.

        'For good moves, take the earlier one.
        If Result.GameRank < UNREACHABLE _
                And BetterThan.GameRank < UNREACHABLE Then

            'Settle good moves by time.
            If Result.MoveCount < BetterThan.MoveCount Then
                Debug.WriteLine("Fox: Result of " & Result.GameRank.ToString & _
                    " is better than " & BetterThan.GameRank.ToString)
                Return True
            Else
                'If need be, add a debug statement here.
            End If
```

```
        End If

        'One or both of the moves is bad.

        'Is this result worse than what we have?
        If Result.GameRank > BetterThan.GameRank Then Return False

        'Is it better?
        If Result.GameRank < BetterThan.GameRank Then
            Debug.WriteLine("Fox: Result of " & Result.GameRank.ToString & _
                " is better than " & BetterThan.GameRank.ToString)
            Return True
        Else
            'Break ties based on move count.
            If Result.GameRank < UNREACHABLE Then
                'Make good things happen sooner.
                If Result.MoveCount < BetterThan.MoveCount Then
                    Return True
                End If
            Else
                'Make bad things happen later.
                If Result.MoveCount > BetterThan.MoveCount Then
                    Return True
                End If
            End If
        End If
        'Default to false.
        Return False
    End Function
```

The fox uses this code when looking ahead, which is to say when it is trying to
break the line. This code would not work when the line is broken. The same
routine for the hounds is critical for them, as the discussion of the evaluation
function showed. Add the following code to the Internal Stuff region:

```
    Private Function BetterHoundsMove(ByVal Result As GameState, _
            ByVal BetterThan As GameState) As Boolean
        'Anything is better than nothing.
        If BetterThan Is Nothing Then Return True

        'Are they both good moves?
        If BetterThan.GameRank >= UNREACHABLE And _
                Result.GameRank >= UNREACHABLE Then
```

```
        'Faster is better; slam the door first, win later.
        If Result.MoveCount < BetterThan.MoveCount Then
            Debug.WriteLine("Hounds a " & Result.GameRank.ToString & _
                " at move " & Result.MoveCount.ToString & _
                " is better than a " & BetterThan.GameRank.ToString & _
                " at move " & BetterThan.MoveCount.ToString)
            Return True
        Else
            Debug.WriteLine("Hounds a " & Result.GameRank.ToString & _
                " at move " & Result.MoveCount.ToString & _
                " is worse than a " & BetterThan.GameRank.ToString & _
                " at move " & BetterThan.MoveCount.ToString)
            Return False
        End If
    End If

    'Are the moves tied?
    If Result.GameRank = BetterThan.GameRank Then
        'Break ties based on move count.
        If Result.GameRank >= UNREACHABLE Then
            'Make good things happen sooner.
            If Result.MoveCount < BetterThan.MoveCount Then
                Return True
            End If
        Else
            'Make bad things happen later.
            If Result.MoveCount > BetterThan.MoveCount Then
                Return True
            End If
        End If
    End If

    'Larger rank is better for hounds.
    Return Result.GameRank > BetterThan.GameRank
End Function
```

The Fox's Move

The AI module now has the support services the two AIs will call upon. It is time to add the two-part AI for the fox. The AI will go in a separate region. Add the following code to the module:

```vbnet
#Region "With Lookahead"
    Private Function Fox2(ByVal GS As GameState, ByVal depth As Integer, _
                ByVal WantMove As Boolean) As GameState

        'Move to lowest steps square if I have one.

        'I'm not moving if I already won or lost.
        If GS.GameRank = 0 Or GS.GameRank = TRAPPED Then
            Debug.WriteLine("Fox2: Game already over, not moving.")
            Return GS
        End If

        'Get my potential moves.
        Dim ss As Integer
        Dim SortedMoves As New Collection
        'The fox can move to any neighbor...
        For Each ss In Moves.Neighbors(GS.FoxAt)
            '...that is not blocked.
            If Not GS.HasChecker(ss) Then
                'We have a potential move, represented by its game state.
                'Store it in the sorted list.
                AddGameStateKeepSorted(GS.ProposeFoxTo(ss), SortedMoves)
            End If
        Next

        'If I can't move, return the existing game.
        'This should never happen since it means I'm trapped
        'but it protects the rest of the code that follows.
        If SortedMoves.Count = 0 Then
            Debug.WriteLine("########################" & _
                "Fox2: not trapped, but no candidates.")
            Return GS
        End If

        'Look at the lowest steps move as our first candidate.
        Dim Candidate As GameState
        Candidate = CType(SortedMoves(1), GameState)

        'Is freedom reachable?
        If GS.GameRank < UNREACHABLE Then
            'I need to win - for now, follow shortest path.
            'This means fox never looks ahead when hounds
            'have to look ahead.
```

```
            Debug.WriteLine("Fox following shortest path to " & _
                    Candidate.FoxAt.ToString)

        Return Candidate
Else
        'Look-ahead code - only when hemmed in:

        'If they asked for a move and we only have 1,
        'no need to look ahead. If they didn't ask
        'for a move, we look ahead to evaluate the quality
        'of our one move.
        If WantMove And SortedMoves.Count = 1 Then
            Debug.WriteLine("Fox OPTIMIZING: Only one move at depth " & _
                    depth.ToString)
            Return Candidate
        End If

        'I need to break that line (or die trying).

        'At the moment, nothing looks good. (Pun alert).
        Dim BestCurrentMove As GameState = Nothing
        Dim BestFutureResult As GameState = Nothing

        'What does the future hold for each move I can make?
        For Each Candidate In SortedMoves
            'Ask the future.
            Dim FutureGame As GameState = FoxLookAhead(Candidate, depth)
            'Is it the best future?
            If BetterFoxMove(FutureGame, BestFutureResult) Then
                BestCurrentMove = Candidate
                BestFutureResult = FutureGame
            End If
        Next Candidate

        'I should always have a best move.
        If BestCurrentMove IsNot Nothing Then
            'Debug.WriteLine(depth.ToString & _
            '        " Fox2: Fox's best move is to " & _
            '        BestCurrentMove.FoxAt.ToString)

            'Did the caller want the move or the result?
            If WantMove Then
                Return BestCurrentMove
```

```
            Else
                 Return BestFutureResult
            End If
        End If
    End If

    'This is not a good sign to be here; make the message stand out.
    Debug.WriteLine("#################### Fox2: " & _
        "hit default return.")

    'Default is the first move in the list, given that things are bad.
    Return CType(SortedMoves(1), GameState)
    End Function
#End Region
```

The first thing to notice is that the code is heavily commented and liberally sprinkled with debug output, both commented and not. Recursive code should be written with care and treated as broken until proven working. For all of that, the routine is simple at its core once the defensive coding is ignored. Looking at the code from the top down, we see that the goal is to get the fox to a square with a lower number of steps to freedom. Squares with 0 steps are green squares that no hound can get to, which means that making it to a 1 is also an assured victory.

The first chunk of code checks to see if the game is already over. There is no need to move if the outcome has been decided. If the game is in play, then the fox creates a game state for every valid move that it can make and stores those games in a sorted list. What follows is a defensive chunk of coding. The passed-in game state claims not to be a victory for the hounds. Therefore, the fox should have a move. If the passed-in game state has an incorrect rank, the fox will try to make moves when it has none. Now we are ready to evaluate the available moves.

We start with the first game in the sorted list. This candidate will have the lowest rank, which the fox likes. How the fox acts depends on whether it is hemmed in. When not hemmed in, the AI uses the heuristic of taking the shortest path to freedom and does not bother looking ahead. In such cases, the first candidate is the best next move.

Things get interesting when the fox is forced to look ahead. The first part of the look-ahead checks if the fox only has one move and the caller wanted a move instead of a result. The look-ahead is optimized away; when only one move is possible, it is the best move. This situation happens late in the game and can be seen in Figure 6.10. This board is seen after the hounds take move 40 in an AI

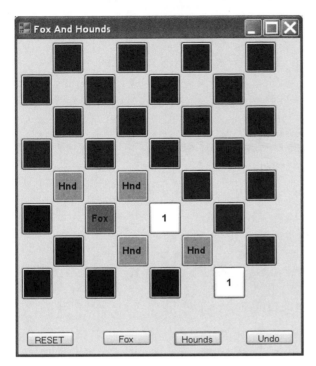

Figure 6.10
The fox is behind a line with only one move.

versus AI game. The fox needs to look ahead to break the wall, but it has only one move, so that is the move it must take. Most of the time, there are multiple moves to ponder.

The fox then creates storage for the best move and for the future result that the best move yields. Then, for each move it has, it asks the future for the outcome of that move. Each result is used to decide whether the move is best. Once all the moves are checked, there should always be a best move, and the code returns either the move or the result of the move, depending on what the caller requested.

If something went wrong and no move or result was returned, the code complains with an easily seen error message in the debugging output. These messages are never seen when the current bug-free code executes, but the code was not always bug free. Professionals never assume that code is bug free.

The Fox's Look-Ahead

All of this sounds perfectly reasonable, except that bit about asking the future. Let us see what asking the future looks like in code. Add the following to the region:

```
'Tell me the future outcome of this move.
Private Function FoxLookAhead(ByVal GS As GameState, _
                ByVal depth As Integer) As GameState

    'Evaluate the candidate they passed in.

    If GS.GameRank < UNREACHABLE Then
        Debug.WriteLine("**************** FoxLookAhead: line is " & _
            "broken, so why am I looking ahead?.")
        Return GS
    End If


    'If you set the depth too low, it won't see how to break the wall.
    'It needs at least 5. It can break the line from the start in
    '5 moves at square 8, in 7 moves at square 10, and in 10 moves at 14.
    If depth > 5 Then
        'Debug.WriteLine("Terminating Fox on depth.")
        Return GS
    End If


    'I'm not moving if I already won or lost.
    If GS.GameRank = 0 Or GS.GameRank = TRAPPED Then Return GS

    'I'm enclosed, or I would not be here. I can't tell one
    'enclosed move from another, so I need to see the hounds' response.
    Dim TheirMove As GameState = Hounds2(GS, depth, True)

    'If I broke them, it's a great move.
    If TheirMove.GameRank < UNREACHABLE Then
        Debug.WriteLine("Fox can break the line at " & GS.FoxAt.ToString & _
            " in " & depth.ToString & " moves.")
        Return TheirMove
    End If
    'I am looking ahead, I give back results from the future.
    Return Fox2(TheirMove, depth + 1, False)
End Function
```

Much like the Fox2() function, the FoxLookAhead() function starts by checking that the code is operating as expected. The job of this routine is to foretell how good the move passed in will turn out to be. Early on it checks for how deep the search is going. The fox needs five levels of search to see the first place it can break the line when the fox starts at the back row. There are later moves that break the line that will exist then, but there is no point in waiting for them. At any point in the game, five is enough to see the next break if one exists.

Then the look-ahead checks to see if the game it was passed in wins for one side or the other. It is not an error for this to happen here, but it certainly terminates the search for good or ill. If the fox is still in the game and looking ahead, it needs to break the line. Fox moves by themselves do not break the line. A fox move can force the hounds to break the line, but it is always a hound's move that opens any hole. So the look-ahead asks the hounds to make their next move so that the fox can see if it has forced a hole.

Before your brain melts, remember that when the fox is looking ahead from behind an unbroken line, the hounds know exactly what to do. They know to keep the line intact if they can and squeeze the fox out of squares it can move to. Failing that, they know that of the moves that break the line, the one that puts the hole the farthest from the fox is best. The hounds do not need to use look-ahead to do this.

If the hounds' best move breaks the line, the fox knows that this is a great move, so it returns as a result the board provided by the hounds that shows them breaking their line. The look-ahead was able to say, "This is the best result of the move you gave me." If the hounds did not break their line, then the look-ahead asks the fox to return the future result of their best countermove by calling Fox2() with a False parameter, indicating that the look-ahead wants a result, not a move. The fox will spread out a tree at most five fox moves deep into the future, looking for boards that break the line.

We mentioned the calming fact that the hounds do not need to look ahead when the fox is looking ahead. This happens to be true for us, and that heuristic goes a long way to manage computational complexity, but it is not really required. The task might not be suitable for beginners, but with careful analysis, the code can be changed to accommodate both sides looking ahead at the same time. Search depth limits still work, but a problem can arise. If the fox is looking ahead past when the line is broken, it will see that in the future the line will be reformed. At one point it will decline to take the early break in the line in favor of a later break because with the later break it cannot see far enough into the future to see the hounds reforming the line after the later break. With the early move, it sees freedom followed by enclosure, and with the later move it sees freedom but can't see the enclosure that surely follows. A sure cure to this is to let the fox see the future all the way to the end. This is computationally expensive, and in this context pointless. We know in advance that the early break is better. We also know in advance that the fox loses unless the hounds make a blunder. We know that the later break is as doomed as the early break, but the AI does not. Without that foreknowledge, the AI would be correct in avoiding the doomed early break in favor of the later break with the uncertain future. We optimize that away with search depth to make a more interesting and effective AI. An AI that correctly refuses to try anything because it knows it will fail is not very much fun. By taking the early breaks, the fox is trying to force the hounds into a mistake instead of letting them take an easy win.

The point here is that both sides could easily need to look ahead in other games. *Fox and Hounds* is too straightforward and too full of rich heuristics to need it, but other games will certainly call for it. *Tic-Tac-Toe* is one such game; looking ahead on both sides is not limited to large and complex games.

The Hounds' Move

Having seen how the fox will look ahead, the hounds should be reasonably easy to understand. Once we do the code for the hounds, we will be able to watch the two AIs play each other. We start with the basic code that asks the hounds to take a move. Add the following code to the region:

```
'Move a hound.
Private Function Hounds2(ByVal GS As GameState, ByVal depth As Integer, _
        ByVal WantMove As Boolean) As GameState

    'I'm not moving if I already won or lost.
    If GS.GameRank = 0 Or GS.GameRank = TRAPPED Then
        Debug.WriteLine("Hounds2: Game already over, not moving.")
        Return GS
    End If

    'Look for move that has max fox steps/highest rank.

    Dim ss As Integer
    'We need to store the moves.
    Dim SortedMoves As New Collection
    Dim i As Integer
    Dim Hounds() As Integer = GS.HoundsAt()
    'Go through all four hounds . . .
    For i = 0 To 3
```

```
            '...checking for possible moves...
        For Each ss In Moves.MovesDown(Hounds(i))
            '...that are not blocked.
            If Not GS.HasChecker(ss) Then
                'Store them away in the sorted list.
                AddGameStateKeepSorted(GS.ProposeHoundTo(i, ss), _
                    SortedMoves)
            End If
        Next
    Next

    'If I can't move, return the existing game.
    If SortedMoves.Count = 0 Then
        Debug.WriteLine(depth.ToString & " Hounds2:  CANNOT MOVE.")
        Return GS
    End If

    'Look at the highest steps move (the last one).
    Dim Candidate As GameState
    Candidate = CType(SortedMoves(SortedMoves.Count), GameState)

    'Did I win or keep the fox in black?  No need to look further.
    If Candidate.GameRank >= UNREACHABLE Then
        'It's a good move for the hounds.

        If GS.GameRank < UNREACHABLE Then
            'Oh, happy day, this move fixes a broken line.
            Debug.WriteLine(depth.ToString & _ "
                "Hounds found a way to win or restore the line.")
        End If
        'Here is where the naive counting of black squares leads to trouble.
        'The bad moves wind up last in the list when there are ties.
        'The better count doesn't have the problem.
        Return Candidate
    End If

    'If we are here, the line is already broken or about to break.

    'Is the line about to break?
    If GS.GameRank >= UNREACHABLE Then
        'Simple rule when we break the line - put the fox farthest
        'from the hole.
```

```
            'MIGHT WANT TO DO SOME TIE BREAKING BY LOOKING AHEAD HERE?
            'Not really, the final result doesn't fail.
            Return Candidate
        End If

        'Line is already broken, we have to look ahead.

        'Initialize the variables.
        Dim BestCurrentMove As GameState = Nothing
        Dim BestFutureResult As GameState = Nothing

        'What does the future hold for each of my moves?
        For Each Candidate In SortedMoves
            'Ask the future.
            Dim FutureGame As GameState = HoundsLookAhead(Candidate, depth)
            'Is that the best?
            If BetterHoundsMove(FutureGame, BestFutureResult) Then
                BestCurrentMove = Candidate
                BestFutureResult = FutureGame
            End If
        Next Candidate

        'I should always have a best move.
        If BestCurrentMove IsNot Nothing Then
            'Debug.WriteLine(depth.ToString & _
            '    " Hounds2: Hounds's best move is a " & _
            '    BestCurrentMove.GameRank.ToString)

            'Did the caller want the move or the result?
            If WantMove Then
                Return BestCurrentMove
            Else
                Return BestFutureResult
            End If
        End If

        'This is not a good sign to be here; make the message stand out.
        Debug.WriteLine("###################### Hounds2: " & _
            "hit default return.")

        'Best we have in a broken situation.
        Return CType(SortedMoves(SortedMoves.Count), GameState)

    End Function
```

The analysis of this code is very similar to the fox's move code. It begins with a quick victory check and then goes on to catalog the available moves. After the same defensive code, it checks to see if it can employ a heuristic on moves without doing any looking ahead. Putting the line back together is always a good thing for the hounds. The sorting, when combined with the final version of the evaluation function, makes it very easy for the hounds to pick among their good moves. It also helps when they have to break the line. Putting a broken line back together involves the exact same kind of look-ahead that the fox uses; just ask the future about the results of the candidate moves.

Hounds' Look-Ahead

The hounds' look-ahead carries the same structure as the fox's look-ahead. There are some differences worth pointing out, however. Add the following code to the region:

```
'Give me the future result of this move.
Private Function HoundsLookAhead(ByVal GS As GameState, _
                ByVal depth As Integer) As GameState
    'Evaluate this hounds move they gave me.

    If GS.GameRank > UNREACHABLE Then
        Debug.WriteLine("*************** HoundsLookAhead: line is good, " & _
            "so why am I looking ahead?.")
        Return GS
    End If

    'It can reform the first broken line in 11, 10, and 5 moves.
    If depth > 6 Then
        'Debug.WriteLine("Hounds: terminating early at " & Depth.ToString)
        Return GS
    End If

    'I'm not moving if I already won or lost.
    If GS.GameRank = 0 Or GS.GameRank = TRAPPED Then Return GS

    'I need to put the line back together, which I can't do
    'until I see the fox move.

    Dim TheirMove As GameState = Fox2(GS, depth, True)
    'If they win, this move stinks and all futures based on it are
```

```
            'equally bad.
            If TheirMove.GameRank <= 1 Then
                'Debug.WriteLine(depth.ToString & _
                '    " HoundsLookahead found a losing move.")
                Return TheirMove
            End If

            'We are still in the game.

            'I am looking ahead, I give back results from the future.
            Return Hounds2(TheirMove, depth + 1, False)
        End Function
```

The code starts with the expected ways to abort the look-ahead. Depth is limited to 6 instead of 5, since earlier versions of the code had trouble with 5. Since a fox victory is a very important condition in determining the quality of a prior move, the extra depth keeps the hounds out of trouble. The look-ahead expects that the move it is evaluating still involves a broken line (or Hounds2() would not have called). Unlike the fox with its shortest path, the hounds get no other guidance on intermediate moves when reforming the line, so it simply asks for the result of the hounds' next move now that the look-ahead knows what the fox will do with the current move. Eventually, one of those future moves will reform the line.

Run the code in the debugger. Click on the Fox and the Hounds buttons in turn, starting with the Fox button. Watch the debugging output carefully in the output window. The hounds' AI should play a perfect game against any opponent. If the human intervenes, the fox can win. One way to do this is to make the hounds move three times in a row with no fox moves between.

Chapter Summary

If the computational complexity can be managed, look-ahead provides real "smarts" to the game AI. It can be easily toned down for less of a challenge to the player. There are certainly some challenges for the programmer, but pruning and heuristics help mitigate them. Possibly the hardest task for the programmer is coming up with an evaluation function that works reliably. The nuances to an evaluation function need careful examination. If nothing else, look-ahead provides a concrete method for fighting Artificial Stupidity.

Chapter Review

Answers are in the appendix.

1. What does an evaluation function do? How is it similar to or different from a goal?

2. What is a heuristic? How do heuristics help?

3. What is pruning and how does it help?

4. What is the most common drawback to look-ahead?

Exercises

1. Have the fox look ahead when the line is broken. Note if this improves the AI for the fox.

2. Change the way black squares are counted and examine the effects on the end of the game.

References

[Dill08] Dill, Kevin. "Embracing Declarative AI with a Goal-Based Approach." *AI Game Programming Wisdom 4*, pp. 229–238. Charles River Media, 2008.

[Knuth74] Knuth, Donald. "Structured Programming with go to Statements." ACM Journal Computing Surveys, Vol 6, No. 4, Dec. 1974. p. 268.

[Wikimedia04] Gdr (original uploader). 2004. Available online at http://en.wikipedia.org/wiki/File:Tic-tac-toe-game-tree.png.

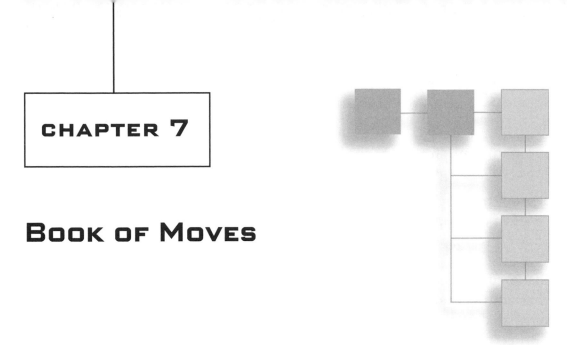

CHAPTER 7

BOOK OF MOVES

In American football, teams do not just play football. They execute predefined plays. Coaches and players do not just make it up as they go, except in "broken" plays, which are usually bad and only occasionally glorious. Indeed, the word "playbook" is common in sports. Likewise, it has a place in game AI. In fact, a book of moves is applicable to game AI beyond the sports games that require one.

At best, a book of moves encapsulates brilliant play and makes it available to the AI when conditions are right. At other times, the book can provide a selection of reasonable, if not brilliant, starting points when the cost of computing them is too high. Opening moves in *Chess* fit this description. A book of moves can guide look-ahead AI to search potentially fruitful paths.

The first thing we will do in this chapter is clear up any confusion between a book of moves, heuristics, and rule-based AI. Once that is done, we will examine the rationale for a book of moves, with the idea of encapsulating killer moves leading the charge. A book can provide more than killer moves; as part of a hybrid AI, we will see how a book can make it possible to have a reasonable AI at all in a complex game like *Twixt*. We will also show how a book of moves can empower our already effective *Minesweeper* AI with low-risk opening moves. After summarizing the advantages and disadvantages of the method, we have two projects: a simple book of opening moves for *Fox and Hounds* and a more complex one for *Minesweeper*.

This Seems Familiar

You may be asking, "Aren't the moves the same thing as heuristics?" You might also be wondering, "Isn't this the same thing as a rule-based AI?" Before we dive into the details, we should shed some light on how to tell a book of moves from other AI concepts. We will compare them to heuristics first.

For our purposes, a book of moves strongly emphasizes what the AI should *do*. Most of the heuristics we have seen so far have been about how the AI should *think*. If we think back to the *Fox and Hounds* AI from Chapter 6, "Look-Ahead: The First Step of Planning," we recall that the heuristics focused on the evaluation function. The way the AI distinguished between possible moves was through the evaluation function and not by anything particular to one move compared to another. If a person walked into a restaurant and told the waiter, "Bring me a taste of everything, and after I taste everything, I will let you know what I like best," they would be using an evaluation function to decide the best move. The evaluation might be guided by heuristics such as, "Most red sauces do not agree with me." This time-consuming and costly method of dining would be avoided if the person exploited the menu. The menu in this case is a book of moves.

The AI in *Fox and Hounds* would benefit from a book of moves. The first entry would be the opening sequence. Rather than looking ahead for its initial moves, the fox could simply head to square number 8, the left-most square of the third row from the top. That is the square that can force the earliest possible break in the line of hounds, and the hounds cannot do anything fatal to the fox if the fox blindly heads there. Similarly, it is difficult, if not impossible, for the fox to find itself unable to exploit any fatal mistakes that the hounds might make if the fox heads blindly for square number 8.

The distinction we are making here is not absolute. One heuristic used by the fox is close to a gray area between how the AI should think and what the AI should do. When there is an opening, the heuristic for the fox is to take the square with the lowest number. It could be argued that this is still about how the AI should think, as in, "Find the lowest number," which is different from how it should act, which might be "Go up and to the left," but the distinction hardly matters. Moves have an emphasis on what the AI should do, and heuristics can pertain to just about anything.

The difference between a book of moves and a rule-based system is also straightforward, although at first glance it may be difficult to distinguish between the two. Although a book of moves may lend itself to a rule-based implementation, the focus of this chapter is on hybrid AI in which the book of moves supplements a more general AI system, which need not be rule based. Our hybrid AI can "order from the menu" using the book of moves or it can "send requests to the kitchen" using the general AI. It is easy to think of the book as a set of narrowly focused, highly effective responses to specific circumstances, but they need not be that restrictive; the book can also contain typical moves that the player will expect to see. We will look at some broader, complex applications before looking in depth at how a book of moves might apply to more accessible AI. That said, rule-based systems and a book of moves are conceptually quite close, and fine distinctions between them may not be terribly enlightening.

Killer Moves

Composers today might consider Mozart unfair competition from beyond the grave, but the truth is that anyone who can read music has full access to Mozart's genius. Similarly, with a book of moves, game AI need not compute genius moves; it just has to be able to use them appropriately. If programmers can implement the AI equivalent to sheet music, they can then exploit any form of brilliant play they can codify. Moves tend to be specialized; Mozart's music might not be appropriate to the instruments of a rock band. Good moves need not always be hard to find.

Imagine an in-game cut scene for the aftermath of a great battle. On one side, we see the local religious authority give the words for the living and the dead. On the other side, we see a similar figure giving similar but different appropriate words. There is no reason for the AI programmer to write either set of words; found in the back of countless hymnals and religious books are brilliant but relatively unknown writings, perfectly suitable for funerals. The selection of good words throughout the ages is rather quite rich, translation issues aside. The really old ones tend not to be familiar, making them novel when reused. As an added bonus, the copyrights on the oldest works have expired.

A similar case can be made for battle speeches, though more care must be taken:

"And gentlemen in England, now abed,
Shall think themselves accursed they were not here,
And hold their manhoods cheap whiles any speaks
That fought with us upon Saint Crispin's day."

The words are stirring enough, and the year it was written—1599—predates modern copyright law by a good 110 years, but the utter familiarity of the St. Crispin's Day speech from Shakespeare's *Henry V* makes it a poor choice for most computer games. The good news is that the game AI need not compute brilliance; it only needs to be able to import it and use it for its own.

All that being said, computer games lack the benefits of 3,000 years of written history and scholarship. Cutting-edge games sport novel forms of gameplay, employing rules of play that are less than two years old and known only within the development studio working on them. These rules might not stabilize until the gold master disk is burned. Where does the AI programmer get expertise when no experts exist? One potentially risky place is from early reviews of the core gameplay.

Games are supposed to be fun. Because games are financially quite risky to produce—indeed, few games break even—many studios review the core gameplay early and often to validate that the fun is there and stays there. These reviews and play-test sessions are where the earliest expertise with the game will be forged. This expertise may be rendered useless as the game evolves, but some of it may survive. Play-test sessions can be mined for good moves if care is taken from the outset. An observant set of players willing to write things down might be all that is needed. If the games are all logged and the scores are reported, promising candidates can be found and replayed for in-depth analysis. As the game develops, special AI can be used to probe and experiment. This AI need not be limited by the constraints of the regular AI; it can take longer to think or use more memory or even use a farm of machines to help. Recall from Chapter 6 that naïve AI methods applied to simple games can generate run times that compare poorly to the heat decay death of the universe; no farm of AI machines is large enough to explore a space that large. For any particular new game and the studio developing it, there will be a balance point between investment and return.

A final consolation in the search for brilliance is that the AI does not have to be brilliant all of the time. As long as it is rarely stupid, the AI can thrive with occasional flashes of brilliance punctuating otherwise solid play. As we shall see, sometimes the book of moves itself enables the solid play.

Having great moves is only part of the task. The code that uses the book has to ensure that any move selected is good for the current situation. In sports, selection failures are characterized as "Good team, bad coach." Recall Horatio, our opera singer who broke into song at a funeral? What if he was *supposed* to sing at the funeral? The pattern-matching problem goes from the general problem of "Do I sing now?" to the more subtle and finer-grained problem of "*What* do I sing now?" If Horatio has a hybrid AI, the general AI has correctly figured out that it is time to sing, and it is handing the situation off to a specialized book of moves AI for song selection. Since he is a tenor and not a baritone, he is not likely to belt out the difficult, well-known line, "Figaro! Figaro! Figaro!" But just the same, as an opera singer, his book of moves is deeply loaded with equally stunning but equally inappropriate songs. The right selection might not be Rossini or even Mozart, despite the awesome quality of their songs, but something well known from a church hymnal. The pattern-matching problems we examined in Chapter 4, "Rule-Based Systems," are still with us.

Hybrid AI

Here, the term *hybrid AI* means a combination of more than one kind of AI so that the different forms mitigate the weak areas of the others. Coaches might call plays, but players execute them. The players react in real time, adjust and make changes, and do their best to exploit the unexpected. A book of moves by itself is not commonly used as a complete AI, although the line blurs in rule-based systems composed of both general rules and highly specific ones. One of the particular strengths of a book is the ability to recognize the value or peril of a situation that a more general system overlooks. We will see this in various applications.

Chess

Chess is well suited to a hybrid approach. The Deep Blue *Chess* computer combined powerful search capabilities with an opening book of 4,000 positions, an extended book drawn from 700,000 grandmaster games, and a database of endgames [Campbell02]. In 1997, this software, running on massively parallel hardware that included custom *Chess* chips, was the first *Chess* program to beat a reigning world champion *Chess* player. The evaluation function of the search was astoundingly rich, but the various books helped detect situations the search would rank improperly or spend too much time evaluating.

While interesting as a thought problem, *Chess* is hardly suited for programmers just starting to write AI. Games with simpler rules might appear more approachable, but it depends on the game. *Go* is harder for machines than *Chess*, but steady improvements suggest that in 20 years, machines may be able to achieve parity with professional players. The game *Arimaa* uses *Chess* pieces on a *Chess* board. It was specifically developed to be easier than *Chess* for humans and far harder for computers; opening books and endgame databases have little or no utility in a game without fixed starting positions, where all of the pieces can still be on the board at the end of the game. *Twixt* is another simple game that is hard for computers, but it does lend itself to a book of moves, as we shall see.

Twixt

Twixt was widely published as a 3M bookshelf game, was later picked up by Avalon-Hill, and is now out of print in the U.S. The goal of the game is to form a chain of links between opposite edges of the board; one player attempts to link the top and bottom edges, while the other player tries to link the left and right edges. Links may not cross, so if one side achieves its goal, the other side is prevented from doing so. The simple rules make for complex gameplay, and draws are very rare. The game is easy to learn, hard to master, and brutally unforgiving of mistakes. *Twixt* is a very tactical game. One of the few strategies is to force the other side to waste one or more moves by cutting off pegs and links from the border or isolating some of the opponent's pegs and links, preventing your opponent from connecting to other pegs and links. This strategy is hinted at in Figure 7.1, where it appears that if black makes more horizontal links in the middle of the board, black will block white from building a vertical chain to the bottom of the board. We will look at the board and see if the complexity of the game can be tamed.

The Game Board

Twixt is usually played on a square pegboard grid of 24 holes on a side. The opposite pairs of border rows can be played by only one color, and the corners are not playable at all. For the board pictured in Figure 7.1, white needs to connect the top and bottom, and black needs to connect the left and right. This leaves a 22×22 grid of 484 holes, which both sides can fill with their pegs. Pegs of the same color can be linked if the two pegs are arranged in a "knight's move" from *Chess*. This is known as a "Twixt" move in *Twixt*. Such moves place the pegs on opposite corners of a vertical or horizontal 2×1 rectangle. The moves in *Twixt* are often denoted by the size of the rectangle they make, larger number first, so a Twixt move is denoted as a (2–1) move. Just as a knight in *Chess* has access to every square on a *Chess* board, pegs that are not a Twixt move apart can be connected by a sequence of Twixt moves if there are no obstructions. Those

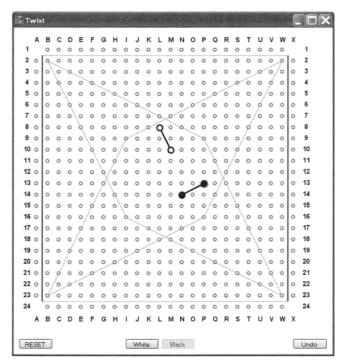

Figure 7.1
A full size *Twixt* board with two Twixt moves.

sequences and the art of obstructing them provide the core of the gameplay. Common sequences are known as setups, and setups make the claim, "These pegs do not connect now, but you will have a very hard time stopping me from connecting them later."

In order to make it easier on the players, the rows and columns are often given numbers and letters to assign each hole a unique code. In Figure 7.1, there are white pegs at L8 and M10 and black pegs at N14 and P13. Another welcome addition to the original board is the diagonal lines to the corners of the open playing field, which make it easier to visualize how a race to a corner will turn out. The lines are on the same 2:1 bias that characterizes the basic Twixt move. A peg at a corner cannot be prevented from connecting to its border row. Winning the corner with a chain of links forces the opponent to block the other end of the chain or lose. Blocking an opponent's chain from reaching its border is often done by forcing that chain against your border. This must be accomplished at the corner or before; whoever wins the corner race blocks the other. The diagonal lines make the outcome of such races easier to see. The diagonal lines also create an octagon, delineating the critical center area of the board.

There are boards of other sizes in use. An 18×18-hole board is less intimidating and easier for beginners as well as game AI. A quarter-size board, with 12 holes per side, is good for demonstration purposes—the *Twixt* resources available on the Web often make use of these smaller boards—but is too small to allow interesting play to develop.

Complexity

We will start with brute-force look-ahead and then exploit the tools we have to see if we can get the complexity of the game down to something that computers can handle in reasonable amounts of time. As you might expect, the initial computations show an impossibly complex game. The goal will be to get the complexity down to something playable. To compute complexity, we will make some simplifying approximations, all based on the idea of "which is at least as big as." If we multiply or add together simple numbers that are smaller than the actual numbers, we will get a result that is smaller than the actual complexity. Simple smaller numbers make for simpler computations. If our result using the simple small numbers is too large to be practical, then we know that the larger, actual result is likewise too large to be practical. Only when the approximation suggests that an approach might be practical will we need to use actual numbers to prove it. Approximations like these are often called "back-of-the-envelope" because they do not need a whole sheet of paper to compute them.

The naïve evaluation of *Twixt*'s computational complexity yields enormous numbers. If you could somehow fill every hole in the board, there would be 484! combinations, which is so large it is not worth computing. It is time for our first heuristic.

In a very long *Twixt* game, each side will make 25 moves for a total of 50 moves. Are the numbers more tractable if the search depth is limited to 25 rounds of move, counter-move? There are 484 starting moves. After taking 49 moves, we have 434 possible 50th moves. The actual complexity can be computed by multiplying the 50 different numbers from 484 to 434 together. If we approximate the 50 numbers between 484 and 434 as all being at least as large as 100, we will vastly underestimate the result, but we also get a much easier math problem.

$484 * 483 * 482 \ldots * 436 * 435 * 434 =$ a very hard to compute number

$100 * 100 * 100 \ldots * 100 * 100 * 100 = 100^{50} = 10^{100}$ (smaller, easier to compute)

Our approximation yields a google (a one with 100 zeroes after it). Recall from Chapter 6 that numbers this large will lead to execution times that compare unfavorably with the estimated time until the heat decay death of the universe.

> Math note: $100 = 10 * 10 = 10^2$. So with two 10s multiplied together in every 100, we get $100^{50} = (10^2)^{50} = 10^{100}$

Maybe some more heuristics will help. Any serious *Twixt* play exploits three-move combinations called setups. Not only are the setups good moves, players certainly expect the AI to use them. So if the AI wants to see the opponent's response to its next three moves, the AI needs to look ahead six moves total instead of 50. If we again approximate the numbers between 484 and 479 as all being larger than 100 and multiply everything, we get a trillion (a one followed by 12 zeroes). The actual number is over 12,000 trillion. This number is still hopeless, but far better than a google.

> $484 * 483 * 482 * 481 * 480 * 479 = 12,461,242,792,078,080$
>
> $100 * 100 * 100 * 100 * 100 * 100 = 100^6 = 10^{12}$ (smaller, easier to compute)

Maybe we can prune. Because we are assuming that the play is based on setups, let us look at the complexity of the setups. The collection of basic setups goes in our book of moves. Once the first peg is placed, assume the best future moves are based on setups starting with that peg. Let us examine the four setups given in the original rules for *Twixt*. These setups, diagrammed in Figure 7.2, are known as "Beam" (4–0), "Tilt" (3–3), "Coign" (3–1), and "Mesh" (2–0). (There are other setups, including four-move and five-move setups, but these are the basic ones from the original rules.) The white pegs show the first and second moves, and the black pegs show the two possible third moves. Either third move links to both the first and second moves (known as double linking). The setups shown are for white, which wants to connect the top and bottom rows of the board.

After the first peg is placed, there are two possible follow-up moves that start a Beam (one toward the top of the board and one toward the bottom), four follow-up moves each to start a Tilt or Coign, and two for a Mesh. That is a total of 12 likely follow-up moves for the side that placed the first peg, which is far fewer than 482. If the opposition attacks the setup ineffectually, there will be exactly one move available to complete the setup. If the opposition does not attack the setup at all, there is no need to waste a move by completing the setup using either of the two available third moves, and the AI should look for the next setup that connects to this one.

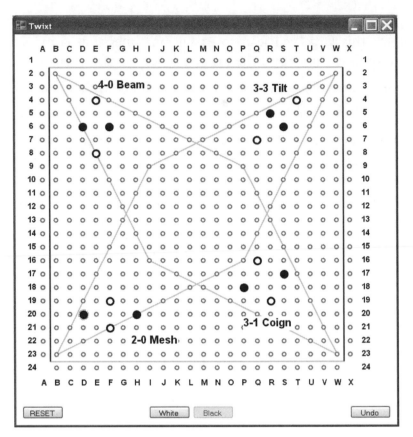

Figure 7.2
A full-size *Twixt* board with the four basic setups.

What should the opponent AI do in the face of these possible setups? When possible, the most common counter is to "hammer" the first peg placed by putting an opposing peg directly adjacent to the first peg in the setup and linking to the newly placed peg. This requires that the opponent have an existing peg from a prior move that is close enough to make the link to the new peg. While the first side is setting up fancy moves, the opposing side is foiling them or cutting them off with a carefully placed Twixt move. There are at most eight holes in which to attempt to hammer the first peg, and not all of them are likely to be a Twixt move from an existing peg from a prior move. If a hammer attack is possible at all, there will usually be only a few holes that make it work. Looking for a hammer attack narrows our search for a counter-move from hundreds to a few. The hammer attack goes into the book of moves alongside the four setups.

There are 484 opening moves, and we would like to trim that number down to a more manageable number. In classic *Twixt*, the opening move is best placed roughly in or near the octagon created by the diagonal lines when they reach the center of the board. Opening moves here are so powerful that modern *Twixt* has the "pie" rule: "You cut the pie it into two pieces, and I pick which one I want." If the opening move is particularly strong, on the second move (and only the second move) the side that did not go first can take the opening move as played as if it were its opening move and force the other side to make the second move against it by switching colors. "I'll play your color, so that makes it your move, with you switching to my original color." Even without the pie rule, three quarters of the opening board can be eliminated due to symmetry when looking for an opening move. If we restrict our opening moves to the 80 holes in the center octagon, symmetry reduces that number to 20, which again is far fewer than 484. We could probably get by with 10 opening moves.

With a book of moves, our AI will not search at all for an opening move. It will have opening moves that it likes in the book of moves, along with the best counter-move in case the pie rule is invoked. Some of these strong opening moves can be used as a second move against a weak opening move as well. For other moves, our search strategies will be guided by the book of moves. We avoid a general search of over 400 open holes and concentrate on the few holes that we think will matter. So how much does this improve the complexity? We might see something like the following:

One opening move (selected at random from the book)

One counter-move (based on the opening move)

Twelve holes that are a setup to the opening move

Eight holes to hammer the previous move or 12 holes to do our own setup

One or two holes to complete the setup based on the opening move, or 12 holes to do another setup

What happens when we multiply numbers like these? Our low numbers are 1 and 2; our high numbers are 8 and 12. Let us use 10 to approximate all of them and compute how expensive six moves of look-ahead would be:

$$10 * 10 * 10 * 10 * 10 * 10 = 10^6 = 1,000,000$$

One million is a very tractable number on current hardware. Playing by the book using look-ahead should make it possible to create a *Twixt* AI that is fast enough to play against, even if it does not ensure that such an AI is powerful against human players who employ four-move and five-move setups. The book of moves has taken us from "clearly impossible" to "maybe." The code for the *Twixt* game shown in the figures is on the CD included with this book. Adding AI to the game is left as an exercise for the motivated reader. While the book of moves for *Twixt* appears straightforward, the rest of a hybrid AI that exploits that book is a daunting challenge.

Minesweeper

The AI for *Minesweeper* given in Chapter 4 proved to be pretty awesome once the player got it started. So how could it benefit from a book of moves when the general rules seemed to get nearly all of the deterministic moves? One question that comes to mind is, "What is the best first move at *Minesweeper*?" That question might initially get the response of "The first move is safe, so why does it matter?" But the best first move is one that either exposes the most squares or that gives the best follow-up moves when the player is forced to start taking chances. So if the first move did not expose more than one square, a good second move needs to be a move that can quickly generate the highest number of deterministic moves. We will look at the numbers and apply them to the various first moves to see if we can come up with something useful.

The Basic Numbers

In *Minesweeper*, there are 99 mines in 480 squares. After the first move, that reduces to 479 squares. This gives a density of 0.207 mines per square on average, which is the same as having a 79.3 percent probability of being clear. These numbers are averages; the mines are not evenly spread out. We can use these numbers to give an expected value of how many mines surround a square before we click it. We will add or multiply these numbers as needed to evaluate different moves that could go into our book of moves. We will not compute the exact values of all the numbers needed to exactly evaluate the different first moves in order to keep the statistics from interfering with the analysis.

A Middle First Move

For our purposes, a middle move has two or more squares between it and any edge. As a first move, it either exposes eight more squares or presents the user with a number between one and eight. The player has a 0.793^8 chance of getting lucky on his or her first move and selecting a square with zero surrounding mines. That works out to getting eight squares 15.7 percent of the time. The average yield of the first move in isolation is thus 1.26 squares. The other 84.3 percent of the time,

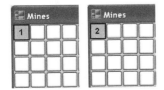

Figure 7.3
Starting in the corner does not produce a good second move.

the player is stuck making numerous risky moves to clear out an area big enough to yield deterministic moves. The problem with a middle first move is that most of the time, it gives a long series of poor follow-up moves.

A Corner First Move

There is a 0.793^3 chance that a corner has no mines in the three surrounding squares. This computes to a 50 percent chance to get three squares, for an average yield of 1.50 squares, so it is better than the middle as a first move by itself. But as shown in Figure 7.3, the other half of the time it leaves the player with at least one mine to place in three squares for a typical chance of failure on the second move of 33.3 percent or worse. The corner is a good place for generating deterministic moves, but playing the corner as a first move leads to a risky second move when better alternatives are available.

An Edge First Move

There is a 0.793^5 chance that a general edge square has no mines around it in the five surrounding squares. This is a 31.4 percent chance to get five squares, for an average yield of 1.57 squares, making it the best first move so far. The other 68 percent of the time, the player has one or more mines nearby, typically one or two. A second move away from the edge, if successful, can yield deterministic moves. How risky is that second move? It has a risk of 20 percent times the number revealed by the first square. Twenty percent is slightly lower than the 20.7 percent risk of a random move, so if a 1 was revealed, the edge gives safer moves than any random guess. If a 2 or higher was revealed, the surrounding squares are more risky than a random guess. The edge is superior to a corner, with higher initial yield on the first move and lower risk on the second move.

One Square Away from an Edge

With eight surrounding squares, this kind of first move has the same initial yield of 1.26 squares that a move to the middle has if the player gets lucky. As shown in

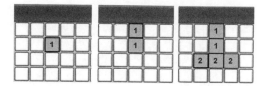

Figure 7.4
Crossing the T produces three moves but stops there.

Figure 7.4, this move often creates a far better second move the 84.3 percent of the time there is a nearby mine. On average, there are 1.66 mines in the surrounding squares, making the most common revealed number a 1 or 2. A revealed 1 makes the risk on the second move 12.5 percent, almost half the risk of a random move. A revealed 2 means a risk of 25 percent. Although this is worse than the 20.7 percent risk of a random move, this is mitigated when you consider the gain of a well-placed second move. If the revealed number is less than 3, then a second move should be the neighboring square that is on the edge. There is a chance the second move will reveal a 0 and four free moves, a happy event that we will ignore for now. The second move cannot reveal a number higher than the number revealed by the first move. If the first move revealed a 1, the second move is a mine, a 0 or a 1. If these two squares leading out of an edge have the same revealed number, then there are three safe moves that "cross the T" of the first two moves. The number revealed by the second move is constrained by the number revealed by the first move, so if the second move was safe enough to take and it did not fail, it has a very high chance of giving the three free moves. The idea here is that we have created a low-risk second move with a possible three- or four-square payoff.

One Square Diagonally Away from a Corner

All the initial numbers for this case compute the same as in the previous case, but the location of the second move should be the corner. As shown in Figure 7.5, a

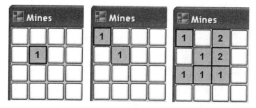

Figure 7.5
The corner produces five moves and more after that.

revealed 1 means that a second move should certainly be taken. A revealed 2 is less rosy. The second move itself might reveal a 0, yielding two free squares. This configuration of a square of four cleared tiles tends to yield deterministic moves. If the second move reveals the same number as the first move, the second move generates five free moves. In either case, the resulting shape of the perimeter gives a superior board to play from. This is shown on the third board of Figure 7.5, where there is a pair of cross the T moves available for two more squares. The equally lowest-risk second move available here yields more follow-up moves and far better playing position.

Can We Apply This?

An AI that computes these numbers on the fly to evaluate openings to *Minesweeper* would be far more involved than the AI we used in Chapter 4. It would involve both statistics as well as some look-ahead, which we covered in Chapter 6. If the exact statistics were beyond the skills of the AI programmer, Monte Carlo methods mentioned in Chapter 5, "Random and Probabilistic Systems," could be used to home in on the right moves. None of these methods would run faster or give a better result than simply adding a highly specialized set of rules to the AI that already has the right moves coded in.

Note that we did not do the full-up, no-holds-barred statistical analysis to prove that the first moves rank in the order presented. Besides lowering the complexity of the analysis we did, this effort was intentionally skipped to let us drive the following point home: The AI does not always have to have the exact optimum move if it has moves that are good enough. Mozart might be the best great composer whose music is in the public domain, but he is not the only great composer whose music is free.

When adding a book of moves to an AI, the programmer must pay as much attention to the integration as to the parts. A good integration is seamless, making it hard to detect when the AI is playing from the book or playing from a more general method. A thin book that has a small number of stellar moves added to modestly good general AI will be obvious to the player and not always entertaining. If the player stumbles from the conditions where the AI plays using the modestly difficult general AI into the conditions where the AI plays from the expert-level book of moves, the player may feel blindsided or be convinced that the AI cheated once it saw the player getting ahead. Going the other way may not be any better, leaving the player wondering why a challenging AI decided to roll over and play dead. Thankfully, the programmer does have the option to turn moves on and off to tune the difficulty.

Advantages

A book of opening moves and endgames provides a tremendous speed increase to the AI. It also can embody brilliant play and effectively leverage the play of experts. It can recognize situations that more general methods improperly evaluate. The book of moves can provide expected moves that the regular AI might miss, such as flanking or ambushing. Moves in the book can be selectively engaged to adjust the difficulty level of play. And finally, a book of moves can guide the search of look-ahead.

Disadvantages

A book of moves is often an aid to another AI, but less often the complete AI. This can mean having two different AIs to write and maintain. The book of moves makes sense only when it is appreciably better than the regular AI it advises in some way, such as quality of play or speed. A really good regular AI might not need the book. Even an AI that needs help from the book will suffer if the expertise level of the moves in the book is not up to the task. Finding that expertise can be harder than programming it into the AI. Finally, killer moves are of no use if they are improperly employed; great plays need great coaches selecting them.

Having two AI systems means more than the effort of writing both; it means that the integration needs to be tuned as well. A "flashes of brilliance" AI can be as frustrating to the player as it is entertaining.

Projects

There are two projects for this chapter. For our first project, we will add an opening book for the fox in *Fox and Hounds*. Our book will have only one move, so we can hard-code the AI for it instead of using a rule-based system. Our second project is more extensive; adding a book of opening moves to *Minesweeper*. The *Minesweeper* book is nearly as easy, requiring only a modest amount of code.

Fox and Hounds

Open your *Fox and Hounds* project from Chapter 6 or from the CD-ROM. Edit the file AI.vb and add the following region to the module between the last #End Region and the End Module lines.

```
#Region "Book of Moves"
    Private Function ConsultFoxBook(ByVal GS As GameState) As GameState
        'We only have one move in our book, only at the beginning.
        'We get there on move 8, since the moves start at 0.
        If GS.MoveCount > 8 Then
            Return Nothing
        End If

        Dim bestMove As Byte = 64 'Higher than any square on the board.
        Dim ss As Byte
        'The fox will move up and left to get to square 8.
        For Each ss In Moves.Neighbors(GS.FoxAt)
            'Don't consider a blocked square.
            If Not GS.HasChecker(ss) Then
                'The smaller the ss the better.
                If ss < bestMove Then bestMove = ss
            End If

        Next
        Return GS.ProposeFoxTo(bestMove)
    End Function
#End Region
```

The code is very simple and takes advantage of the way the squares are numbered. Square 8 is the first square of the third row since we start at 0 at the top left. The smallest numbered square is always above and if possible to the left. It takes the fox to square 8, but not if we forget to call the new code. Add the following lines near the top of the Fox2() function in the same file just below the initial check for a game either side has won and before where the fox gets its potential moves.

```
            'Check the book of moves.
            Dim Candidate As GameState = ConsultFoxBook(GS)
            'If the book gave a move, use it.
            If Candidate IsNot Nothing Then Return Candidate
```

You will need to comment out the declaration for the variable Candidate further down in the routine. Do this by adding a single quote character in front of the statement. The declaration comes right after a comment. After you comment out the declarations, the two lines will look like the following.

```
'Look at the lowest steps move as our first candidate.
'Dim Candidate As GameState
```

Now you can run the game and test the new code using the Fox button. See how much faster the book move is than the look-ahead? Note that the fox stops trying to go up when it gets to square number 8 or after eight moves have elapsed.

Minesweeper

The opening moves for *Minesweeper* that we have discussed can be reduced to, "Click a square in a particular untouched area. If you get a 1, click a particular neighbor of that square, hoping to get a 1 or a 0." So our book expects to have to try a first move and then a second move. Our book also expects to operate only in places where no squares have been clicked. This is different from the rule-based AI from Chapter 4 that operates only on revealed squares. This gives us two reasons not to use the existing rule-based framework for our new code. The first reason is that the existing framework doesn't work with blank squares. The second reason is that we do not want the general AI to make risky moves unless the player directly tells it to. Since the book of moves is small and reasonably simple, we will just use some hard-coded AI. Just because a book of moves often fits very well into a rule-based approach does not mean that it always has to be implemented that way.

Open your *Minesweeper* project from Chapter 4. The code on the CD has an AI Auto button, and we will see it in Figure 7.6. The AI Auto button is very handy. After every book move, you should click the AI Auto button to make sure that you take any risk-free moves before going back to the book. The bulk of our code is in three routines. We need a first move routine, a second move routine, and something to execute them. We will put the move routines in the file AI.vb. Open that file and add the following code just above the End Module statement:

```
#Region "Book of Moves Code"

Public Function BookFirstMove(ByVal FirstSq As Square, _
    ByVal SecondSq As Square, ByVal theField As PlayingField) As Integer

    'Did somebody already click first move?
    If FirstSq.IsRevealed Then Return 0
```

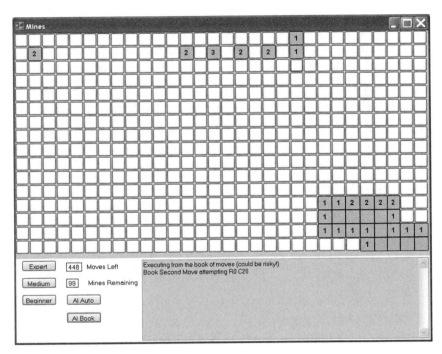

Figure 7.6
The board after a number of book moves.

```
            'First move must be unmarked.
            If FirstSq.Text <> "" Then Return 0
            'The follow-up move must be unmarked.
            If SecondSq.Text <> "" Then Return 0
            'First square needs eight unclicked neighbors.
            Dim Sq As Square
            For Each Sq In theField.NearNeighbors(FirstSq.R, FirstSq.C)
                If Sq.IsRevealed() Then Return 0
            Next
            'First move looks good, try it.
            theField.MoreThoughts("Book First Move attempting R" & _
                    FirstSq.R.ToString & " C" & FirstSq.C.ToString)
            Call FirstSq.LeftClick()
            'We took one move.
            Return 1
        End Function
    #End Region
```

The whole point of this routine is to take a first move and second move pair and check that this is a good place to take both moves. If the first move has been taken, the square would be revealed already, and we obviously cannot take the first move again. We don't want to take the first move if somehow somebody has already clicked the second move or marked the second move as being a mine. The code checks for the second square's text, instead of checking to see if it is revealed. If it is revealed with no text, that means it is a zero square, and we should let the regular AI take the first move since it is free. If the second move has text, that text is either a number or a flag marker, both of which we want to avoid. For the same reason, we want all the surrounding squares not to have been clicked. We are hoping the first move reveals a 1, and for the sake of the second move we want the maximum number of squares to be available to hold that one mine, minimizing the chances that the second move is the one holding it. If the square meets all our needs, we click it (and hope).

The first move is a risky move that usually does not tell us a whole lot. The second move is likewise risky, but hopefully it tells us something useful. Add the following code to the same region:

```
Public Function BookSecondMove(ByVal FirstSq As Square, _
    ByVal SecondSq As Square, ByVal theField As PlayingField) As Integer
    'Take the second move if the first move looks good.

    'First move has to have revealed a minimally risky number.
    If FirstSq.Text <> "1" Then Return 0
    'First square needs eight unclicked neighbors.
    Dim Sq As Square
    For Each Sq In theField.NearNeighbors(FirstSq.R, FirstSq.C)
        If Sq.IsRevealed() Then Return 0
    Next
    'First move was perfect, attempt the second move.
    theField.MoreThoughts("Book Second Move attempting R" & _
            SecondSq.R.ToString & " C" & SecondSq.C.ToString)
    Call SecondSq.LeftClick()
    'We took one move.
    Return 1
End Function
```

The second move code has the same idea: Make numerous checks and, if they pass, take the second move. The first move has to have shown a 1. The surrounding squares have not been revealed, so the one mine has the lowest probability of being on the second move's square. If that is the case, the second move is worth taking. Now we need to code to execute these first and second moves.

Switch to the file PlayingField.vb. There is a code tab and a design tab; we will do the code first. Find the AI Related region and add the following code to it:

```
Public Sub ExecuteBook()
    'Store the pairs of moves in collections.
    Dim FirstSquares As New Collection
    Dim SecondSquares As New Collection

    'Add in pairs of moves to the collections in order.
    'Add in the corners first.
    'Add the upper-left corner.
    FirstSquares.Add(Field(1, 1))
    SecondSquares.Add(Field(0, 0))

    'Add the lower-right corner.
    FirstSquares.Add(Field(NumRows - 2, NumCols - 2))
    SecondSquares.Add(Field(NumRows - 1, NumCols - 1))

    'You can figure out from here how to add the other two corners.

    'Then add some edge moves, from center outward.
    Dim Col As Integer
    For Col = 1 To NumCols \ 4
        'Add moves on upper edge going right.
        FirstSquares.Add(Field(1, NumCols \ 2 + Col))
        SecondSquares.Add(Field(0, NumCols \ 2 + Col))
        'Add moves on upper edge going left.
        FirstSquares.Add(Field(1, NumCols \ 2 - Col))
        SecondSquares.Add(Field(0, NumCols \ 2 - Col))

        'You can figure out how to add the lower edge.

    Next
    'If we wanted the left and right edge, we'd add them here.

    'Now walk down the list in two passes.
    Dim pass As Integer
    For pass = 1 To 2
        Dim FirstMove As Square
        Dim SecondMove As Square
        Dim i As Integer
        For i = 1 To FirstSquares.Count
```

```
'Get the first and second moves out of the collections.
FirstMove = FirstSquares(i)
SecondMove = SecondSquares(i)
If pass = 1 Then
    'Check for follow-up moves first; they pay off better.
    If BookSecondMove(FirstMove, SecondMove, Me) > 0 Then Return
Else
    'Look for first moves.
    If BookFirstMove(FirstMove, SecondMove, Me) > 0 Then Return
End If
        Next
    Next
End Sub
```

That chunk of code can be divided into two parts. The first part collects the pairs of first-move and second-move squares and stores them in the order we want them checked. It does the corners first and then the edge moves. The edge moves concentrate on the middle of the edge, hoping for a good breakout pattern in three directions. We include only two of the four corners, and we do only the top edge. If we try all four corners, there is a non-trivial chance that our code will hit a mine near a corner before it tries an edge move. For the sake of instruction, we want a good chance at seeing the code take multiple book moves before hitting a mine. All these moves are low risk, but none of them are risk free.

The second part of this code loops through the pairs of moves in order, stopping as soon as one of them executes. Notice that it looks for second moves in the first pass before it looks for first moves in the second pass. This is not a coding error. The second move is the one most likely to net us deterministic safe moves. We take the risk of the first move only so that we can execute the second move and make some headway. So we always check for moves we *want* to take before we resort to moves we *have* to take. In any case, since the code takes only a single move before it chickens out, it has to check for second moves first; otherwise, it will risk every possible first move in the collection before doing a follow-up second move. On any run of the code, the code does not know what first moves have been taken. Even if the AI kept track of first moves that it took, the player could have taken some first moves that the AI would not know about, so we always check to make sure.

All we need now is some user-interface code to enable the user to try these risky moves. Switch to the design view of PlayingField.vb and add a button. Change the name of the button to BookButton and the text to AI Book. Set the enabled property to false. (Figure 7.6 shows the button in place.) Then switch back to the Code view and add the following code:

```
Private Sub BookButton_Click(ByVal sender As System.Object, _
          ByVal e As System.EventArgs) Handles BookButton.Click
    'Make sure the book button gets enabled and disabled.
    FirstThought("Executing from the book of moves (could be risky!)")
    Call ExecuteBook()
End Sub
```

All that remains is a few details. Add the following line of code to the EndGame() routine:

```
BookButton.Enabled = False
```

Add the following line of code to NewGame():

```
BookButton.Enabled = True
```

Now we are ready to test. Run the code and start an expert-level game. Click the AI Book button until the AI hits a mine or until it successfully executes a second move. Let the regular AI take over if it can. If the regular AI gets stumped, go back to the AI Book button.

With a new game, see if you can click the AI Book button enough times that the AI runs out of book moves to attempt before it hits a mine. This may require you to run a large number of failed games before it happens. This illustrates why we did not add all the possible combinations to the collections; it will be rare to exhaust them all without gaining some traction for the regular AI. This can be seen in Figure 7.6. Note the every-other pattern you get on the top row. The book of moves won't attempt adjacent squares, so it skips a square. If the book finally gets in a second move, this every-other pattern gives the regular AI a fighting chance to make additional moves via RuleTwoFar in the regular AI.

Our hybrid AI has a reasonable opening book and a very solid rule-base for general play, but it lacks an endgame AI. Endgame in *Minesweeper* often boils down to, "You have to make *N* fifty-fifty guesses to complete this board." Our code demonstrates how a book of moves can provide a powerful adjunct to a good AI, but there is no book of moves, and there are no general rules that will help when it comes down to just guessing.

Chapter Summary

A book of moves can make all the difference in a game AI. It can improve the speed or quality of play that the more general methods provide. A book is very good at providing the player with expected actions from the AI. When backed up by a good general AI, it need not have the perfect move for every occasion. It makes demands on the programmer, especially when used in games with completely new gameplay.

Chapter Review

Answers are in the appendix.

1. Describe how moves in a book of moves and heuristics are similar and how they are different.

2. How is a book of moves similar to a rule-based AI? How would you decide which label to use on a particular system?

Exercises

1. Make a list of moves for your favorite sport. In addition to the moves, categorize the situations where each move is a great response, a mediocre response, and a bad response.

References

[Campbell02] Campbell, M.; Hoane, A. J.; and Hsu, F. 2002. Deep Blue. *Artif. Intell.* 134, 1-2 (Jan. 2002), 57-83. DOI= http://dx.doi.org/10.1016/S0004-3702(01)00129-1. Available separately online at http://sjeng.org/ftp/deepblue.pdf.

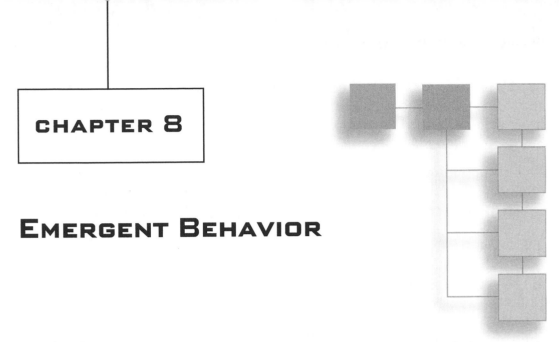

CHAPTER 8

EMERGENT BEHAVIOR

One of the more welcome outcomes in computer AI is emergent behavior. It is very well suited to control simulated flocks of birds or crowds of people. For our purposes, we will bend the classical definition of emergence to mean behaviors that were not explicitly programmed into individual software agents but are exhibited by a group of interacting agents. Early examples are found in the video *Eurythmy* produced at the Ohio State University Computer Graphics Research Group [Girard85] and in Craig Reynolds' "boids," used to make *Stanley and Stella in: Breaking the Ice* [Reynolds87]. Since then, countless others have made use of this technology in movies and games.

The impact of the emergent behavior that arises from simple steering forces is best experienced with animated visual media. The *Lord of the Rings* movies are so engaging as films that it is difficult to study the computer-generated hordes in motion, but the boids demonstration on Craig Reynolds' Web site [Reynolds01] is accessible to anyone with a Java-enabled browser. The paper airplane–shaped triangles are not particularly engaging, but the motion they exhibit certainly is. For anyone who has never seen the demonstration, a few minutes watching the motion and a glance at the explanation would be time well-spent.

Emergence is a welcome technology for two main reasons: It looks very realistic, and it can be computationally cheap. Reynolds programmed three simple behaviors into each boid. These behaviors told each boid to stay with its local group, to go where its local group is going, and to avoid getting too close to nearby neighbors. Not only are these behaviors simple, they do not involve the entire flock—just the local group. Because one of the behaviors avoids crowding, it provides a limit to the complexity of the computations required for a single boid, *regardless of how high the total number of boids goes*.

This computationally cheap algorithm produces lifelike results. The motion is often described as *organic* or *realistic*, even when simulated birds are drawn with simple triangles that look more like paper airplanes. Two similar but not identical flocks flying the same route will usually behave visibly—but not wildly—differently. It can be maddening to attempt this level of realism with other AI methods, particularly those with a centralized control mechanism.

While the life-like results are computationally cheap, so are any undesired behaviors. Emergent behavior can be hard to predict, difficult to tune, hard to control, and generally frustrating. The simplicity of the methods can be stymied by complex situations, something demonstrated to anyone who has seen a simple-minded bird trying to escape from the inside of a complex building.

This chapter is devoted to giving our software agents lifelike interactions. While the easiest way to do this is to copy the state of the art, we will examine what goes on under the hood in modest depth. We will use a freeway-simulation project, *Cars and Trucks*, as an example to illustrate some of the real-world issues that arise. Thankfully, this kind of AI is conceptually simple and rather robust. It even applies to behaviors outside of steering.

Give My Creature ALife!

In various versions of the Frankenstein story, Dr. Frankenstein pounds his fist or exhorts to the thundering skies, "Give my creature life!" It does not turn out quite like he planned, however. Indeed, in some versions, it appears not to happen at all—at least not at first.

Anyone can make boids flock, but game developers are in the business of creating new and engaging interactions that no one has experienced before. Without a known-good cookbook recipe, a game AI programmer has to traverse uncharted territory in search of good, usable emergent behavior. And of course, completely new software agents do not come with guarantees as to what will emerge when they interact. (Recall that the results Dr. Frankenstein achieved did not meet his goals.)

This creates two critical concerns for AI programmers. The first concern is dealing with their game designer. Much like Dr. Frankenstein, a game designer who demands complete and total control over AI behavior will not gracefully deal with an AI gifted with all of the controllability of a herd of cats. If the designer's task is to achieve a very specific entertainment experience, he or she may not be able to realize it with these methods. Designers with more leeway bring a more daunting challenge to the AI programmer—hence the AI programmer's second concern. When this more flexible designer says, "That concept is too cool to leave out. Put it in and we'll design around it if we have to," the AI programmer is committed to making it happen. This second concern cannot be overemphasized. Any novel application seeking emergent behavior is a high-risk endeavor. Early prototyping and proof-of-concept work is mandatory. Early winemakers knew that grape juice usually turned itself into wine if they left it alone, but they also knew that sometimes it just went bad.

Fortunately, there are some guiding principles worth examining when there is no recipe. Start with the interactions of simple behaviors, searching for the potentially narrow zone between no results and an unstable system. As part of the search, you may need to carefully explore the interactions not only for balance but also for the right timing.

Proven Recipes

New systems that resemble existing systems are likely to show similar emergent behavior. Tanks and birds have substantial differences, but tank platoons and bird flocks can benefit from very similar code [VanVerth00]. Steering behaviors for groups of individuals are the poster child for emergent behavior. Besides keeping a group in formation, steering behaviors also excel at obstacle avoidance. Variations on this theme rarely destroy the desired emergent behavior. Failures in behavior are possible, but they tend to be moderately benign and reasonable. Car drivers caught in exit-only lanes are forced to leave the freeway when they do not want to. Game AI that makes mistakes that leave the player thinking, "That could have happened to me . . ." are more well regarded than AI that makes more unfathomable errors. Not all failures are benign; agents can get stuck, run in circles, or even into walls.

The problem of getting good emergent behavior is harder when the issue at hand docs not relate to movement. In computer science, a classic method of attack is to transform a new problem into a better-known problem. If the two problems are truly isomorphic—that is to say, one can be transformed to another without loss of something important—then any reasoning that can be applied to the known problem also can be applied to the new problem.

Here's an example: Although financial systems and flying birds hardly seem similar, the herd mentality of the stock market is a known phenomenon. Ponzi schemes might be modeled this way: "Some of the birds around me are flying this way. This way appears to be taking us closer to the goal." As more "birds" (investors) "fly this way" (invest in the scheme), the purported value of their investments rises. The movement of some individuals in that direction attracts more "birds" and further reinforces the appearance of getting closer to the goal. As we have seen in prior chapters, the AI programmer has to be able to visualize the problem at hand in the terms of any particular proposed solution. We will cover these facets in detail.

Interaction

Emergence comes from interaction of multiple influences. With multiple agents, the multiple influences felt by each agent are typically tied to the other agents. If the influences between agents are going to be meaningful, then clearly the agents need to be able to interact in meaningful ways. In the case of boids, the actions each boid takes change its direction of flight and thus position. All the surrounding boids are paying attention to both properties. The boids see the actions, they act on the actions, and their own reactions cause further actions. Another analogy is nuclear fission. One atom splits and ejects high-speed neutrons. Those neutrons might or might not hit other fissionable atoms. Those atoms might or might not split, yielding more high-speed neutrons. With too little interaction, the reactor is a very expensive warm pile. With the right amount of interaction, large but manageable quantities of usable heat are available to make power. If there is too much interaction, the expensive reactor melts down. So it goes with software agents and emergent behavior; too much or too little interaction will not give desirable results.

To a first-order approximation, a resting herd of buffalo on the prairie resembles scattered boulders in the high grass. Things change when one buffalo spots a hunting predator and gives the alarm. The herd self-organizes spatially, calves heading for larger members of the herd and males interposing between the herd and the threat. The individuals acting on their own interact, giving the herd coherence as a herd. Without interactions between individuals, there would be no herd behavior; as best we can tell, bison do not get instructions from any centralized sources.

Half of a randomly aligned buffalo herd will not see a hunting predator (buffalo ignore wolves that do not appear to be hunting) because they are pointed the wrong way. Their safety depends on actions taken by the rest of the herd. A deaf buffalo will not hear snorts and other signals; unless some action takes place where it is looking, it will not react with the herd. *Its failure to react also means fewer cues for it neighbors.* A deaf buffalo exhibits inferior individual actions, but it also weakens herd behavior due to its diminished *interactions*.

There is a chain in all of these examples. It goes like this: Agent A acts, Agent B notices the action, Agent B reacts, Agent A notices the reaction.... Unlike reactors, bison do not seem to have major problems if the chain of herd reactions result in a stampede.

In the *Cars and Trucks* freeway-simulation project for this chapter, each vehicle pays attention to the lane, speed, and position of the vehicles around it and reacts by changing its speed and/or its selected lane. The simulation moves the cars and trucks every animation frame, so differences in speed create changes in relative position. Thus, the actions taken by each vehicle cause interactions with the nearby vehicles. The agents could be programmed to do many other things, such as select a radio station, but the other agents would ignore these behaviors, and thus they would not cause any interactions.

Simple Behaviors

The basic design for systems that create emergent behavior seems to be, "Toss in a few rules and turn them loose." This exploits the simplicity of the system and keeps the programmer from investing in code that later proves superfluous. Boids only needed simple behaviors.

Simple behaviors do not always imply that they are simple to code. Simplicity was a design goal for the *Cars and Trucks* freeway simulator project for this chapter. It has three basic behaviors: The vehicles are not allowed to change lanes into another vehicle, the vehicles prefer the fastest lane possible, starting on the right, and the vehicles try to keep a safe following distance for their speed. Avoiding collisions when changing lanes proves to be relatively easy to implement. Determining the speeds available in nearby lanes is also quite simple.

Establishing a safe following distance is more involved and depends on many factors, however, as we will see in the code. The math for vehicles on a straight section of freeway is far simpler than the math for birds in flight.

When looking for new emergent behavior, start with the simplest interactions. The code should resemble general rules more than a book of moves. It is hard to force emergence, and it can be easy to over-think the problem; tightly scripted behaviors are too organized to allow new behavior to emerge.

Between Order and Chaos

Individual goal-directed boids do not compute the most direct path to their goal and take it. They are not striving for optimal behavior; they are settling for reasonable behavior. Optimization drives toward order, fewer choices, and predictability. There is little or no room for new behaviors to emerge when everything that is not mandatory is prohibited. This is fine if the AI is for battle droids marching in lockstep formation, deterred from conforming only by their own destruction. It certainly will not be lifelike. Optimal behavior can be hard or impossible to compute, turning this "close enough is good enough" approach into a virtue.

The flip side of too much order is none at all. If what emerges is to be termed *behavior*, it needs to have some minimal amount of coherence. Conflicting directives need a rational resolution. If the interaction inputs drown out the agent's internal checks and balances, the system will probably not be stable. Ponzi schemes eventually collapse, stock-market bubbles burst, and bank runs are stopped by government authorities. If all agents disregard their internal checks and balances, the system crashes. In contrast, a system in which the agents disregard their internal checks and balances to varying degrees might exhibit large swings but on the whole remain stable. Getting the checks and balances right is one of the new challenges presented when dealing with emergent behavior.

The messy middle ground between order and chaos is a hallmark of living things. If we want our agents to have organic credibility, they must also appear to live in this messy middle ground. Programmers and designers who abandon the need for total control may find that emergent behavior gives them the lifelike appearance that they are after. Most people take steps to manage their time and their finances. While nearly everyone knows how they can further optimize their time and their finances, few find that they can comfortably live within the tighter constraints that additional optimization imposes.

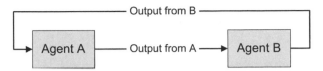

Figure 8.1
Simple feedback between two agents.

Feedback and Control

The study of complex systems is beyond the scope of this book, but some of the basic ideas from feedback and control systems can be illuminating. Aside from the nuclear reactor example in which the atoms are destroyed, the actors in our examples can act upon the actions in others that were triggered by the original actor. "I do something, you react to it, and then I react to you." This is known as *feedback* and is shown in Figure 8.1.

Figure 8.1 has been simplified to show only the feedback. Both agents could have other inputs. Both agents are free to decide what they do with any of the inputs, including ignoring some or all of them. We will ignore those complexities as much as we can. Timing and reinforcement are the key properties of feedback that we need to examine.

Reinforcement

In Figure 8.1, if the reaction of Agent A to feedback is to do more of what it did in the first place, this is known as *positive feedback*. If left unchecked, positive feedback results in chaos or system failure. Reactors melt, bison stampede at full speed into places where going slow or perhaps turning might be prudent, and children act out in ever more outrageous ways. Of course, not all positive feedback is bad; in fact, positive feedback is one of the ways that good ideas get turned into innovation. "That's a great idea! We should do that!" is positive feedback.

In Figure 8.1, if the reaction of Agent A to feedback is to do less of what it was doing, we call it *negative feedback*. Your intuitive ideas about positive and negative feedback are probably correct; feedback and control theory examine them in exacting detail. Negative feedback can also be good or bad. "I'd love to go boating, but there are small craft warnings out," is probably wisdom. "Great idea, none of us has time for it," has prevented countless innovations from becoming reality. Also called *dampening*, negative feedback is required to keep systems stable, but too much of it yields the ultimate in order in which nothing happens.

It should be obvious that stable systems need a balance between positive and negative feedback. Boids balance the need to stay with the flock against the need to avoid overcrowding. When designing a stable system with emergent behavior in mind, you should examine the interaction behaviors. Every positive-feedback input is a potential source of instability; it must be balanced in some manner. With a few simple behaviors, it should be easy to prove that the system will find a balance point. As the number of behaviors increases, proof becomes impossibly hard. The programmer is reduced to "flight testing" the system, looking for a stable regime and then programming in guards against excursions outside the stable envelope.

Timing

Both kinds of feedback are beneficial in emergent systems. Positive feedback drives emergence, and negative feedback keeps it from going out of control. Hidden in all of this is the effect of timing. How fast should the feedback loops operate? It should come as no surprise that the answer is neither too fast nor too slow, but just right. Our project simulation can provide some concrete insights into timing.

Fast Feedback

In the military, feedback is known as a *decision loop*, and the Holy Grail is to have a faster decision loop than the enemy. The idea is that the fast side acts, forcing the slow side to react. The fast side can then turn that reaction into a mistake before the slow side can adapt. If the advantage is extreme, the fast side can avoid destructive force-on-force styles of combat and still defeat the enemy. This works, however, only if the forces of the fast-thinking side are nimble enough to exploit the advantages of thinking faster. Many systems can think faster than they can act.

Faster feedback is not always better. Computer games need to stay at human-compatible speeds. In the case of boids, if the reaction times are too short, the flock will appear to vibrate instead of undulate. Short times imply higher frequencies, and at some point the frequency is too fast for human perception. Shorter feedback loops also carry an inherent disadvantage even if the system would benefit from them. Faster and faster feedback tends to result in decisions with less and less input data, because there is not enough time between decisions to gather enough data. You may need to analyze the data from several cycles of the decision loop to reliably discern any trends. In this case, you also need to determine the minimum number of data points required.

The stock market illustrates this dilemma quite well. Trades can be executed in about a minute. But how long does it take to reliably determine a trend? For a day-trader, five minutes may suffice. For a buy-and-hold, fee-averse investor, the answer may be one quarter or even one year. For the first investor, one hour is an eternity, and for the second investor, one hour is insignificant.

To be effective, feedback loops need to take long enough that real trends can be distinguished from noise. In the case of our software agents, our feedback loops need to take enough time that the agents can meaningfully act in ways that will cause interactions. Games do have an inherent upper limit on effective feedback speed, which we will see shortly when we look at feedback in *Cars and Trucks*.

Slow Feedback

Slow feedback loops give rise to plodding systems such as freight trains that often travel for miles before appreciably changing their speed. Technically, the feedback part is fast, but the control part is slow. The train engineer can hit the air brakes or the throttle very quickly, but the train needs time to change speed. For our purposes, we are combining feedback and control for simplicity and because software systems are far less constrained on the control side than physical systems are. If the feedback loop for a flock of boids takes too long, a boid that is too close to its flock mates will fly away from them long enough that it will no longer regard them as flock mates. A boid that is correcting for excess separation may collide with all the other flock mates that are making the same correction.

Slow feedback fights against the interaction needed for emergent behavior to appear. An e-mail exchange would be too slow for use in most games. Instant messaging provides far faster feedback and enables a sense of "being there" to emerge. Face-to-face conversation provides feedback at a rate that encourages a wide range of emergent behaviors.

Fast feedback loops give rise to frenetic systems such as mayflies, constantly darting here and there at the slightest input; slow feedback gives us freight trains. Neither would be satisfactory at controlling an automobile. The timing of the feedback has to be appropriate to the situation. Our project gives a good example to analyze. The physics implementation suggests a minimum think speed, as we shall see.

Feedback in Cars and Trucks

In the *Cars and Trucks* simulation, we will have independent control over the frame rate and the AI's thinking rate. While many games have a single update loop for animation, AI, and game input, others split one or more of them out. We get reasonable animation as low as six frames per second. We get reasonable AI performance at two thoughts per second. The latter number was arrived at by tuning the system after examining the various options.

It makes no sense to have the think rate higher than the frame rate. The vehicles move forward only once per animation frame. The vehicles change lanes and speed every time they think, but they only move when the animation calls for them to move. Thinking faster than the system can react is pointless, as one would expect. In terms of the military decision loop, this is the equivalent of generals pounding their desks in frustration at their slow-reacting forces.

All games have this same upper limit. While you may or may not need to have the AI think at the frame rate, there is never any need to exceed the frame rate. To be more precise, the AI need not think faster than important things change. Most games have animation and physics running in lockstep, so the basic rate of change *is* the frame rate. Resource-limited mobile games that have small bits of rapid animation but slow overall movement can let the AI slow down to the movement rate. PCs and consoles left such limits behind years ago, making the frame rate the basic change rate.

In *Cars and Trucks*, thinking almost as fast as the system can react did not prove to be optimal, either. The cars changed lanes too often. We got the mayfly effect. Some dampening was added to the code to make staying in the current lane more acceptable if the car in front was too close but pulling away. In visual terms, all the drivers appear to drive like indecisive maniacs; this might be a reasonable model for some drivers but not for all drivers. Even after dampening the lane changes, fast AI updates made it hard for the user to see what the AI was thinking. The AI graphically shows what it is thinking, and the user can absorb that information only so fast. The simulation would get smoother if the AI ran more often, but the user would have a hard time keeping up with what the AI is doing to each car. *Game design can place limits on how fast the AI should react.*

A think rate of one thought per second proved slightly slow. The vehicles miss opportunities that go by them as they daydream. This rate was still fast enough to be safe, but the drivers sometimes appeared lethargic, letting openings go by that they could have safely taken. A think rate as slow as one thought every two seconds would have resulted in collisions or the possibility that some vehicles could drive right through other vehicles in their lane. You can replicate the effects of tuning the AI by completing the exercises at the end of the project.

The thinking speed not only has an impact on the AI, it has wider impacts that need to be examined. AI is one part of the game, and all parts must balance. There is give and take available among the major parts of the game; our simulation, as simple as it is, has enough of the right elements to illustrate this.

If the AI can make certain demands of the simulated physics, our simulation never has collisions. Once the code was debugged, collision detection was restricted to the think cycle, not the animation cycle. Given the right physics and a properly working AI, the collision detection can be skipped altogether. This is an engineering decision balancing fun, realism, and computational demand. It would clearly be unacceptable if there were humans driving any of the cars, for example.

Without certain guarantees, collisions could happen any time there is motion, which asks that collision detection be performed every frame. During debugging, collision detection was run every frame. Collision detection is physics, not AI, but in a virtual world everything is under software control. When working properly, our "physics" and AI provide certain guarantees that let us move collision detection out of the animation loop and then make it completely optional. There are three ways a vehicle can collide in our simulation: It can run into the back of a slower vehicle in its lane, it can change lanes directly into another vehicle, or it can change lanes into the path of an oncoming faster vehicle. We will look at the impact of each of these.

Our AI looks forward two seconds' worth of travel distance at the vehicle's current speed to see what it might hit in its lane. As long as what passes for physics in our simulation allows the AI to cut the vehicle speed in half before the next second of travel, a given vehicle will not collide when it comes up on a slower vehicle already in its lane, even if that vehicle is at a dead stop. We get a realistic-looking behavior with the fast drivers slowing down over many think cycles as they come up on slow traffic and match speeds while keeping a safe distance. The realism suffers when very high speed vehicles shed an unrealistic amount of speed in the initial braking. If the blocking vehicle is moving at a reasonable rate, this drawback is far less noticeable as the overtaking vehicle smoothly matches speeds. Note that cars can never travel backward in our simulation. They can stop if they have to, but on our freeway they never back up.

Physics can suggest a minimum feedback speed. In our case, a car that halves its speed every second needs one second of travel distance to stop. If you sum the sequence that begins one-half plus one-fourth plus one-eighth..., you get a number that is almost one. So our stopping distance is one second of travel distance, but we also have to factor in reaction time. The car needs to see the obstacle before it can get within one second of travel distance. So the AI must look ahead more than one second, with two seconds travel distance being the minimum. That minimum works only if the AI thinks at least once a second.

Our AI guarantees that it won't change lanes into another vehicle, avoiding direct side-swipe collisions. In addition, it always makes sure that there is a safety margin of about half a car length of daylight in front and behind before it changes lanes right in front of or right behind another car. Since it only changes lanes to increase or maintain speed, it tends not to change lanes to get behind a slower car that it is now in danger of hitting. This is no help to overtaking drivers a little farther back in the new lane. Giving the overtaking car a full second of clearance would have been much more considerate.

The worst problem area for the simulation is when a slow vehicle changes into the lane of a very-high-speed vehicle. If it cannot change to a clear lane, our fast-vehicle AI needs to dump enough speed to keep it from slamming into the back of the slower vehicle that instantly appeared in front of it. When it happens, it appears unrealistic, even by the admittedly loose standards of our simulation. The slow-vehicle AI could check for more than half a car length of daylight behind it when it changes lanes and not change lanes into the clear zone in front of an overtaking faster car, but the simulation is slanted toward a more enter-taining American "My taxes paid for that lane, I'm taking it" style of freeway driving than a German Autobahn style, where pulling into the path of an overtaking car moving at nearly twice your speed is clearly suicidal.

As you might expect, the problem shows up when there are large differentials in speed. Vehicles moving at speed of 50 to 85 pixels per second merely appear rude to each other, but when they interact with vehicles travelling at 120 or 180 pixels per second, it looks more like a death wish. If our rude vehicles were more considerate and gave the overtaking vehicle at least a one-second buffer, we could use the same realistic-appearing deceleration the normal overtake code uses and avoid having the high-speed vehicles conduct panic stops. Our simulation amusingly treads on the physics so that it avoids collisions altogether and so that the AI can think at a more leisurely pace.

To summarize, we actively balance realism, frame rate, fun, and AI think rate. We traded realism to protect frame rate. We could have made the AI more considerate, easing the unrealistic demands on physics, but it is more entertaining to watch the fast drivers stand on their brakes when they get into traffic. In many games, the limits on the amount of CPU available to the AI will place limits on how often it is allowed to think. This is always a potential issue, but with emergent behavior in the mix, it has a direct impact on the limit to feedback speed. Fortunately, as we have seen, slower feedback loops often work better. The point should be emphasized strongly that the real-time constraints the game places on the AI must be carefully considered when tuning the feedback loops that control emergent behavior.

So with the right feedback, we can get the interactions we want between our agents. The simple behaviors are sufficient, and they cause the group to exhibit a pleasing group behavior. All positive feedback is balanced by a negative feedback to keep the system in balance. While we were not striving for flocking behavior, by basing our simulation on similar behaviors, we started with good assurances that we would get a decent group behavior.

Beyond Steering

Steering behaviors are one very accessible way to exploit emergent behavior. Flocking just looks right. With the proper architecture, we can get emergent behavior in places other than motion control. Consider the *Day in the Life* project from Chapter 5, "Random and Probabilistic Systems." Each actor is influenced by up to five inputs (cash on hand plus four pieces of data per job). In the original simulation, the inputs were fixed for every job. There were no pay raises, and the job descriptions never changed. What happens when the jobs begin changing? Will we get behaviors that we did not explicitly plan to get? If the chance of success for crime goes from 30 percent to 59 percent, Barry will give up the stunt show for a life of crime. Getting more criminals when crime is more enticing hardly seems unexpected. Similarly, the numbers for stunt show and day job are "close," and minor changes will cause Eddy and Barry to change jobs in a predictable manner. How can we get something unexpected?

What happens when we add interactions and some feedback? We could run the simulation for all of our available actors simultaneously, and we could make the jobs and cash change according to what the actors were doing. As soon as the current actions of the actors change the data upon which the same actors base their future decisions, we have created feedback. When the current actions of the actors influence the future decisions of other actors, we have created interactions. What would that give us? Let us look at some examples.

The money that criminals steal ought to come from somewhere. If the money gained by each successful criminal action came from the cash on hand of others, it would slow down or even stop the steady Eddys of our world from ever making it to retirement as a financier. Successful rock stars, lotto winners, and criminals who have moved on to become financiers might have to leave their comfortable life of retirement if large amounts of their cash are stolen all at once. The richest financiers can tolerate a certain steady level of theft if the criminal Carls of the world have their successes spread out over time, but if some criminals got lucky at the same time, it would take the retirees below the minimum level needed to play the market. This still seems predictable.

If the job market itself was influenced by the actions of actors, we could expect waves and trends of activity that would be completely unpredictable. Using simple supply and demand, jobs where the supply of workers is less than the demand for work to be done will see rising wages as employers compete for workers. Jobs with an oversupply of workers will see wages drop. We already know from Chapter 5 that many of our workers are sensitive to the relative wages of the different jobs. The number of various jobs could shrink and grow, and the values used to define every job could change with every tick of the simulation. For example, entertainment jobs such as stunt show and rock star might be more sensitive to the average level of cash on hand in the population than day job or financier; a well-off population has discretionary money available for entertainment, and a struggling population does not. The simulation might get stuck if the interactions are heavily dampened, or it might become unstable if positive feedback loops are not balanced by negative influences. The basic architecture has each actor acting on four outside and one inside influences; with some feedback it is reasonable to predict that we could get emergent behavior from the *system*. We expect the *job market* part of the simulation to exhibit emergent behaviors driven by the actors. As written for Chapter 5, the actors are heavily optimized for specific behaviors. Some of the actors and some of the jobs are "close" in terms of how easy it is to get an actor to give up his or her expected job if another job changes slightly, but the bulk of the system is meant to be stable. Along with the feedback, a richer set of actors and a richer set of jobs may be required to get a critical mass of interactions. It certainly appears plausible that with a few changes, we could get the job market part of the simulation to give us emergent behavior.

This example illustrates the critical concerns with emergent behavior. Since we do not have running code, we do not know if we will get emergent behavior at all. We think that we can get it, but we cannot predict if we will like what emerges. Even if we like it, the architecture offers little guidance as to how we will control it or tune it. Experience from Chapter 5 suggests that some numbers and some equations will be more sensitive to change than others. That experience also suggests that we will see substantial run-to-run variations in the outcomes. That variation causes a particular fear for AI programmers; what if the players play the game differently from how it was tested, and a new and utterly inappropriate behavior emerges after the game ships? The fact that other AI techniques can exhibit a similar vulnerability is a small consolation.

Advantages

Good emergent behavior gives the illusion of higher-order organization and coordination than are actually present. The method can be very cheap to program and is robust. The results typically have lifelike qualities that would be extremely difficult to achieve using other methods.

Disadvantages

The drawbacks to emergent behavior tend to relate to the unknowns. Game designers and quality-assurance staff tend to place a very high value on control and predictability. Neither group will be pleased if the herd of water buffalo wanders out of the mouth of the ravine and makes itself unavailable for a stampede that would kill the evil tiger that the player has lured into place. The unknowns increase if the envisioned system is far from what others have done before; the AI programmer does not know if he or she will obtain good emergent behavior until after the system is programmed.

The *Cars and Trucks* Project

The *Cars and Trucks* project differs from a typical flocking implementation in that the vehicles are not expected to stay in a flock. The desired speeds of our vehicles cover a wide range—from 50-pixels-per-second trucks to

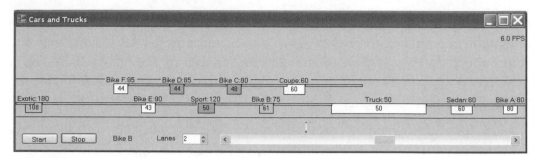

Figure 8.2
Cars and Trucks running on two lanes.

180-pixels-per-second exotic cars to the barely subsonic 600-pixels-per-second collision test vehicle. The player controls the number of available lanes as the simulation runs. Because the vehicles that have identical desired speeds are reasonably separated, as long as there are two or more lanes available, the vehicles eventually sort by speed as you would expect. Realistic group behavior results; the exotic car can get stuck in the slow lane when it attempts to pass on the right and fails to make it to a gap in time. When the 55-pixels-per-second truck passes the 50-pixels-per-second truck on a two-lane road, the rest of the convoy bunches up and jockeys for the best lane position. If the player adds three extra lanes, the really fast cars cannot clear off until the cluster of four bikes doing between 80 and 90 sort themselves out enough to clear an open lane. When the head of a line of cars gets an opening, the line behind accordions very realistically as the cars hold off on acceleration until the gap in front of them starts to open safely, as shown in Figure 8.2.

The simulation starts with the vehicles in a single lane. Those behind the truck start dangerously close together, forcing them to drop to a low speed. The upper lane was added a few frames before the screenshot was captured. The vehicles that change to the upper lane do so at a speed in the low 40s. In the upper lane, the Coupe leads, and with nothing ahead of it quickly makes it to its desired speed of 60. With a stable speed, it has a white background. Behind it is Bike C at a speed of 48 and climbing. The dark backgrounds of Bike C and Bike D are green when seen in color. Bike D can only accelerate when Bike C starts pulling away, so Bike D is at a speed of 44 and climbing. The 60–48–44 sequence of speeds shows the accordion effect as acceleration in vehicles ahead makes for increased clearance, calling for acceleration in the current vehicle.

As seen in Figure 8.2, our vehicles will be drawn as boxes using Label and TextBox controls. The position of a vehicle is the leading edge of the box. Inside each box is a number showing the current speed of the vehicle. The box will have a white background if the AI did not change speed the last time it thought. If the AI slowed down, the background will be reddish; if the AI accelerated, the background will be greenish. Projecting in front of each vehicle is a headlight—a narrow beam that projects forward two seconds' worth of travel distance at the current speed. This is similar to the feelers or probes often seen in flocking demos. The vehicle ignores anything ahead of it beyond the reach of the headlight. Above each box is the vehicle's name and its desired speed. All vehicles have a length, in pixels. (The bikes are too long, but a shorter bike body will not hold a two-digit number.) The sport and the exotic vehicles are the minimum size to hold a three-digit number.

Alongside the road is a "pixel marker," equivalent to a mile-marker road sign. You can see it above the scrollbar and below and between Bike B and Truck in Figure 8.2. When the simulation is running, the display is centered on a reference vehicle, which is Bike B in Figure 8.2. The marker goes flying by at the equivalent of the road speed of the reference vehicle. When the marker falls off the left edge, it is redrawn at the right. The vehicles travel left to right; a wide-format monitor enables you to see more of them.

Position is stored in absolute pixels. This makes the motion and display math easy to understand. In each animation frame, the vehicles are moved and then drawn. For movement, the internal position of the vehicles is updated according to their speed in pixels per second, and the frame rate in frames per second. Lane changes take place on AI think time, not animation time. To draw, the three labels that make up a vehicle have their Top property set according to the selected lane and their Left property set to a value reflecting the vehicle's relative position to the reference vehicle. Setting properties of labels and text boxes is rather rudimentary, but it is sufficient for our animation needs.

Two timers are used to control the AI and the animation. (Do not expect this method to be commonly used in commercial games.) The AI timer typically fires every half second to run the AI code. The animation timer typically fires 6 to 12 times a second, depending on the desired frame rate. This gives us the equivalent of complex, multi-threaded game code without the coding complexity. Performance will depend on the number of vehicles, but it will also depend greatly upon whether the code is run in the debugger or as an independent executable. In the code, comments identify the core five vehicles needed for initial testing. Using all 14 will have a speed impact on the simulation. Debugging statements, when turned on, will have a serious impact on speeds. A particularly fast computer is not required. (This book was written on an eight-year-old computer with dual 1.2GHz Athlon MP processors and 2GB of RAM running numerous background server processes at all times.)

The code has two parts: the road and the vehicles. We will develop both of them together. First we will put some cars on the road; then we will animate them. The last thing we will do will be to make them think.

The code uses LineShape controls to mark the edges of the pavement. These controls are part of the Visual Basic PowerPack, a free download from Microsoft. It is available at http://msdn.microsoft.com/en-us/vbasic/bb735936.aspx. Check the Toolbox window in Visual Basic to see if you already have the controls installed. If you do not have them and you do not want to download the PowerPack, the project will operate properly without the two lines. Simply do not add them when called for and do not add any code that manipulates them. The text will note these optional additions.

The Road and the Vehicles

Launch Visual Basic and create a project called *CarsAndTrucks*. Then follow these steps:

1. Change the name of Form1.vb file to Road.vb. Set its Text property to Cars and Trucks.

2. Resize the form. 1,050 × 300 is a good size. Depending on your monitor width, you may want to unpin the Solution Explorer or the Toolbox to gain width. Wider is better.

3. Double-click My Project in Solution Explorer. Go to the Compile tab and set Option Strict to On. Option Strict turns off silent type conversions that could fail and forces us to make them explicit. Being mindful of type conversions as we write the code helps prevent bugs.

4. Save all. Do this on a regular basis as we go.

Add a class to the project and call it Vehicle.vb. Our vehicles will keep a modest amount of data, most of which will be private. To start with, we will want to be able to create a vehicle and draw it. We start with the data that each vehicle needs. Add the following code to the Vehicle class.

```
Public Const VehicleWidth As Integer = 20

'We keep most of the vehicle data private.
Private myName As String
'Speeds are in pixels per second.
Private myDesiredSpeed As Integer
'Length is in pixels.
Private myLength As Integer
'Use floating point so that we can accumulate fractions.
Private Xpos As Double = 0
Private myLane As Integer = 1
'Actual speed in pixels per second.
Private currentV As Integer

'Visually, a vehicle is two Label controls and a TextBox control.
'We want to react when the body is clicked, so it is WithEvents.
Dim WithEvents Body As TextBox
Dim HeadLights As Label
Dim NameTag As Label
```

Most of the data that a Vehicle class object stores will be known when the vehicle is created. The New() function will have many parameters, so we have a certain amount of work to do to create our vehicles. Add the following code to the class:

```
'Create a vehicle.
Public Sub New(ByVal length As Integer, ByVal desiredSpeed As Integer, _
        ByVal parent As Road, ByVal X As Integer, ByVal V As Integer, _
        ByVal callMe As String)

    'Store the basic data.
    myName = callMe
    myDesiredSpeed = desiredSpeed
    currentV = V
    Xpos = X
    myLength = length

    'Create our three controls.
    Body = New TextBox
    HeadLights = New Label
    NameTag = New Label
```

```
        'Not moving? Side of the road please.
        If desiredSpeed <= 0 Then
            'Only signs have no speed.
            NameTag.Visible = False
            myLane = 0
        End If

        'Put the controls on the form.
        Body.Parent = parent
        HeadLights.Parent = parent
        NameTag.Parent = parent

        'Get their sizes right. (Note that the
        'width of a vehicle is height on a control;
        'our vehicles are sideways on the form.
        Body.Height = VehicleWidth
        HeadLights.Height = VehicleWidth \ 4

        'The same way that vehicle length turns into
        'control width.
        Body.Width = length
        HeadLights.Width = 2 * desiredSpeed

        'Auto-size the name tag.
        NameTag.Text = myName & ":" & desiredSpeed.ToString
        NameTag.AutoSize = True

        'Color them.
        Body.BackColor = Color.White
        HeadLights.BackColor = Color.Transparent
        NameTag.BackColor = Color.Transparent

        'Outline them or not.
        Body.BorderStyle = BorderStyle.FixedSingle
        HeadLights.BorderStyle = BorderStyle.FixedSingle
        NameTag.BorderStyle = BorderStyle.None

        'Tweaks for the body since it is a TextBox control.
        Body.TextAlign = HorizontalAlignment.Center
        Body.ReadOnly = True

        'Put us on the map.
        Me.Draw(-200)
    End Sub
```

The careful eye will have noticed that the code for the width of a headlight uses a backslash (\) instead of a forward slash (/) when dividing by 4. The backslash is an integer divide with fractions truncated. The result does not need type conversion when assigned to an integer variable. We want narrow headlights, and we do not care if they are one pixel narrower than rounding would call for.

Also worth noting is that our road is sideways. That means we have to deal with the fact that height on the form turns into the width of our vehicles. The length of our vehicles is the width of the controls that draw them. The drawing code will also have to keep this transformation in mind. We will have our class speak in terms of X position and vehicle length to avoid confusion.

The development environment will complain about Me.Draw(−200) because we have not added that chunk of code. The −200 value will make more sense when we see the positions we use to place the initial vehicles on the road. Without the draw call, all the controls would wind up in the top-left corner of the form. This way, we can take a glance at our starting data before things move. Add the following code to the class.

```
Public Sub Draw(ByVal offset As Integer)
    'Headlights go out twice our speed.
    HeadLights.Width = 2 * currentV

    'Position us in the proper lane.
    Body.Top = VehicleWidth * (10 - 2 * myLane)
    'Headlights same as the body.
    HeadLights.Top = Body.Top
    'Name tag above the body.
    NameTag.Top = Body.Top - NameTag.Height

    'And at the right spot along the way.
    'Everything gets the offset.
    'Body is a Label control. Its width is our
    'vehicle's length. Our right edge is at X, so
    'our left is our length further back.
    Body.Left = Me.X - Body.Width - offset
    'Headlights have their left edge at our position.
    HeadLights.Left = Me.X - offset
    'Center the name tag.
    NameTag.Left = Body.Left + Body.Width \ 2 - NameTag.Width \ 2

    'Show how fast we are going.
    Body.Text = currentV.ToString
End Sub
```

This code deals with the sideways road, but it needs help from the class in terms of the X position. Our virtual world is one of integer values, usually in terms of pixels, made possible by our flat, 2D simulation. We use a floating point value to store position so that we can accumulate fractions of a pixel of motion because our frame rate and speeds do not always divide evenly. Aside from that, everything is integer pixels, so we will provide a function that converts our floating-point position to the closest integer. While we are doing that, we will provide the rest of the functions used to get read-only access to the internal data of the vehicle. Add the following code to the Vehicle class.

```
Public Function ID() As String
    Return myName
End Function


'Where along the road is it?
Public Function X() As Integer
    Return CInt(Xpos)
End Function


'How fast am I going?
Public Function Speed() As Integer
    Return currentV
End Function


'How long is my car?
Public Function Length() As Integer
    Return myLength
End Function


'What lane am I in?
Public Function Lane() As Integer
    Return myLane
End Function
```

That gives us a good start on vehicles. We can test the code by adding some code to the Road form to create a few vehicles. We need to change our focus from the Vehicle class to the Road form. View the code of the Road.vb and add the following code:

```
#Region "Public Stuff"
    'A place to keep our car collection.
    Public ToyBox As New Collection
```

```
#End Region

    Private Sub Road_Load(ByVal sender As System.Object,_
            ByVal e As System.EventArgs) Handles MyBase.Load

        'Keep this list in sorted X order, ascending.
        '(length, desired speed, parent, X pos, initial speed, name)

        'The barely subsonic vehicle for crash testing (250 is a
        'more realistic top speed).
        ToyBox.Add(New Vehicle(35, 600, Me, -3025, 50, "F1+"))

        'To get serious speed differences.
        ToyBox.Add(New Vehicle(35, 180, Me, -1025, 50, "Exotic"))

        'Various fast bikes.
        ToyBox.Add(New Vehicle(30, 95, Me, -605, 50, "Bike F"))
        ToyBox.Add(New Vehicle(30, 90, Me, -545, 50, "Bike E"))
        ToyBox.Add(New Vehicle(30, 85, Me, -485, 50, "Bike D"))

        'Also shows good speed differences.
        ToyBox.Add(New Vehicle(35, 120, Me, -425, 50, "Sport"))

        ToyBox.Add(New Vehicle(30, 80, Me, -365, 50, "Bike C"))

        'These five make good initial test vehicles.
        ToyBox.Add(New Vehicle(30, 75, Me, -305, 50, "Bike B"))
        ToyBox.Add(New Vehicle(45, 60, Me, -240, 50, "Coupe"))
        ToyBox.Add(New Vehicle(200, 50, Me, 0, 50, "Truck"))
        ToyBox.Add(New Vehicle(45, 60, Me, 70, 50, "Sedan"))
        ToyBox.Add(New Vehicle(30, 80, Me, 120, 50, "Bike A"))

        'A two-truck slow pass up ahead.
        ToyBox.Add(New Vehicle(200, 55, Me, 1000, 50, "Truck"))
        ToyBox.Add(New Vehicle(200, 50, Me, 1400, 50, "Truck"))

    End Sub
```

Now we are ready to test. We have created numerous vehicles with widely varying capabilities. (Feel free to comment out vehicles to make things simpler as you debug your code.) We keep all of the vehicles in the toy box so that we have them in one convenient place. We keep the toy box sorted so that the AI and collision detection can run a great deal faster. If a given vehicle is not hitting the vehicle

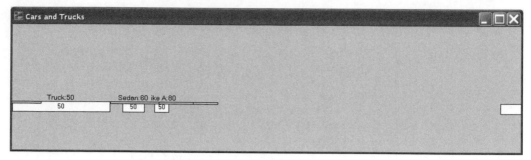

Figure 8.3
An initial test run of *Cars and Trucks.*

directly in front of it, it could hardly be hitting any vehicle in front of both of them. We will have to sort the toy box every time we want to go through it in order, but the sort should be quick because the list retains a great deal of order between sorts. Run the code in the debugger. You should see something resembling Figure 8.3.

If you look at the X positions we loaded and hunt for the −200 value in the list, you will see that there is a 200-pixel-long truck located at X=0. On the left side of the form, we see the tail end of that truck at −200. The −200 number we fed to the initial Draw() calls in New() was picked for this reason. We get a static view. If we extend the size of the form, we can see the two trucks up ahead, but there is no way to see the convoy of vehicles behind. They would be a lot easier to see if they were moving.

Movement and Animation

We loaded all the vehicles at a speed of 50 pixels per second. Without any AI, they cannot change speed. If we did not put any of them on top of another, we can defer collision detection until after we get them to move.

We will program in a variable frame rate. Each frame, every vehicle, starting from the front, is moved forward by its speed in pixels per second divided by the frame rate. Floating-point math keeps track of fractions for us, giving us some freedom in setting the frame rate. The upper limit to frame rate will depend on the particulars of your system. After moving everything, we draw it in its new place. Animation frames are initiated by a timer. We will start with the user-interface elements. Switch to the Design view of Road.vb; then follow these steps:

1. A glance at Figure 8.2 may be helpful as you place controls. Drag a Label control from the Toolbox to the upper-right corner of the form. Change its

Name property to FpsLabel. Change the Text property to FPS. Change the Anchor property to Top, Right. This label will show how fast our animation actually runs.

2. Drag a Button control from the Toolbox to the lower-left corner of the form. Change its Name property to StartButton. Change its Text property to Start. Change its Anchor property to Bottom, Left. This button will start the simulation.

3. Drag another Button control from the Toolbox and place it next to the Start button. Change its Name property to StopButton. Change its Text property to Stop. Change its Anchor property to Bottom, Left. This button will stop the simulation.

4. Drag a Timer control from the Toolbox onto the form. When you let go, it will jump to the bottom of the editing pane. Timers have no visible user interface elements, so they are held at the bottom. Change the Name property of the timer to AnimationTimer.

5. Drag another Timer control to the form. Change its Name property to ThinkTimer. We do not need it to move the vehicles, but we want it on the form so that we do not have to revisit some of the code we are about to write.

6. Drag a HScrollBar control from the Toolbox to the bottom-right corner of the form. Change its Name property to PanScrollBar. Change the Small-Change property to 10. We will resize it later, after the rest of the controls are on the form.

7. Drag a Label control to the form and place it to the right of the Stop button. Change the Name property to RefLabel.

We need to track some data if we are going to compute the frame rate. We also need to set the frame rate. Once we do that we can turn on the Start and Stop buttons and ask our vehicles to move. Switch to the Code view of Road.vb and add the following code inside the class:

```
'Some constants we can tweak.
Dim FrameRate As Integer = 6
Dim ThinkRate As Integer = 2

'We need a start time to compute frame rate.
Dim startTime As Date
Dim framecount As Integer
```

```vb
Private Sub StartButton_Click(ByVal sender As System.Object, _
            ByVal e As System.EventArgs) Handles StartButton.Click
    'Store values for computing frames per second.
    startTime = Now
    framecount = 0
    'Initialize and enable animation.
    AnimationTimer.Interval = CInt(1000 / FrameRate)
    AnimationTimer.Enabled = True
    'Initialize and enable AI.
    ThinkTimer.Interval = CInt(1000 / ThinkRate)
    ThinkTimer.Enabled = True
    'Don't show FPS when running.
    FpsLabel.Visible = False
    'Do not scroll when running.
    PanScrollBar.Enabled = False

End Sub


Private Sub StopButton_Click(ByVal sender As System.Object, _
            ByVal e As System.EventArgs) Handles StopButton.Click
    'Stop animation and AI.
    AnimationTimer.Enabled = False
    ThinkTimer.Enabled = False

    'Compute frames per second.
    Dim stopTime As Date = Now
    Dim min As Integer = stopTime.Subtract(startTime).Minutes
    Dim secs As Integer = stopTime.Subtract(startTime).Seconds + 60 * min
    'Avoid a divide by zero.
    If secs < 1 Then secs = 1
    'Compute the rate and show it.
    FpsLabel.Text = Format((framecount / secs), "0.0") & " FPS "
    FpsLabel.Visible = True
    'Allow scrolling.
    PanScrollBar.Enabled = True
End Sub
```

The buttons turn the timers on and off. They also disable and enable the scrollbar. Once we get the vehicles moving, we will switch from a static ground view of the vehicles going by to a vehicle-relative view so that we can stay with a particular vehicle. We need to ask the vehicles to move because they hold their position values internally. Switch to Vehicle.vb and add the following code:

```
Public Sub MoveForward(ByVal FrameRate As Integer)
    Xpos += currentV / framerate
End Sub
```

What remains is to ask the vehicles to move when the animation timer fires. Switch back to the code for Road.vb and add the following code:

```
Private Sub AnimationTimer_Tick(ByVal sender As System.Object, _
        ByVal e As System.EventArgs) Handles AnimationTimer.Tick
    Dim Toy As Vehicle

    'Increment drawn frames.
    framecount += 1

    Dim offset As Integer = CInt(Me.Width / 2)

    'Move them forward and draw
    For Each Toy In ToyBox
        Toy.MoveForward(FrameRate)
        'Track the reference vehicle when we get it.
        Toy.Draw(-offset)
    Next

    'Our floating marker will need to move when we put it in.
End Sub
```

Before we run the code, a word or two about timers, frame rate, and performance is in order. The timers we use have a maximum resolution of 55 milliseconds. This has an impact on how well the system can deliver the desired frame rate. Running the code in the debugger will not help matters. Our two timers will interact; the animation may lose smoothness when the AI runs. While the VB code itself is reasonably fast, changing the positions of controls using the native Windows desktop is a known choke point. The Microsoft DirectX technology exists for this very reason. These timers should give reasonable performance at our low frame rates. These timers do provide a number of concrete benefits to the beginning AI programmer. These are the simplest timers available. They let us control the think rate and the frame rate independently. We do not have to deal with threading issues or the need to write a time-locked core graphics loop.

We will add more to this code later as indicated by the comments. Run the code in the debugger. Start and stop the simulation and note the frame rate. Aside from rounding and the occasional glitch, it should stay near six frames per second. Change the frame rate to something very high, such as 60, and run again. The animation should be much smoother, but note that it does not run at 60 frames per second. If you run the executable outside of the debugger, the maximum frame rate will improve. Although the most demanding modern games strive for 60 frames per second, numbers in the 9 to 12 range are good enough for our purposes. The original *Quake* had a design goal of staying above 10 frames per second. When running the code in the debugger, six frames per second gives the system enough time to output any debugging data that you might need. If need be, reduce the number of vehicles to the five core vehicles mentioned in the code and retest. In any case, do not place extreme concern on the frame rate.

Let us switch from the ground view to a vehicle-relative view. When we do this, we will need a ground feature to indicate how fast we are going, so we will implement a sign at the edge of the road. Add the following code to the Road class.

```
'Who are we tracking?
Private refVehicle As Vehicle
'Let's have a mile marker go by.
Dim FloatingMarker As New Vehicle(2, 0, Me, 0, 0, "Floating Marker")
```

Now we can draw relative to the reference vehicle. We will set the reference vehicle later, but we can change the animation timer code to its final form now. Find the following line in the animation timer event handler:

```
Toy.Draw(-offset)
```

Change that line to read as follows:

```
Toy.Draw(refVehicle.X - offset)
```

Just below that code is a comment about the floating marker. Add the following code below the comment.

```
'Move the floating marker and draw.
FloatingMarker.MoveFloatingMarker(refVehicle, FrameRate, offset)
FloatingMarker.Draw(refVehicle.X - offset)
```

We will update the Vehicle class to implement the code needed to move the floating marker later. For now, we will stay with the Road.vb file.

Find the `Public Stuff` region and add the following code. We want to be able to click on a vehicle to make it the reference vehicle, so the `Vehicle` class will need a way to tell the form that a vehicle got clicked.

```
Public WriteOnly Property ReferenceVehicle() As Vehicle
    Set(ByVal value As Vehicle)
        refVehicle = value
        RefLabel.Text = refVehicle.ID
    End Set
End Property
```

Find `Road_Load`, the form's `Load` event handler, and add the following code to it after the code that adds the last vehicle. At startup, the reference vehicle is the middle one.

```
'The middle vehicle is our starting reference vehicle.
Me.ReferenceVehicle = CType(ToyBox(1 + ToyBox.Count \ 2), Vehicle)
```

Switch to Vehicle.vb. We need to handle the floating marker, and we need to react if the user clicks a vehicle to make it the reference vehicle. Add the following code to the class:

```
Public Sub MoveFloatingMarker(ByVal refV As Vehicle, _
        ByVal Framerate As Integer, ByVal halfSize As Integer)
    If refV.Speed = 0 Then Return
    'Markers appear to go backward.
    Xpos -= refV.Speed / Framerate
    'After it falls off the back end, put it back on the front.
    While Xpos < refV.X - halfSize
        Xpos += 2 * halfSize
    End While
    'If the user changed the refV, the marker may be too far ahead.
    While Xpos > refV.X + halfSize + 1
        Xpos -= 2 * halfSize
    End While
End Sub

'Let the user tell us which car to follow.
Private Sub Body_Click(ByVal sender As Object, _
        ByVal e As System.EventArgs) Handles Body.Click
    Dim theRoad As Road = CType(Body.Parent, Road)
    theRoad.ReferenceVehicle = Me
End Sub
```

Run this code in the debugger. Notice that on the first animation frame, the view jumps from −200 to center on the reference vehicle. Click a vehicle and watch the view center on that vehicle. You can walk up and down the chain this way. Below the vehicles, you can see the marker fly by at 50 pixels per second.

Now we will finish adding the final user-interface elements. While we have not yet added the AI, we can predict that the richness of the interactions will be greatly enhanced if we can have more than a single lane. Take a glance at Figure 8.2 and then switch to the Design view of Road.vb.

1. Drag a Label control to the form and place it to the right of the RefLabel. Change the Text property of the new label to Lanes.

2. Drag a NumericUpDown control next to the new label. Resize the control and make it smaller because it has to display only a single-digit number. Change the Name property to LanesUpDown. Change the Maximum property to 5 and the Minimum property to 1.

3. Enlarge the PanScrollBar control so that it takes up all of the rest of the available space.

4. If you have the PowerPack, drag a LineShape control to anywhere on the form. Change its Name property to FastLineShape. Drag another LineShape control to the form and change its Name property to SlowLineShape.

Switch to the Code view of Road.vb and locate the Public Stuff region. The AI will want to ask the form how many lanes there are. Add the following code to the region:

```
'Tell others how many lanes.
Public Function Lanes() As Integer
    Return CInt(LanesUpDown.Value)
End Function
```

If you have the PowerPack and added the two LineShape controls to the form, add the following code to the form:

```
Private Sub Road_Resize(ByVal sender As Object, _
            ByVal e As System.EventArgs) Handles Me.Resize
    'Get the slow line into place.
    SlowLineShape.X1 = 0
    SlowLineShape.X2 = Me.Width
```

```
    SlowLineShape.Y1 = Vehicle.VehicleWidth * 19 \ 2
    SlowLineShape.Y2 = SlowLineShape.Y1

    'Get the fast line into place (it moves).
    FastLineShape.X1 = 0
    FastLineShape.X2 = Me.Width
    FastLineShape.Y1 = Vehicle.VehicleWidth * 19 \ 2 - _
        2 * Vehicle.VehicleWidth * Lanes()
    FastLineShape.Y2 = FastLineShape.Y1
End Sub

Private Sub LanesUpDown_ValueChanged(ByVal sender As System.Object, _
        ByVal e As System.EventArgs) Handles LanesUpDown.ValueChanged
    'The AI can think for itself. The fast lane stripe needs our help.
    Call Road_Resize(Nothing, Nothing)
End Sub
```

If you added the lines, run the code in the debugger and change the number of lanes. The fast line should respond correctly to the number of lanes specified by the control. The slow line should be in place half a car width below the line of cars. If you did not add the lines, there will not be any visible effect until we add the AI.

As a precursor to the AI, we need to add some helper code to the code in Road.vb. We will add two routines: one to sort the cars and another to check for collisions. A side effect of sorting the cars is that we can figure out how to set the scrollbar so that when the simulation is stopped, we can scroll around and see all the vehicles. Add the following code to Road.vb:

```
'The AI and the collision detection need a sorted list.
    Private Sub SortToys()
        Dim swapped As Boolean = True
        Dim Behind As Vehicle
        Dim Ahead As Vehicle

        'This is the sorting loop.
        While swapped
            swapped = False
            Dim i As Integer
            For i = 1 To ToyBox.Count - 1
                'The back has a lower subscript.
                Behind = CType(ToyBox(i), Vehicle)
```

```
                              'The front has a higher subscript.
                              Ahead = CType(ToyBox(i + 1), Vehicle)
                              'Are they out of order?
                              If Ahead.X < Behind.X Then
                                    'The one we thought should be ahead is not;
                                    'we need to swap them.
                                    swapped = True
                                    'Debug.WriteLine("*** " & Behind.ID & _ " has passed " &
                                          Ahead.ID)
                                    ToyBox.Remove(i + 1)
                                    ToyBox.Add(Ahead, , i)
                              End If
                    Next
              End While

        'Grab the leader and trailer to set the scrollbar.
        Behind = CType(ToyBox(1), Vehicle)
        Ahead = CType(ToyBox(ToyBox.Count), Vehicle)

        'The world is half a form bigger on each side of the pack.
        Dim offset As Integer = CInt(Me.Width / 2)

        'The slow vehicle sets the minimum.
        PanScrollBar.Minimum = Behind.X - offset
        'The fast vehicle sets the maximum.
        PanScrollBar.Maximum = Ahead.X - offset
        If refVehicle IsNot Nothing Then
              'Get the value right.
              PanScrollBar.Value = refVehicle.X - offset
        End If

        'This more properly belongs on the resize event.
        PanScrollBar.LargeChange = Me.Width \ 4

        'Protective code to check that our code works OK.
        Call CollisionDetect()

End Sub

'Run any time the list is sorted.
Private Sub CollisionDetect()
      Dim Toy As Vehicle
```

```
'The bag holds groups of vehicles by lane.
Dim Bag As New Collection
'We use myBag to access one of those groups.
Dim myBag As Collection
Dim key As String
For Each Toy In ToyBox
    'Convert the lane to a string so that we can
    'use it as a key.
    key = Toy.Lane.ToString
    If Not Bag.Contains(key) Then
        'This is the first one in that lane we've seen.
        'Create the group.
        Bag.Add(New Collection, key)
    End If
    'Get my group out of the bag...
    myBag = CType(Bag(key), Collection)
    '...and put me in it.
    myBag.Add(Toy)
Next

'Since we started with a sorted ToyBox, all
'the groups have to be sorted.

Dim Behind As Vehicle
Dim Ahead As Vehicle

Dim i As Integer
For Each myBag In Bag
    For i = 1 To myBag.Count - 1
        'Grab two vehicles.
        Behind = CType(myBag(i), Vehicle)
        Ahead = CType(myBag(i + 1), Vehicle)
        'My nose is ahead of your nose, so if my tail is
        'behind your nose, we conflict.
        If Ahead.X - Ahead.Length <= Behind.X Then
            Debug.WriteLine("###### COLLISION: " & Behind.ID & _
                        " is hitting " & Ahead.ID)
        End If
    Next

Next
End Sub
```

The code needs to be called to be effective. We will call it when the ThinkTimer ticks. To see that it is working, we will turn on the scrollbar. Add the following code to Road.vb:

```
Private Sub ThinkTimer_Tick(ByVal sender As System.Object, _
            ByVal e As System.EventArgs) Handles ThinkTimer.Tick
    'Passing happens; we need this to think, not to draw.
    Call SortToys()
    'Real AI code goes here.
End Sub

Private Sub PanScrollBar_Scroll(ByVal sender As System.Object, _
        ByVal e As System.Windows.Forms.ScrollEventArgs) Handles _
        PanScrollBar.Scroll
    'Redraw at our new place.
    Dim Toy As Vehicle
    For Each Toy In ToyBox
        Toy.Draw(PanScrollBar.Value)
    Next Toy
End Sub
```

Run this code, making sure to start the simulation. Let it run a second or two and then stop the simulation. The scrollbar should allow you to scroll back to the F1+ vehicle way in the back. Going the other way should take you to the lead truck. The call to SortToys() also calls CollisionDetect(). The AI needs the sort, so we must sort before the AI runs because the animation moved the vehicles, and they could have been passing each other. However, when debugging, you can call the sort after every animation frame to make sure that everything works and no collisions have taken place. Be sure to watch the Immediate window for debugging output; the collision message will go there.

It is time to add that real AI code promised by the comment in the ThinkTimer Tick event handler. Replace that comment with the following code:

```
    'Now do the AI.
    Dim Toy As Vehicle
    Dim i As Integer

    'Debug.WriteLine("Thinking...")
    'Run the AI, front to back.
    For i = ToyBox.Count To 1 Step -1
        Toy = CType(ToyBox(i), Vehicle)
```

```
        Toy.Think(i, Me)
    Next
```

We need to switch to the Vehicle.vb file to get the vehicles to think. The AI will need a variety of helper functions. The AI is interested in what vehicle is ahead of or behind it. The vehicles also have a limit to how hard they can accelerate. That limit allows high acceleration from low speed and lower acceleration when the vehicle is near its desired speed. The formula used is a simplification of actual acceleration curves. As you might expect, trucks have too much low-end pickup, and the exotic vehicles have too much high-speed charge. That said, even this token nod toward realism gives the right impression. Add the following code to the Vehicle class:

```
'Institute acceleration limits.
Public Function BestNextSpeed() As Integer
    'Acceleration drops with speed.
    Dim a As Integer = CInt(0.1 * (2 * myDesiredSpeed - currentV))
    'But even the slowest truck can do 1.
    If a < 1 Then a = 1
    Dim newV As Integer = currentV + a
    'Don't go faster than desired.
    If newV > myDesiredSpeed Then newV = myDesiredSpeed
    Return newV
End Function


'Who is ahead of me in a given lane?
Private Function CarAhead(ByVal desiredLane As Integer, _
        ByVal myIndex As Integer, ByVal theRoad As Road) As Vehicle
    Dim i As Integer
    Dim OtherGuy As Vehicle
    For i = myIndex + 1 To theRoad.ToyBox.Count
        'Ahead of me in the lane we are checking.
        OtherGuy = CType(theRoad.ToyBox(i), Vehicle)
        If OtherGuy.Lane = desiredLane Then
            Return OtherGuy
        End If
    Next
    Return Nothing
End Function

'Who is behind me in a given lane?
Private Function CarBehind(ByVal desiredLane As Integer, _
```

```
                    ByVal myIndex As Integer, ByVal theRoad As Road) As Vehicle
        Dim i As Integer
        Dim OtherGuy As Vehicle
        For i = myIndex - 1 To 1 Step -1
            'Behind me in the lane we are checking.
            OtherGuy = CType(theRoad.ToyBox(i), Vehicle)
            If OtherGuy.Lane = desiredLane Then
                Return OtherGuy
            End If
        Next
        Return Nothing
    End Function
```

Now that the AI can get answers about the cars around it and the capabilities of the vehicle itself, it is time for the AI to do some thinking. The AI has two parts. The first part picks the best speed from the available choices. It depends on the part that computes the best speed in a given lane.

```
    'The next two are where the AI lives.
    Public Sub Think(ByVal myIndex As Integer, ByVal theRoad As Road)

        'Find the best lane:
        'Which lane is fastest for me?
        'Look from right to left.
        Dim newlane As Integer = myLane - 1
        'No lane is this bad:
        Dim newspeed As Integer = -100

        Dim i As Integer
        'Go through up to three lanes.
        For i = myLane - 1 To myLane + 1
            'Don't let cars below lane 1.
            If i > 0 Then
                Dim otherspeed As Integer = SpeedInLane(i, myIndex, theRoad)
                If otherspeed > newspeed Then
                    newspeed = otherspeed
                    newlane = i
                End If
            End If

        Next
        'Color based on speed changes.
        If currentV = newspeed Then Me.Body.BackColor = Color.White
```

```
        If newspeed > currentV Then Me.Body.BackColor = Color.LightGreen
        If newspeed < currentV Then Me.Body.BackColor = Color.Pink

        'Execute the decisions.
        currentV = newspeed
        myLane = newlane

    End Sub

    Private Function SpeedInLane(ByVal somelane As Integer, _
              ByVal myIndex As Integer, ByVal theRoad As Road) As Integer
        'Want some daylight between our bumper and bumpers in other lanes.
        Dim CUTOFF_BUFFER As Integer = 21

        'Does the lane exist?
        If (somelane > theRoad.Lanes()) Or (somelane < 1) Then
            'Debug.WriteLine(Me.ID & " checking lane " & somelane.ToString & _
            '        " which does not exist.")
            Return 0
        End If

        'If it's not our current lane, we have to prevent side swiping
        'a car in the other lane whose nose is behind our nose.
        Dim BlindSpot As Vehicle = CarBehind(somelane, myIndex, theRoad)
        If somelane <> myLane Then
            'Only if there is somebody in that lane behind me.
            If BlindSpot IsNot Nothing Then
                'Will I hit them?  Add some padding to prevent
                'cutting them off.
                Dim tail As Integer = Me.X - Me.Length - CUTOFF_BUFFER
                'If they are behind me and my tail is behind their nose,
                'I'll hit them.
                If tail < BlindSpot.X Then
                    'Debug.WriteLine(Me.ID & " sees that lane " & _
                    '    somelane.ToString & " is blocked by " & BlindSpot.ID)
                    Return -1
                End If
                'Are we thinking about being rude?
                'I could change this to 1x their speed and actually
                'decline the lane, but we'll just cut them off instead.
                tail += CUTOFF_BUFFER - BlindSpot.Speed * 2
                If tail < BlindSpot.X Then
                    'Debug.WriteLine("++++" & Me.ID & " considers cutting off " & _
```

```
                        '        & BlindSpot.ID & " in lane " & somelane.ToString & ".")
                End If
        End If
End If


'Is there anyone in front to worry about?
Dim OtherGuy As Vehicle = CarAhead(somelane, myIndex, theRoad)
If OtherGuy Is Nothing Then
        'Debug.WriteLine(Me.ID & " finds lane " & somelane.ToString & _
        '" is open for an available speed of " & BestNextSpeed().ToString)
        Return BestNextSpeed()
Else
        'Will we hit his tail end? (Should never happen in our own lane.)
        If myLane <> OtherGuy.Lane Then
                Dim tail As Integer = OtherGuy.X - OtherGuy.Length - _
                    CUTOFF_BUFFER
                If tail < Me.X Then
                    'Debug.WriteLine(Me.ID & " sees that lane " & _
                    '    somelane.ToString & " is blocked by " & OtherGuy.ID)
                    Return -1
                End If
        End If

End If


'The lane is usable.  How fast is it?



'We like a distance that is numerically equal to twice our speed.
Dim deltaX As Integer = OtherGuy.X - Me.X - OtherGuy.Length
Dim matchSpeed As Integer = deltaX \ 2

'Is the other guy faster than we are?
'This is not worth changing lanes over - only applies in our
'lane. Not checking this in other lane dampens maniacal lane
'switching so we only switch into a lane with non-compromised
'clear distance ahead. In our lane, we'll take a compromise if
'it is safe.
If OtherGuy.Lane = Me.Lane Then

        'If he's pulling away we don't slow down
        If OtherGuy.Speed > Me.Speed Then
            If Me.Speed > matchSpeed Then
```

```
                matchSpeed = Me.Speed
            End If
        End If


        'Is the other guy a nutcase?
        If OtherGuy.Speed > myDesiredSpeed Then
            'He's going faster now than we want to go, ignore him
            'and floor it.
            matchSpeed = myDesiredSpeed
        End If
    End If


    'Go to match speed if we can and if we want that much.
    If matchSpeed > BestNextSpeed() Then matchSpeed = BestNextSpeed()
    'Debug.WriteLine(Me.ID & " can do " & matchSpeed.ToString & _
    '        " in lane " & somelane.ToString & " behind " & OtherGuy.ID)


    Return matchSpeed
End Function
```

At this point, you should give the code a thorough thrashing. If your code misbehaves, there are numerous debug messages commented out that can be turned on. Some of them are split over multiple lines for readability, so you will need to uncomment all the lines involved. The easiest way is to select the lines using the mouse and then click the Uncomment button in the toolbar. Look at how the vehicles behave in tight groups and then open another lane and watch how they react. Watch an inbound, high-speed unit slow and match speed over many seconds. If you reduce the number of lanes, the cars in the closed lane come to a screeching halt and then dart into traffic as soon as they get an open window ahead of them, often cutting off oncoming cars. All sorts of accordion behaviors can be demonstrated. In a two-lane situation with the fast lane at 55 pixels per second and the slow lane at 50 pixels per second (easily arranged with the two leading trucks), you can watch the last car in the slow lane change lanes after the faster line gets past, which in turn keeps the slow line pinned to the slow lane until the new last car in the slow line can make the same maneuver.

Is any of this emergent behavior? Who really cares? Much of the behavior here can be deduced by studying the AI code of the individual agents. But some of the patterns, such as accordion speed changes and fighting for a newly opened fast lane, are not directly programmed in. In any case, the method gives realistic-looking (if somewhat rude) behaviors quite cheaply—the hallmarks of emergent behavior. Consider how hard it would be to orchestrate the same behaviors with a top-down, coordinated approach. As a thought problem, try to see if you can define these behaviors without resorting to using terms equivalent to the interactions of independent agents. Forcing these formations would be hard; letting them happen is simple.

Chapter Summary

Emergent behavior yields realism at a low run-time cost, especially when applied to group movement. More innovative uses will require exploration and tuning to achieve the maximum effectiveness of the method, but even these efforts are quite reasonable. AI built this way tends to degrade gracefully in the face of overly constraining circumstances, but it is not free of its own set of peculiarities. Every AI programmer considering these methods should keep in mind the unpleasant behaviors seen when a real bird gets trapped in an unfamiliar environment.

Chapter Review

Answers are in the appendix.

1. List the elements and characteristics of a system that allows and encourages emergent behavior.

2. Describe the effects of feedback and the effects of feedback rates.

Exercises

1. Adjust the tuning settings for the AI think rate. A rate of one thought per second is the slowest that is still safe for the simulation. Note how the drivers miss open slots. Increase the rate above two until it matches the frame rate. Note how this makes it harder to see what the drivers are doing.

2. Change the SpeedInLane() function to allow the drivers to change into lanes with compromised clear distance. The comment above an If statement talks about dampening maniacal lane changes; make that If statement always true instead of true only when the lane being evaluated is the current lane. Run the code and note the amount of ruthless lane changing it generates. Notice how two lanes will swap with each other when a car cuts off another; this creates a better hole for the car that got cut off, thus creating a ripple

effect down the two lanes. Note how this interacts with tuning the AI in Exercise 1; a fast AI will cause constant lane changing but little increase in speed overall.

3. Add the check to `SpeedInLane()` that declines a lane change if it would cut off an oncoming car within the oncoming car's one-second zone. The existing code has a commented-out debug statement that is triggered if the lane change treads on a two-second zone. Changing the multiplier to 1 and declining the lane change instead of issuing a debug output will make the drivers far less suicidal about pulling out in front of high-speed inbound traffic.

References

[Girard85] Girard, M; Amkraut, S; Karl, G. "Eurythmy," (Computer Graphics Video), *SIGGRAPH Video Review*, Issue 21, second entry. 1985.

[Reynolds01] Reynolds, Craig. "Boids: Background and Update," Web page available online at http://www.red3d.com/cwr/boids/ last updated 2001.

[Reynolds87] Reynolds, Craig. "Flocks, Herds, and Schools: A Distributed Behavioral Model, in Computer Graphics," 21(4) (SIGGRAPH '87 Conference Proceedings) pages 25–34. Also available online at http://www.red3d.com/cwr/papers/1987/boids.html.

[VanVerth00] Van Verth, Jim; Brueggemann, Victor; Owen, Jon; McMurry, Peter. "Formation-Based Pathfinding with Real-World Vehicles," *Proceedings*, 2000 Game Developers Conference. Also available online at http://www.essentialmath.com/vanverth00formationbased.pdf.

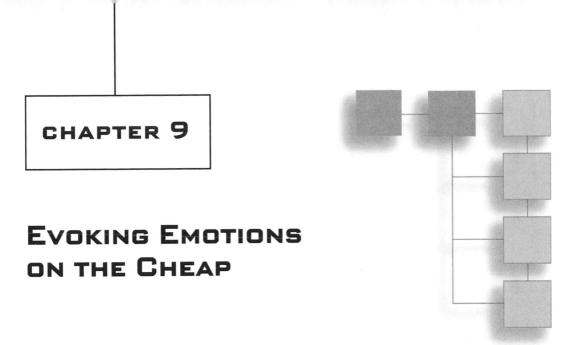

CHAPTER 9

EVOKING EMOTIONS ON THE CHEAP

One of the most difficult tasks in a computer game is to convey emotion. While some games have no room for emotional content, many more benefit greatly from it. Modern computers finally have the processing power and graphics capability needed to show a realistic-looking human face. Players have been conditioned since birth to instantly read nuances of human expression, but technology to show them is relatively new. With motion-capture data touched up by a professional animator, a simulated face and body stance can convey nearly anything. Things change when the AI is in charge.

The AI programmer's first protest is quite clear: "It's all I can do to get them to decide what to do. You mean I have to get them to decide what to *feel*?" Upon rising to face that challenge, the AI programmer faces the next hurdle: "How do I get the AI to show what it is feeling?" Many AI programmers lack professional training as artists, psychologists, and actors; worse yet, many of them are introverts, outside their comfort zone when dealing with emotionally charged content. Inexperienced AI programmers who also lack those skills and a wide comfort zone could easily conclude that there is no way for them to model and show emotions under the control of game AI. They would be wrong on both counts.

To start with, they are trying to solve the wrong problem. The core problem is *not* how to model and show emotion in games. Showing emotions is the core problem in realistic simulations such as the virtual Bosnian village given in [Gratch01]. Showing emotion is a secondary problem in games. This may sound completely counterintuitive; what could be more emotionally engaging than showing emotion? The real problem to solve in games is evoking an emotional response *in the player*. How we get there is a secondary problem and a free choice. In simulation, showing emotions is primary. Evoking emotions is secondary, but it is a strong indicator of success. As luck would have it, modeling emotions in games is not a particularly difficult problem. To varying degrees of fidelity, we can make our game AI feel at a level comparable to how well our AI thinks. We do need to keep foremost in our minds that the feelings that count are the player's feelings.

AI game programmers are afforded great liberties with the AI's "feelings." Everything from faking it to sophisticated models beyond the scope of this book is perfectly acceptable. Modeling feelings may be unfamiliar, but it is closely analogous to modeling thinking. In games, we are not required to particularly care about the AI's feelings. Even if the AI programmer creates a high-fidelity emotion system, the game designer may override the AI's feeling at any time. We are familiar with overrides from the behavior side already; the designer says, "Make it do *this, here*, regardless of what the AI thought it should do." The designer does this for dramatic impact. The designer may also say, "Make it feel angry here, regardless of what it wants to feel." The AI might have decided to feel depressed, or it might be coldly planning future retribution, but the designer wants anger for the emotional impact.

While we do not particularly care about what the AI is feeling, we care deeply about what the player is feeling. We especially care when the player has feelings about the virtual characters in the game. "I've saved them! I've saved them all!" the player shouts. On occasion, we can get the player to be affected by the feelings attributed to the virtual characters. "Oh, no! She's going to be really angry at me!" the player says. These are emotional responses from the player. They do not require emotions to actually be present in the virtual characters. People attach sentimental value to non-feeling objects in real life; they even attribute feelings to inanimate objects. Often, children worry about how lonely a lost toy is going to be more than they worry about how sad they will be if they never get it back.

The game succeeds when players feel compelled to describe their playing experiences to their friends with sentences that start out, "I was so..." and end with words like "pumped," "scared," "thrilled," or even "sad." Evoked emotions do not always have to be positive to be meaningful. Games are an art form capable of a wide range of expression, for good or ill. We have already seen that the real problem with bad AI is that it frustrates, annoys, or angers the player. We would like to avoid evoking those particular emotions in the player. The AI can be the most frustrating part of a computer game, but with some effort, it can also be one of the parts that evokes the strongest positive emotions.

Showing human faces expressing simulated emotions is a tremendously powerful tool for evoking an emotional response in the player, but it is far from being the only tool. There are other, less direct means—many of which are far cheaper to implement. Novice AI programmers might not want to start with the most complex tool available. We can evoke emotion via music, mood, plot, and even camera control. This is only a partial list; the AI can creep into nearly everything, giving the game better chances at evoking an emotional response from the player. These tend to be design elements, but they have to be controlled somehow, and that somehow is AI.

Before delving into other tools, we should recall our definition of game AI to see if what we will be doing is really AI. Our AI reacts intelligently to changing conditions. Things that will never change have no need of AI. A face that never changes expression or lighting that never changes or even music that never changes require no decisions. These static elements start out purely as art, music, and level design. These elements need not be static, but once they start changing, they raise the question, "How do we control the changes?" This is the realm of AI—even if artists, musicians, and level designers do not always think that way at first. Like any part of game AI, once it is well understood, it stops being AI to many people. Everyone knows how to go somewhere, but pedestrians, drivers, and pilots have different skills, levels of training, and available tools to get themselves someplace else. The job of the AI programmer is to bring intelligence into any part of the virtual world that would benefit from it. Doing so gives the entire creative team a richer palette of tools with which to craft an emotionally engaging experience. They all know how to "walk" but the AI programmer provides them a "pilot and plane" when they need one.

Before we get into how we might evoke an emotional response from the player, we will consider what emotions games evoke. After that, the bulk of this chapter will go over tools that can be used to evoke an emotional response in the player other than body posture and facial expression. These more indirect methods have an impact on what the AI programmer needs to know about other team member's jobs. This chapter concludes with a treatment of modeling emotional states using techniques ranging from simple to sophisticated. The projects for the chapter start out with simple touches, progress to an FSM for emotions, and finish with a relationship model loosely based on *The Sims*. In prior chapters, we have shown that beginners can learn how to program game AI for behaviors. In this chapter, we will show that modeling emotions can be just as accessible.

What Emotions Do Popular Games Invoke?

As a programmer, you may be thinking something along the lines of, "I'm a programmer, not a psychologist." But the emotions we are dealing with make a pleasantly short list. Our list, shown in Table 9.1, is taken from XEODesign's research into why people play games [Lazzaro04]. They observed people playing popular games and studied the players' responses and what triggered them. Words with a non-English origin are marked. This list is not meant to be exhaustive. For example, relief is not listed. Relief may be thought of as the removal of fear or feelings of pressure. This list was also aimed at emotions that come from sources other than story.

Table 9.1 Emotions and Their Triggers

Emotion	Common Themes and Triggers
Fear	Threat of harm, an object moving quickly to hit player, a sudden fall or loss of support, or the possibility of pain.
Surprise	Sudden change. Briefest of all emotions, does not feel good or bad. After interpreting the event, this emotion merges into fear, relief, etc.
Disgust	Rejection, as with food or behavior outside the norm. The strongest triggers are body products such as feces, vomit, urine, mucus, saliva, and blood.
Naches/kvell (Yiddish)	Pleasure or pride at the accomplishment of a child or mentee. (Kvell is how it feels to express this pride in one's child or mentee to others.)
Fiero (Italian)	Personal triumph over adversity. The ultimate game emotion. Overcoming difficult obstacles. Players raise their arms over their heads. They do not need to experience anger prior to success, but the accomplishment does require effort.
Schadenfreude (German)	Gloat over misfortune of a rival. Competitive players enjoy beating each other—especially a long-term rival. Boasts are made about player prowess and ranking.
Wonder	Overwhelming improbability. Curious items amaze players at their unusualness, unlikelihood, and improbability without breaking out of realm of possibilities.

The research showed these emotions link to the following four different ways of having fun [Lazzaro07]. It should hardly be a surprise that the most popular titles incorporate at least three of the four.

- **Hard fun:** The fun of succeeding at something difficult

- **Easy fun:** The fun of undirected play in a sandbox

- **Serious fun:** "Games as therapy": fun with a purpose

- **People fun:** The fun of doing something with others

Game designers must be fluent in these areas, and AI programmers should at least be familiar with them. The AI will be tasked with supporting these kinds of fun and evoking these emotions in the players. When designers ask for some "good AI," the AI programmer should ask if they mean "hard to beat" or "fun to play with" or something altogether different. In order for AI programmers to implement a good AI, they have to implement the *right* AI. Let us consider the many ways such an AI can express itself.

Music

Musicians will tell you that half the emotional content of a film is in the musical score. Music is a powerful tool for evoking a full range of responses in the player. Games have incorporated it since shortly after the first PC sound cards became available. Unlike films, games can exhibit a fluid control over their music and change it in response to player actions. Games can do more than pick what music fits a scene. Back in 1990, the game *Wing Commander* not only made smooth transitions in the music every two to four bars on beat boundaries, but it also transitioned instantly when there was a serious change in the game state, such as a missile chasing the player [Sanger93].

Something has to decide what to play and when. That something is just another form of AI with new outputs. At its simplest, music follows a fixed script with no changes based on player interaction. The designer says, "This is the music I want for this level." If the designer wants more out of the game, he or she will want player interaction to drive as much of the experience as possible. Interaction is the key differentiator between games and other media. "I need this game to react to what the player does and do something appropriate" are the marching orders for the AI, whether it is doing resource allocation in a strategy game or music selection in a flight simulator.

Music has similar drawbacks to facial expression. Music is complex and dynamic and hard to describe, but people almost innately respond to it. That is to say, critical listeners are far more common than skilled practitioners. Skilled game musicians are rarer still, but they exist, and the industry is growing. Designers will want to place certain demands on music. The AI programmer should be part of the process—and the earlier, the better. Because music is such a powerful tool, the designer may demand total control of all music changes. AI programmers might think that this takes them out of the loop, but they may be the people tasked with translating the designer's demands into code. As the designer's vision expands beyond the simplest triggers, the need for code to reason and react will increase. A holistic approach that includes considering "music AI" ensures that even if the music only has the simplest of changes, no creative capability was unintentionally excluded because no one thought about designing it in.

Mood

Mood here is a catch-all intended to pick up static elements, usually of a visual nature, that need not be static. Consider the possibilities when AI controls clothing, lighting, and even the very basic texture maps on the objects in the world. These are virtual worlds, after all, and the game studio has control over every bit of it. Mood elements easily play to fear, relief, wonder, and occasionally to surprise. They provide subtle support to the bold dramatic elements of the game.

Clothing

Clothing can be under AI control if there are sufficient art assets to support it. *Dress for Success* was originally published in 1975, but wardrobe designers for theatre have long used costuming as visual shorthand to communicate unspoken information to the audience. People are used to thinking about facial expressions, but wardrobe expression shows at longer ranges and uses less detail. By using a consistent wardrobe palette, especially one that is well understood by the public, the game designer can communicate information to the player in more subtle ways than facial expression, dialog, or music. That information can carry emotional content or evoke an emotional response. Players who are less tuned in can be clued in via dialog. Consider the following exchange:

"Uh, oh, this is going to be bad. He's wearing his black pin-stripe power suit."
"What do you mean?"

"He wears that to fire people and when he doesn't have a choice about ram-rodding something down people's throats. He wears his less-threatening navy-blue suit when he's selling something that actually needs our cooperation."

"That doesn't sound very friendly."

"If he wants you to relax, he'll shed the jacket or maybe even loosen the tie. That's when he asks you if you need to take some time off because your kid is in the hospital or something. He's not actually friendly unless he's wearing a golf shirt someplace other than here."

After that dialog, the game designer has prepped the player for the desired interpretations of the wardrobe choices presented. The designer has seeded potential emotional reactions that can be evoked by the game. Fear and trepidation get matched to the black pin-stripe suit. This is hardly new, but once again we have a venue for AI control. Scripting may provide enough control to manage wardrobe; after all, once upon a time it used to be sufficient for the entire AI of a game. Game AI in large part has left scripting behind for more dynamic techniques. These techniques are then applied to the more static elements as designers envision effective ways to exploit them.

Lighting

Lighting falls into our category of mood as well. Lighting used to be static because computers lacked the processing power to do anything else. But these days, dynamic lighting is a fact of life in games; watching your shadow on the floor shorten as a rocket flies toward your retreating backside warns you in a very intuitive way of your impending demise. Just like clothing selection, AI control puts lighting selection in the designer's bag of tricks.

One day, all designers are going to ask, "Can we get the AI to do the lighting selection?" A shifty character AI knows to turn off lights and meet only in dark places like poorly lit parking garages. A naïve community activist AI prefers brightly lit places and broad daylight. If we can teach the AI to tell time and to use a light switch, the AI can do its own lighting selection. If the activist AI likes candlelit dinners, we will have to teach the AI about candles as well. A virtual character who actively lights candles and turns lights off fishes for an emotional response from the player more directly than if the character simply meets with others in dark and spooky parking garages. The action is more noticeable than the ambience. The AI of the activist could also decide that it is annoyed and turn the lights back on and blow out the candles. Seeing that is likely to evoke an emotion in the player as well. Even if the AI can't handle candles, the emotional payloads delivered by turning the lights down and then back up compared to the low cost of having an AI that knows the difference between business and pleasure makes a strong case for AI-controllable lighting. An FSM might be all that is needed to model the emotional state of the AI.

The level of AI devoted to lighting control varies from the simple controls described earlier to the baked-into-the-game control seen in *Thief 3, Deadly Shadows* [Spector04]. AI-controlled dynamic lighting shows great promise for a more engaging player experience, especially with non-gamers and casual gamers. The ALVA lighting control system given in [El-Nasr09] improved player performance and lowered player frustration.

Unlike clothing, the additional asset cost for AI-controlled lighting is quite low. Light fixtures and light switches would already be in the level. Compared to outfits, soft lighting is cheap. Lighting is just as visual as clothing selection.

Texturing

Virtual characters are not the only things in a level that wear "clothing." As noted by Chris Hecker when he posited that one day there would be a *Photoshop of AI*, graphics rendering in games is done via texture-mapped triangles [Hecker08]. For those unfamiliar with graphics, a texture is an image that is applied to the geometric skin of an object, and that skin is built using triangles. A flat wooden door and a flat metal door might share the same geometric skin, but they use different textures to make that skin look like wood or metal. The graphics system can switch between those skins easily after an artist has created them both and they are loaded into the system. This takes us down the same rabbit hole into Wonderland that the rest of the chapter falls into. If it can be changed, that change will need control, and why not have the AI manage some of it?

This one really could take us to Wonderland. We start out being able to change the color of the leaves, which happens in the real world, and wind up wherever the crazed minds of artists and designers can take us. Imagine a world in which an unlimited supply of spray paint (including transparent) and wallpaper can be applied instantly to anything and everything, changing every time you blink or close your eyes. Shapes remain constant, but appearances change instantly.

Luckily, we do not have to go all the way into this Wonderland. More subtle and skilled artists could take us partway there, to a world where things change when we are not looking at them. Imagine a game featuring a house shared by a strange old man and his daughter. When he is home, the place is dirty and dingy, complete with the occasional cobweb on the inside and graffiti on the exterior. When she is home, it is clean and shiny; no cobwebs and no graffiti. What kind of emotional reactions are we evoking in the player when they interact with either character? Presume nothing bad ever happens to the player when he or she visits the house or interacts with either character. Given the cumulative effect on the player of exposure to countless horror movies of questionable value, what kind of emotional response is the player going to have every time he or she visits this house?

This kind of world inspires new genres of games. Imagine a God game in which the player is responsible for carrying out the orders of a capricious god modeled on some stereotypical gamer. The very walls of the buildings seem happy when the god is happy; you would certainly know who is recently out of favor and who has recently regained favor. This is fertile ground for evoking emotions in the player, limited by the imagination of the game designer, the skills of the artists, and the abilities of the AI programmer to keep it under control. Typical AI tries to simulate thoughts turning into actions. It is only a modest leap to transform this into simulating feelings and turning them into effects. We need only modest fidelity in the simulated feelings as long as the effects evoke the right emotions in the players.

Plot

The emotional responses we listed earlier were taken from gameplay outside of story. Plot provides rich opportunities for evoking emotions in the player. Consider a game in which the player runs a fragment of a conflict-torn country. He is joined by an advisor, who comes with supporting forces. The advisor gives sound advice and offers good ideas for the player to consider. Sometime later, the advisor betrays the player and goes over to the other side, helping lead the enemy. A typical emotional response to this is a feeling of betrayal, followed by an urge for revenge that revitalizes the player and prompts him or her to play the game to completion to defeat the traitor. If the betrayal is part of a fixed script, this setup is a plot device and not part of the AI. But what if the game design does not require the betrayal? What if the game decides whether or not to use this device? We are back to AI, possibly some very easy AI to write.

A rich game would use the same betrayal device both ways. A skilled player gets betrayed as described, but a struggling player would be gifted with the other side's advisor changing sides, bringing with him plans, support, and gratitude. This is just as likely to cause an emotional response in the player as being stabbed in the back. The positive feelings can be reinforced if the advisor occasionally thanks the player and offers up advice or volunteers to do dangerous missions.

The game AI could pick which way the betrayal works, or even if the betrayal happens at all. An experienced game designer will point out that branching scripts are hardly new and might claim that they are not AI. They are, as we saw in Chapter 2, "Simple Hard-Coded AI." They just do not require an AI programmer to script them. The scripting system itself is probably the work output of an AI programmer. The AI programmer does need to make sure that the scripting system does not get in the way of the designers, but instead frees and inspires them. Their needs might require the techniques of other chapters. The AI programmer may not have training as a playwright, but the AI programmer can ask the designers what tools they need to ensure that they can evoke an emotional response from the player. Someone else may write the script, but AI owns the action. It is possible for the AI to own the script, but this is rare.

In the game *Façade*, the AI owns the entire plot sequence. The AI interprets player input as best it can and reacts accordingly. In this one-act interactive drama, the AI has access to 27 plot elements, called *beats* in dramatic writing theory, and any particular run-through of the game typically encounters about 15 of them [Mateas05]. *Façade* certainly succeeds as interactive drama, but it is not the first thing people think of when they think about computer *games*. While it does not fit this chapter's "on the cheap" emphasis on techniques that are accessible to beginners, it does show just how far AI-controlled plot has already gone. For many designers, there are serious issues beyond abandoning control to the AI; *Façade* shows at most 25 percent of its total available content in any given run, often less. Unless the experience provides a compelling reason for repeated play, the rest of the assets are effectively wasted.

Somewhere between simple branching scripts and total AI control, designers find their particular sweet spot for AI interaction with the plot. This is the spot that the AI programmer must support. The simplest techniques can be added as necessary, but more complex capabilities must be designed in from the start.

Camera

It's no surprise that computer games are often called video games; this is due in part to their history, but also to the fact that games have such strong visual elements to them. We touched on camera AI in Chapter 2. Camera scripts allow the designer to take control of what the player sees and from what perspective. Camera scripts can be used to make sure that the player can appreciate all the work the art team has put into the game. Between the scripts and the artwork, there should be no problem with evoking emotions in the player. Did the runway survive the combat unscathed? A touch of camera AI at the right point in the game brings relief or dismay to the player without saying a word or showing a face.

There are two kinds of camera AI to consider. The camera AI described earlier is on behalf of the designer, who wants to achieve dramatic impact. Like many of the items in this chapter, the AI is simple to provide, and the real emphasis is on game design. There is also camera AI that is on behalf of the player. Such AI need not exist in first-person games, but when we leave first person for another point of view, we need camera AI. Third-person viewpoints, particularly the chase camera view, present interesting problems to the camera AI. The first problem to consider is when the camera hits a wall.

To fully appreciate the problem, a quick graphics refresher may be in order. Think of the objects in a 3D world as if they were blow-up balloons. Their geometry "blows them up" to their final shape, and we paint textures on the outside surfaces. In order to save CPU time, we don't paint on the inside surfaces; they might as well not exist. Real balloons are closed, so they hold air, and we want our objects to be closed so that no one can see inside them and spoil the illusion that they are solid objects.

Our objects can be as interesting as the real balloons seen in the Macy's New Year's Day Parade or as mundane as a flat sheet of wallboard. We use a mesh of flat triangles instead of curving air-tight fabric. It takes a large number of triangles to build a detailed world, particularly when our objects appear curved. The more triangles we consider and the longer we consider them, the slower our system draws.

One very easy way to reject a triangle is to check which way the triangle is facing. If the painted outside surface, known as the front face, is facing away from us, we do not need to draw the triangle. The unpainted back face is facing us, and no one is ever supposed to see it. As long as our object is closed—it "holds air"— and we are not inside it, we know that there is a front face somewhere on this object that is closer to the camera than the back face we are considering. This technique is called *back-face culling* and has been used to speed up rendering since the dawn of time in computer graphics. Roughly speaking, back-face culling lets us reject half the triangles of every object in the scene.

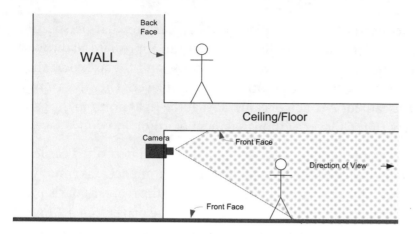

Figure 9.1
A third-person perspective camera is about to conflict with a wall.

Figure 9.1 shows an over-the shoulder camera view inside a two-story building. The figure on the first floor is the player. The player's views above and below are blocked by the front faces of the floor and ceiling. The player is facing away from the thick exterior wall shown. The shaded area indicates what the camera can see.

What happens if the player puts his back to the wall? We can either make the camera change viewpoint or let the camera penetrate the wall. At first blush, letting the camera penetrate the wall seems enticing. Back-face culling effectively removes the wall, so we will still see the player exactly as before. Figure 9.2 shows

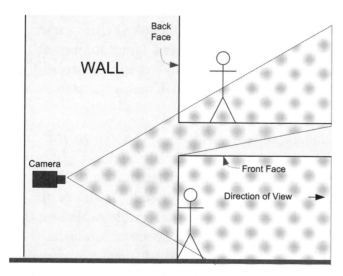

Figure 9.2
A camera inside the wall sees too much.

potential problems that happen when we let the camera get "inside" the geometry. We want it to look through the back face of the wall to show us the player, but the camera can also see through the back face of the floor above, showing us the lower half of the figure on the second floor. The field of view has extended past the corner of the ceiling and the wall, giving a partial view of the second floor. The front face of the ceiling still blocks the rest of the second floor. The problematic corner configuration seen in the side view of the wall and ceiling also shows up in top-down views when one wall meets another wall. When walls meet, a camera pushed inside the wall sees sideways past the walls of the current room.

The thick exterior wall makes this point of view possible. Because the first-floor ceiling does not extend into the wall, its front face no longer prevents us from seeing part of the upstairs. Extending the ceiling into the wall has two drawbacks. The first is that it adds triangles that will rarely be seen, making work for our artists and for our graphics pipeline for very little gain. The second is that if we put our back to the other side of the wall, the camera would again go into the wall; we would see the extended ceiling, *and there is not supposed to be a ceiling there!* Note that on the left side of the wall, the view is open to the sky; this is an exterior wall. This thick wall creates problems!

As shown in Figure 9.3, a thin wall presents problems, too. Figure 9.3 makes it clear that we cannot let the camera punch through walls from the inside heading

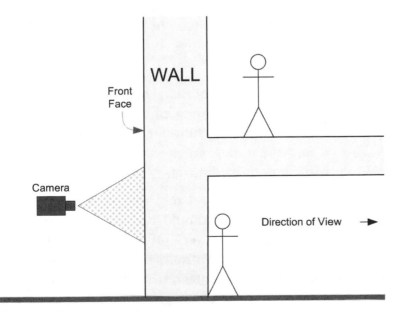

Figure 9.3
Thin walls present their own camera problems.

back out, or all we will see is a close-up of the other side of the wall we have our back to. It is clear that something must be done.

We might consider fighting the issues presented by Figure 9.2 and Figure 9.3 with tightly constrained level designs and careful attention to camera placement. A tall room with waist-high furniture gives the camera more space than the player has, keeping it out of trouble. A camera that is close to the player can penetrate walls without punching through the back side or seeing around corners. A narrow field of view keeps the camera from peeking into places other than where the player happens to be. All those limitations go out the window when a designer says, "That's too constraining, and third-person is too good to give up. Make the camera smart enough to keep itself out of trouble." Even if the designer allows a constrained level, the camera could conflict with mobile objects such as a taller character walking up behind the player. The view from inside a character is just as jarring as the view from inside a wall, and the camera needs to be smart enough to avoid it. This is camera AI on the player's behalf. The designer is really saying, "Keep the player's eyes out of trouble." It can be done, but great care must be taken to do it well.

Early camera AI of this type had some teething problems. The camera would make sudden and hard-to-anticipate changes in viewpoint to keep it out of trouble with the surrounding walls. Players fought against the camera AI as much as they fought off their enemies. The changing viewpoint changed the player's aim point, making combat while moving an exercise in frustration. All of this evoked an emotional response in the player, but disgust probably was not what the game designer had in mind.

Other games incorporated camera AI from the outset. The system described in [Carlise04] used steering behaviors and scripting to control the camera. They envisioned adding rules to the system for more "film-like" transitions. Effective camera AI adds to the player's enjoyment. Beyond effective camera AI, there is room for the camera AI to provide emotional impact.

The lesson for camera AI is that it is a powerful tool that needs to be used carefully. Taking control of the player's eyes should be done sparingly and carefully. Otherwise, it is easy to frustrate the player. (Of course, preventing the player from coming to harm while the AI is controlling the camera would be considerate.) But with the proper care and an integrated approach, having full control over the player's eyes is too powerful a tool to ignore, especially when the game is trying to create an emotional response in the player.

A Wide Skill Set

Cross-pollination is not possible without something to cross with. AI programmers do not have to be expert designers, artists, musicians, set designers, writers, or costume designers, but all of those skills are helpful. We could also add a touch of psychology and ergonomics for completeness. If the AI programmer lacks these skills, he or she needs to be able to ask the right questions of the team members who have them. The programmer also needs to be careful to always offer up his or her own special skills—making things think, or possibly making things feel—to the rest of the team. Working together, the team can produce games in which the richness of the interactivity produces a wide range of emotions in the players. To the player, having done something is fine, but having done something and felt good about it is better.

Much as the interactions of software agents give us emergent behaviors, so do the interactions between team members on a game cause a game to emerge. This is why good communication skills are commonly listed on job openings. For AI programmers, having a wide range of knowledge in other areas improves communication with the members of the team who are working in those areas. There is a great deal of synergy, particularly when AI programmers and animators work closely together to solve each other's problems. AI programmers should exploit the expertise of the sound designer if the team is blessed with one. Recall that emergent behavior depends on the richness of the interactions; if the agents do not react to other agents' behaviors, then nothing emerges. The first step for the AI programmer is speaking "their" language; the next steps are seeing things their way and offering his or her own abilities as a solution to their problems. If the AI programmer can talk to the rest of the team, one of the problems that he or she can help solve is when a designer says, "I'd like the player to feel. . . ."

Modeling Emotional States

Computer games have modeled emotions for a very long time. In 1985, *Balance of Power* modeled not only integrity, but pugnacity and nastiness as well [Crawford86]. While the first two might be deemed merely an observation of the facts, nastiness is close enough for our purposes to be considered as a modeled emotion. Since then, games have made great strides in modeling emotions.

Most of this chapter talks about evoking an emotional response in the player. Some of the methods imply that the AI itself has emotions to display. How do we model the emotional state of the AI? For many AIs, an FSM is sufficient to model emotional states. *The Sims* does not directly model emotions, but it does model relationships. More complex systems store emotional state as a small collection of numeric values, each indicating the strength of the feeling. A single emotion might range from 0 to +100. Opposing emotions such as fear and confidence can be interpreted from a single stored value. This might call for a range of −100 to +100. The different emotions that can coexist are each stored as a separate value. Numerical methods can then be applied to the collection to determine how the emotional state should affect actions. We will examine a range of emotional models, starting with a simple addition to an FSM.

An FSM works for emotions as long as we only need a single emotion at a time. Recall from Chapter 3, "Finite State Machines (FSMs)," that FSMs work best when we have short answers to "I am. . . ." Our simple-minded monster was attacking, fleeing, or hiding. The simplest possible way to make our monster feel would be to map a single emotion to each of the existing action states. It could be angry when attacking, afraid when fleeing, and happy when hiding. These are all believable for the conditions, and the amount of effort to implement them is extremely low. We get into trouble when we lack a clear mapping between what our AI is doing and what it is feeling, or when we are not already using an FSM.

The next level of sophistication would be to use a separate FSM for the emotional state of the AI. This allows a more sophisticated AI for actions than an FSM. A sports-coach AI might use a book of moves for action selection but could be augmented with an FSM for feelings. One coach AI may exhibit questionable judgment when it is upset or angry. A different coach AI might be programmed to show brilliance only when under pressure. In both cases, the emotional state of the AI is influencing its actions. If the game foreshadows these traits before using them and telegraphs the AI's feelings when they are active, the player enjoys a richer experience.

The killer weaknesses of an FSM are that it can only be in one state at a time and that there are no nuances for a given state. For this reason, an FSM should be used only for the very simplest of emotional models. An FSM used this way does not allow the time-honored device of emotions in conflict. When we need to model more than one emotion at a time, and those emotions need a range of intensity, we are forced to use other techniques. Thankfully, those techniques present a range of complexity.

The game *The Sims* does not directly model emotions at all [Doornbos01]. But the Sims make friends, fall in love, and acquire enemies. How can they do that without emotions? The Sims do not have emotions, but they do have needs, preferences (traits), and relationships. Friends, lovers, and enemies are a function of the relationships between the Sims. The psychological model for the Sims is that a strong positive relationship is created between Sims that meet each other's needs through shared interests. As a basis for relationships, real-world experience suggests that this one is pretty bulletproof. The Sims all have needs such as needs for food, comfort, fun, and social interactivity. Each individual Sim has a small number of traits selected from a much longer list of possible traits. These traits provide each Sim with individual preferences. Each Sim keeps its own relationship score with every other Sim it has met. Relationship scores need not be mutual. The relationship score runs from -100 to $+100$.

Positive interactions build the relationship score, and negative interactions reduce it. All Sims act to meet their most pressing need. The interaction that one Sim prefers to use to meet a need might not be an interaction preferred by the other Sim. The preferences color the interaction, changing each Sim's relationship score with the other. If both Sims like the interaction, they both react positively. Thus, meeting needs through shared preferences builds positive relationships. It is not modeling emotions, but it certainly has proven effective.

Instead of modeling needs, other systems directly model emotions. The same -100 to $+100$ range that *The Sims* uses for needs is instead used for emotions. Often thought of as "sliders" (vertical scrollbars), each one carries a pair of opposed emotions. One might be joy versus sadness. Other pairs include acceptance versus disgust or fear versus anger. A small number suffices because the number of combinations grows very rapidly as more sliders are added. The system deals with all of the emotions combined, so look at the combinations to see if two emotions that are directly modeled give you an emotion that you are thinking of adding.

On this core data, an input and output system is required. It is pointless to model an emotion that the system cannot show. It is equally pointless to model a feeling that is only subtly different from other feelings. If the player cannot tell the difference, there is no difference. Just as in personality modeling, a broad brush is required. A few archetypes suffice. The system can output feelings directly into expression and posture if the animation assets to support them exist. It can output them indirectly through the kind of techniques described earlier in this chapter.

The input system has to make emotional sense of the world. Strong emotions fade over time, but the AI has to react to events in the world around it. The simplest methods concentrate on the impact of what directly happens to the AI. Taking damage causes anger or fear. Winning the game causes joy. Restricting emotions to direct inputs gives rise to a lack of depth in characters. If the AI has more depth, it needs to respond emotionally to events in the world that happened to something else.

More sophisticated AIs, particularly AIs that have plans and goals, can evaluate how events will affect their plans and goals and react with appropriate emotions [Gratch00]. This makes intuitive sense to people. Consider two roommates sharing their first apartment. The first roommate has a car, and the second one occasionally borrows it. What kind of emotional responses do we get when something goes wrong? "What do you mean, it's no big deal that you got a flat and they will come out and fix it tomorrow? Of course you're paying for it, but you don't understand! I was going to drive to my girlfriend's tonight!" The AI had a plan in place to achieve a goal, and that plan has been ruined. This is a perfect place for a negative emotion on the part of the AI. If the AI had a different plan to achieve the same goal, it would have a much different emotional response. "It's a good thing she's picking me up tonight. They better have it fixed by noon when I need to drive to work." AI that deals in plans and goals is briefly touched upon in Chapter 10, "Topics to Pursue from Here." As you study them, keep in the back of your mind how to incorporate emotional modeling into the AI. Writing an AI that voices its feelings using the spoken lines that illustrate this paragraph remains a very hard problem, even for experts. The point here is not to have an AI that speaks its feelings. The spoken text is used here as a vehicle to convey the emotional response of the AI to events that affect the AI's plans. As we have seen, modeling emotions is not particularly difficult. Modifying a planning AI to help drive the emotional model is not a task for beginners, but it should present far fewer challenges to an AI programmer experienced with planning AIs.

As we have seen, the core data needed to model emotions is the easy part. The input and output systems carry more complexity. As you might expect, tuning the system as a whole is critical. There are some general guidelines. The first is that a handful of modeled emotions is enough. The range of 0 to +100 is also enough. Finer gradations do not improve the system. The hard stop of +100 or −100 is also perfectly acceptable; people can only get so angry, and as long as they do not have a stroke, more bad news will not make them any angrier. Less obvious is that effects—both input and output—need not be linear. The effect of the food need in *The Sims* is not linear. The difference in happiness between a fed Sim and a very well fed Sim is very small, even if one carries a need of +10 and the other a need of $+100$. The difference in drive between a hungry Sim (-10) and a starving Sim (-100) is far more than a linear difference. The same idea could be applied to how anger affects good judgment; a small amount of anger creates a small impairment in inhibition, but serious anger drives the AI into actions that provide immediate satisfaction, regardless of their long-term cost. There is a wide array of non-linear curves suitable for modeling emotions. The behavioral mathematics of game AI is the subject of an entire book [Mark09]. Beginning AI programmers should know that simple linear equations will not be enough. Evaluation and selection functions are prime candidates for implementing these emotional effects.

Advantages

Concentrating on evoking an emotional response from the player instead of on displaying the emotional states of AI agents gives game designers considerable latitude if they wish to exploit it. A holistic approach leaves no stone unturned in the quest to pack impact into the game. For many of the avenues, the costs are reasonable and the technical risks quite low. When games also demand good modeling of emotional states, they can pick a level of sophistication appropriate to their needs. The net effect of actively managing emotional content is a game to which players will have much stronger reactions than any otherwise equivalent competition.

Disadvantages

The fact that emotional content under the control of some form of AI can be packed into nearly all aspects of a game means that doing so will have a schedule impact across the board. A number of low-cost items may not sum to an acceptable overall cost. Paying that cost is a gamble. Not all players will react in the same way to the emotional content of a game. Players who are sensitive and observant will have markedly different reactions from players who are not. There are players who are clueless about clothing, lighting, or even the impact of a dirty environment compared to a clean one. It is a well-understood concept in game AI circles that the AI can be too subtle to be appreciated.

Evoking emotions on the cheap does not free many games from the need to directly model emotions and display them graphically through facial expression and body stance. Games that put emotional content front and center this way may not have the budget to pack emotion into every possible additional avenue available. The designer may decide that having a main character show emotion is all that is required.

Dealing in emotions at all forces a broad swath of people to become aware of the potential to deliver emotional content, like it or not. Even when AI can accurately make the decisions, the rest of the game has to be able to exploit them. It may be the case that the rest of the team is not equipped with the analytical skills needed to judge the emotional impact of their work so that they can create multiple alternatives.

The emotional payload of the more nuanced effects requires a cultural context. The difference between a black pin-stripe suit and a navy-blue one will be lost in cultures where no one wears a suit. Worse than an "I don't get it" response is when the cues confuse or worse yet offend the player. These techniques can easily be the unwitting vehicle of hidden stereotypes and unintentional disrespect. A nuanced world in front of a clueless player is wasted effort. A clueless design in front of a sensitive player has the all of the makings of a perfect Internet flame storm. The last thing any game company needs is an eloquent player who feels disrespected and yanked around emotionally.

Projects

Pac-man showed us that simply changing the color of the ghosts not only told the player that the ghosts were vulnerable, it helped imply that they were afraid of the player. For our project we will add some color to our FSM monster AI from Chapter 3. That way, we can tell how it is feeling. After we do that, we will give the emotions their own FSM that is separate from the FSM that controls actions. After giving our monster emotions, we will model the relationships between passengers on a cruise ship.

Using Action States for Emotion States

We will model the emotional state of our monster using the same states it uses for thinking. Our monster, when it attacks, is healthy and angry, so we will use pink as our color for that state. When out monster flees, it is wounded and afraid; we will use light gray for that state. When our monster is calmly hiding, its protective camouflage turns it green. We can do this with three lines added to the entry functions of the three states.

Open the project and edit the AttackState.vb class. Add the following line to the Update() routine:

```
World.BackColor = Color.Pink
```

Switch to the FleeState.vb class. Add the following line to the Update() routine:

```
World.BackColor = Color.LightGray
```

Switch to the HidingState.vb class. Add the following line to the Update() routine:

```
World.BackColor = Color.LightGreen
```

Run the code and watch the background of the form change color with the state of the AI. We have no visual representation of our monster, but we can tell at a glance how it is feeling. Unfortunately, this forces our monster to be happy any time it is hiding, even if it is near death and unwilling to fight. The mapping between our action states and the emotional states is imperfect. It is time to give our monster a more sophisticated set of feelings.

Using a Separate FSM for Emotions

Comment out or completely remove the three lines you just added and run the program to make sure that all of them are inoperative. We are going to add a separate FSM to model the monster's feelings. We will need three new states, but we can reuse the existing transitions. Once we have created the states, adding them to the AI will be very easy. Add a new class to the project and name it FeelHappy.vb. Just inside the class definition, add the following code:

```
Inherits BasicState
```

After you press Enter, VB will populate the required skeletons. Add code until your file looks like the following:

```
Public Class FeelHappy
    Inherits BasicState

    Public Sub New()
        Dim Txn As BasicTransition
        'Get angry if I see intruders while healthy.
        Txn = New SeePlayerHighHealthTxn()
        'Set the next state name of that transition.
        Txn.Initialize(GetType(FeelAngry).Name)
        'Add it to our list of transitions.
        MyTransitions.Add(Txn)
```

```
        'I react to health - if low, be afraid.
        Txn = New LowHealthTxn()
        'Set the next state name of that transition.
        Txn.Initialize(GetType(FeelAfraid).Name)
        'Add it to our list of transitions.
        MyTransitions.Add(Txn)
    End Sub

    Public Overrides Sub Entry(ByVal World As Monster)
        World.Say("I feel happy now.")
    End Sub

    Public Overrides Sub ExitFunction(ByVal World As Monster)

    End Sub

    Public Overrides Sub Update(ByVal World As Monster)
        World.BackColor = Color.LightGreen
    End Sub
End Class
```

VB will complain because we have transitions to states that do not exist yet. Add a new class to the project. Name it FeelAfraid.vb and make it inherit from BasicState. Add code until your file looks like the following:

```
Public Class FeelAfraid
    Inherits BasicState

    Public Sub New()
        Dim Txn As BasicTransition

        'Order is important.
        'Get angry if I see intruders while healthy.
        Txn = New SeePlayerHighHealthTxn()
        'Set the next state name of that transition.
        Txn.Initialize(GetType(FeelAngry).Name)
        'Add it to our list of transitions.
        MyTransitions.Add(Txn)

        'If healthy and no intruder, I am happy.
        Txn = New HighHealthTxn()
        'Set the next state name of that transition.
        Txn.Initialize(GetType(FeelHappy).Name)
```

```
      'Add it to our list of transitions.
      MyTransitions.Add(Txn)
   End Sub
   Public Overrides Sub Entry(ByVal World As Monster)
      World.Say("I feel afraid!")
   End Sub

   Public Overrides Sub ExitFunction(ByVal World As Monster)

   End Sub

   Public Overrides Sub Update(ByVal World As Monster)
      World.BackColor = Color.LightGray
   End Sub
End Class
```

We only need one more state. Add a new class to the project. Name it FeelAngry.vb and make it inherit from BasicState. Add code until your file looks like the following:

```
Public Class FeelAngry
   Inherits BasicState

   Public Sub New()
      Dim Txn As BasicTransition

      'Order is important - react to health first.

      'I react to health - if low, be afraid.
      Txn = New LowHealthTxn()
      'Set the next state name of that transition.
      Txn.Initialize(GetType(FeelAfraid).Name)
      'Add it to our list of transitions.
      MyTransitions.Add(Txn)

      'If healthy and no intruder, I am happy.
      Txn = New NoPlayersTxn()
      'Set the next state name of that transition.
      Txn.Initialize(GetType(FeelHappy).Name)
      'Add it to our list of transitions.
      MyTransitions.Add(Txn)

   End Sub
```

```
    Public Overrides Sub Entry(ByVal World As Monster)
        World.Say("I feel so angry!")
    End Sub

    Public Overrides Sub ExitFunction(ByVal World As Monster)

    End Sub

    Public Overrides Sub Update(ByVal World As Monster)
        World.BackColor = Color.Pink
    End Sub
End Class
```

What remains is to put those states into an FSM and wire that FSM to the user interface. We need a new FSM for the feelings. Switch to the code for Monster.vb and locate the declaration for the monster's Brains. Add code for feelings so that we have two FSMs as follows:

```
'We need an FSM.
Dim Brains As New FSM
'We need to feel as well as act.
Dim Feelings As New FSM
```

Now that we have a new FSM machine for feelings, we need to load it with states. Add the following lines to Monster_Load() below the lines that states into Brains:

```
'Load our feelings (make the start state appropriate).
Feelings.LoadState(New FeelHappy)
Feelings.LoadState(New FeelAfraid)
Feelings.LoadState(New FeelAngry)
```

Now we have to tell our monster to examine its feelings. Locate ThinkButton_Click() and add the following line to make our monster feel each time it thinks:

```
Feelings.RunAI(Me)
```

Now run the project. Lower the monster's hit points first and watch it become afraid while hiding. When we piggy-backed the monster's feeling onto its actions, we could not make it feel that way while it was hiding. Run it through the rest of the transitions to make sure that its feelings match the conditions. If we need finer-grained control, we could have the feeling FSM react to different levels of hit points than the action FSM machine uses. Our monster might be in combat, take damage, feel afraid but stay in combat, take more damage, and then flee.

Our monster provides better feelings when the feelings are controlled in their own FSM. We still use the simple display techniques, but we improved the emotional model. Our monster is not very sophisticated, so an FSM fills its emotional needs easily.

Now that we have a separate emotional model, we can use the emotional state to influence the behaviors of the AI. We are attempting to directly express emotions with color, but we can also indirectly express emotions with altered behaviors. Direct expression of emotion is more accessible to the player, but indirect expression may be more accessible to the AI programmer. Good AI practice is to attempt both; if the player sees that an AI character is visibly angry, the player will expect the AI character to *act* angry as well. (See Exercise 3 at the end of the chapter.)

Modeling Needs and Relationships

For our final project, we will model needs and relationships instead of modeling emotions directly. As with *The Sims*, meeting needs through shared interests will build relationships. Our project purports to be the social director of a cruise ship. The director mixes people into pairs to share activities together. The director uses a mix of intentional and random elements when selecting matchups and activities. The director makes sure that people with strong needs get those needs met. The director randomly picks partners for the people with strong needs. The activities are selected at random from those activities that will meet the need. Over time, the interactions will build relationships. Let us examine the details needed to make this general description clear.

We will model only three needs: exercise, culture, and dining. Everyone starts with random values for each of their three needs. Needs can range from -100 to $+100$, with negative values implying an unmet need and positive values implying a met need. We will make sure that everyone starts with the sum of all of their needs equal to zero. This is a design decision that is tunable. We also will limit the initial range of any one need to -20 to $+20$, another tunable design decision. Each turn, every need is reduced in value by 10. Every time a person does an activity, the corresponding need is incremented by 30, exactly balancing the net drop to be zero, keeping our system in balance.

Each need will have three activities that meet that need. Exercise is met by swimming, tennis, and working out. Going to the movies, on a tour, or to a play meets the culture need. The available dining pleasures include French cuisine, Asian cuisine, and pub fare. We will keep these activities in a mini-database.

Each person will have a full set of randomly picked individual preferences, one for every activity available. This differs from *The Sims*, which has a small number of traits selected from a far larger list. The preferences are used along with needs to judge how a person will react to a given activity. Preferences range from -2 to $+2$, another tunable design decision. Positive values denote the person liking the activity. The net sum of all preferences is not constrained; the simulation includes people with both positive and negative viewpoints on life as a whole.

Everyone also tracks one-way relationship scores with all the people they have interacted with. This score starts at 0 and has no limit. Relationships are not required to be mutual. The scores are updated every time two people interact. A positive score implies a positive relationship.

There are three terms that influence the relationship score with each shared activity. The first term can be thought of as the "we think alike" term. If both parties share a positive or negative preference for an activity that they do together, it is a positive influence on the relationship. With this term, "We both hated it" builds relationships just as well as "We both loved it." This term is computed by multiplying the two preference values together. For example if one person dislikes (-1) pub fare and his partner strongly dislikes (-2) it, this term yields $+2$ for their relationship every time they get to dislike it together.

In addition to mutual preferences, individual preferences also count, giving us a second term to add into our relationship score. If either of the individuals likes the activity, it adds to their relationship score; if they do not like the activity, it subtracts. This "I like it" term allows our people to take their own opinions into account. Note that this second term need not be the same for both people. Whether the two people think alike or not, each individual still has independent preferences and wants to be catered to.

The third term in the score is need based instead of preference based. As a bonus, if the activity matches to an unmet need in *both* people, it adds to the relationship; regardless of the food, hungry people prefer to dine with other hungry people. All together, positive relationships are built between people who have shared preferences, do things they like to do, and meet shared needs. This bonus "we needed that" term picks up on any shared needs.

Unlike *The Sims*, our people do not get to pick what they do or who they do it with. Each round, our cruise director puts everyone into a pool of candidates. The director selects the person in the pool with the strongest need. The director randomly picks that person's partner, but the activity picked matches the first person's strongest need. The activity is also randomly picked. The pair is removed from the pool, and the selection process is repeated until the pool of people is empty. The random pairing and selection drives toward all the people doing all the activities with all the other people. This is not intended as a game mechanic, but as a way to validate the simulation by driving toward good coverage of the interaction space. We know that left to themselves, people would self-select toward their own preferences and established friends.

In addition to the needs, preferences, and relationships, we will compute some other scores to help us make sense of the simulation. Our people have their own views on life, computed as the simple sum of all of their preferences. We expect people with a positive view on life to more easily build positive relationships because they like to do more things. We expect the reverse as well. We will also compute how opinionated each person is by taking the average of the sum of the squares of their preferences. Strongly opinionated people might be candidates for strong relationships, positive or negative. We certainly expect people with weaker opinions to build their relationships more slowly. The final derived score we keep is compatibility. Compatibility between two people is computed by multiplying the matching preferences of each person and summing the result. Since the first term of the relationship score is based on multiplying the two values of a single preference, we expect compatibility to help predict strong relationships.

Why do we compute the extra numbers? The derived values are to help us predict and tune. Our system mixes determinism with random chance, so trends may be slow to emerge. The preferences and needs for our people will be randomly initialized; these numbers will make it easier for us to see if any particular set of people will make for interesting interactions. Compatibility score is one of our better predictors; without some strong values in the mix, the simulation is boring. This has game design implications; randomly generated characters are fine so long as they are not all boring randomly generated characters. Let us build the simulation and see how they turn out.

User Interface

Our user interface will be quite simple, as shown in Figure 9.4.

1. Launch Visual Basic if it is not already running.

2. Create a new Windows Forms Application project and name it CruiseDirector.

Figure 9.4
The user interface for the CruiseDirector project.

3. In the Solution Explorer window, rename Form1.vb to Cruise.vb.

4. Click the form in the editing pane and change the Text property to Cruise Director.

5. Add a button to the form. Change the Text property to People and the Name property to PeopleButton.

6. Add another button to the form. Change the Text property to Dump and the Name property to DumpButton.

7. Add a third button to the form. Change the Text property to 1 Time and the Name property to Button1Time.

8. Add a fourth button to the form. Change the Text property to 100 Times and the Name property to Button100Times. You may need to make the button wider to fit the text.

9. Save the project.

Helpers

We will begin our design from the core data and work our way outward. To do that, we start our thinking from the outside and work inward. We will need a class for people. We know that each person has needs, preferences, and relationships to store. The values for all three kinds of data are integers, but we would like to tag them with names and pass them around. Our lowest-level chunk of data will be a simple name-value pair object. Our people class will use it, and our mini-database will need it, too. The data is so simple that we will let other code manipulate it directly.

Add a class to the project and name it NVP.vb. When the editor opens, add two lines of code to the file as follows:

```
Public Class NVP
    Public name As String
    Public value As Integer
End Class
```

Needs and preferences will be initialized to random integer values when we create a person. To get those random values, we need a helper function. We will use the concept of rolling an N-sided die to get our integer random values. The code is extremely useful in a variety of games. Add a module to the project and name it Dice.vb. Add code to the file as follows:

```
Module Dice
    'Get one roll on an N-sided die.
    Public Function getDx(ByVal dots As Integer) As Integer
        Return CInt(Int((Rnd() * dots) + 1))
    End Function
End Module
```

The Mini-Database

Between the name-value pair helper object and VB's Collection object, we are ready to make our mini-database. The database stores the available activities along with the need each activity meets. The database also keeps a list of needs met by the activities. We will use the database when we create a person. From the list of needs, it can create a set of randomly initialized needs for a person. Likewise, it can create and initialize a set of randomly initialized preferences from the list of activities. We will also use the database to help the cruise director. When the director gets the strongest need, the director will want a random activity to meet that need. And when we print out the relationship data, we will need a list of available activities. The mini-database simplifies the rest of the code considerably; if it gets initialized cleanly, everything else just works.

Add a class to the project and name it MiniDB.vb. Add initialization code so that it resembles the following:

```
Public Class MiniDB
    'ToDo is activities grouped by need (a collection of collections).
    Dim ToDo As New Collection
    'Simple list of names of needs.
```

```
    Dim Needs As New Collection
    'Simple list of names of activities.
    Dim ActivityNames As New Collection

    Public Sub Add(ByVal Activity As String, ByVal Satisfies As String)
        Dim Category As Collection
        If Not ToDo.Contains(Satisfies) Then
            'Must be a new need.
            Debug.WriteLine("Creating " & Satisfies)
            Needs.Add(Satisfies)
            'Different needs get their own category.
            Category = New Collection
            ToDo.Add(Category, Satisfies)
        Else
            Category = CType(ToDo.Item(Satisfies), Collection)
        End If

        'Now add the activity to the category.
        If Not Category.Contains(Activity) Then
            Debug.WriteLine("Adding " & Activity & " to " & Satisfies)
            Category.Add(Activity, Activity)
        End If

        'Keep a simple list of names of activities.
        If Not ActivityNames.Contains(Activity) Then
            ActivityNames.Add(Activity, Activity)
        End If
    End Sub
End Class
```

When our main code initializes the database, it will add each activity with its need to the database. The ToDo collection of collections lets us use a need name to get a collection of activities that meet that need. The name of the need is used as a key in ToDo to find the subtending collection. Along the way, we keep simple lists of activities and needs so that other code can iterate through them. Much of the rest of the code keeps us from adding the same thing twice or does explicit type conversions.

Since everything depends on the database, we should see if we can initialize it. Switch to the Code view of Cruise.vb and add code as follows:

```
Public Class Cruise
    Dim Roster As New Collection
    Dim MDB As New MiniDB
```

```
Private Sub Cruise_Load(ByVal sender As System.Object, _
          ByVal e As System.EventArgs) Handles MyBase.Load
    Randomize()

    'Load up the database.
    MDB.Add("tennis", "exercise")
    MDB.Add("swimming", "exercise")
    MDB.Add("workout", "exercise")
    MDB.Add("movie", "culture")
    MDB.Add("tour", "culture")
    MDB.Add("drama", "culture")
    MDB.Add("French cuisine", "dining")
    MDB.Add("Asian cuisine", "dining")
    MDB.Add("pub fare", "dining")

    'Add people using the people button code.
    'Call PeopleButton_Click(Nothing, Nothing)
  End Sub
End Class
```

Our cruise director needs a database and people, so the first thing we did was to declare variables for them. Upon form load, the Randomize() call reseeds the random number generator so that we get a different run every time. Then the code adds activities to the database. At the end, it will eventually add a new group of people by using the PeopleButton_Click event handler. For now, we leave that call commented out. Run the code in the debugger and check the debugging output in the Immediate window. You should see each activity load in the proper place.

Now that our database can be created, we can add the code that accesses the data. Switch back to MinDB.vb in the editor. We will start with the database code needed to help create a person. People will require needs and preferences; we will add them in that order. Add the following code to the MiniDB class:

```
'Give some person a set of initialized needs.
  Public Function SetOfNeeds() As Collection
      Dim PersonalNeeds As New Collection
      Dim net As Integer = 0
      Dim need As String
      Dim thisNeed As NVP = Nothing
      For Each need In Needs
          thisNeed = New NVP
          thisNeed.name = need
```

```
        'These variability parameters are tunable!
        thisNeed.value = 21 - getDx(41)
        PersonalNeeds.Add(thisNeed, need)
        net += thisNeed.value
    Next
    'Everyone has a net of zero; adjust a random need.
    'Net of zero is another tuning parameter!
    If Needs.Count > 0 Then
        'Get the random need.
        thisNeed = CType(PersonalNeeds(getDx(Needs.Count)), NVP)
        'Adjust it to make our net be zero.
        thisNeed.value -= net
    Else
        Debug.WriteLine("cannot create SetOfNeeds: No needs in database.")
    End If
    Return PersonalNeeds
End Function

'Give a person a set of individual preferences.
'Preferences run from -2 to +2.
Public Function SetOfPreferences() As Collection
    Dim PersonalPreferences As New Collection
    Dim Activity As String
    For Each Activity In ActivityNames
        Dim thisPreference As New NVP
        thisPreference.name = Activity
        'The variability here is a tuning parameter.
        'Five minus three gives -2 to +2.
        thisPreference.value = getDx(5) - 3
        'Seven minus four gives -3 to +3.
        'thisPreference.value = getDx(7) - 4
        PersonalPreferences.Add(thisPreference, Activity)
    Next
    Return PersonalPreferences
End Function
```

Note in the comments where it calls out the tunable parameters. Initial values for needs are restricted to −20 to +20 in range, except that a random need is forced to yield a net of zero. Both the range and the net of zero are tunable and will make a difference in the simulation. Recall that we give a bonus to relationships if both parties have an unmet need that the activity in question satisfies. If we move the balance point up from zero, that bonus becomes less likely. If we make the net sum of the need values a negative number, the bonus will become more likely; if everyone is always hungry, they will always enjoy eating together. If we allow extreme ranges in the starting values, some of the people will be quite single-minded for the first part of the simulation, and it will take longer for the true long-term trends to emerge. If we do not allow somewhat extreme values, our people will lack interesting diversity.

Preferences are also tunable. Because preference values will be added sometimes and multiplied other times, the range is important. Increasing the range of preference values makes strong preferences more dominant in the relationship score. The code for a range of −3 to +3 is given as comments. Running the simulation with the wider range is left as an exercise, but it is well worth doing. So far, our simulation has three tuning knobs to adjust, and it is a good experience for AI programmers to try their hand at tuning a simulation.

The cruise director needs the database to pick an activity and to give the list of activities. We will add that code now to finish up the database. Add the following to the MiniDB class:

```
'Get a random activity for this need.
Public Function ActivityForNeed(ByVal Satisfies As String) As String

    'Find the collection of activities for this need.
    If ToDo.Contains(Satisfies) Then
        'We have a collection for this need, get access to it.
        Dim category As Collection = CType(ToDo.Item(Satisfies), Collection)
        'Pick a random item.
        Dim i As Integer = getDx(category.Count)
        'The lower-level collection holds activity names (strings).
        Return CStr(category(i))
    Else
        Debug.WriteLine("Error: MiniDB unable to meet need " & Satisfies)
        Return ""
    End If
End Function

'What is the master list of activities?
Public Function ActivityList() As Collection
    'Give them a copy of our list instead of our actual list.
    Dim alist As New Collection
    Dim activity As String
    'Copy from our list to theirs.
    For Each activity In ActivityNames
        alist.Add(activity, activity)
```

```
        Next
        Return alist
    End Function
```

That completes the code for the mini-database. We can now initialize the needs and preferences of our people, so we should work on people next.

The Person Class

Create a class and call it Person.vb. We start with the data we store and the code that does initialization. Add code to the class as follows:

```
Public Class Person
    Dim myname As String
    Dim myNeeds As New Collection
    Dim myPreferences As New Collection
    Dim myRelationships As New Collection

    Public Sub New(ByVal name As String, ByVal MDB As MiniDB)
        myname = name
        'Load all of the needs.
        myNeeds = MDB.SetOfNeeds
        'Load my preferences.
        myPreferences = MDB.SetOfPreferences
    End Sub
End Class
```

All our people require to start is their name and a database from which to get their needs and preferences. People will lack any relationships until they start to interact. The cruise director needs to know their highest need. Add the following to the Person class:

```
    'What is my highest need? We need both the name and value.
    Public Function HighestNeed() As NVP
        'Default to our first need.
        Dim highNeed As NVP = CType(myNeeds(1), NVP)
        Dim someNeed As NVP
        For Each someNeed In myNeeds
            'If we find a bigger need use it instead.
            If someNeed.value < highNeed.value Then highNeed = someNeed
        Next
        Return highNeed
    End Function
```

In addition, the simulation will want to call for adjustments to the needs. Needs get stronger over time and interactions satisfy a need. Add the following code to the Person class:

```
'We interacted to meet some need.
Public Sub EaseNeed(ByVal Need As String)
    Dim someNeed As NVP = CType(myNeeds(Need), NVP)
    '30 is picked to balance 3 needs that drop 10 each turn.
    someNeed.value += 10 * myNeeds.Count
    'Clip at +100.
    If someNeed.value > 100 Then someNeed.value = 100
End Sub

'Every turn we need more.
Public Sub IncAllNeeds()
    Dim someNeed As NVP
    'All my needs get 10 points worse.
    For Each someNeed In myNeeds
        someNeed.value -= 10
        'Clip at -100.
        If someNeed.value < -100 Then someNeed.value = -100
    Next
End Sub
```

The code for meeting a need is self balancing. It knows that all needs get stronger by 10 each turn, so the amount of satisfaction has to be 10 times the number of needs to maintain balance. Keeping balance and having all needs act the same way is a design decision. We start with a balanced and conservative simulation. We can give it wider swings and variability if it proves unsatisfactory. Needs change when people interact, but so do relationships. Add the following code to the Person class:

```
Public Sub UpdateRelationship(ByVal theirName As String, _
        ByVal howMuch As Integer)
    Dim thisRelation As NVP
    'Have we met?
    If myRelationships.Contains(theirName) Then
        'Update the existing relationship.
        thisRelation = CType(myRelationships(theirName), NVP)
        thisRelation.value += howMuch
    Else
        'Create a new relationship.
        thisRelation = New NVP
```

```
          thisRelation.name = theirName
          thisRelation.value = howMuch
          'Store the relationship.
          myRelationships.Add(thisRelation, theirName)
      End If
  End Sub

  'A simple Boolean when the caller does not care about magnitude.
  Public Function NeedsSome(ByVal need As String) As Boolean
      Dim someNeed As NVP = CType(myNeeds(need), NVP)
      Return (someNeed.value <= 0)
  End Function

  'Return HOW MUCH they like an activity.
  Public Function Likes(ByVal activity As String) As Integer
      Dim somePref As NVP = CType(myPreferences(activity), NVP)
      Return somePref.value
  End Function
```

The NeedsSome() function is used when computing the relationship score for an interaction. The third term in the computation was a bonus if both parties had an unmet need satisfied by the activity. So we need to be able to ask a person if a particular need was unmet. The other parts of the relationship score need a person's preference value for an activity, which is provided by the Likes() function.

The final code for a person handles the various ways outside code interrogates a person in order to print out results. The simulation will make use of these in debugging statements that let us see our results. Add the following code to the Person class:

```
  Public Function CurrentRelationship(ByVal theirName As String) As Integer
      'If we have met them...
      If myRelationships.Contains(theirName) Then
          Dim rel As NVP = CType(myRelationships(theirName), NVP)
          '...then return the value of our relationship.
          Return rel.value
      End If
      'Return 0 if we haven't met yet.
      Return 0
  End Function

  'Give back my name and my needs in a compact form.
  Public Function ShortDump() As String
```

```
        Dim sn As String = myname & "["
        Dim someNeed As NVP
        For Each someNeed In myNeeds
            sn = sn & " " & someNeed.value.ToString
        Next
        sn = sn & " ]"
        Return sn
    End Function

    Public Function LongDump() As String
        Dim ld As String = ""
        Dim opinionated As Double = 0.0
        Dim view As Integer = 0

        Dim attr As NVP
        For Each attr In myPreferences
            'Strong preferences count more.
            opinionated += attr.value * attr.value
            'Keep the sign when building their total outlook.
            view += attr.value
            'Build the string of preferences.
            ld = ld & " " & attr.name & "=" & attr.value.ToString
        Next
        Return (Me.ShortDump & " View=" & view.ToString & " Op=" & _
            Format(opinionated / myPreferences.Count, "0.00") & "; " & ld)
    End Function

    Public Function Name() As String
        Return myname
    End Function
```

Now that we can create a database and some people, we are ready for the cruise director to make an appearance.

Finishing the Cruise Class

Switch to the Code view of the Cruise class. Add code as follows:

```
Private Sub PeopleButton_Click(ByVal sender As System.Object, _
            ByVal e As System.EventArgs) Handles PeopleButton.Click
    Dim people() As String = {"Drackett", "Jones", "Lincoln", _
                        "Morrill", "Stradley", "Taylor"}
```

```
        Dim surname As String

        Debug.WriteLine("+++++++++ LOADING NEW PEOPLE.")
        'Remove prior people.
        Roster.Clear()
        'Load up the roster with new people.
        For Each surname In people
            Roster.Add(New Person(surname, MDB))
        Next
    End Sub
```

Uncomment the call to PeopleButton_Click that is near the end of the Cruise_Load event handler. We had commented it earlier because we lacked any people code. Now that we have the Person class complete, we can do more testing.

Run this code in the debugger and look at the output in the Immediate window. Click the People button. The code claims to be loading new people. We would like to see these people. Stop debugging and add the flowing code to the Cruise class:

```
    'Dump all of the people and their relationships.
    Private Sub DumpButton_Click(ByVal sender As System.Object, _
             ByVal e As System.EventArgs) Handles DumpButton.Click
        'Dump all of the pair-wise relationships.
        Dim PersonA As Person
        Dim PersonB As Person

        'Do all of the people.
        For Each PersonA In Roster
            'Make some blank space for readability.
            Debug.WriteLine("")
            'Dump my personal stats.
            Debug.WriteLine(PersonA.LongDump)
            'Do all of the pair-wise relationships.
            For Each PersonB In Roster
                '(With everyone but me.)
                If PersonA IsNot PersonB Then
                    Call DumpRelationship(PersonA, PersonB)
                End If
            Next
        Next
    End Sub
```

```
'Dump a single relationship.
Private Sub DumpRelationship(ByVal PersonA As Person, _
            ByVal PersonB As Person)
    'How compatible are these people?
    Dim compatibility As Integer = 0
    Dim activity As String
    For Each activity In MDB.ActivityList
        'Use their preferences to add to their score.
        compatibility += PersonA.Likes(activity) * PersonB.Likes(activity)
    Next
    Debug.WriteLine("[C: " & compatibility.ToString & ", R+R: " & _
        (PersonA.CurrentRelationship(PersonB.Name) + _
        PersonB.CurrentRelationship(PersonA.Name)).ToString & "] " & _
        PersonA.Name & " (" & _
        PersonA.CurrentRelationship(PersonB.Name).ToString & ") (" & _
        PersonB.CurrentRelationship(PersonA.Name).ToString & ") " & _
        PersonB.Name)
End Sub
```

Run the code in the debugger and click the Dump button. In the Immediate window, you will see blocks of data, one block per person. The block begins with the person's own internal statistics. Let us look at an example:

```
Taylor[ -14 -13 27 ] View=9 Op=1.89; tennis=2 swimming=1 ...
```

The string begins with the person's name. In square brackets are the three need values for exercise, culture, and dining, in that order. View is the numeric sum of the person's preferences. Taylor in this run is a pretty positive person, since the expected value is 0. The next value is how opinionated the person is. Taylor in this run is modestly opinionated. Remember that opinionated values are computed as the average of the squares of the preferences. As a result, strongly opinionated people have a value above 2 and approaching 3. Following that is a list of the person's personal preference values.

After the person's own statistics are his relationship statistics. Without interactions, only the compatibility number has a value. Let us look at the output and go through it.

```
[C: -7, R+R: 0] Taylor (0) (0) Morrill
```

The first value in square brackets is the mutual compatibility score. The second value is the sum of their individual relationship scores. Taylor and Morrill are mildly incompatible. Values within 10 points of 0 are too low to be accurate predictors of future relationships. Values in the teens are strong predictors, but smaller values less so. The simulation is slightly biased toward positive relationships due to the bonus term when both parties need an activity. Taylor is more likely to have positive relationships because Taylor likes nearly everything. Taylor's partners might not share that view, but in general, Taylor is a positive person in this run. Between Taylor and Morrill in parentheses is how they feel about each other. Taylor's score for Morrill is next to Taylor's name, and Morrill's score for Taylor is next to Morrill's name. Since they have not interacted yet, both are 0. These are the two values that are added to get the R+R number out front.

Scroll through your output. If no two people have a compatibility value in the teens (including in the negative teens) or larger, the interactions might not produce strong results. Click the People button and the Dump button a few times to get an interesting set of people. A compatibility score of 17 can produce twice the relationships score of a compatibility of 12. To see this, we will have to make our people interact. Add the following code to the Cruise class:

```
'Have two people interact.
Private Sub Interact(ByVal PersonA As Person, ByVal PersonB As Person, _
                ByVal Need As String, ByVal Activity As String)
    Dim RCa As Integer
    Dim RCb As Integer
    Dim bonus As Integer = 0
    'We like it more if we both need it.
    If PersonA.NeedsSome(Need) And PersonB.NeedsSome(Need) Then bonus += 1
    RCa = PersonA.Likes(Activity) * PersonB.Likes(Activity) + _
            PersonA.Likes(Activity) + bonus
    RCb = PersonA.Likes(Activity) * PersonB.Likes(Activity) + _
            PersonB.Likes(Activity) + bonus

    Debug.WriteLine(PersonA.ShortDump & " tries " & Activity & "(" & _
            PersonA.Likes(Activity).ToString & ", " & _
            PersonB.Likes(Activity).ToString & ") with " & _
            PersonB.ShortDump & " result (" & RCa.ToString & ", " & _
            RCb.ToString & ")")
    PersonA.UpdateRelationship(PersonB.name, RCa)
    PersonB.UpdateRelationship(PersonA.Name, RCb)

    PersonA.EaseNeed(Need)
    PersonB.EaseNeed(Need)
End Sub
```

That provides the basic interaction, but we need to wrap a few layers around it. We need to be able to run a complete round of interaction, and we need to hook the interactions to the user interface. Add the following code to the Cruise class:

```
Private Sub OneRound()
    Dim Pool As New Collection
    Dim PersonA As Person = Nothing
    Dim NeedyPerson As Person

    'Load the pool from the roster, increment all needs.
    For Each PersonA In Roster
        Pool.Add(PersonA, PersonA.Name)
        Call PersonA.IncAllNeeds()
    Next

    While Pool.Count >= 2
        'Grab the person with the highest need.
        'Default to the first person.
        NeedyPerson = CType(Pool.Item(1), Person)
        'We keep both the person and their need.
        Dim BigNeed As NVP = NeedyPerson.HighestNeed
        'Look for a person with a higher need.
        For Each PersonA In Pool
            Dim Aneed As NVP = PersonA.HighestNeed
            If Aneed.value < BigNeed.value Then
                NeedyPerson = PersonA
                BigNeed = Aneed
            End If
        Next
        'Take the needy person out of the pool.
        Pool.Remove(NeedyPerson.Name)
        'Pick a random partner.
        PersonA = CType(Pool(getDx(Pool.Count)), Person)
        'Take them out of the pool.
        Pool.Remove(PersonA.Name)
        'Make them randomly interact to meet the highest need.
        Dim activity As String = _
                MDB.ActivityForNeed(NeedyPerson.HighestNeed.name)
        Interact(NeedyPerson, PersonA, BigNeed.name, activity)
    End While
End Sub

Private Sub Button1Time_Click(ByVal sender As System.Object, _
        ByVal e As System.EventArgs) Handles Button1Time.Click
```

```
            'Test the interaction code.
            Call OneRound()
        End Sub

        Private Sub Button100Times_Click(ByVal sender As System.Object, _
                ByVal e As System.EventArgs) Handles Button100Times.Click
            'Enough interactions to get trends.
            Dim i As Integer
            For i = 1 To 100
                Call Debug.WriteLine("Round " & i.ToString)
                Call OneRound()
            Next
            Call Debug.WriteLine("")
        End Sub
```

Run the project in the debugger. Click the Dump button and then click the 1 Time button and look at the debug output. Following is an example line of interaction output. Your numbers will vary.

```
Taylor[ -15 -23 8 ] tries drama(2, -2) with Lincoln[ -3 -19 -8 ] result (-1, -5)
```

Needs are in square brackets after each name. Here we see that Taylor and Lincoln have culture needs of −23 and −19, respectively. Recall that needs are listed as exercise, culture, and then dining. Their preferences are in parentheses between them. Taylor strongly likes drama (+2), and Lincoln strongly dislikes (−2) it. In terms of their relationship, the "we think alike" term comes out to −4 and the bonus "we needed that" term gives +1. That gives −3, to which we add each individual "I like it" value to get the final change in relationship. Taylor adds +2 to get a total of −1. Lincoln adds −2 to get a total of −5, which is listed in that order as the result at the end.

Check your output to see that the highest-need person was picked first. Work through the computations to make sure that the relationship's changes are correct. Click the Dump button and look to make sure that each person has the correct relationship value as given by the single interaction. If all is correct, click the 100 Times button and then dump again. Look at the output and compare the relationships scores of different pairs of people who have similar compatibility scores. Note also that positive relationships are more common. What are these numbers telling us?

As we alluded to before, compatibility is not a strong predictor until the value gets away from 0. The simulation has other factors that can dominate the relationship score. The "we needed that" bonus term adds an average of half of one point every interaction. We know that the first person in every pair was picked on the basis of need. Because our needs average to 0, we expect the first person to nearly always have an unmet need. Because the person's partner is picked at random, that partner is equally likely to have any need be met as unmet. So half of the time, we expect to see the "we needed that" bonus to apply. In the absence of strong personality matches or conflicts, the bonus gently eases our simulation toward positive relationships. We can think of this as "most people get along, even if they don't actually like each other."

Another influence on our system is that our people have a full set of preferences that are picked without bias. This means that on the average, any given person's net preference value is near 0. It also means that with so many pairs of potential interactions available, we will see a good deal of cancelations. Statistically, this is known as "reversion to the mean." We could change our people so that they only held strong opinions or did not care. In the code, we would turn any $+1$ or -1 values for preferences to 0.

Along that same line, our range of preferences is notably constrained. If we increased the range from the current -2 to $+2$ to -3 to $+3$ or even more, we will see different results. Note that this would completely change the scaling of the compatibility number; simulations with one range would be tuned differently than with the expanded range. The expanded range can also be combined with the preceding idea of strong opinions only.

Another driver toward the mean is our cruise director. By pushing toward full coverage of all the possible interactions, we suppress weaker trends that might appear if our people had a chance to pick who they interacted with and what interactions they tried. The flip side of this is that the strong trends we see—those between people with compatibility scores in double digits—indicate that our simulation does deliver what we expect. If you do not see these trends, try different sets of people. Just click the People button and dump the new roster. Repeat until you see one or more compatibility scores in the teens, positive or negative. A value of 17 or higher is especially informative.

A final note on tuning is that this whole process is driven purely by numbers and simple equations. These numbers belong in a spreadsheet and on charts for better clarity. Statistical analysis may seem to be far removed from emotions, but for game AI, these heartless tools are a warmly welcomed help.

Chapter Summary

The job of the AI programmer is twofold. The first is to drive the capability to make intelligent changes to the game in every nook and cranny that will become richer for having it. The second is to infect the "creative" sides of the game with the idea that *everything* might be subject to intelligent manipulation. All these manipulations can be bent toward realizing all the creative goals for the game, including evoking emotional responses from the player. This simply might not apply to some games; for example, no one really expects any emotional content attributable to the black and white stones used to play the game of *Go*. But if the opponent is displayed as a virtual human, that virtual human needs virtual emotions. Once any decision is made about the emotional content of a game, a certain amount of care is called for.

Chapter Review

Answers are in the appendix.

1. Many aspects of a game have an emotional payload. What additional attribute is required to make these aspects part of the overall AI?

2. Describe the critical difference between games and simulations with regard to what they are trying to do with emotions.

3. Some of the techniques in this chapter are subtle. How can the game make sure the player catches on?

4. List some general categories of places where some AI control adds to the ability of the game to deliver emotional content.

5. Expand the range of preferences for our people on the cruise and examine the numbers. Consider trying to balance for some sense of "realism" to your sense of "fun."

Exercises

1. Create a list of wall colors and the emotions they evoke.

2. Not only do clothes convey information, but accessories do as well. Make a list of the impact from different kinds of footwear, sunglasses, rings,

watches, and jewelry. List aspects of the accessories that would take them from mundane to noteworthy. Why is a plain wedding band different from a wedding ring with a multi-carat diamond or a pinky ring?

3. Change the Brains state machine transitions for the monster so that they are influenced by the emotional state of the monster.

4. What emotions does trash in a neighborhood evoke?

References

[Carlisle04] Carlisle, Phil. "An AI Approach to Creating an Intelligent Camera System," *AI Game Programming Wisdom 2*, edited by Steve Rabin, pp. 179–185. Charles River Media, 2004.

[Crawford86] Crawford, Chris. *International Politics as the Ultimate Global Game*, Microsoft Press, 1986. Available online at http://www.erasmatazz.com/library/Balance%20of%20Power.txt.

[Doornbos01] Doornbos, Jamie. "Those Darn Sims: What Makes Them Tick?" in lecture, Game Developers Conference, 2001. Similar material can be found online at http://www.cs.northwestern.edu/~forbus/c95-gd/lectures/The_Sims_Under_the_Hood_files/frame.htm.

[El-Nasr09] Seif El-Nasr, Magy; Vasilakos, Thanos; Rao, Chinmay; Zupko, Joseph. "Dynamic Intelligent Lighting for Directing Visual Attention in Interactive 3D Scenes," *IEEE Transactions on Computational Intelligence and AI in Games*, Vol 1, No. 2, 2009.

[Gratch00] Gratch, Jonathan. "Émile: Marshalling Passions in Training and Education." Proceedings of the Fourth International Conference on Intelligent Agents, Barcelona, Spain. June 2000.

[Gratch01] Gratch, Jonathan; Marsella, Stacy. "Tears and Fears: Modeling Emotions and Emotional Behaviors in Synthetic Agents" Proceedings of the Fifth International Conference on Autonomous Agents, pp. 278–285. ACM Press, 2001. Available online at http://people.ict.usc.edu/~gratch/agents01-emotion.pdf.

[Hecker08] Hecker, Chris. "Structure vs Style." In lecture, 2008 Game Developers Conference, San Francisco, CA. Slides and audio available online at http://chrishecker.com/Structure_vs_Style.

[Mateas05] Mateas, Michael; Stern, Andrew. "Structuring Content in the *Façade* Interactive Drama Architecture." Presented at AIIDE 2005. Available online at http://www.interactivestory.net/papers/MateasSternAIIDE05.pdf.

[Lazzaro04] Lazzaro, Nicole. "Why We Play Games: Four Keys to More Emotion Without Story" 2004. In lecture, Game Developers Conference 2004, San Jose, CA. Available online at http://www.xeodesign.com/xeodesign_whyweplaygames.pdf.

[Lazzaro07] Lazzaro, Nicole. "The 4 Most Important Emotions of Game Design." In lecture, Game Developers Conference 2007, San Francisco, CA. Slides available online at http://www.xeodesign.com/gdc2007/Lazzaro_GDC07-100n030607.zip.

[Lazzaro08] Lazzaro, Nicole. "Halo vs. Facebook: Emotion and the Fun of Games." In lecture, Game Developers Conference 2008, San Francisco, CA. Slides available online at http://www.xeodesign.com/halo_v_facebook_2008/halo_vs_facebook_xeodesign_102n033108.zip.

[Mark09] Mark, Dave. *Behavioral Mathematics for Game AI*, Course Technology PRT, March, 2009.

[Sanger93] Sanger, George "The Fatman." At an audio roundtable discussion. 1993 Computer Game Developers Conference, Santa Clara, California. Confirmed in private e-mail.

[Spector04] Spector, Warren. "Thief: Deadly Shadows Interview." Given at E3 Conference, 2004. Available online at http://gamespot.com/video/528587/6099282.

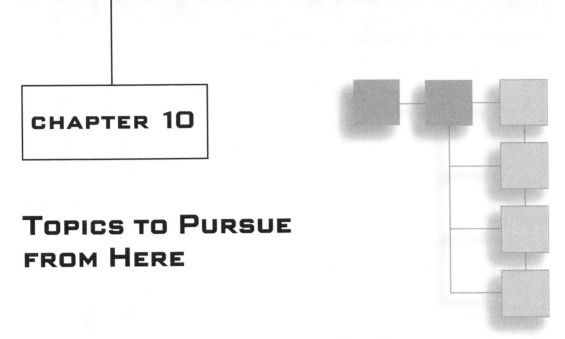

CHAPTER 10

TOPICS TO PURSUE FROM HERE

The topics in this chapter range from next steps (A* path finding) to topics at the leading edge in game AI (planning, behavior trees). In between is machine learning. All these are of interest to AI programmers and are the subject of articles and even whole sections in the four volumes of the *AI Game Programming Wisdom* series of books. Besides being the topics of game-industry–focused publications, game AI issues have been picked up by academia as vehicles for research. Game AI is too broad for one book to cover, so we will wrap up with a selection of topics.

A* Path Finding

This topic might be considered the graduation exercise for the readers of this book. The algorithm is one that all AI programmers need to have mastered. Rather than provide a project with code, just the algorithm is given. Armed with an understanding of how it works and aided by the numerous free resources available on the Internet, you should be able to write your own implementation of A*.

A* (pronounced *A-star*) is the algorithm of choice for general path finding in most games. Path finding answers the question, "What's the best way to get from here to there?" If there are only a few places in your game, you can precompute the paths between them and store the paths.

Precomputed paths are cheaper than A* paths, but two major issues crop up quickly. The first issue is that the number of paths explodes as the number of places increases. The number of paths is related to the square of the number of places. The second issue is that precomputed paths require knowing all the places in advance. They cannot be used with dynamically created maps. Precomputed paths fail if elements such as bridges can be rendered unusable during play. When you lack a static map with a small number of places, you need a general path finder, and A* is hard to beat.

A* works with two core concepts. The first is, "I know how much it costs to get from the starting point to here," for any particular "here" to which the algorithm has progressed. The second concept is, "I can estimate the cost of getting from here to the goal," again for any particular "here." In technical terms, A* is a best-first graph search algorithm to determine the lowest cost path between two nodes. We will examine what all these words mean and why they are important.

The best-first part is one of the major reasons why A* is so popular. A* is reasonably fast, and that speed comes from examining the most promising steps first. A character standing in a building would first check if he or she can walk directly toward his or her goal. If the character is standing in an open-air gazebo, this will in fact be the best way to go. If the character is standing in a room with walls and doors, the extremely high cost of going through a wall would force the character to examine less direct paths. If there is a door in the wall blocking the direct path, that door will probably be checked before other doors that lead away from the goal.

"Reasonably fast" is a relative term. A* is a search method, and search as a computational problem is not cheap. The difference between "cheaper than the alternatives" and "cheap" should be kept in mind.

A* is a graph search algorithm. For navigation purposes, most virtual worlds are not really contiguous. Unlike on Earth, in games, the concept of "here" is not a set of coordinates such as latitude and longitude that can always be more finely specified. In games, "here" is some discrete space, perhaps a triangle. Board games often use squares or hexagons for this purpose; they are spaces that cannot be subdivided. Whether in board games or computer games, every "here" has some neighboring places that are directly connected to it. To A*, a graph is a set of points and a set of lines connecting those points to their neighbors. These points represent the "here" for any location in the virtual world; in graph-theory terms, these are called nodes. Every square or hexagon in a board game becomes one node in a graph. The lines connecting the nodes, called edges of the graph, have costs associated with them. A roadmap showing only the distance between cities is a familiar example of this kind of graph; the roads are drawn as simple straight lines, and the cities are drawn as circles. Our discrete computer-game world can be modeled as a graph like this. Outside of navigation, our game may have a very finely detailed and continuous definition, but for navigation purposes there are powerful motivations for minimizing the number of nodes in the graph. A* is going to search for a path through the nodes, and having fewer nodes yields a faster search.

As long as certain givens remain true, A* will produce the lowest-cost path between the two nodes if any legal path exists. So what are the certain givens about A* that need to remain true? The big one is the heuristic upon which A* depends. A* uses a heuristic to make decisions using imperfect data. Perfect data would be expensive to compute, and much of it would be thrown away. The heuristic in A* tells the algorithm that from any point in the graph, the distance to the goal is *at least* a certain amount. Of the two core concepts in A*, this is the estimate part. For driving on roads, a good heuristic is the direct straight-line overland distance to the goal.

There are two major requirements for a good heuristic. The first is that it needs to be admissible, and the second is that it needs to be as close as possible to the actual distance. An admissible heuristic is one that is never larger than the actual distance.

As an example, imagine that our heuristic was the direct straight-line overland distance. Because driving is restricted to roads, the actual path will generally be longer than the heuristic. But we know that the actual path is rarely shorter (a tunnel through a mountain could be shorter than the direct path over the mountain). If we have no tunnels, the heuristic is admissible; if we have tunnels, the heuristic is inadmissible.

It should be easy to get a heuristic that never overestimates the actual distance between two nodes, but we also want it to be as large as possible without going over. We will see the importance of this when we get to some examples. If the roads are all set on hillsides, none of them will ever be anywhere near as short as a straight line, so we should adjust the heuristic to something larger than the direct distance.

Both parts of a good heuristic have a profound impact on the performance of A*. We can use Figure 10.1 to walk through an example of how A* works.

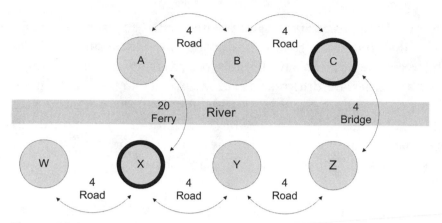

Figure 10.1
Transportation graph between river towns.

An A* Example

On some major rivers such as the Rhine, there are few bridges and many ferry stops. Let us consider a journey from C to X in Figure 10.1. Presume that all the towns are regularly spaced to make the math simpler. It takes only four minutes to drive on the roads between two neighboring towns, but using the ferry takes 20 minutes. If you could drive it, B and X would be 5.66 minutes apart, taking the diagonal into account.

A* starts at the beginning and evaluates the nodes around it. So if the trip is from C to X, the algorithm starts with C, which has neighbors B and Z. Because we start at node C, the cost to get there is 0. In A* terms, this is **g**, the known lowest cost to get to a node. This is the first of the core concepts of A*: knowing the actual cost to get someplace. The cost to get to B is 4. Because the bridge and the road are equally fast, the cost **g** to get to Z is also 4.

Is it faster to take B or Z to get to X? We do not know, but we can use a heuristic to make a guess. In A* terms, the heuristic is **h**, the estimated cost to the goal. For this example we will use straight-line driving time, which is directly proportional to distance, as our heuristic. Obviously we cannot use the actual driving time; if we do not yet know what the shortest path is, how can we know how long it will take to drive?

The heuristic **h** tells us that Z is 8 minutes away from X, and using a direct diagonal path, B is 5.66 minutes away from X. Our heuristic is reasonable, but it does mislead us from time to time. No actual cost is lower than our heuristic, a required given if the algorithm is to function optimally. A* uses the sum of the known cost and the estimate of the remaining cost supplied by the heuristic to give $\mathbf{f} = (\mathbf{g} + \mathbf{h})$, the "fitness" of the node in A* terms. The fitness is used to decide what node to pursue next. This is where the best-first part of the algorithm comes into play; fitness tells us the best node to examine next. Let us examine the values we have so far.

We started with node C, but because it is not the goal and we have added all its neighbors to the list of nodes to examine, we are done with C. After we dealt with node C, we had B and Z to pick from.

Node B: $\mathbf{f} = \mathbf{g} + \mathbf{h} = 4 + 5.66 = 9.66$

Node Z: $\mathbf{f} = \mathbf{g} + \mathbf{h} = 4 + 8 = 12$

At this point, we can offer some commentary on our heuristic. At node B, we estimated 5.66 as the cost to X. The actual value using the ferry is 24. Even if there had been a bridge instead of the ferry, the actual would have been 8. This amount of underestimation is making B look more enticing than it is. We will waste time exploring from B before we decide to abandon it and go through Z.

If we know that our nodes exhibit a regular grid pattern and lack diagonals, we can use the "Manhattan distance" as our heuristic. Instead of using Pythagoras' theorem to compute the hypotenuse of a right triangle from the lengths of the sides, we simply add the lengths. On the streets of a city with a grid pattern of streets, this is the distance that will be covered to get from one place to another.

In our example, using Manhattan distance makes the estimate for node B equal 8. A larger but admissible estimate makes us more likely to abandon suboptimal nodes earlier, and that is a serious performance gain. In this case, it puts node B and Z on equal footing. Tuning the heuristic to the particulars of the application is an important optimization. Let us return to the algorithm using our original heuristic.

Node B is more promising at this stage, so it will be examined first. We will keep Z around in case B does not work out. Node B is not our destination, so we have to add its neighbors (in this case, just node A) to the list of nodes to examine. We do not add nodes we have already visited, such as node C; driving in circles never makes a path shorter. Getting to node A adds 4 to the known cost to the goal, $\mathbf{g}$, and the estimated cost ($\mathbf{h}$) to get from node A to node X is 4 (because that is the straight-line distance to cross the river).

Node A: $\mathbf{f} = \mathbf{g} + \mathbf{h} = 8 + 4 = 12$

With that, we are done with node B. Nodes A and Z have the same estimated cost, so we could investigate either one next. Since it doesn't matter which we choose, let's look at node A next. The only new neighbor to add to our list is node X. Getting from node A to node X costs 20 (since we have to take the ferry), so we add that to 8, the known cost for node A, giving us a g of 28. Since node X is the goal, h is zero.

Node X (via A): $f = g + h = 28 + 0 = 28$

When we compare the 28 to the values we have, we find that we have paths with a potentially lower cost. Node Z is claiming 12 for its estimated total cost. As long as that path can stay under 28, we will continue pursuing it. Going from Z to Y adds 4 to g, the known cost thus far to the goal.

Node Y: $f = g + h = 8 + 4 = 12$

That finishes node Z. The path using node Y is still below our 28, so we continue. Going on to X from Y adds 4 to g, the known cost thus far to the goal. Since X is the goal, we have the following:

Node X (via Y): $f = g + h = 12 + 0 = 12$

There are no paths left that might come in lower, so we have the shortest path. By using best-first, A* can still pursue blind alleys, but it abandons them as soon as their cost rises above alternatives. It does not foresee obstacles, but it will avoid them as they appear.

Details in the Lists

Implementing A* is harder than understanding how it works. The details in this section will be of particular interest to those readers who will need to implement their own A*. We will go over the lists used to make A* work, and we will comment on how admissibility of the heuristic has a performance impact.

We keep two lists in A*: the open list and the closed list. The open list holds nodes that might need further examination. We need to be able to easily find the node with the best fitness from the open list because that is always the next node to examine. To hold nodes that are no longer on the open list, we have the closed list. Once we have put the neighbors of a node on the open list, we can take that node off the open list and put it on the closed list. The two lists make things easier to juggle.

To start with, we added C to the open list. Each step involves removing the fittest node from the open list and checking its children to see if they get updated and belong on the open list. In the evaluation of node C, we removed C from the open list after we added nodes B and Z to the open list and updated their values. B and Z had not been looked at before, so their values were set, and they went onto the open list. New nodes always go on the open list. Neighboring nodes already on the open list will have their numbers updated only if the new numbers are better. Neighboring nodes on the closed list go back on the open list only if their numbers improve, but this will never happen if the heuristic is good, and the cost always increases with additional steps. Since most applications have the cost increase with each step, the only concern is with the heuristic.

For simplicity, we did not show in the discussion the fact that when we evaluated node B, the algorithm considered going back to node C since node C is a neighbor of node B. Node C was given a 0 value for **g** when we started. A path that goes from node C to node B back to node C will want to give C a **g** value of 8, which is worse than what is already there. For path finding related to travel in time or space, the costs always increase, so looping paths will automatically be worse than non-looping paths. C is a neighbor of B, but C will not go back onto the open list unless it can do so with better numbers than it already has. This never happens in our example because cost is monotonic (taking another step can only increase cost) and our heuristic is admissible. Because it never happens, we can safely ignore any neighbor that has made it to the closed list. Real implementations of A* would not have computed the cost of going to node C; instead they would first see if node C was on the closed list, and if it was they would ignore node C.

Being able to ignore nodes on the closed list is a huge performance win! Once again, this optimization is made possible by having an admissible heuristic and monotonically increasing cost. Monotonically increasing cost is usually a given, but admissibility of the heuristic is a design decision.

If the estimate provided by the heuristic is sometimes higher than the actual cost, not only do we no longer have a guarantee that the path we get will be the shortest one, but we may also find that we need to move nodes that are on the closed list back to the open list in pursuit of the shortest path. It is extremely unlikely that any real implementation of A* will ever allow backtracking by reexamining nodes on the closed list.

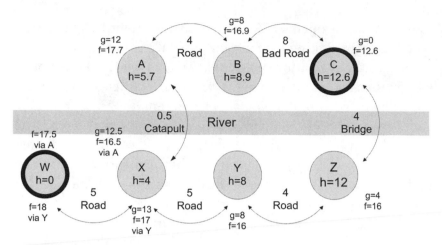

Figure 10.2
A somewhat more varied transportation graph between river towns.

Let us change our example to see what happens if the heuristic is not always admissible and we still want the shortest path. We will have to take some liberties with the graph to make this happen, yielding the revised graph shown in Figure 10.2. In order to shorten travel times, the cities at node A and node X have commissioned a catapult service to fling travelers across the river extremely quickly. This makes our heuristic inadmissible. The move to catapult service was sparked by heavy rains that forced the cancellation of the ferry service and caused major damage to the road between node B and node C. The roads to and from node X also suffered some minor damage.

We wish that the code should not need to touch any node that it has already touched, but the combination of an inadmissible heuristic and the desire for the shortest path means we need to handle paths that split and then merge differently than before. If a second path makes it to a merge point—a node we have already touched—with a lower **g** value than what the merge point already has, then the first path through the merge point is not the optimal path, and the merge point goes back onto the open list with new values for **g** and **f**. This is the case in Figure 10.2.

Again, we start at C. Our final goal is node W instead of node X. Node X is the merge point. The numbers for the nodes are shown in the figure. Node C goes on the open list first. Being the only node there, its neighbors, B and Z, which are not on any list, go on the open list, and C goes on the closed list. We examine the open list for the most promising node.

Z at 16 beats B at 16.9, so Z is examined next. Z cannot improve C's numbers, so C stays on the closed list. Z puts Y on the open list with B because Y is a new node. We are done with Z, so it joins C on the closed list. Again, we examine the open list for the most promising node.

Y at 16 also beats B at 16.9, so we examine Y. Y cannot improve on Z's numbers, so Z stays on the closed list. X is new, so it goes on the open list. Y is done, so Y joins Z and C on the closed list.

From the open list, B at 16.9 beats X at 17, so we examine B next. B cannot improve C's numbers, so C stays on the closed list. A is new, so B adds A to the open list with X. B gets put on the closed list with C, Z, and Y.

On the open list, X at 17 beats A at 17.7, so we examine X next. X cannot improve Y's numbers, so Y stays on the closed list. X cannot improve A's numbers, so X does not update A on the open list. W is new, so X puts W on the open list. X joins Y, Z, C, and B on the closed list.

On the open list, A at 17.7 beats W at 18, so A is examined next. Here is where we will encounter the effects of an inadmissible heuristic. The catapult method of crossing the river is far faster than the heuristic expects anyone to ever go. This is where the heuristic gives an *inadmissible* estimate of the cost. Node A cannot improve B's numbers, so B stays on the closed list. Node A *can* improve X's numbers, so X is updated and moved from the closed list back to the open list to join W.

An A* implementation that has the normal optimization of ignoring nodes on the closed list would not have touched X again. Nor would it have taken the effort to see if it could improve the numbers of **any** node on the closed list as we did in the preceding paragraphs. Node A goes onto the closed list with B, C, Y, and Z.

The open list is again checked. X at 16.5 beats the existing W at 18, so X is given another chance. X cannot improve A or Y, so they remain on the closed list. X can improve W on the open list, so W goes from 18 to 17.5. X goes to the closed list with all the other nodes except W. Since the goal node has the best score on the open list, it is used as it is.

This example shows that the world does not end if the heuristic is sometimes inadmissible. It can have easily happened that with an inadmissible heuristic, A* will not find the shortest path, regardless of whether it reexamines nodes on the closed list or not (see Exercise 2 at the end of this chapter). This is the penalty for using an inadmissible heuristic. But if catapults are rare and roads are the norm, we might stay with our inadmissible heuristic. We do this because it is more aggressive about discarding paths early, and that is a performance win. The effect in our example would be that sometimes, the pathfinder neglects to exploit catapults when they are off the beaten path. In our example, the catapult is 8 times faster than the heuristic. If we tune for catapults instead of roads, we have to expand our searching by a factor of 8 to get to the point where we say, "Even a catapult won't help you when you are this far away," and that could be a lot of useless searching.

Since reexamining nodes on the closed list does not guarantee getting the shortest path when the heuristic is inadmissible, and reexamining nodes on the closed list is pointless when the heuristic is admissible, the case for reexamining nodes on the closed list is too weak to justify.

Besides holding the **f**, **g**, and **h** numbers, each node also tracks what node came before it in the path. When our code reached X via A, X would store A. When a node is placed on the open list for the first time or updated with better numbers, the node is also updated with the new predecessor in the path. When our example reached X via Y, it updated the costs and also overwrote the stored A with Y. This way, when A* completes, the nodes have stored the best path.

Caveats

A* is popular because it usually performs well and gives optimal results. Performing well does not make it free, however; A* can be costly to run. When no path exists, A* exhibits maximum cost as it is forced to explore every node in the graph. If the usual case is that paths usually exist and obstacles are localized, then dealing with the difference in performance between the usual case and the worst case presents a difficult engineering challenge.

A* also depends heavily on the concept of "here" in the graph. The world may be represented at a low level by a mesh of tiny triangles that can be fed to the graphics engine, but that mesh makes for expensive path finding. A room may have a large number of triangles that make up the floor, but for navigation purposes it can be reduced to a single "here" or a small number of "heres." To help with path finding, many games have a coarse navigation mesh with far fewer nodes than the graphics mesh. The navigation mesh makes the global pathfinder run quickly by greatly reducing the number of nodes. The nodes in the navigation mesh can be forced to have nice properties that make them easier to deal with, such as being convex. Path finding within a node in the navigation mesh is done locally, and simple methods often suffice; if the node is convex, then a straight line is all that is required.

An issue with any pathfinder is that long paths are fragile paths. Bridges get blown up, freeways are subject to being closed by accidents, and fly-over rights can be denied after a flight takes off. Before blindly using A* and expecting all paths to work, you should investigate the methods that are being used to deal with path problems.

Before the novice AI programmer rejoices that path finding is solved, he or she needs to consider the needs of the virtual world. A* will rightly determine that using roads and bridges is better than taking cross-country treks and fording streams. What A* does *not* do is traffic control. Unexpected traffic jams on popular routes and near choke points are realistic, but so are traffic cops. The game's AI might be smart enough to prevent gridlock, but the planning code still has a problem. The planning code has to factor in the effects of the very traffic the planning code is dispatching. If the planning code places a farm tractor, a truck carrying troops, and a motorcycle dispatch rider on the same narrow path in that order, the whole convoy is slowed to the speed of the tractor. A* told the planner that the dispatch rider will get to its destination in far less time than will actually happen. A* told the planner that the troops will get there on time as well. Even worse is the case when opposing traffic is dispatched to both sides of a one-lane bridge. A* by itself may not be enough.

Machine Learning

Machine learning has been "the next big thing" in game AI for many years. The methods have been described as elegant algorithms searching for a problem to solve. The algorithms have been put to good use in other areas of computer science, but they have gained very little traction in game AI. People have been looking for ways of getting around the limits of machine learning in games for some time now [Kirby04].

Realizing the potential of machine learning is difficult. There are many kinds of machine learning. Two of them are popular discussion topics: neural networks and genetic algorithms. Neural networks appear to be very enticing, particularly to novice game AI programmers. They have been a popular topic for over a decade in the AI roundtables at the Game Developers Conference. The topic is usually raised by those with the least industry experience and quickly put to rest by those with many years of experience. The conventional wisdom is that neural networks are not used in commercial games. By contrast, genetic algorithms have gained a very modest toe-hold into game AI, but not in the manner that you might first expect, as we shall see. A major goal of this section is to give beginning AI programmers sufficient knowledge and willpower to enable them to resist using either method lightly.

Before considering the different machine-learning algorithms, it is worthwhile to consider how they will be used. The first big question to ask of any proposed game feature is, "Does it make the game more fun?" If cool techniques do not translate into improved player experience, they do not belong in the game.

The next big question to answer is, "Will it learn after it leaves the studio?" For most machine learning used in games, the answer is a resounding "No!" Quality-assurance organizations do not want support calls demanding to know why the AI suddenly started cheating or why it suddenly went stupid. In the first case, the AI learned how to defeat the player easily; in the second case, the AI learned something terribly wrong. Most ordinary car drivers are happy with the factory tuning of their real-world automobiles, and most players are fine with carefully tuned AI. That being said, the answer is not always "No"; *Black & White* is an early example of a game that turned machine learning in the field into a gameplay virtue.

Learning algorithms are susceptible to learning the wrong thing from outlier examples, and people are prone to the same mistake. *Black & White* learned in the field, and learning supported a core gameplay mechanic. One of the main features of the game was teaching your creature. If teaching is part of the gameplay, then learning is obviously an appropriate algorithm to support the gameplay. How many games can be classified as teaching games? Most games do not employ teaching in their gameplay, and most of those same games have no need of learning algorithms. There may be other gameplay mechanics besides teaching that are a good fit for machine learning in the field, but it will take an innovative game designer backed by a good development team to prove it.

The final question always to ask is, "Is this the right tool for this job?" For neural networks in game AI, the answer is usually an emphatic "No." In some cases involving genetic algorithms, the answer will be a resounding "Yes." One of the clarifying questions to ask is, "Is it better to teach this than it is to program it?"

Of course, "better" can have many different interpretations: easier to program, produces a better result, can be done faster, etc.

Training

The trick with teaching—or *training*, as it often is called—is to make sure that the right things are taught. This is not always a given. A system trained to distinguish men from women at first had trouble with long-haired male rock stars. Another image-analysis system learned to distinguish the photographic qualities of the training data instead of differences in the subjects of the photographs. The system is only as good as the training data; it will faithfully reflect any biases in the training data. Lionhead Studios improved the user interface to the learning system in *Black & White II* to make it explicitly clear to players exactly what feedback they were about to give their creature, solving a major source of frustration with the original game.

The most straightforward way to ensure that learning has taken place is to administer a test with problems that the student has never seen before. This is called an *independent test set*. A system that is tested using the same data that trained it is subject to memorizing the problems instead of working out the solutions. Just as other software is tested, learning systems need test data that covers a broad range of the typical cases, as well as the borderlines and outliers. The system is proven to work only in the areas that the test set covers. If the system will never encounter a situation outside of the training set, the demand for an independent test set is relaxed.

Hidden in this coverage of training is a fact that needs to be made explicit: We are talking about two different kinds of training. The two methods of training are supervised training and reinforcement training. In supervised training, the learning algorithm is presented with an input situation and the desired outputs. The image-analysis system designed to identify men versus women mentioned earlier was taught this way. The system trained against a set of pictures of people, where each picture was already marked as male or female. Supervised training happens before the system is used and not when the system is in use. If there is a knowledgeable supervisor available at run-time, there is no need for the learning system to begin with. The success of supervised training in learning algorithms outside of the game industry has not been echoed within the game industry. Unless otherwise noted, supervised learning is the default when discussing learning algorithms.

Reinforcement learning, by contrast, emphasizes learning by interacting with the environment. The system starts with some basic knowledge and the need to maximize a reward of some kind. In operation, the system must balance between exploitation and exploration. At any given point in time, the system might pick the action it thinks is best, exploiting the knowledge it already has. Or it can pick a different action to better explore the possibilities. Reinforcement learning uses exploration to improve future decision making by making changes to the basic knowledge the system starts with.

A good introduction to reinforcement learning is given in the first chapter of [Sutton98], which is available in its entirety online. Advanced readers will want to study the method of temporal differences (TD); TD(λ) is of particular interest. Reinforcement learning has produced a few notable success stories; in commercial video games, *Black & White* used reinforcement learning. TD-Gammon began as a research project at IBM's Watson Research Center using TD(λ). It plays backgammon at slightly below the skill level of the top human players, and some of its plays have proven superior to the prior conventional wisdom [Tesauro95]. Reinforcement learning creeps into games in small ways as well [Dill10].

Why Don't These Methods Get Used in Games?

Many experienced game AI programmers attribute characteristics of undead vampires to neural networks and genetic algorithms; they are enticing, particularly to the naïve. They keep returning, at least as a topic of conversation, despite heroic efforts to lay them to rest. They cannot be trusted to do what you want them to do, and it takes arcane knowledge and skills to get them to do anything at all. At the end of the project, there is great fear that they will turn to dust should the game ever see the light of day. All kidding aside, what are the real reasons?

There are three basic concerns: control over the AI, lack of past history of achieving a successful AI with these methods in games, and control over the project.

Many game designers demand arbitrary control over what the game AI does. The smarter the AI gets, the more it wants to think for itself. In and of itself, that is not a problem; the problem comes when a designer wants to override the AI, usually for dramatic impact or playability reasons. As we shall see, neural networks effectively are a black box. They might as well carry the standard warning label,

"No user-serviceable parts inside." You can train them (repeatedly if necessary), you can use them, and you can throw them away. For all of the other methods that we have covered in prior chapters, there are places where the AI programmer can intervene. Places where numbers can be altered or scripts can be injected abound in those methods, but not inside these black boxes. They have to be trained to do everything expected of them, and that is often no small task.

Supervised training is notorious for its need of computational resources. In addition, every tweak to the desired outputs is essentially a "do-over" in terms of training. The combination of these two issues is a rather non-agile development cycle. My non-game industry experience with supervised training could be summarized as, "Push the Start Learning button on Monday; come back on Friday to test the results." When a game designer says, "Make it do this!" the AI programmer starts the entire learning process over from scratch. Worse, there is no guarantee that the system will learn the desired behavior. Nor is there any guarantee that old behaviors will not degrade when the system is taught new ones.

Effectively training a learning system is a black art, and expertise comes mainly through experience. Getting the desired outputs is not always intuitive or obvious. This lack of surety makes the methods a technical risk.

Just as building a learning system is an acquired skill, so is testing one. The learning systems I built were never released for general availability until after they had successfully passed a field trial in the real world. Learning systems in games need their own particular test regimes [Barnes02]. The task is not insurmountable, but it does create project schedule risks—the test team has to learn how to do something new.

The issue of completeness also crops up. A neural network operates as an integrated whole. All of the inputs and desired outputs need to be present to conduct the final training. So the AI cannot be incrementally developed in parallel with everything else. Prior versions may not work in the final game. From a project-management perspective, this is usually unacceptable; it pushes a risky technology out to the end of a project, when there is no time left to develop an alternative if learning does not work out. Good project management calls for mitigating risks as early as possible.

Neural Networks

Neural networks loosely mimic the structure of the human brain. As shown in Figure 10.3, a typical network has three layers: the input layer, a hidden layer, and

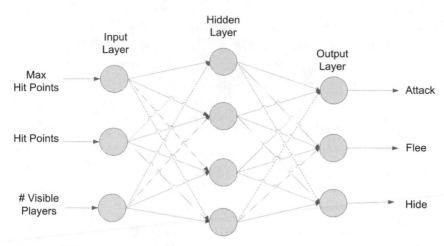

Figure 10.3
A neural network for determining monster state.

an output layer. The hidden layer helps provide a way to create associations among multiple inputs and multiple outputs. Key to exploiting neural networks is knowing that they are classifiers and that they need the right inputs.

Classifiers

Neural networks are classifiers. They take inputs and render an opinion on what they are. As a learning algorithm, they infer relationships instead of requiring the relationships to be explicitly programmed in. This is critical to understanding the utility of the method. When you know the relationships among the inputs, you can get exactly what you want by directly programming them. When you do not, or when they tend to defy an exact definition, it may be easier and more accurate for the network to infer, or learn the relationship.

At this point, we know enough to ask the final question we should always ask, "Is this the right tool for the job?" If the job of our AI is to classify the situation before it, we might still be okay. However, the job of most game AI is to answer the question, "What should I do?" It is not always obvious that the answer to "What is the situation?" that we get from a classifier will directly yield the answer to "What should I do?" that the AI needs to provide.

The neural network show in Figure 10.3 could be used to determine the best next state in the FSM from Chapter 3, "Finite State Machines (FSMs)." The network classifies the world by indicating the next state that is the best fit to the conditions at hand. Using a neural network for this simple example is total overkill, but recall our discussion of complexity in an FSM. The complexity of the transition rules can be the downfall of an FSM that has a manageable number of states. Using a neural network frees programmers from the task of programming the transition rules, provided they can teach the network instead.

An advantage of using a neural net to classify is that the outputs are not fixed to binary values. In our existing monster FSM AI, when the monster is attacking or fleeing, it has no middle ground in which it is considering both. A neural network can be trained to consider two or more different alternatives. If the training data did not have a sharp cutoff between attacking and fleeing, the neural network will reflect that for those inputs that had more than one different valid output. The training data would indicate that sometimes the monster flees players when hit points are at a given level, and sometimes it continues an attack. The FSM code that disambiguates multiple possible next states can weigh the options presented by the outputs. If the highest output is always used, the behavior will be the same as before. If a weighted random selection is used, the behavior will more closely match the proportions in the training data.

Using a different example, the output of a neural network trained to recognize letters might show strong outputs for Q, G, O, and C when presented with a Q to recognize. If the network did not have a strong preference, the next character might be used to assist in the decision. In English, Q is almost always followed by U or u. Having weighted outputs instead of binary outputs coming from the neural network allows the overall system greater leeway in making decisions. This is true of other methods as well.

Classifiers such as recognition systems are *oracles*. When asked a question—any question—they give an answer. On the surface this capability seems impressive, but it is also true of the Magic 8-Ball toy. If you feed text that uses the Greek or Cyrillic alphabet to a recognizer trained on the Roman characters present in English, the recognizer will output what it thinks are English characters. It would make the same attempt when fed Hebrew or Hiragana characters or even Kanji symbols and random applications of the spray-paint tool on a bitmap. One of the more important design decisions to make with such a system is what to do when presented with inputs that have no particular correct response. Such inputs are commonly called garbage, but they include ambiguous input as well.

There are two ways to approach this problem. The simplest is to demand, "Give me an answer, even if it's wrong." In this case, the system is trained with the broadest array of data available and sent into battle. The alternative is to design a system that has an "I don't think so" output. In these systems, the training data includes properly marked garbage. Good garbage for training can be hard to find, and tuning systems that have a garbage output can be a black art. The question for the designer is to ponder the difference between an AI that is resolute, if occasionally stupid, compared with one that sometimes does not know what to do. If the designer says, "All the choices are always good, just sometimes some are better than others," then the resolute system is fine. On the other hand, if there is a good default behavior available to the AI, especially when some of the outputs could be badly inappropriate, then it may be worth the effort to implement a garbage output. Whether it is programmed to recognize garbage or not, a classifier should always be tested with data that has no right answer.

Input Features

Getting the inputs right can make or break a neural network. The inputs are collectively known as the features presented to the network. We could have pre-processed two of the inputs, hit points and max hit points, and used the ratio as a single input instead. In our particular case, a properly engineered network will infer the relationship, but this is not always a given.

Consider a monster that is in combat with a powerful foe. The monster is losing hit points in large chunks. The monster will go from the attacking state to dead without ever having a chance to flee. Our current set of features is not sufficient. If we add rate of change of hit points as an input feature, our monster can act more intelligently. It can know that it can stay in combat longer against a weak foe, even if the monster is hurting. And it will know to flee early if it is being hammered by a potent foe.

Getting the features right is critical if the network needs to deal with time-varying data. The rate of change in a value (the first derivative, in mathematical terms) can be very useful, as we saw in the monster-hit-points example. The rate of change of a first derivative (the second derivative of the value) can be useful as well. When the steering wheel of a car is turned, the car begins to deviate from a straight course and to rotate. The change rate of the vehicle's heading (the first derivative) gives a sense of how fast the vehicle is getting around the corner. The second derivative, combined with other data (notably the position of the steering wheel and its first derivative), tells the driver if he or she has exceeded the available traction and is beginning to spin out. The increasing rate of heading change, easily noticed when the second derivative is positive, means that the car is not only cornering, but spinning as well. Stable cornering has a constant rate of change in heading and therefore a zero second derivative (the rate of change of a constant is zero). The amount of counter-steering required to catch the spin depends on how bad the spin is; the second derivative is a very useful number.

Going the other way and summing data over time may also have merit. If the monster is tracking the cumulative number of points of damage it is dealing out to a foe, the monster may have a good idea of how soon it will vanquish a foe without resorting to cheating and looking at the foe's actual hit points. The monster is guessing at the number of hit points the foe started with, but it will know the cumulative number of hit points that the foe has lost. The cumulative sum is the first integral of damage delivered. The monster may want to decide to stay in a difficult combat because it thinks it can finish off a potent foe before the foe can return the favor. A single value for damage delivered does not tell enough of the story to be useful. Time-varying data typically needs special handling to create effective features to input to a neural network.

As mentioned earlier, using a neural network in place of our familiar monster FSM is total overkill. It is used as a familiar example only. There are better ways than neural networks to do everything we have illustrated so far.

Genetic Algorithms

Genetic algorithms are rarely if ever used for game AI. Instead they are sometimes used for tuning variables in games. Motorsports provide us with a good example [Biasillo02]. A mechanic setting up a car manages many tunable parameters to obtain optimum performance on any particular track. There are the camber, caster, and toe angles to be adjusted when doing a basic wheel alignment. There is the braking proportion between front and rear tires—a setting more easily understood if you consider the rear braking needs of an empty pickup truck compared to a fully loaded one. An empty pickup truck needs minimal rear braking force because the lightly loaded rear tires provide minimal traction. A heavily loaded truck benefits from having a great deal of rear braking force to exploit the greater traction available. This is only a partial list of tuning parameters; as you might expect, there can be interactions between variables.

Genetic algorithms can help us in our search for the optimal settings. Genetic algorithms roughly mimic biological evolution. We start with a population that has different characteristics. Some are more fit than others. Cross-breeding and mutation yield new members with different characteristics. Some of these will hopefully be more fit than any of their parents. The best are emphasized for further improvement, possibly along with a small number of less-fit individuals in order to keep the diversity of the population high. The best need not be restricted to children of the current generation; it could include members from older generations as well. We continue until we have a good reason to stop. Let us expand on the concepts of this paragraph in detail.

In programming terms, our variables to tune are the characteristics of our individuals. Each of the angles used in wheel alignment is a characteristic. The braking proportion is another. For production vehicles, you might think that these values have already been optimized by the factory, but the factory settings may degrade lap times to decrease tire wear or increase stability. Even relatively uncompromising road-legal sports cars such as the Lotus Elise are specified for road use and need to be tuned for optimal track handling; specialized vehicles also offer room for improvement on the track.

Selection requires a way to tell which individual is more fit than another. At first blush, we can pick lap time as the fitness function. Why would lap time not be the best fitness function? Most races run more than one lap. One of the compromises in street specifications for wheel alignment is a trade-off between handling and tire wear. Do racers care about tire wear? Racers care about the lowest total time to complete the race (or the farthest distance traveled in a given time period in endurance racing). There is more to it than stringing together a sequence of fast laps. Time spent changing tires might or might not have an impact. Autocross racers have trouble keeping their tires warm between runs and might not wear out a fresh set of tires in an entire day's competition. Things are very different in NASCAR, especially at tire-hungry tracks such as Talladega. The point is that great care must be taken in selecting a fitness function for a genetic algorithm, or your system will tune for the wrong situation. In motorsports games, as in real life, vehicles are often tuned to individual tracks.

Hidden in the selection criteria is the cost of the fitness function. In our motorsports case, we have to simulate a lap or possibly an entire race with each member of the new population that we want to evaluate. In our case, not only do we have to run a simulated race, but we need a good driver AI. We are going to optimize the car not only for a particular track but also for a particular driver. The cost to mix and match characteristics is typically quite modest when compared to the cost to evaluate them. Not only do we have to select for the right thing, but the very act of measuring for selection must have a reasonable cost.

Crossbreeding in a genetic algorithm involves how we select which parent provides each characteristic of the child. There are a number ways to make the selection, but it is worth emphasizing that the process is selection, not averaging. The child car will not have the toe angle set to the average of the two parents; it will get the exact toe angle value from one of them.

Mutation calls for changing a value in a child randomly to something other than the two values present in the parents. At first glance, it may seem that if the starting population is diverse enough, there is no need for mutation. However, the selection process will tend to suppress diversity as it emphasizes fit individuals who are likely to resemble each other. Diversity is required to keep the algorithm from falsely converging early on a sub-optimal solution.

If we are to keep our population from growing without bound, we need to figure out which individuals are not going to make it to the next run. An obvious method is to replace the worst individuals. Another method would be to replace the members who score closest to the new individuals. Doing selection this way also helps keep a diverse population.

There are many reasons for stopping the algorithm. If the new generations have stopped improving, then perhaps the optimal population has been found, and there is no reason to continue. If the latest generation has individuals that are "good enough," then it may be time to go on to other things. If each generation takes a large amount of computation, time will be a limiting factor. And finally, if the original population contains individuals thought to be optimal, a few generations may be all that is needed to confirm their status.

Genetic algorithms are good at getting close to an optimal solution, but they can be very slow to converge on the most optimal solution. If the problem can be expressed in terms of genes and fitness, the algorithm gives us a way to search arbitrarily complex spaces. It does not need heuristics to guide it or any expertise in the area searched. Our search speed will depend heavily on how expensive our fitness function is to run.

Behavior Trees

Behavior trees made it on to the industry's radar in a big way with Damian Isla's paper at the 2005 Game Developers Conference [Isla 2005]. The paper was about managing complexity in the AI. Behavior trees bring welcome relief to that problem area without introducing any new major problems of their own.

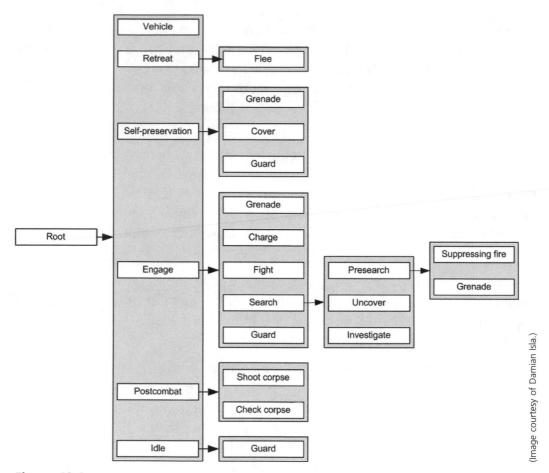

(Image courtesy of Damian Isla.)

Figure 10.4
A subset of the behavior tree used in *Halo 2*.

One of the drawbacks of an FSM is that the number of possible transitions between states grows with the square of the number of states. An FSM with a large-but-manageable number of states may find itself with an unmanageable number of transitions. In Chapter 3, we brushed on hierarchical state machines as a way to control state explosion, with the idea that two-level machines often suffice. If we emphasize the hierarchy more than the state machines, we wind up with something like behavior trees. Behavior trees attempt to capture the clarity of FSMs while reducing their complexity. Behavior trees have been used effectively in some very popular games. Figure 10.4 shows a subset of the behavior tree for *Halo 2*, and Figure 10.5 shows a subset of the behavior tree used in *Spore*.

There are a few important observations to make about the trees. The first observation is that the number of levels in the tree is arbitrary. The second

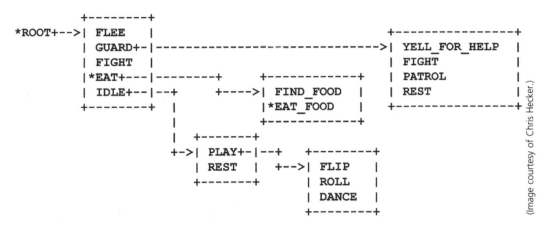

```
              +--------+
*ROOT+-->| FLEE   |                              +----------------+
         | GUARD+-|----------------------------->| YELL_FOR_HELP  |
         | FIGHT  |                              | FIGHT          |
         |*EAT+---|--------+      +-----------+  | PATROL         |
         | IDLE+--|--+      +---->| FIND_FOOD |  | REST           |
         +--------+  |           |*EAT_FOOD   |  +----------------+
                     |           +-----------+
                     |
                     |   +-------+
                     +->| PLAY+-|--+   +--------+
                        | REST   | +-->| FLIP   |
                        +-------+     | ROLL   |
                                      | DANCE  |
                                      +--------+
```

Figure 10.5
A subset of the behavior tree used in *Spore*.

(Image courtesy of Chris Hecker.)

observation is that the tree is not a proper tree in that children can have more than one parent. The careful eye will note that Grenade appears in many places in the *Halo 2* tree. REST and FIGHT appear more than once in the *Spore* tree. These are not different behaviors with the same name; they are the same behaviors with multiple parents in the tree. The third and less obvious observation is that there are no loops in the trees. A final observation is that these diagrams are far easier to understand than an equivalent single-level FSM diagram would be. Behavior trees attempt to keep the best parts of an FSM while managing their drawbacks. We will look at how behavior trees work by looking at the two ways we can evaluate them: top-down and bottom-up.

Top-Down Evaluation

So how do behavior trees work? The *Spore* behavior tree in Figure 10.5 is marked with asterisks to denote the current state of the AI, which is EAT_FOOD. Each time the AI is asked to think, it starts at the top of the tree and checks that the current decision is still a good one. A common arrangement for the items at any level is a prioritized list. Note that IDLE is listed last on both diagrams. All the ways of disambiguating states can come into play here. All the states have a decider that indicates if it wants to activate and possibly how strongly it wants to activate. So in the *Spore* case, FLEE, GUARD, and FIGHT can interrupt EAT. If any of them do want to interrupt, the machine has EAT_FOOD terminate, then EAT is asked to terminate, and then the new sequence is started. With no interruptions at the highest level, EAT continues to run. FIND_FOOD has priority over EAT_FOOD, so it can interrupt EAT_FOOD if it wants in the next level down.

Actual implementations of behavior trees include some subtleties. A number of good ideas from other AI methods find a home in behavior trees as well. The current behavior gets a boost in priority when it is rechecked against alternatives. This helps stop the AI from equivocating between two actions. In actual use, the trees need some help to better deal with events in the world. The sound of a gunshot is an event; it is highly unlikely that the AI will ever "hear" a gunshot by examining the current world state. Instead, the event has to be handled immediately or remembered until the next time the AI thinks, and the behavior tree needs hooks to make that memory happen.

An important subtlety more particular to top-down evaluation in behavior trees is that a high-level behavior cannot decide that it wants to activate unless it knows that at least one of its children will also want to activate. In real life, it is wasted effort to drive into the parking lot of a restaurant if no one in the car wants to eat there. This requirement needs to hold true all the way down the tree to the level of at least one usable behavior. The lowest-level items in the tree that actually do something are the behaviors, and all the things above them are deciders. Deciders need to be fast because they are checked often. The *Spore* diagram only shows deciders. Most of the nodes in the tree we have covered so far do selection; they pick a single child to run. Nodes can also do sequencing, where they run each child in turn.

Bottom-Up Evaluation

If there is sufficient CPU available, we can switch from the top-down evaluation described to a bottom-up evaluation. The top-down method requires the highest-level deciders to accurately predict whether any of their descendants wants to activate in the current situation. This capability is critical. Given that assurance, the tree evaluates very quickly, and top-down evaluation gives better performance. Bottom-up evaluation starts by having the lowest-level leaves of the tree, the behaviors, comment on the current situation and feed their opinions up the tree to the deciders. The deciders no longer have to predict whether one of their descendant behaviors wants to activate; instead, they are armed with sure knowledge that includes *how much* each descendant wants to activate. The deciders are then left with the task of prioritizing the available options. The results are fed up the tree to the highest level for final selection.

What benefit does bottom-up evaluation provide that is worth the performance hit? Bottom-up offers the possibility of better decision making. In particular, nuanced and subtle differences in behaviors can be more easily exhibited in a bottom-up system. The highest-level deciders in a top-down system need to be simple in order to run quickly and to keep complexities from the lowest levels from creeping up throughout the tree. The high-level deciders in top-down make broad-brush, sweeping, categorical decisions. The tree in Figure 10.5 decides between flee, guard, fight, eat, or idle at the highest level *before* it decides how it will implement the selected category of action. It decides *what* to do before it works out *how* to do it. With a bottom-up system, we can let the question of *how* we do something drive the decision *whether* to do it. Let us consider an example of how this might work.

In a fantasy setting, an AI character is being driven by the decision tree shown in Figure 10.6. Decider nodes have italic text, and behavior nodes have bold text. Extraneous nodes have been left out for clarity. A top-down evaluation decides to evade at the highest level. The next level down, it has to decide between running away and hiding. It decides to hide in a nearby building, simplified as the Hide node in Figure 10.6. The next level down, it decides between picking the lock on the door, using a spell to unlock the door, or breaking the door down. If the character has no picks and no spells, the only option is to break the door down. Unfortunately, breaking the door down will be obvious to any pursuers. It would be better to keep running away in this case, but the decision between running and hiding has already been made at a higher level, and hiding is usually better than running. Hiding would have been the best choice if the character had picks or a spell.

A bottom-up evaluation takes care of this problem. Both the Pick Lock behavior and the Cast Unlock Spell behavior return a very strong desire to activate if the

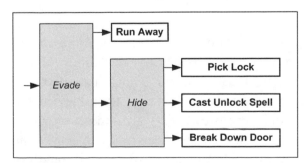

Figure 10.6
A partial decision tree used by a fantasy character.

character is properly equipped and no desire at all to activate otherwise. The Break Down Door behavior always returns a weak desire to activate. The Run Away behavior returns a medium desire to activate. The Hide node will pick the best of the three methods for opening the door and offer them to the Evade node in the next level up in the tree. The selected hiding result will be compared to running away. If the character is properly equipped, hiding will be preferred to running away. If the character lacks picks or spells, the character runs away.

Looking at all the leaves this way may seem vaguely familiar. Bottom-up evaluation in a behavior tree is analogous to a rule-based system with an explicit hierarchical disambiguation system. The argument for or against bottom-up evaluation centers on whether or not nuances are lost by making high-level decisions first. If there are no nuances to lose, top-down evaluation is simple and fast. If low-level complexities keep creeping into the high-level deciders, the system is losing the simplicity and possibly the speed that top-down systems are supposed to deliver. In such a case, the system can be simplified by pushing the detail back down to the leaves where it belongs and evaluating from the bottom up.

Advantages

Behavior trees provide two major advantages: They are easy to understand, and they allow for sophisticated behavior selection. The diagrams shown are easy for AI programmers to understand, and they are easy for experienced game designers to understand. This point is critical; if the vision of the designer is to make it into the AI of the game, the designer needs to understand what the AI will do. Besides being easy for a designer to understand, the diagrams are straightforward for an AI programmer to implement. The method is also easy to debug. All these advantages make for a more productive team, allowing more time to get the AI right because of the clarity provided.

Where does that clarity come from? The diagram partitions the AI problem, allowing the team to look at one node (along with its parents and children) and safely ignore details that are important only to other nodes. FSMs also divide the AI problem, but behavior trees add their hierarchy as an additional way of partitioning the problem that FSMs lack. Hierarchical FSMs are a middle ground between pure FSMs and behavior trees in terms of partitioning. With FSMs, the mindset at any level is finishing the statement, "I am..." yielding a flat diagram. In contrast, a typical behavior tree works on the idea of "The big decisions count the most," yielding an appropriate number of levels in the diagram. In an FSM, the partitioning is done once; in a behavior tree, it is done as many times as needed. *Superior partitioning localizes concerns better.* Graphically, this can be seen if the nodes in a behavior tree have few links and the states in an FSM have many transitions. In addition, behavior trees do not loop.

Like all divide-and-conquer methods, great pains must be taken in the divide. If the divide is not clean, then the conquer is unlikely to succeed. The divide step is also a good time to evaluate which method to use. If your tree has minimal levels and a relatively broad base, an FSM or a hierarchical FSM might be the optimal solution. If your tree has much depth or is uneven, with broad parts here and deep parts there, a behavior tree may be best.

Throughout the discussion, we have tied behavior trees to diagrams. Non-graphical methods of specifying a tree or an FSM may detract from the clarity of the design, but decisions about what AI algorithm you use should be made holistically. Tool support may have a strong influence on those decisions; the *Spore* developers described their particular way of defining their behavior tree as "fairly self-documenting" while at the same time having "the side benefit of compiling extremely rapidly" [Hecker07]. Implicit in that statement is the idea that their design definition was used to generate code, avoiding any disconnect between the design and the code at the potential price of a design that was harder for people to deal with.

The sophisticated behavior selection available does a very good job at handling AI that thinks in terms of "What should I be doing right now?" Whether we evaluate in the typical top-down or the more expensive bottom-up sequence, we arrive at a single thing that the AI should be doing. This is predicated on a fundamental question to ask before considering a behavior tree for your AI: "Can I make high-level decisions or categorizations at all?" Along with that is the question of whether doing just one thing is appropriate.

The benefits to behavior trees come from the fact that they control complexity. If your tree starts with a single root and then explodes immediately into a large number of leaves, you have lost the simplifying power of the method. Put another way, you need to ask, "Can I effectively organize the AI behaviors into a hierarchy?" If there is no benefit to the hierarchy, perhaps another method would be better. If you cannot because you need to string a bunch of behaviors together, a planning architecture may be what you need.

Planning

"Can't the AI just work out all of the steps it needs to pull this off by itself?" is the essential question that brings us to planning. We got a taste of planning in Chapter 6, "Look-Ahead: The First Step of Planning." In general terms, our AI searched for things to do that would take it to some goal. The preceding sentence seems pretty innocuous, but if we analyze it in careful detail, we can examine any planning system.

Note that we used the term search. Recall the astronomical numbers we computed in Chapters 6, "Look-Ahead: The First Step of Planning," and 7, "Book of Moves." Planners do searching as well, so it should come as no surprise that their computational complexity is a serious issue. Writing a planner is no small task, either, but their novel capability of sequencing steps together at run-time make them well worth examining.

You may recall from Chapter 6 that systems that think about the future need a way to represent knowledge that is independent from the game world. This is especially true for planning systems. Good knowledge representation needs to be designed in from the start. The AI is not allowed to change the world merely by thinking about the world; it can only change the world by acting on the world.

Planning AI emphasizes capability instead of action. The elements in a planning system are couched in terms of their results on the world instead of the actions they will perform. Planning elements declare, "This is what I make happen," instead of emphasizing procedure by saying, "This is what I do." They are *declarative* instead of *procedural*. The overall system is tasked with meeting goals instead of performing actions. With planning, the system is given a goal and given the command, "Make it so" instead of telling all the elements what they are supposed to do.

Consider a visitor to a large city who is talking with friends, some old and some recently met. "I need a place to sleep," the visitor says. This is declarative. "You can sleep on my sofa," one friend says, which is the only thing the visitor was expecting. "You can sleep on the other half of my king-sized bed," another friend offers. "I'm the night manager of a hotel; I can get you a room at cost," says a third. None of the other friends speak up. All three options meet the goal, and two of them were unexpected. The visitor decides the best plan. The visitor could have said, "Can I sleep on your sofa?" to the one friend and left it at that. This is procedural. While planners deal with dynamic situations gracefully, other, cheaper methods do as well. Planners' strong suit is more than just picking the single best action.

The biggest benefit of planning comes when the AI assembles multiple actions into a plan. This capability is a reasonable working definition for a planner and the biggest reason to justify their costs. Planning systems search the space of available actions for a path through them that changes the state of the world to match the goal state. Let us look at an example, loosely based on the old children's folk song, "There's a Hole in the Bucket."

The setting is a farm back in the days when "running water" meant someone running out to the well to get water. Our agent, named Henry, is tasked with fetching water. So the goal is to deliver water to the house. There are many objects available for Henry to use, including a bucket with a hole in it. Henry searches for a way to achieve the goal with the objects at hand. He will patch the bucket with straw. The straw needs to be cut to length. He will cut the straw with a knife. The knife needs to be sharpened. He will sharpen the knife on a stone. At this point, we will depart from the song, because in the song you need water in order to sharpen the knife on the stone, and as programmers we despise infinite loops. In our example, the stone will be perfectly fine for sharpening the knife. Our Henry's plan goes like this: Sharpen the knife on the stone. Cut the straw to fit. Patch the bucket with the cut straw. Use the bucket to fetch water.

Just as behavior trees scale better than pure FSMs, planning systems scale better than behavior trees when the need is for sequences of actions. In a behavior tree, the sequences are assembled by the programmer as part of the tree. With a planner, the AI dynamically performs the assembly, although not without cost. Once again, we see an almost Zen-like condition where adding sophistication makes the systems simpler. The execution systems are becoming more abstract and more data driven. This pulls the actions code into smaller, more independent chunks. What used to be code is slowly turning into something more like data. This phenomenon is not restricted to AI; it is a common progression seen in nearly all programming areas. The cost we mentioned was further alluded to when we said, "adding sophistication."

By analogy, consider simple programs that use numbers and strings as input data. By now, every reader of this book has written some of them. Consider the task of writing a compiler, such as the VB compiler we have been using. While at the lowest level the input data to the VB compiler is still simple strings, in reality that data is written at a much higher level. The VB compiler as a program is far more sophisticated than nearly all of the programs it compiles. The output of the VB compiler is far more flexible and wider ranging than the simpler programs it usually compiles. Few of the readers of this book are sufficiently qualified to write a VB compiler. "Adding sophistication" raises the bar for the programmers. We need not debate whether writing a planner is more or less difficult than writing a compiler, but we should again also emphasize that the more-sophisticated programs consume more-sophisticated data. VB code is more than simple strings, and the actions made available to a planner are likewise more than simple strings.

We will examine three planning systems: STRIPS, GOAP, and HTN. The latter two (along with behavior trees) are very current topics among industry professionals.

STRIPS

STRIPS stands for the Stanford Research Institute Problem Solver and dates to 1971 [Fikes71]. The basic building blocks in STRIPS are actions and states. From these, we can develop plans to reach goals. Let us examine these states, goals, actions, and plans. Along the way, we will touch on conditions as well.

States are not the states of an FSM, but the state of the virtual world. States can be partial subsets of the world state. States in this sense are a collection of attributes that have specific values. A state for nice weather might call for clear skies and warm temperatures.

Goals are specified as states in this manner. A goal state is defined by a set of conditions that are met when the goal is reached. Goal states differ from other states in that the AI places importance on achieving the goal states, and it does not particularly care about other states along the way to the goal.

Actions have preconditions and postconditions. An action cannot be performed unless all its preconditions are met. If an action succeeds, all the postconditions of the action will become true, whether they were previously true or not. As far as the planner is concerned, only things expressed in the preconditions or post-conditions matter. Planners are results oriented.

Let us examine the sharpen knife action from Henry's plan to mend the bucket earlier in this section. It would have two preconditions: Henry has to possess the knife, and he has to possess the stone. As a postcondition of the action, the knife will be sharp.

Table 10.1	Hole-in-the-Bucket States
State	**Conditions**
World	Kitchen has no water.
	Bucket has a hole.
	Have straw.
	Straw is too long.
	Have a knife.
	Knife is dull.
	Have a stone.
Goal	Kitchen has water.

A plan is a sequence of actions leading to a goal. Every precondition of every action that is not forced to be true by a prior action in the plan must be true in the initial state that is used to develop the plan. If those conditions are true and the plan is successfully executed, then the world state will match the goal state at the end.

Let us revisit our example of Henry and the bucket. Our states are given in Table 10.1. We have two states of interest: the state of the world and our goal state. The goal state only has one condition: showing that most states are far simpler than the world state.

To transform the world state so that it also matches the goal state, we have the actions listed in Table 10.2. The column order shows how the action transforms the state of the world; start with the preconditions and perform the action to get the postconditions.

Table 10.2	Hole-in-the-Bucket Actions	
Precondition	**Action**	**Postcondition**
Bucket is mended	Use bucket	Water is delivered.
Cut straw is available	Mend bucket with straw	Bucket is mended.
Have a knife		
Have straw		
Knife is sharp	Cut straw to length	Cut straw is available.
Have a stone		
Have a knife	Sharpen knife	Knife is sharp.

We start with the goal. The only action that transforms the world state to the goal state is the "use bucket" action. The precondition for using the bucket is not met, so we seek actions that will transform the world state to one where the preconditions are met.

The mend the bucket action has the postcondition of the bucket being mended, which meets the preconditions needed for using the bucket. This might not be the first time that the bucket needed to be mended. If the world state had included leftover straw from the last time the bucket was mended, all of the outstanding preconditions would be met, and we would get a shorter plan that used the state of the world instead of more actions. In our case, we do not have cut straw.

The cut straw to length action has that as a postcondition. To make use of this action, we need to meet three preconditions. The state of the world provides us with a knife and with straw meeting two of the preconditions, but the knife is dull, giving our plan another outstanding precondition. If we cannot find a way to meet this outstanding precondition, this particular plan will fail.

The sharpen knife action can meet the outstanding precondition, but it adds two preconditions of its own. The world state provides both the knife and the stone, meeting all of our outstanding preconditions. This leaves us with a workable plan; the world state, when transformed by a string of actions, meets the goal state.

Our simple example illustrates chaining actions together into a plan but leaves out dealing with alternatives and failures. We might also have scissors capable of cutting the straw but lack a sharpening stone. As you might expect, an initial plan to use the knife would fail to meet all of its outstanding preconditions, and the planner would explore using the scissors instead. We will see these facets of planning in the sections on GOAP and HTN planners.

The ideas behind STRIPS are reasonably easy to grasp. The complexities of programming the system are not trivial. A great deal of effort needs to be applied to the knowledge-representation problem presented by states, preconditions, and postconditions. The knowledge-representation issues have implications about the interface between the planning system and the game. STRIPS is not widely used in games.

GOAP

If Damian Isla's presentation on behavior trees at the 2005 Game Developers Conference put that method on the radar of game AI programmers, then Jeff

Orkin's articles and presentations did the same thing for goal-oriented action planning (GOAP) [Orkin03], [Orkin06]. For our purposes, GOAP (rhymes with soap) can roughly be considered as STRIPS adapted to games and uses the same vocabulary. We will look at how GOAP is typically applied to games.

When used in games, actors controlled by GOAP systems typically have multiple goals, but only one goal active at a time. The active goal is the highest-priority goal that has a valid plan. For independent agents, this single mindedness is not a major drawback. Some games require that multiple goals be active at the same time. In this case, the planner needs to be more sophisticated. It may want to accept a higher-cost plan for one goal so that other goals can be pursued in parallel. It may need to ensure that the many plans have no resource-contention problems. It is up to the game designer to decide whether the game is better served by having a wise AI that plans around these issues or a potentially more realistic AI that correctly models the problems. Adding such a capability adds complexity to an already complex algorithm, and it adds CPU demands to an algorithm that is already demanding of uncomfortable amounts of processing power.

Note

These are real-world problems; a full-scale review by the U.S. military many years ago found that in one scenario, the combined demands of the worldwide commands collectively called for five times the total airlift capacity of the Military Airlift Command and deployment of the Rapid Deployment Force simultaneously to 10 different locations.

In games, GOAP actions are typically simplified so that each action can report a cost value associated with it that can be used to compare that action to other actions. These costs can be used to tune the AI's preference of one action over another. The lowest-cost action might have a cost of 1. If costs tend to be roughly comparable, the planner will prefer plans with fewer steps. It will accept Rube-Goldberg–style plans only when there are no simpler means of accomplishing the goal. The actions themselves are implemented with scripts or small FSMs that are restricted to doing just the one action. FSMs work quite well because the implementation of the action is often heavily tied to animation sequences, and those sequences are often easily controlled by FSMs.

Given those simplifications to the actions, GOAP planners in games can use the now-familiar A* algorithm to search the action space for a path between the goal and the current state. With A*, the direction in which we search has an impact. To use A* at all, we need a heuristic. We will examine both of these facets in detail.

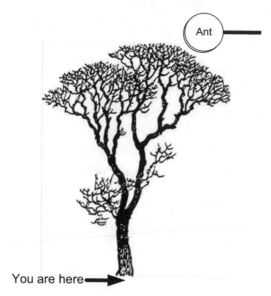

Figure 10.7
The direction of the search matters.

Note the direction of search, from the goal to the current state. This is for performance reasons. As long as A* has a good heuristic, it will find the lowest-cost path, but the performance will vary, depending on which end of the final path the search starts. The typical GOAP or STRIPS case gives the actor many possible actions that might be checked if we start by acting on the current state. Most of those actions will not take us closer to our goal, which gives us a large search space to examine and discard. If we start at the goal, we are far more likely to see only a few actions that need to be searched to take us toward the current state. As Figure 10.7 suggests, if you start at the base of a tree looking for an ant that is on the tip of one of the leaves, it would be easier for the ant to find you at the base of the tree than it will be for you to find the ant.

If all the actions are simple enough that each one changes only a single post-condition, then we can create a good heuristic for A* to use when estimating. That heuristic is that the minimum cost to finish A* from any point is the number of conditions that need to change. If the minimum cost of a step is 1 and the actions can change only one condition, this heuristic holds true. Plans could cost more if the designer gave some steps higher weight than the minimum to help steer the search. Plans could also cost more if there are no direct paths. Indirect paths happen when the steps that lead to the goal add extra unmet conditions that will need to be satisfied by later actions. A real-world example might be in order.

A farmer who stands at the door of his house wants to go out into the night to find out what is making noise in the barn. A single action, "GOTO," would take him to the barn. That action has a precondition, "has light to see by," that is unmet. The lantern has the capability to change that condition, but it also has preconditions for being in hand, for fuel, and for being lit. Since the lantern has fuel, the precondition for fuel does not count. The precondition of being lit does count because the lantern in not currently lit. The matches have the capability to light things on fire, and they carry the precondition of being in hand. So the final plan will have grown to get matches, get the lantern, light a match, light the lantern, and finally go to the barn. The designer might have included a flashlight object that has a much lower cost than the lantern, making it preferable because a dropped flashlight is less likely to cause a barn fire than a dropped lantern. In this case, the flashlight has no batteries, and there are no batteries in the house, so the A* stopped progress on the path using the flashlight when it hit the high cost of driving into town to get more batteries.

A* connected the dots to form a plan to meet the goal. The AI programmer did not have to do it himself or herself the way he or she would have for an FSM. The programming paradigm shifts to something like, "Toss in capabilities in the form of actions and stir them with goals to see what plans you get." The simplicity of the actions is supposed to make programming the set of them simpler in total than trying to program the equivalent capability in an FSM or a behavior tree.

Knowledge representation is critical to the success of the method. The actions have to be able to get all the inputs they need from the state representation and make concrete changes to it. Notice that many of our preconditions and postconditions are simple Booleans that can be represented by one bit of a bit field. Performance of the knowledge representation is critical, and bit fields are a common way to help achieve it. Goal-oriented agents coded this way resemble goal-driven people; they do not stop to smell the flowers along the way, but they do get the details right.

HTN

"Don't we have a plan for that? Or something close?" One of the caveats that we gave about A* is that although we appreciate its performance, we know it is not free. A* connects the dots for us in GOAP. Maybe there is a way to save and reuse chunks of plans the way we might pre-compute popular paths. Each of the travelers who passed through the Cumberland Gap or crossed the Rocky

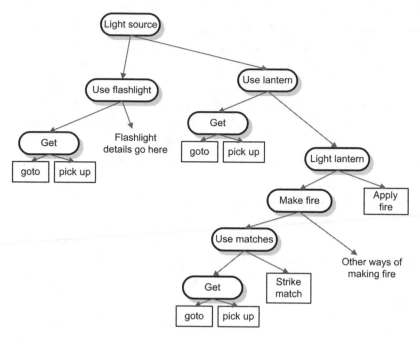

Figure 10.8
A subset of a hierarchical task network.

Mountains on the various trails did not come up with a brand-new plan before setting out (with the possible exception of the disastrous Donner party). We might like our AI to have a deep bag of tricks to use in terms of pre-computed plans while still being able to re-plan when things go decidedly wrong.

At the lowest level, a hierarchical task network (HTN) resembles the other planners we have mentioned. We have actions that can be directly executed if their preconditions are met, providing us with a change to the state of the world. These are often referred to as *primitive tasks*. HTNs also include a task library. Any task that is not a directly executable primitive task is called an *abstract task*. The abstract tasks in the task library decompose into lower-level abstract tasks and finally into primitive tasks. An example might be in order.

As shown in Figure 10.8, our farmer from the GOAP example has a "light source" abstract task in his task library. That task decomposes into the "use lantern" and "use flashlight" abstract tasks. The "use lantern" abstract task decomposes into a "light lantern" abstract task and the highly useful "get" abstract task. As they must, all the remaining abstract tasks similarly reduce to primitive tasks, although for simplicity, the diagram does not show the full decomposition of everything. Details of the flashlight and other methods for making fire are not shown.

The decompositions are hierarchical. In a rich environment, there will be many such decompositions to choose from for each task; our farmer has a flashlight and a lantern at his disposal for use as a light source, and probably more than one means of making fire. The task library is comparable to a rich script library [Kelly07] and can be computed offline [Kelly08]. There are some compelling advantages to HTN: The plans can be rapidly forward searched, and they deal gracefully with changing conditions. While they can be computed offline, designers can create plans to their liking as well.

The highest-level abstract tasks tend to be a very close match to typical goals that might be presented to a STRIPS or GOAP planner. Instead of running A* from the end goal back to the current state, we can more rapidly find matching high-level abstract tasks that take us to our goal, a welcome performance improvement. Instead of hoping that the ant on the leaf finds us at the base of the tree, we pull out the closest thing we have to an ant-locator plan and follow it directly to the ant. The forward search with HTN is faster than the backward search with GOAP.

Because of their forward and hierarchical nature, HTNs are also part of plan execution. Again using our farmer example, suppose the farmer starts to use the flashlight, and the batteries fail before he gets out the door. The light source task needs to re-plan, but nothing higher in the hierarchy has to change. The basic plan for getting to the barn and exploring the noises is sound. Only the part about getting some light has to change. A GOAP or STRIPS planner would have to restart the search because its plans do not natively retain the dependencies explicitly or keep alternatives that were discarded along the way. Once a GOAP or STRIPS planner discovers the flashlight in our example, it will discard using the lantern. Even if a clever implementation were to recognize that only a portion of the plan had failed, GOAP or STRIPS would need to search through all actions for alternative means of making light. The HTN planner in Figure 10.8 has the alternative light sources encoded in the abstract tasks.

To make sure everything works properly, HTNs include a new feature known as *critics*. Critics detect conflicts early in an effort to minimize backtracking. Instead of going out to investigate noises in the barn, suppose our farmer was going out after dark to light a bonfire for roasting marshmallows. Critics would detect the fact that he might not have enough matches to both light the lantern and light the bonfire.

HTN planners are gaining traction in real-time–strategy games [Brickman08] [Cerpa08] and other genres. The potential for better performance is always welcome in computer games. The increase in intelligence is equally welcome; not only do agents make workable plans, but they re-plan when things go wrong.

Resources

The hot topics among professional game AI programmers are always the subject of presentations at the Game Developers Conference (GDC), particularly at the AI summits that have been held in recent years. Along with academics and various other people outside of the industry, this same group of professional game AI programmers has authored the articles in the *AI Game Programming Wisdom* series of books. They also present at other conferences such as AIIDE and AAAI. Some of them even run Web sites devoted to game AI.

The first volume of the *AI Game Programming Wisdom* series, edited by Steve Rabin, has an entire section devoted to A*. Machine learning is the subject of the articles in section 10, and neural networks are the subject of the articles in section 11 in *AI Game Programming Wisdom 2*, although by volume 4, the editor openly asks, "What happened to Learning?" [Rabin08]. The entire four-volume series was written by and for industry professionals, so some of the articles may be hard going for novice AI programmers. A full list of the articles in the series as well as from many other sources can be found at http://www.aiwisdom.com/.

The noteworthy Web sites for game developers are too numerous to keep track of, so we will mention only a few:

- **http://www.gamedev.net.** The AI section of gamedev.net is reasonably extensive.

- **http://aigamedev.com.** The aigamedev.com site is focused entirely on game AI at a professional level, although some of the articles require paid membership to view.

- **http://www.gamasutra.com.** The gamasutra.com site tends to collect GDC-related material; Damian Isla's behavior tree paper is available there.

- **http://www.wikipedia.org.** While in no way guaranteed to be academically rigorous *or even factually correct*, Wikipedia is probably the best place on the Internet to read about a topic for the first time, including AI-related topics. Although Wikipedia is a good place to get the first clue about a topic, all articles should be read whilst wondering what mistakes are in it. The references section of the articles that have them is a rich hunting ground for good information, often pointing to papers of higher quality than the Wikipedia article citing them.

- Your favorite search engines.

Chapter Summary

This chapter covers a wide range of topics. Every game AI programmer needs to be fluent in A*. From there, we find that the more sophisticated topics have to be judged on the basis of whether they will be useful in a project. The important point is not that machine learning or planning systems are cool, which they are, but whether they are the right tool for the job. Unlike the topics in prior chapters, these were not picked for near-universal applicability or ease of understanding. By the same token, there is no VB code project for a neural network or some flavor of planner. They are topics that aspiring AI programmers who have made it this far should strive toward. The code for them would not be in keeping with the non-threatening nature of the code in this book, particularly for those novice AI programmers who come from a background other than hard-core programming, such as animators, producers, or even managers who have worked thus far to gain solid background in game AI.

Chapter Review

Answers are in the appendix.

1. What are the two concepts in A* that let us perform the best-first search?

2. What conditions could cause a node to move from the closed list back onto the open list in A*?

3. When is a machine-learning system easier to implement than a directly programmed system?

4. What is the major advantage of behavior trees over FSMs?

5. Why does the search run backward in a GOAP system and forward in an HTN system?

Exercises

1. Search for A* on the Internet. Write an A* implementation that directs the fox in *Fox and Hounds* when there is an opening.

2. Change the graph in Figure 10.2 so that the catapult service is between node A and node W at cost 0.5. Reduce the cost of road travel to or from node X back to 4. A path from node C to node W through A now has an actual cost of 12.5, while a path through node Z has cost 16. Prove to yourself that regardless of whether the algorithm reexamines nodes on the closed list, the inadmissible heuristic will cause the algorithm to return the longer path.

3. Search for neural network implementations on the Internet. Write one in VB for our monster. When training the network, leave out training data with hit-point values between the always fight and always flee levels. Watch the network outputs in the transition area.

References

[Barnes02] Barnes, Jonty; Hutchens, Jason. "Testing Undefined Behavior as a Result of Learning," *AI Game Programming Wisdom*. Charles River Media, 2002.

[Biasillo02] Biasillo, Gari, "Training an AI to Race," *AI Game Programming Wisdom*, Charles River Media, 2002.

[Brickman] Brickman, Noah; Nishant, Joshi. "HTN Planning and Game State Management in Warcraft II." Available online at http://users.soe.ucsc.edu/~nishant/CS244.pdf.

[Fikes71] Fikes, Richard; Nilsson, Nils. "STRIPS: A New Approach to the Application of Theorem Proving to Problem Solving." *Artificial Intelligence*, v2, pp. 189–208. 1971.

[Hecker07] Hecker, Chris. *Liner Notes for Spore/Spore Behavior Tree Docs*, Web page 2007. Available online at http://chrishecker.com/My_Liner_Notes_for_Spore/Spore_Behavior_Tree_Docs.

[Isla05] Isla, Damian. "Handling Complexity in the Halo 2 AI." Proceedings of the 2005 Game Developers Conference. CMP Media, 2005. Available online at http://www.gamasutra.com/view/feature/2250/gdc_2005_proceeding_handling_.php.

[Cerpa08] Cerpa, David; Obelleiro, Julio. "An Advanced Motivation-Driven Planning Architecture." *AI Game Programming Wisdom 4*, pp. 373–382. Charles River Media, 2008.

[Dill10] Dill, Kevin. Comments regarding Axis & Allies and Kohan 2 in private correspondence, 2010.

[Kelly07] Kelly, John-Paul; Botea, Adi; Koenig, Sven. "Planning with Hierarchical Task Networks in Games." Proceedings of the Seventeenth International Conference on Automated Planning and Scheduling, American Association for Artificial Intelligence, 2007. Available online at http://www.plg.inf.uc3m.es/icaps-pg2007/papers/Planning%20with%20Hierarchical%20Task%20Networks%20in%20Video%20Games.pdf.

[Kelly08] Kelly, John-Paul; Botea, Adi; Koenig, Sven. "Offline Planning with Hierarchical Task Networks in Video Games." Proceedings of the Fourth Artificial Intelligence and Interactive Digital Entertainment Conference, American Association for Artificial Intelligence, 2008. Available online at http://www.aaai.org/Papers/AIIDE/2008/AIIDE08-010.pdf.

[Kirby04] Kirby, Neil. "Getting Around the Limits of Machine Learning." *AI Game Programming Wisdom 2*, pp. 603–611. Charles River Media, 2004.

[Orkin03] Orkin, Jeff. "Applying Goal-Oriented Action Planning to Games." *AI Game Programming Wisdom 2*, pp. 217–228. Charles River Media, 2003.

[Orkin06] Orkin, Jeff. "Three States and a Plan: The A.I. of F.E.A.R." Proceedings of the 2006 Game Developers Conference. Available online at http://web.media.mit.edu/~jorkin/gdc2006_orkin_jeff_fear.pdf.

[Rabin08] Rabin, Steve. Preface, *AI Game Programming Wisdom 4*. pp. x. Course Technology, 2008.

[Sutton98] Sutton, Richard; Barto, Andrew. *Reinforcement Learning: An Introduction*. The MIT Press, Cambridge, Massachusetts, 1998. Available online at http://webdocs.cs.ualberta.ca/~sutton/book/ebook/the-book.html.

[Tesauro95] Tesauro, Gerald, "Temporal Difference Learning and TD-Gammon," Communications of the ACM, volume 38, Association for Computing Machinery, 1995.

ANSWERS TO CHAPTER REVIEW QUESTIONS

Most of the review questions have straightforward answers. Others call for opinions, and opinions may vary. The answers given here are one set of opinions.

Chapter 1: What Is Game AI?

1. *What are the three parts to our definition of game AI?* The AI has to be able to act, it has to be intelligent, and it has to deal with changing conditions.

2. *Why is game physics not game AI?* All choices are forced in physics, so there is no room for intelligence.

Chapter 2: Simple Hard-Coded AI

1. *What are the common drawbacks to hard-coded AI?* Hard-coded AI lacks a formal methodology for determining which behavior to employ. Without formal organization, hard-coded AI tends to grow quickly in size and complexity. It can be very difficult to change or maintain.

2. *What are the advantages to hard-coded AI?* Hard-coded AI is intuitive and can be fast to write and fast to execute.

3. *Complexity can be as low as the sum of the parts and as high as the product of the parts. What is the relationship between the parts when complexity is*

the sum? What is it when complexity is the product? When complexity is the sum of the number of parts, the parts are independent. When it is the product, all the parts are interrelated.

4. *What is the design of the data called when the data is information the AI uses to help it think about (or even imagine about) the world?* It is called knowledge representation.

5. *Critique the expediencies in the code that interrogates the world in the four-set-point thermostat. Comment on the dangers versus the additional complexity needed to mitigate the risks.* In general, the wrapper code knows the internal implementation of the world. It does not ask the world for values; it goes in and finds those values. The world code and the wrapper code are two separate files that must be kept synchronized. If the wrapper asked the world via a function in the world code, the world code could change however it liked as long as it kept the function valid. The function would be in the world-code file. It is easier to keep one file consistent than it is to keep two files synchronized. Internally in the wrapper, the parallel arrays are very handy, but they must be kept synchronized. In addition, the settings are in time-sorted order, and the search for the right setting silently depends on this fact. If the settings were allowed to be changed, the code that stores the new settings would have to sort them. Expediencies should be kept localized; within a routine is fine, within a file is tolerable, and across files is questionable.

6. *Why is the side effect in the code that gets the set-point temperature in the four-set-point thermostat important?* The side effect of showing the temperature used helps let us see what the AI is thinking.

Chapter 3: Finite State Machines (FSMs)

1. *Define a finite state machine and tell what each part does.* A finite state machine is composed of states and transitions. The transitions are used to change from one state to another. The states are used to define the different things the machine will do.

2. *What are the advantages of a finite state machine compared to hard-coded AI?* The formal organization combats complexity by making the states

independent. The transitions remain, but they are organized into a regular system. The code is less fragile.

3. ***What are some indicators that a finite state machine is inappropriate to use?*** An FSM has fundamental problems when it needs to be in more than one state at a time. It has problems if the states are not inherently discrete. If the complexity rises past a certain level, other methods may be easier to implement.

4. ***What do we mean by ambiguous transitions?*** When more than one transition is valid, they are ambiguous.

5. ***What do we call it when ambiguous transitions exist? What are three ways of dealing with them?*** When there are ambiguous transitions, we have a race condition. We can ignore them (which is free), we can fully specify the transitions (this is usually a very bad idea), or most likely we will prioritize the transitions.

Chapter 4: Rule-Based Systems

1. ***What are the two parts of a rule in a rule-based system?*** The rules have a matching part and an execution part.

2. ***What does the framework do in a rule-based system?*** The framework presents the current conditions to the rule base, selects a rule (or rules) to execute, and executes it. If more than one rule is to execute, the framework ensures that there are no conflicts between them.

3. ***Why is it that a rule-based system can play like both a human and a machine at the same time?*** The rule-based system plays like a human when it exploits human-sourced behaviors. It plays like a machine in that it never gets tired of picking the same best way to respond to a given situation.

4. ***What makes a rule-based AI appear intelligent? What makes it appear stupid?*** A rule-based system appears intelligent when it comes up with a good or possibly even great response for a situation. It appears stupid when the rules are too sparse and the best response it has is not appropriate for the situation. It also has issues when it lacks good defaults or the ability to recognize when to use them.

Chapter 5: Random and Probabilistic Systems

1. *What are three ways to get odds for a game?* You can get odds for a game by precomputing them, by Monte Carlo methods, or by faking them and tuning to suit.

2. *What are the drawbacks to these methods?* The first potential drawback to these methods is that they demand good numbers and possibly a large number of them. Furthermore, tuning those numbers is an acquired skill.

Chapter 6: Look-Ahead: The First Step of Planning

1. *What does an evaluation function do? How is it similar to or different from a goal?* An evaluation function attempts to comment on how good an indeterminate situation is. The function should correspond in some way to how close the situation is to a goal, but it does not require that the goal be in sight.

2. *What is a heuristic? How do heuristics help?* Heuristics are general guidelines. They can help guide the search toward fruitful paths and away from poor ones. They can help evaluate indeterminate situations.

3. *What is pruning and how does it help?* Pruning is the act of discarding paths deemed to have low potential for success. It narrows the search space, allowing a deeper look down higher-potential paths.

4. *What is the most common drawback to look-ahead?* There is rarely enough processor time to search every promising path.

Chapter 7: Book of Moves

1. *Describe how moves in a book of moves and heuristics are similar and how they are different.* Both can guide the AI, but moves tend to be concrete actions posed in game terms, and heuristics can be more abstract and generalized. Moves are about how the game is played, and heuristics tend to be about how the game is evaluated.

2. *How is a book of moves similar to a rule-based AI? How would you decide which label to use on a particular system?* The book of moves is a specialized form of a rule-based AI. A system that uses rules for basic AI is

probably a rule-based system, particularly if it includes general rules and defaults. An AI that is assisted by a specialized rule base might be said to be using a book of moves.

Chapter 8: Emergent Behavior

1. *List the elements and characteristics of a system that allows and encourages emergent behaviors.* Systems that feature independent agents who employ simple behaviors and interact tend to exhibit emergent behaviors.

2. *Describe the effects of feedback and the effects of feedback rates.* Feedback is what enables continued interaction. If the rate is too slow, the interaction will fade. If the interaction is too fast, the system may not allow any significant variations to develop.

Chapter 9: Evoking Emotions on the Cheap

1. *Many aspects of a game have an emotional payload. What additional attribute is required to make these aspects part of the overall AI?* They have to be changeable in order for the AI to have anything to do.

2. *Describe the critical difference between games and simulations with regard to what they are trying to do with emotions.* Simulations attempt to model emotions accurately as a first priority. Games attempt to evoke emotional responses in the players as a first priority.

3. *Some of the techniques in this chapter are subtle. How can the game make sure the player catches on?* The most straightforward way is to tell them in some more direct manner.

4. *List some general categories of places where some AI control adds to the ability of the game to deliver emotional content.* The AI can help control music, ambient settings (mood), plot, and even the camera itself.

Chapter 10: Topics to Pursue from Here

1. *What are the two concepts in A* that let us perform the best-first search?* A* tracks the cost so far and estimates the cost remaining to the goal. It is useful to have an admissible heuristic, but tracking and estimating cost allows the algorithm to be best-first.

2. *What conditions could cause a node to move from the closed list back onto the open list in A*?* This can happen when the heuristic is inadmissible and there are branching paths that can rejoin. This never happens if the algorithm is written with the usual optimization to ignore all nodes on the closed list.

3. *When is a machine-learning system easier to implement than a directly programmed system?* Machine learning is superior when it is easier to teach the machine than it is to directly program the machine.

4. *What is the major advantage of behavior trees over FSMs?* They control complexity better, allowing faster iteration cycles in development.

5. *Why does the search run backward in a GOAP system and forward in an HTN system?* In GOAP the number of actions that are close to the goal is typically smaller than the number of actions that are close to the agent. A* is faster when it has fewer branches to explore. HTN task libraries are designed to present goal states to the agents, making a forward search faster.

INDEX

pixels, absolute, 257
placement
  of controls, 8, 24
  of mines, 109
planning, 356–358
  goal-oriented action planning
    (GOAP), 361–363
  hierarchical task networks
    (HTNs), 365
players
  interfaces, enabling, 189–197
  views, 294. *See also* views
PlayingField class, 88
playing fields, 79–80
  initialization, 86
  squares, adding, 82–84
PlayingField.vb file, 237
playing *Minesweeper,*
  92–98
plot, 291–292
precomputing, 127–128
  paths, 330. *See also* A*
predictions, Monte Carlo
  methods, 126–127
primitive tasks, 364
Private keyword, 53
probabilistic systems
  analysis, 130
  design, 130
probabilistic systems, 125
  advantages, 130
  disadvantages, 130–131
productive guesses, 119
programming, 52–53. *See also*
  code
projects, 22–40
  Day in the Life, 131–148
  emotions, 302–328
  Fox and Hounds, 163–214
  FSMs (finite state machines),
    52–73
  hit point calculator, 5–17
  mines, 80
  Minesweeper, 79–121
  MonsterAI, FSMs (finite state
    machines), 55–73
  moves, 232
  running, 16
  Thermostat, 23–40
  analysis, 30–32

implementation, 32–39
state of the art, 39–40
properties
  BackColor, 11, 26
  BorderStyle, 26
  Done, 76
  Name, 7
  ScrollBars, 100
Properties window, 6
pruning, 153–154
  heuristics, 154–157
public arrays, 32
public interfaces
  adding, 58
  AI, 199–200
Public keyword, 53, 58, 175
Public Methods region, 191
PublicStuff region, 269
Pythagoras theorem, 333

Q

Quake, 2
quality, interactivity, 2
questions, answers to review,
  371–376

R

Rabin, Steve, 366
race conditions, 47
radio buttons, 37
  character class, adding, 10
  Mage, 15
random events, Monte Carlo
  methods, 127
random number generators, 89
random systems, 125
  advantages, 130
  analysis, 130
  design, 130
  disadvantages, 130–131
rates, frames, 264, 267
read-only access, 262
realism, balancing, 253
real-time constraints, 253
refactoring, 22
reforming lines, 161
regions, 58
  AI Related, 237
  No Lookahead, 197

Public Methods, 191
PublicStuff, 269
reinforcement of emergent
  behavior, 247–248
relationships
  classifiers, 344
  models, 307–325
representation, knowledge (KR),
  25, 162
resources, 366–367
REST, 351
results, *Day in the Life* project,
  147–148
Revealed variable, 95
rich script libraries, 365
roads, *Cars and Trucks,*
  258–264
Rock Band occupation, *Day in
  the Life* project, 133–134
routines
  AI, 200–203
  ColorMe, 173
  IncrementMineCount,
    adding, 86
  Matches, 104
  NewGame, 93
  rules, loading, 107
rule-based systems, 75
  advantages, 78
  AI implementation, 99–121
  analysis, 77–78
  design, 77–78
  disadvantages, 78–79
  implementation, 79–99
  Minesweeper project, 79–121
  overview of, 75–77
RuleOne class, 104
rules
  design, 101–106
  need for, 119–121
  routines, loading, 107
  for single-square evaluation,
    103–106
  testing, 106
  for two-square evaluation,
    108–110
RuleTwoNear class, 118
running
  Minesweeper, 92–98
  projects, 16

License Agreement/Notice of Limited Warranty

By opening the sealed disc container in this book, you agree to the following terms and conditions. If, upon reading the following license agreement and notice of limited warranty, you cannot agree to the terms and conditions set forth, return the unused book with unopened disc to the place where you purchased it for a refund.

License

The enclosed software is copyrighted by the copyright holder(s) indicated on the software disc. You are licensed to copy the software onto a single computer for use by a single user and to a backup disc. You may not reproduce, make copies, or distribute copies or rent or lease the software in whole or in part, except with written permission of the copyright holder(s). You may transfer the enclosed disc only together with this license, and only if you destroy all other copies of the software and the transferee agrees to the terms of the license. You may not decompile, reverse assemble, or reverse engineer the software.

Notice of Limited Warranty

The enclosed disc is warranted by Course Technology to be free of physical defects in materials and workmanship for a period of sixty (60) days from end user's purchase of the book/disc combination. During the sixty-day term of the limited warranty, Course Technology will provide a replacement disc upon the return of a defective disc.

Limited Liability

THE SOLE REMEDY FOR BREACH OF THIS LIMITED WARRANTY SHALL CONSIST ENTIRELY OF REPLACEMENT OF THE DEFECTIVE DISC. IN NO EVENT SHALL COURSE TECHNOLOGY OR THE AUTHOR BE LIABLE FOR ANY OTHER DAMAGES, INCLUDING LOSS OR CORRUPTION OF DATA, CHANGES IN THE FUNCTIONAL CHARACTERISTICS OF THE HARDWARE OR OPERATING SYSTEM, DELETERIOUS INTERACTION WITH OTHER SOFTWARE, OR ANY OTHER SPECIAL, INCIDENTAL, OR CONSEQUENTIAL DAMAGES THAT MAY ARISE, EVEN IF COURSE TECHNOLOGY AND/OR THE AUTHOR HAS PREVIOUSLY BEEN NOTIFIED THAT THE POSSIBILITY OF SUCH DAMAGES EXISTS.

Disclaimer of Warranties

COURSE TECHNOLOGY AND THE AUTHOR SPECIFICALLY DISCLAIM ANY AND ALL OTHER WARRANTIES, EITHER EXPRESS OR IMPLIED, INCLUDING WARRANTIES OF MERCHANTABILITY, SUITABILITY TO A PARTICULAR TASK OR PURPOSE, OR FREEDOM FROM ERRORS. SOME STATES DO NOT ALLOW FOR EXCLUSION OF IMPLIED WARRANTIES OR LIMITATION OF INCIDENTAL OR CONSEQUENTIAL DAMAGES, SO THESE LIMITATIONS MIGHT NOT APPLY TO YOU.

Other

This Agreement is governed by the laws of the State of Massachusetts without regard to choice of law principles. The United Convention of Contracts for the International Sale of Goods is specifically disclaimed. This Agreement constitutes the entire agreement between you and Course Technology regarding use of the software.